DATE DUE

MY 1 5 '09			

DEMCO 38-296

LEGAL RESEARCH
IN A NUTSHELL

By

MORRIS L. COHEN
Librarian (Retired) and Emeritus Professor of Law
Yale Law School

KENT C. OLSON
Lecturer and Assistant Librarian for Public Services
University of Virginia School of Law

SIXTH EDITION

ST. PAUL, MINN.
WEST PUBLISHING CO.
1996

Nutshell Series, In a Nutshell, the Nutshell Logo and the WP symbol
are registered trademarks of West Publishing Co. Registered in the
U.S. Patent and Trademark Office.

COPYRIGHT © 1968, 1971, 1978, 1985, 1992 WEST PUBLISHING CO.

COPYRIGHT © 1996 By WEST PUBLISHING CO.
610 Opperman Drive
P.O. Box 64526
St. Paul, MN 55164–0526
1–800–328–9352

All rights reserved
Printed in the United States of America

Library of Congress Cataloging-in-Publication Data

Cohen, Morris L., 1927–
    Legal Research in a nutshell / by Morris L. Cohen, Kent C. Olson.
— 6th ed.
      p. cm. — (Nutshell series)
    Includes bibliographical references and indexes.
    ISBN 0–314–09589–6
    1. Legal research—United States. I. Olson, Kent C. II. Title.
III. Series.
KF240.C54 1996
340 ' .072073—dc20
                                      96–8770
                                      CIP

ISBN 0–314–09589–6

TEXT IS PRINTED ON 10% POST
CONSUMER RECYCLED PAPER

PREFACE

Now in its sixth edition, *Legal Research in a Nutshell* has been revised more times than any other volume in the Nutshell series. Over the course of its several editions, legal research has changed dramatically—faster than almost any area of legal doctrine. Each new edition focuses increasingly on electronic methods of research. This edition contains extensive coverage of research using online databases, and adds expanded treatment of CD-ROM and Internet-based resources.

The Nutshell nonetheless devotes most of its attention to printed, or "traditional," legal resources. While electronic methods are essential in today's legal research, they have not yet supplanted the sophisticated editorial tools that form the basis of our legal literature. Many online sources are based on printed works and thus incorporate their structure and logic. An understanding of the books is required for effective research, whether in print or electronic media. Successful research also requires an appreciation for the computer's ability to execute powerful search approaches impossible with print materials. The resulting symbiosis of the two methods pervades most of the chapters that follow, and shapes the actual practice of legal research today.

The basic organization of our book mirrors the structure of both the law school curriculum and the legal literature. We begin with case law and statutes and then work out to secondary sources and other research tools.

While secondary sources are often the first materials consulted in actual research, we feel that an understanding of the basic case law and statutory texts is essential to successful use of the law reviews and treatises which analyze these texts. New chapters in this edition on "Specialized and Practice Materials" and "Reference Resources" are designed to aid in practical research situations.

We also include discussion of international and comparative law materials. While these chapters may be beyond the scope of many introductory courses in legal research, we feel that no consideration of legal resources is quite complete without recognizing the place of the United States in a larger community. Our discussion of international and comparative law recognizes their increased role in practice and in scholarship. These chapters include coverage of newly developing organizations such as the European Union and the World Trade Organization.

The Nutshell is designed not as a reference book but as a practical teaching tool, for use by individuals or in legal research courses. In either case, simply reading this book will not make you an effective researcher. Skill in legal research can only be achieved by combining knowledge with experience. Reading in the Nutshell should be accompanied by practice using the books and databases described and the methods suggested.

We are pleased that the Nutshell now has a partner in research instruction. Ruth McKinney's excellent new workbook, *Legal Research—A Practical Guide and Self-*

Instructional Workbook (1996), can be used as a companion volume to this work and contains extensive cross-references to relevant sections of this Nutshell.

We hope that with the extensive revisions incorporated in this new edition, this Nutshell will continue to provide an effective introduction to American legal research.

MORRIS L. COHEN
KENT C. OLSON

New Haven, Connecticut
Charlottesville, Virginia
March, 1996

*

ACKNOWLEDGMENTS

The authors wish to express their gratitude to law library colleagues at Yale and the University of Virginia for supporting the preparation of this new edition, and to students in Advanced Legal Research courses for suggesting ways to improve this text.

Reprint permission for sample excerpts from *ALR5th* (Exhibits 21–23), *ALR Quick Index* (Exhibit 24), *American Jurisprudence 2d* (Exhibit 26), *Auto-Cite* (Exhibit 34), *Michigan Civil Jurisprudence* (Exhibit 27), *New York Reports* (Exhibit 8), *United States Code Service* (Exhibit 41) and *United States Supreme Court Reports, Lawyers' Edition* (Exhibit 5) has been granted by the copyright holder, Lawyers Cooperative Publishing, a division of Thomson Legal Publishing Inc.

Material in Exhibit 6 is reprinted with permission from *The United States Law Week*. Copyright by The Bureau of National Affairs, Inc. (800–372–1033).

Copyrighted material from *Shepard's Atlantic Reporter Citations* (Exhibit 20), *Shepard's Code of Federal Regulations Citations* (Exhibit 68), *Shepard's Georgia Citations* (Exhibits 45–46), *Shepard's Maryland Citations* (Exhibits 18–19), and *Shepard's United States Citations* (Exhibit 32) is reproduced by permission of Shepard's, a subsidiary of The McGraw-Hill Companies. Further reproduction of any kind is strictly prohibited.

Material in Exhibits 29, 31 and 58 is reprinted with the permission of LEXIS-NEXIS, a division of Reed Else-

ACKNOWLEDGMENTS

vier Inc. LEXIS® and NEXIS® are registered trademarks, and KWIC™ is a trademark of Reed Elsevier Properties Inc.

The statutes reprinted in Exhibit 44 are taken from the *Official Code of Georgia Annotated,* Copyright © 1926 through 1930, 1982, 1986, 1990, 1994, 1995 by the State of Georgia, and are reprinted with the permission of the State of Georgia. All rights reserved.

Material in Exhibits 53–55 is reproduced from *CIS/Index,* Copyright © 1995 Congressional Information Service, Inc. Used with permission. All other reproduction is strictly prohibited without the express written consent of CIS.

Material is reproduced with permission from *CCH Congressional Index* (Exhibits 56 and 83) and *CCH Food Drug Cosmetic Law Reports* (Exhibits 73–76), published and copyrighted by CCH Incorporated, 2700 Lake Cook Road, Riverwoods, Illinois 60015.

Copyrighted material from *Congressional Quarterly Weekly Report* in Exhibit 57 is reprinted with permission of Congressional Quarterly, Inc.

Material reprinted from *Restatement of the Law (Third), Unfair Competition* in Exhibit 70, Copyright © 1995 by The American Law Institute. Reprinted with the permission of The American Law Institute.

Index to Legal Periodicals & Books, 1994–1995, page 873, Copyright © 1994 by The H. W. Wilson Company. Material in Exhibit 71 reproduced with permission of the publisher.

ACKNOWLEDGMENTS

Material in Exhibit 72 is reprinted with permission from *Current Law Index*™. Copyright © 1996 by Information Access Company.

An excerpt from *Martindale-Hubbell*® *Law Digest,* Reed Elsevier, Inc. is reproduced in Exhibit 77 with permission from the publisher. All rights reserved.

Copyrighted material from *Encyclopedia of Associations* in Exhibit 79 is reprinted with permission of Gale Research Inc.

*

OUTLINE

APPENDICES

*

LEGAL
RESEARCH
IN A NUTSHELL

*

CHAPTER 1

THE RESEARCH PROCESS

§ 1–1. INTRODUCTION

Good research makes for good lawyering. It gives the attorney the knowledge with which to build a successful case or to provide accurate and insightful advice. Efficient research saves time for other aspects of lawyering and time for life beyond the law.

Legal research is the process of finding the laws that govern most of our life activities and the materials which explain or analyze these laws. Research is essential in legal practice to determine both the impact of past actions and the implications of contemplated actions. Through research, lawyers find the sources needed to predict how courts will act, and to persuade them to take particular actions. Nonlawyers perform legal research for a variety of reasons, from settling a boundary dispute

to challenging a traffic ticket. Because the literature of the law is a central part of our history, legal research is also important to academic pursuits in law schools and in universities generally.

Applying the law to a particular situation requires expertise in legal analysis. A lawyer should be able to analyze a factual situation and apply legal doctrines developed in analogous or similar situations. These doctrines may conflict with each other, making it necessary to weigh their importance and relevance to a particular problem. Most of the law school curriculum seeks to develop this expertise.

Finding the law to apply, on the other hand, requires expertise in legal research, and that demands an understanding of which resources to consult for each situation, as well as the relative value of the resources available. Experienced legal researchers know which sources are authoritative or useful for what purposes.

Legal research involves the use of a variety of printed and electronic sources. The printed sources include court decisions, statutes, administrative documents, scholarly commentaries, and practical manuals. Computer databases containing many of these materials have dramatically changed legal research, but they have not eliminated its complexities. The volume and variety of legal literature continues to grow, making the researcher's choice of tools and tactics for each problem difficult. A thorough knowledge of available legal resources, both published and computerized, is necessary. There are as many procedures as there are problems, and no single approach can work every time.

§ 1–2. THE FORMS OF LEGAL LITERATURE

Legal sources differ in their relative authority. Some are binding; others are only persuasive in varying degrees; and some are only useful as tools for finding other material. These variations require that researchers evaluate the sources they study. Whether researching by book or by computer, one must be familiar with the three broad categories of legal literature: (a) primary sources; (b) finding tools; and (c) secondary materials.

a. Primary Sources

Primary sources of law are those recorded rules which will be enforced by the state. They are found in constitutions, in decisions of appellate courts, in statutes passed by legislatures, in executive decrees, and in regulations and rulings of administrative agencies.

Law is made by many governmental agencies (judicial, legislative and executive) in a variety of jurisdictions (the federal government, fifty states, and a host of local counties and municipalities). Treaties, and even some norms of international law accepted by our courts, are also included among our primary sources.

One major category of primary sources is judicial decisions. The United States is a "common law" country. Its law is expressed in an evolving body of doctrine determined by judges on the basis of cases which they must decide, rather than on a group of abstract principles. As established rules are tested and adapted to meet new situations, the common law grows and changes over time.

Our judicial system consists of hierarchies of courts, including, in most jurisdictions, a number of trial courts,

one or more intermediate appellate courts, and a court of last resort, usually the *Supreme Court* of the jurisdiction. This system incorporates the processes of appellate review, in which higher courts review the decisions of lower courts, and judicial review, in which courts determine the validity of legislative and executive actions.

The products of legislative actions, *statutes,* are another major primary source. Statutes have come to govern a great variety of human activities. The ruling principles in some subject areas are determined wholly by case law; other areas are governed partly by case law and partly by statute, or by statutes as construed and interpreted by the courts.

A third important primary source is administrative law, contained in the regulations and decisions of government agencies. Federal and state agencies promulgate regulations governing activity within their areas of expertise. Agencies also act in a "quasi-judicial" capacity by conducting hearings and issuing decisions to resolve particular disputes.

American primary sources share a number of characteristics which have pervasive importance to legal research. They are issued *chronologically* in either official or unofficial publications. Thus the researcher requires some means of subject access to find the law applicable to a particular factual situation. The law is constantly changing as thousands of new decisions, statutes and regulations are issued each year. These changes require frequent updating of legal resources. On the other hand, the development of the law involves a quest for certainty and stability, as reflected in the doctrine of *stare decisis*. This gives primary materials a continuing relevance long

beyond their initial publication. They remain in effect until they are expressly overruled or repealed.

The primary sources relevant to any problem may range from the earliest enactments of law-making bodies to the most recent decisions, statutes and rulings. A current decision can rely on a precedent many generations old, and an executive order may be based on a statute of another century. Since primary sources retain their force and effect until expressly overruled or repealed, even the earliest materials must remain accessible. However, because the law is constantly changing, access to the *most recent* legal sources is also a prerequisite to effective legal research.

b. Finding Tools

Because an enormous volume of decisions and statutes have been issued chronologically since the beginning of our legal history, the researcher needs some means of subject access into this large body of law. The effective operation of the doctrine of precedent requires that prior decisions be found easily by subject. Without a topical approach, researchers could not find existing decisions or statutes on point.

Fortunately a varied group of finding tools provides such access. *Digests* reprint headnotes summarizing points of law from court decisions in a subject classification, and *citators* list later sources that have relied upon or mentioned a particular precedent. *Annotations* and *legal encyclopedias* provide narrative explanations of case law. *Annotated codes* collect both legislative amendments and notes of court decisions applying statutes. *WESTLAW* and *LEXIS,* two comprehensive and competing computer-based legal research systems, provide the

capability to search for cases and other documents by using practically any word or combination of words.

The purpose of these tools is not to persuade, nor do they themselves have any primary or persuasive authority. Finding tools are only a means for locating primary sources. Those sources must then be read to determine their applicability to a particular situation. In legal research, as in other aspects of the lawyer's work, one must use a highly developed sense of relevance—a keen appreciation of which sources are legally and factually relevant to the specific inquiry.

c. Secondary Materials

Works which are not primary authority but which discuss or analyze legal doctrine are considered *secondary materials*. These include treatises, hornbooks, restatements, and practice manuals. Much of the most influential legal writing is found in the academic journals known as *law reviews*. Secondary materials vary widely in purpose and quality, ranging from authoritative treatises by great academic scholars to superficial tracts by hack writers. The best of these works have a persuasive influence on the law-making process by virtue of the prestige of their authors or the quality of their scholarship. Secondary sources can help analyze a problem, and their footnotes provide references to both primary sources and other secondary material.

Relevant secondary materials can be found through law library catalogs, legal periodical indexes, and other bibliographic aids. In addition, court decisions and other secondary sources frequently provide citations to persuasive treatises and law review articles. Some treatises,

periodicals and appellate records and briefs can also be found as online databases or in CD–ROM form.

§ 1–3.　THE IMPACT OF TECHNOLOGY

Electronic access to information, first through the on-line databases of WESTLAW and LEXIS and more recently through CD–ROM and the Internet, has had a dramatic impact on the way legal research is conducted.

The ability to search the full text of documents for specific combinations of terms has freed researchers from total reliance on the editors who create indexes and digests.　Each research situation presents a unique set of factual and legal issues, and the computer makes it possible to find documents which address this specific confluence of issues.

Yet editors have hardly been put out of work.　Researchers forced to work only with an uncontrolled mass of electronic data would quickly find themselves drowning in raw information.　Digests and indexes continue to provide the invaluable service of sorting material by subject and presenting it in a comprehensible fashion.

Electronic research has significantly affected the process of legal research.　The computer can integrate a variety of tasks that are conducted with separate print sources, such as finding cases, checking the current validity of their holdings, and tracking down secondary commentary.　Hypertext links between documents make it possible to follow various leads and ideas as they arise rather than following one linear research path.

Computerized research has also blurred the distinctions between different types of information and broadened the scope of legal inquiry.　Traditionally research in

case law, for example, was a process quite distinct from research in secondary commentary or social sciences. Using electronic databases it is much more convenient and natural to switch from one information source to another and back again, bringing to legal research more empirical experience and a wider range of scholarly commentary.

§ 1–4. LEGAL LANGUAGE

The law has developed its own terminology over the centuries. For an understanding and mastery of the language of the law, a good law dictionary is a necessity for the beginning student. The leading American law dictionary is *Black's Law Dictionary* (6th ed. 1991). In addition to definitions, it provides references to relevant cases and statutes. *Black's* can also be searched on Westlaw. *Ballentine's Law Dictionary* (3d ed. 1969) is the major competitor to *Black's*, but it is considerably out of date. Several shorter dictionaries are also available. Among the best are Steven H. Gifis, *Law Dictionary* (3d ed. 1991) and Daniel Oran, *Law Dictionary for Non–Lawyers* (3d ed. 1991). Others of similar size and approach can be found in any law library.

David Mellinkoff's *The Language of the Law* (1963) offers a learned and often witty introduction to the history and peculiarities of legal expression. Bryan A. Garner's *A Dictionary of Modern Legal Usage* (2d ed. 1995) is an entertaining guide to its complexities and nuances.

Both traditional and computer-based research depend on the selection of effective search terms. Two thesauri can aid the researcher in identifying and choosing appropriate words: William C. Burton, *Legal Thesaurus* (2d

ed. 1992) and William P. Statsky, *West's Legal Thesaurus/Dictionary* (1985).

To cope with the complex shorthand of legal citations, guides to proper citation form and usage are essential. *The Bluebook: A Uniform System of Citation* (15th ed. 1991), published by the Harvard Law Review Association, is the generally accepted standard. Many of its rules are seen as archaic or inflexible, and advocates of a simplified citation form have countered with *The University of Chicago Manual of Legal Citation* (1989), also known as the *Maroon Book*. Although *Bluebook* practice still prevails, the *Maroon Book* has pushed it in its newest edition to a somewhat more reasonable approach. Present controversy over reform of citation practice may lead to yet more simplification in the near future.

Abbreviations of many kinds are widely used in legal writing, and aids to their understanding are frequently needed. *Black's Law Dictionary* includes an extensive list of abbreviations. The *Bluebook* contains many explanatory lists of abbreviations and citations on a jurisdiction by jurisdiction basis.

Two specialized abbreviations sources by Mary Miles Prince, *Bieber's Dictionary of Legal Abbreviations* (4th ed. 1993) and *Bieber's Dictionary of Legal Citations* (4th ed. 1992), provide far more extensive coverage of obscure and cryptic abbreviations. Donald Raistrick, *Index to Legal Citations and Abbreviations* (2d ed. 1993) is also recommended, particularly for English sources.

§ 1–5. BEGINNING A RESEARCH PROJECT

This book presents legal materials in order of their traditional importance. Court reports and their finding

tools are discussed first because of their central place in the American legal system and in legal education. Statutory publications, some of which include very useful case-finding features, are discussed next, followed by administrative sources, secondary materials, and finally international and foreign law.

When studying legal research, it is essential to understand the workings of the basic primary sources such as court reports and statutes. In practice, however, the order in which resources are consulted by an experienced researcher is generally quite different.

Often the hardest part of the research process is finding the first piece of relevant information. One document frequently leads to other documents. Cases cite earlier cases as authority; a statute's notes provide useful leads to decisions, other statutes, legislative history, and secondary sources; and a periodical article may cite to a variety of sources. Finding the first piece of the puzzle, though, can be a challenge.

Where does a researcher begin when working on a new problem? To some extent, this is a matter of personal preference and relative familiarity with particular tools. It makes sense to use material which you can use most effectively. There are, however, some guidelines for beginning a research problem which will make your task much easier.

Before looking anywhere, step back and study the problem carefully. Determine whether the jurisdictional focus is federal or state. Be sure you understand the terms in which the problem is stated; if not, consult a good dictionary or other reference source. Formulate *tentative* issues, but be prepared to revise your statement

of the issues as research progresses and you learn more about the legal background.

Generally, begin researching by going to a trustworthy secondary source—a legal treatise or a law review article. The mass of primary sources can seem forbidding, and using a subject index or digest to find cases or statutes on point is often frustrating. Primary sources by themselves often are not very straightforward. Secondary materials, on the other hand, try to *explain* and *analyze* the law. They offer easier access, while providing food for thought. They summarize the basic rules and the leading primary sources and place them in context, allowing the researcher to select the most promising primary sources to pursue. One must be careful, however, to allow for the biases of the author.

The choice of the appropriate starting point should be influenced by the nature of the problem. When researching a new or developing area of law, start by looking for a recent periodical article. A law review article can provide an overview of the field, references to important cases and statutes, and a relatively current perspective. Moreover, the indexes to periodicals are among the easiest and most useful tools for subject access to legal literature.

When researching an issue that fits within a traditional area of legal doctrine, begin by consulting a subject treatise or hornbook in the area. A good treatise explains the major issues and provides a context in which related issues might be raised or considered. The names of some of the most famous treatises, such as Corbin on Contracts or Tribe on Constitutional Law, are familiar to any law student. Treatises in other areas can be found

by checking a law library's catalog or asking a reference librarian.

If no treatise is available, a legal encyclopedia such as *American Jurisprudence 2d* or *Corpus Juris Secundum* can be a useful first step. These works attempt to cover the entire field of legal doctrine, so their focus is rather diffuse. They do, however, outline the basic rules in each area and provide extensive references to primary sources.

When it is apparent that the issue to be researched is one of public law (i.e., involves substantial governmental regulation), it may be most efficient to begin with the statute underlying the area of regulation. Public law includes most issues of constitutional and administrative law, as well as antitrust, banking, labor, taxation, and several other areas. Beginning with the statutory base deprives the researcher of an organized introduction to the field, but an annotated code leads directly to most of the relevant primary sources. If the statute is studied in a looseleaf service, an introduction is often provided by the publisher.

In most situations it is best to begin research by using printed resources, in order to get an overview of an area and to minimize cost at this early stage. There are times, though, when the computer databases of LEXIS or WESTLAW may be the best starting point. If you are generally familiar with an area of law and are researching a narrow question or a particular combination of issues, use of the databases may be the most effective way of focusing your research. Because the researcher defines the terms to be searched, computers provide far more flexibility than other tools.

There are still times when the first research step will be the major case-finding tools to be discussed in this book, such as digests and annotations. These tools are specifically designed to gather together cases with similar facts or issues, and can be great resources for finding relevant court decisions. With digests, however, it is not always easy to find the appropriate place to look. For that reason it is often easier to use digests once a few cases have been found by other means. References in these cases will provide leads into the digest system or annotated reports.

Finally, sometimes the first step of research does not involve using the library at all. Instead it may be more efficient to make a telephone call or two. Government agencies and professional associations are staffed with experts who can answer questions, provide invaluable references, or send essential documents. There are several directories of government agencies, and resources such as the *Encyclopedia of Associations* list professional and trade groups by subject.

These various options are the sort of choices one must make in any research process. It is important to remember that there may be professional help available to guide you in the choice of the first resource. Most law libraries are staffed with librarians trained to provide just this sort of assistance. While law librarians are not permitted to interpret the law or provide legal advice to library users, they are trained to assist patrons in tracking down the relevant sources.

§ 1–6. COMPLETING A RESEARCH PROJECT

For many researchers it can be just as difficult to know when to stop researching as it is to know where to begin. Yet every research situation demands that the researcher determine when it is time to synthesize the information found and produce the required memorandum, brief, or opinion letter.

Often the limits to research are set by the nature of the project. Some assignments are limited to a specified number of hours or a certain amount of money. In such instances the ability to find information quickly and accurately is essential.

The more difficult situation arises when there is no clear limit to the amount of research to be done. In such cases you must do enough research to be confident that your work will be based on information that is complete and accurate. The surest way to achieve this confidence is to try several approaches to the research problem and compare results. If a review of the secondary literature, a digest search, and online queries produce different conclusions, more research is necessary. When these various approaches lead to the same primary sources and a single conclusion, chances are better that a key piece of information has not eluded you.

Confidence in your research product is a result of confidence generally in your research skills. Familiarity with legal resources and experience in their use will produce the confidence that your research is complete and accurate.

§ 1-7. CONCLUSION

As we will see in the following chapters, the law has a voluminous literature and a wide range of highly developed research tools. Some of these tools are the result of centuries of development in improving access to primary sources. Others are the product of recent technological innovations.

Many practitioners of legal research understand little about the tools they use. As a result they spin their wheels and overlook aids and shortcuts designed to help them. Learn how legal information resources work as you encounter them, hone your skills through practice, and this mastery will save you from needless waste of valuable time and effort.

CHAPTER 2

COURT REPORTS

---

§ 2–1. INTRODUCTION

Judicial decisions are one of the most important sources of legal authority in the common law system. Over the course of time, judges shape legal doctrines to address the complex issues of changing society. Case law retains its vitality today despite the ever increasing scope of legislative enactments. Even statutes which may appear straightforward at first must be read in conjunction with cases which construe and apply their provisions.

The reporting of judicial decisions is related to the quest for certainty and fairness in the law. The records of earlier legal controversies provide guidance to later courts faced with similar cases, and aid in preventing

16

further disputes. The doctrine of *precedent*, or *stare decisis* ("let the decision stand"), seeks to ensure that people in like circumstances are treated alike. Courts follow this doctrine so that people can study earlier disputes, evaluate the legal impact of planned conduct, and modify their behavior to conform to existing rules.

The earliest evidence of law reporting in England closely follows the Norman conquest of 1066, although many of the oldest cases are known only from early legal texts such as those by Glanville (c. 1190) and Bracton (c. 1250). The *Plea Rolls,* beginning with the reign of Richard I in 1189, contain fragmentary reports, and the *Year Books,* covering the long period from 1285 to 1537, include both transcripts of proceedings and brief summaries of decisions. The *Year Books* constitute a rich body of legal literature, much of which has been translated from its original Law French, edited, and republished in scholarly series by the Selden Society and similar groups.

Following the *Year Books* came the *nominate* or *nominative* reports, that is, court reports named for the person who recorded or edited them. The earliest known reporter was probably James Dyer, whose reports were published around 1550. *Plowden's Reports,* first published in 1571, are considered among the finest and most accurate, while the reports of Sir Edward Coke were perhaps the most influential of the period.

The American colonies inherited the English legal system and its common law tradition. No decisions of American courts were published during the colonial period, so lawyers and judges had to rely on English precedents. After independence many states enacted *reception statutes* adopting the English common law and

statutes as part of the law of the state, excluding those portions which were considered repugnant to the new American system. The first volume of American decisions, *Kirby's Reports* in Connecticut, was published in 1789. *Official* court reporting (reports published pursuant to statutory direction) did not begin until 1804 when Massachusetts, New York and Kentucky authorized the publication of official reports.

As the country grew in the 19th century, the number of reported decisions increased dramatically and the overburdened official reporting system soon lagged further and further behind. The need for improved and more rapid access to cases was met by commercial publishers. In 1876, one of these publishers, John B. West, began publishing selected decisions of the Minnesota Supreme Court in a weekly leaflet, the *Syllabi*. Three years later he launched the *North Western Reporter,* covering five surrounding states as well as Minnesota. This was the first component of what became West Publishing Company's *National Reporter System*. By 1887 it covered every state and the federal system.

West reporters continue to be widely used today, while many official reports have ceased publication. Besides publishing cases sooner than the remaining official reports, West's reporters also include editorial features which make it easier to find and understand the court decisions. Each case is prefaced with a one-paragraph summary of its holding, called a *synopsis,* and with numbered editorial abstracts, or *headnotes,* of the specific legal issues. Each headnote is assigned a legal topic and a number indicating a particular subdivision of that topic. This classification plan, known as the *key number system,* allows uniform subject access to the cases of

different jurisdictions. The headnotes are reprinted by subject in *digests*, which will be discussed in Chapter 3.

This century's major development in access to court decisions is electronic dissemination, through a variety of computerized means. New decisions are available electronically long before they are published in print form, and the full text of decisions can be searched for specific word combinations. Among the most widespread electronic resources are the commercial databases WESTLAW, from West Publishing Company, and LEXIS–NEXIS, a division of Reed Elsevier Inc. An increasing number of recent court decisions are also available through noncommercial sources on the Internet, and several companies publish collections of decisions on CD–ROM. Case research using these electronic resources will be discussed in Chapter 5.

To use court reports effectively, it is necessary to understand the hierarchical structure of the American judicial system. Litigation usually begins in a *trial court*. The jurisdiction of these courts may be based on geography (the U.S. District Courts in the federal system, or county courts in many states) or subject (the U.S. Tax Court, or state family courts and probate courts). In the trial court, *issues of fact* (such as which of two cars entered an intersection first) are decided by the factfinder (either the judge or a jury). These findings are binding on the parties and cannot be appealed. *Issues of law* (such as whether a witness's statement is admissible at trial) are decided by the judge, and a party who disagrees with these rulings can appeal them to a higher court.

Appeals from the decisions of trial courts are generally taken to an *intermediate appellate court* (the U.S. Courts

of Appeals and similar state tribunals). An appellate court usually consists of three or more judges, who confer and vote on the issues after oral argument and written briefs from the lawyers for each side. One of the judges writes an opinion summarizing the question and stating the court's holding. Dissenting judges may write separate opinions outlining their views.

The *court of last resort* in each jurisdiction (called the *supreme court* in the federal system and in most states) usually reviews cases from the intermediate appellate courts, but may take appeals directly from the trial court. Its role in the judicial system is to craft policy and establish legal rules, rather than to resolve every individual dispute. The court of last resort's decisions on issues of law are binding on all trial and intermediate appellate courts in its jurisdiction.

Court reports consist of these judicial decisions, or written determinations of issues of law. Very few trial court decisions are published. Trial court decisions on issues of fact have no precedential effect and usually do not even result in written judicial opinions. A jury verdict at the end of a trial, for example, produces no published decision unless the judge must decide a motion challenging the verdict on legal grounds. A few trial court decisions on issues of law are published, but most reports consist of appellate decisions. Selected decisions from intermediate appellate courts, and nearly all decisions from courts of last resort, are published both in printed volumes and in computer services.

The first appearance of a new decision is the official *slip opinion* issued by the court itself, usually an individually paginated copy of a single decision. These opinions are most readily available through commercial online

databases, and a growing number of appellate courts are now making their decisions available through the Internet. Slip opinions provide the text of new cases, but they are difficult to cite because they have no volume and page numbers. Several jurisdictions and organizations are in the process of developing "medium-neutral" citation systems that allow a researcher to refer to any printed or electronic resource. At this point these developments are neither widespread nor standardized, but it is clear that they will be the norm in the near future.

Published court reports provide both a permanent record of judicial decisions and an easily cited source. They usually appear first in weekly or biweekly pamphlets known as *advance sheets*, containing a number of decisions paginated in a continuous sequence, and then in bound volumes. The volumes consolidate the cases from several advance sheets, and usually contain subject indexes and alphabetical tables of the cases reported. They are numbered consecutively, often in more than one series. When the volumes of a reporter reach an arbitrary number (such as 100 or 300), publishers frequently start over with volume 1, second series. Some reporters are now in their third or fourth series. If a reporter is in a second or later series, that must be indicated in its citation in order to distinguish it from the same volume number in the first series. *People v. Harris*, 570 N.E.2d 1051 (N.Y.1991), for example, is from the second series of the *North Eastern Reporter*.

Court reports vary somewhat between publishers, but several standard features are important in case research. Exhibit 1 shows a variety of these features in a case from the New York Court of Appeals, as published in a West reporter:

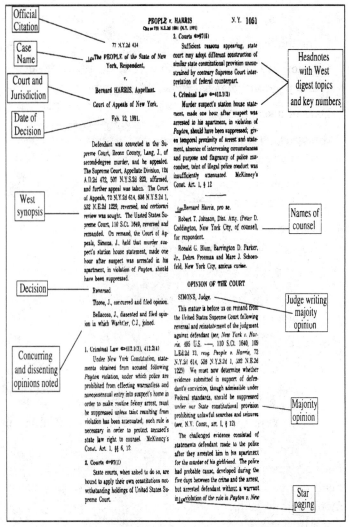

Exhibit 1: A decision of the New York Court of Appeals, as published in the *North Eastern Reporter*, showing several standard features in court reports.

Case name (sometimes called *caption* or *style*) listing the parties involved.

Citation indicating the volume number, reporter series, and page number at which the case appears.

Date of decision.

Synopsis, or brief descriptive paragraph of the case's facts and holding.

Headnotes summarizing the points of law discussed, with digest classification numbers.

Name of the judge writing the majority opinion, and of concurring or dissenting judges, if any.

Names of lawyers who represented the parties.

Full text of majority opinion and of any additional opinions.

Star paging, if available, providing references in unofficial reporters to page numbers in official reports.

§ 2–2. SUPREME COURT OF THE UNITED STATES

The Supreme Court of the United States is one of the nation's preeminent lawmaking bodies. It stands at the head of one of the three coordinate branches of government, and determines the scope and interpretation of the Constitution. Its decisions are studied not only by lawyers but by political scientists, historians, and citizens interested in the development of social and legal policy.

The Supreme Court is the court of last resort in the federal court system and has the final word on federal issues raised in state courts. The Court exercises a tight control over its docket and has wide discretion to decline review, or to *deny a writ of certiorari* as it is called in most cases. The Supreme Court usually accepts for consideration only those cases that raise significant policy issues. In recent years it has issued opinions in fewer than 150 cases during its annual term, which begins on the first Monday of October and ends in late June or early July.

The reports containing the decisions of the Supreme Court have a long history. These decisions are now available in three permanent bound reporters, in two looseleaf services for prompt access to new decisions, and through several electronic sources.

a. The *United States Reports*

Begun in 1790 as a private venture, the *United States Reports* (cited as U.S.) became official in 1817 and continues today as the official edition of United States Supreme Court decisions. Several volumes of *U.S. Reports* are published every year. The official court reporter prefaces the text of each decision with a *syllabus,* preliminary paragraphs summarizing the case and the Court's holding. Following the general pattern of publication, the decisions appear first in slip opinion form, followed by an official advance sheet (called the "preliminary print"), and finally the bound *U.S. Reports* volume. Unfortunately, as with many government publications, the *U.S. Reports* tends to be published quite slowly. Almost three years pass before a decision appears in the preliminary print, and another year or more before its inclusion in a bound volume. (In contrast, the decisions

are available on WESTLAW and LEXIS within a few minutes of their issuance.)

The early volumes of Supreme Court decisions are now numbered sequentially as part of the *U.S. Reports* series, but for many years they were cited only by the names of the individual reporters.   Even now citations to these early cases include a parenthetical reference to the nominative reporter volume, as in *Marbury v. Madison,* 5 U.S. (1 Cranch) 137 (1803).   Some familiarity with the following reporters' names and their periods of coverage will make it easier to read and understand older citations:

Nominative Reports			**U.S. Reports**
Dallas	1–4	(1790–1800)	1–4
Cranch	1–9	(1801–1815)	5–13
Wheaton	1–12	(1816–1827)	14–25
Peters	1–16	(1828–1842)	26–41
Howard	1–24	(1843–1860)	42–65
Black	1–2	(1861–1862)	66–67
Wallace	1–23	(1863–1874)	68–90

After volume 90 (1874), cases are normally cited only by volume number of the *U.S. Reports.* Thus the official citation of the Supreme Court's decision in *New York v. Harris* is 495 U.S. 14 (1990), meaning the case beginning on page 14 of volume 495 of the *U.S. Reports.*   The opening pages of the official report of *New York v. Harris* appear in Exhibits 2 and 3.   Note that this is the same case which the New York court considered on remand in Exhibit 1.

NEW YORK *v.* HARRIS

CERTIORARI TO THE COURT OF APPEALS OF NEW YORK

No. 88-1000. Argued January 10, 1990—Decided April 18, 1990

Police officers, having probable cause to believe that respondent Harris committed murder, entered his home without first obtaining a warrant, read him his rights under *Miranda* v. *Arizona*, 384 U. S. 436, and reportedly secured an admission of guilt. After he was arrested, taken to the police station, and again given his *Miranda* rights, he signed a written inculpatory statement. The New York trial court suppressed the first statement under *Payton* v. *New York*, 445 U. S. 573, which held that the Fourth Amendment prohibits the police from effecting a warrantless and nonconsensual entry into a suspect's home in order to make a routine felony arrest. However, the court admitted the second statement, and Harris was convicted of second-degree murder. The Appellate Division affirmed, but the State Court of Appeals reversed. Applying the rule of *Brown* v. *Illinois*, 422 U. S. 590, and its progeny that the indirect fruits of an illegal search or arrest should be suppressed when they bear a sufficiently close relationship to the underlying illegality, the court deemed the second statement inadmissible because its connection with the arrest was not sufficiently attenuated.

Held: Where the police have probable cause to arrest a suspect, the exclusionary rule does not bar the State's use of a statement made by the defendant outside of his home, even though the statement is taken after an arrest made in the home in violation of *Payton.* The penalties imposed on the government where its officers have violated the law must bear some relation to the purposes which the law serves. *United States v. Ceccolini,* 435 U. S. 268, 279. The rule in *Payton* was designed to protect the physical integrity of the home, not to grant criminal suspects protection for statements made outside their premises where the police have probable cause to make an arrest. *Brown* v. *Illinois, supra,* and its progeny are distinguishable, since attenuation analysis is only appropriate where, as a threshold matter, courts determine that the challenged evidence is in some sense the product of illegal governmental activity. Here, the police had a justification to question Harris prior to his arrest; therefore, his subsequent statement was not an exploitation of the illegal entry into his home. Cf. *United States v. Crews,* 445 U. S. 463. Suppressing that statement would not serve the purpose of the *Payton* rule, since anything incriminating gathered from Harris' in-home arrest has already been excluded. The principal incentive to obey

Exhibit 2: The beginning of a case in the official *U.S. Reports*, showing the name, docket number, date, and the beginning of the official syllabus.

NEW YORK *v.* HARRIS   15

14   Opinion of the Court

Payton still obtains: the police know that a warrantless entry will lead to the suppression of evidence found or statements taken inside the home. Moreover, the incremental deterrent value of suppressing statements like Harris' would be minimal, since it is doubtful that the desire to secure a statement from a suspect whom the police have probable cause to arrest would motivate them to violate *Payton.* Pp. 17–21.

72 N. Y. 2d 614, 532 N. E. 2d 1229, reversed.

WHITE, J., delivered the opinion of the Court, in which REHNQUIST, C. J., and O'CONNOR, SCALIA, and KENNEDY, JJ., joined. MARSHALL, J., filed a dissenting opinion, in which BRENNAN, BLACKMUN, and STEVENS, JJ., joined, *post,* p. 21.

Peter D. Coddington argued the cause for petitioner. With him on the briefs were *Robert T. Johnson, Anthony J. Girese, Stanley R. Kaplan,* and *Karen P. Swiger.*

Barrington D. Parker, Jr., by invitation of the Court, 492 U. S. 934, argued the cause as *amicus curiae* in support of the judgment below. With him on the brief was *Ronald G. Blum.**

JUSTICE WHITE delivered the opinion of the Court.

On January 11, 1984, New York City police found the body of Ms. Thelma Staton murdered in her apartment. Various facts gave the officers probable cause to believe that the respondent in this case, Bernard Harris, had killed Ms. Staton. As a result, on January 16, 1984, three police officers went to Harris' apartment to take him into custody. They did not first obtain an arrest warrant.

When the police arrived, they knocked on the door, displaying their guns and badges. Harris let them enter.

---

*Briefs of *amici curiae* urging reversal were filed for the United States by *Solicitor General Starr, Assistant Attorney General Dennis, Deputy Solicitor General Bryson, Michael R. Dreeben,* and *Robert J. Erickson;* for the Office of Prosecuting Attorney, Wayne County, Michigan, by *John D. O'Hair* and *Timothy A. Baughman;* and for Americans for Effective Law Enforcement, Inc., et al. by *Fred E. Inbau, Wayne W. Schmidt, James P. Manak, Gregory U. Evans, Daniel B. Hales, George D. Webster,* and *Jack E. Yelverton.*

Exhibit 3: A *U.S. Reports* case continued, showing the end of the syllabus, names of attorneys, and the beginning of the majority opinion.

b. *Supreme Court Reporter* and *Lawyers' Edition*

Because the *U.S. Reports* is published so slowly, the need for more timely publication is met by several commercial versions. Two of these publications, West Publishing's *Supreme Court Reporter* (cited as S.Ct.) and Lawyers Cooperative Publishing Company's *United States Supreme Court Reports, Lawyers' Edition* (known simply as *Lawyers' Edition,* and cited as L.Ed.) are not only published in advance sheets within a few weeks of decision; they also have a permanent value because they are later published in bound volumes with editorial research aids not in the official edition.

The *Supreme Court Reporter* began in 1882, with cases from volume 106 of the *U.S. Reports.* As a component of West's National Reporter System, it includes the publisher's editorial synopses and headnotes. Each headnote is designated by topic and assigned to a numbered subdivision within the topic. Subject access to the headnotes is provided in the *United States Supreme Court Digest,* a companion set to the reporter. Since the same key number system is used for court decisions throughout the country, the same point of law can also be researched in digests covering other federal courts and state courts. The opening page of *New York v. Harris* as it appears in the *Supreme Court Reporter* at 110 S.Ct. 1640 is shown in Exhibit 4 and illustrates these headnotes.

Lawyers' Edition contains all Supreme Court decisions since the Court's inception in 1790. Like the *Supreme Court Reporter,* it contains editorial summaries and headnotes for each case. Its headnotes are reprinted, arranged by topic, in the companion set to the reports,

the officer, whether locked or unlocked. What is left for the "standard criteria"?

[13]It is a proper part of the judicial function to make law as a necessary by-product of the process of deciding actual cases and controversies. But to reach out so blatantly and unnecessarily to make new law in a case of this kind is unabashed judicial activism.

495 U.S. 14, 109 L.Ed.2d 13

[1]NEW YORK, Petitioner

v.

Bernard HARRIS.

No. 88–1000.

Argued Jan. 10, 1990.

Decided April 18, 1990.

Defendant was convicted in the New York Supreme Court, Bronx County, Lang, J., of second-degree murder and he appealed. The Supreme Court, Appellate Division, 124 A.D.2d 472, 507 N.Y.S.2d 823 (memorandum opinion), affirmed. On further appeal, the New York Court of Appeals, 72 N.Y.2d 614, 536 N.Y.S.2d 1, 532 N.E.2d 1229, reversed. Certiorari was granted. The Supreme Court, Justice White, held that, where the police have probable cause to arrest a suspect, the exclusionary rule does not bar the State's use of a statement made by the suspect outside his home, even though the statement is made after a warrantless and nonconsensual entry into the suspect's home.

Judgment reversed.

Justice Marshall filed a dissenting opinion in which Justices Brennan, Blackmun, and Stevens joined.

1. Arrest ⟨key⟩68.5(1)
   Criminal Law ⟨key⟩412.1(3)

Payton violation that occurs when police officers make warrantless and nonconsensual entry into suspect's home to make felony arrest does not automatically require exclusion of statements made by suspect outside premises where police have probable cause to arrest; Payton rule was designed to protect physical integrity of home, not to grant suspect additional protection for statements made outside of home. U.S.C.A. Const. Amend. 4.

2. Criminal Law ⟨key⟩412.1(3)

Arrest made in suspect's home without warrant, but with probable cause, did not render suspect's continued detention unlawful and did not render subsequent statements made at station house after Miranda warnings inadmissible. U.S.C.A. Const.Amend. 4.

3. Criminal Law ⟨key⟩412.1(3), 412.2(3)

Attenuation analysis did not apply in deciding admissibility of statement made by suspect after he received Miranda warnings at station house, even though suspect's arrest violated Payton rule that prohibits warrantless and nonconsensual entry into suspect's home; station house statement was not product or exploitation of illegal entry into home. U.S.C.A. Const.Amend. 4.

4. Criminal Law ⟨key⟩412.1(1, 2), 412.2(3)

Not every statement taken by police while suspect is in legal custody is admissible; statements taken during legal custody would be inadmissible if they were product of coercion, if Miranda warnings were not given, or if there was Edwards violation.

5. Criminal Law ⟨key⟩412.1(3), 412.2(3)

Suppressing statement made by suspect after he received Miranda warnings at station house would not serve purpose of Payton rule that prohibits warrantless and nonconsensual entry into suspect's home to make felony arrest; purpose of rule is to protect the home by requiring exclusion of anything

Exhibit 4: The first page of a case in the unofficial *Supreme Court Reporter*, showing the West synopsis and key number headnotes.

United States Supreme Court Digest, Lawyers' Edition.
The *Lawyers' Edition* classification system, however,
does not appear in other reports, so it is useful only for
Supreme Court research. One *Lawyers' Edition* feature
not found in the *U.S. Reports* or the *Supreme Court
Reporter* is the inclusion of legal analyses, or *annotations*,
on issues arising in about four decisions per volume.
(The use of these annotations as case-finding tools will be
discussed in Chapter 4.) *Lawyers' Edition* also includes
summaries of selected briefs submitted by the lawyers
who argued the cases, but these summaries are far too
short to provide much insight. The annotations and
briefs of counsel are grouped together in a separate
section at the end of each volume, with references to
their location at the beginning of the decisions. Exhibit
5 shows the first page of *New York v. Harris* as it
appears in *Lawyers' Edition,* including these references
at the bottom of the page. Note that *Lawyers' Edition* is
now in a second series, so that *New York v. Harris* is
cited as 109 L.Ed.2d 13 (1990).

Both the *Supreme Court Reporter* and *Lawyers' Edition* are published first in biweekly advance sheets, long
before the official preliminary print is available. At the
end of the annual term they are then published in
"interim editions" bound volumes. The permanent
bound volumes are not published until the cases appear
in the *U.S. Reports* volumes, so that the commercial
editions can include *star paging* with references to the
official *U.S. Reports* page numbers. Star paging allows
the researcher to use the commercial volumes while
citing directly to the official text. Exhibit 4 shows this
star paging in the *Supreme Court Reporter,* at the end of

NEW YORK v HARRIS
(1990) 495 US 14, 109 L Ed 2d 13, 110 S Ct 1640

[495 US 14]
NEW YORK, Petitioner

v

BERNARD HARRIS

495 US 14, 109 L Ed 2d 13, 110 S Ct 1640

[No. 88-1000]

Argued January 10, 1990. Decided April 18, 1990.

Decision: Fourth Amendment exclusionary rule held not to bar use at trial of statement made by suspect at police station after police had entered suspect's home without warrant or consent and had arrested him there.

SUMMARY

Police officers investigating a murder had probable cause to believe that the accused had committed the offense. Without obtaining an arrest warrant, three officers went to the accused's apartment to arrest him. They knocked on the door and displayed their guns and badges to the accused, who let them enter. After being informed of his Miranda rights, the accused reportedly admitted to the murder. He was arrested and taken to the station house, where he was again informed of his Miranda rights and signed a written inculpatory statement. He was subsequently given Miranda warnings a third time and was videotaped in an incriminating interview with a district attorney, even though he had indicated that he wanted to end the interrogation. At the accused's trial in a New York state court, his first statement (his initial admission to the murder) and his third statement (the videotaped interview) were suppressed, but his second statement (the written inculpatory statement) was deemed admissible by the court. The accused was convicted of second-degree murder. The Appellate Division of the New York Supreme Court affirmed the conviction (124 AD2d 472, 507 NYS2d 823). The New York Court of Appeals reversed. Accepting the trial court's finding that the accused did not consent to the officers' entry into his home and that his warrantless arrest therefore violated the rule adopted in Payton v New York (1980) 445 US 573, 63 L Ed 2d 639, 100 S Ct 1371 (holding that the Fourth Amendment prohibits the police from making a warrantless and nonconsensual entry into a suspect's home in order to make a routine felony arrest), the Court of

---

SUBJECT OF ANNOTATION

Beginning on page 787, infra

When is evidence which is obtained after unconstitutional search or seizure sufficiently remote from such search or seizure so as not to be tainted by, and not to be inadmissible as fruit of, such search or seizure

---

Briefs of Counsel, p 786, infra.

13

Exhibit 5: The first page of a case in the unofficial *Lawyers' Edition*, showing the summary and references to related annotation and briefs.

the previous decision and at the very beginning of *New York v. Harris.*

The digests to both *Supreme Court Reporter* and *Lawyers' Edition* include extensive case tables listing Supreme Court cases by name, so that it is quite easy to find a case knowing only the names of its parties. *Lawyers' Edition* is also accompanied by a *Quick Case Table with Annotation References*, a paperback volume listing opinions by name and providing references to the U.S., L.Ed. and S.Ct. citations.

c. Looseleaf Services

While *Supreme Court Reporter* and *Lawyers' Edition* are published much sooner than the official *United States Reports,* there is still a lag of several weeks while their synopses and headnotes are prepared. Two other publications provide access to Supreme Court cases much sooner in a looseleaf format. Both reproduce the official slip opinions without adding headnotes, and mail them to subscribers the day after they are announced. These services are *The United States Law Week* (cited as U.S.L.W.), published by the Bureau of National Affairs, and the *U.S. Supreme Court Bulletin,* published by CCH Incorporated (formerly Commerce Clearing House). Both publications also provide information about the Supreme Court's docket, arguments, and other developments, making them comprehensive sources of current information about the Court's activities.

Of these two sources, *U.S. Law Week* is far more widely used. It is the standard source for information on cases pending on the Court's docket. Its Topical Index

and Table of Cases can be confusing at first, because they provide page references only if an opinion has been issued. Other entries (for cases which are pending on the docket or for which review has been denied) simply provide a docket number; to find more information it is necessary to turn to a Case Status Report table for page references. These index features are indicated in Exhibit 6, showing entries referring to *New York v. Harris* in the 1990 *U.S. Law Week* volume.

U.S. Law Week also includes weekly coverage of "General Law" in a separate binder, summarizing major new cases from federal and state courts and noting other important legal developments. For law students seeking clerkships, this is a popular source of information on judicial nominations and confirmations. A *daily* edition of *U.S. Law Week* is available online but not in print.

Double jeopardy, statements by defendant while in custody taken without Miranda warnings, motion to suppress denied, judge sua sponte and without defense consent declaring mistrial on concluding some inadmissible: manifest necessity, No. 89-1528

Exclusionary rule

—Abolition because resulting in suppression on ground statements not credible; credibility as relating to guilt or innocence, whether issue for jury, No. 89-547

—Entry of suspect's residence to effect routine felony arrest without warrant or consent, violation of Fourth Amendment rule, Payton v. N.Y., does not require suppression of statement made by suspect after removal from residence if arrest supported by probable cause, No. 88-1000, ▷ 4457

"Focus" of investigation, whether voluntary polygraph examination became "custodial" under Miranda when, as result of statements made, investigation "focused" on own conduct, suppression of statements given without new warnings; standard forms signed at start of examination as basis for continued questioning, No. 89-45

Fruit of poisonous tree

—Subjective beliefs of person contacted by police, bearing, if any, on whether person was seized within Fourth Amendment or whether evidence later obtained admissible as fruit of contact, No. 89-40

New York; Birnbaum v., 89-1108
New York; Catalanotte v., 88-1875
New York; Corrigan v., 89-1804
New York; Delaware v., 111 Orig.
New York v. Harris, 88-1000, ▷ 4457
New York v. HHS, 89-1392
New York; Manno v., 89-1781
New York; Oneida Indian Nation of New York v., 88-1915
New York; Oneida Indian Nation of Wisconsin v., 88-1758

88-986	filed (12/12/88) 58:3033, sum 58:3061, judg vac (03/05/90) 58:3564
88-995	filed (12/12/88) 58:3033, sum 58:3050, rev grant (02/27/89) 57:3570, oral arg (10/04/89) 58:3256, ▷ 58:4003 (11/07/89)
88-1000	filed (12/12/88) 58:3033, sum 58:3041, rev grant (04/17/89) 57:3687, order (06/12/89) 57:3812, amicus brief filed (06/26/89) 57:3841, oral arg (01/10/90) 58:3479, ▷ 58:4457 (04/18/90)
88-1031	filed (12/20/88) 58:3033, sum 58:3052, order (04/17/89) 57:3687, amicus brief filed (06/04/90) 58:3769, rev den (06/04/90) 58:3769
88-1037	filed (12/17/88) 58:3033, sum 58:3054
88-1042	filed (12/19/88) 58:3033, sum 58:3057, order (04/17/89) 57:3687, rev den (11/06/89) 58:3305

Exhibit 6: Index entries for Supreme Court cases in BNA's *United States Law Week*, showing cross-references from topical index and case table to list of docket numbers.

d. Electronic Resources

Under a program started in 1990 called Project Hermes, Supreme Court opinions are transmitted electronically to a dozen organizations as soon as they are announced. Two of the participants in this program are WESTLAW and LEXIS, which make the opinions available to their subscribers within minutes. Also involved is an educational consortium based at Case Western Reserve University, which provides free access to the opinions over the Internet through a variety of means.

In addition to speedy access to the latest opinions, LEXIS and WESTLAW also offer complete historical coverage of the Supreme Court since 1790. Every Supreme Court case since its inception can be searched for keywords, parties' names, or names of justices.

Several publishers offer CD–ROM versions of Supreme Court opinions. Some of these begin coverage only in 1990, but West's *Supreme Court Reporter* and Michie's *Federal Law on Disc* provide complete coverage since 1790.

§ 2–3. LOWER FEDERAL COURTS

The federal court system has grown extensively from the thirteen District Courts and three Circuit Courts created by the Judiciary Act of 1789. The general trial courts in the federal system are still known as United States District Courts, but there are now ninety-four districts, with one or more in each state. In addition, there are several specialized trial courts, such as the

Bankruptcy Courts, the Court of Federal Claims, and the Court of International Trade. The intermediate appellate courts in the federal system are the United States Courts of Appeals. These appellate courts are divided into thirteen circuits, consisting of the First through Eleventh Circuits (each covering several states), the District of Columbia Circuit, and the Federal Circuit. The map in Exhibit 7 shows the jurisdiction of these circuits.

There is no counterpart to the *U.S. Reports* for the decisions of the U.S. District Courts and Courts of Appeals. The only officially published sources are the individual slip decisions issued by the courts themselves. There are, however, commonly used unofficial reports and extensive coverage in electronic sources.

The only comprehensive printed sources for lower federal court decisions are reporters from West Publishing Company. In 1880 West's *Federal Reporter* began covering decisions of both the district and circuit courts. Over 1300 volumes later it is still being published, and is now in its third series (cited as F.3d). In 1932, with the increasing volume of litigation in the federal courts, West began another series called *Federal Supplement* (F.Supp.) for selected U.S. District Court decisions, leaving the *Federal Reporter* to cover the decisions of the U.S. Courts of Appeals. (*Federal Supplement* now also includes decisions of the U.S. Court of International Trade and rulings from the Judicial Panel on Multidistrict Litigation.) Like the *Supreme Court Reporter,* both of these reporters contain editorial synopses and headnotes with key numbers, allowing researchers to find cases through West's series of digest publications.

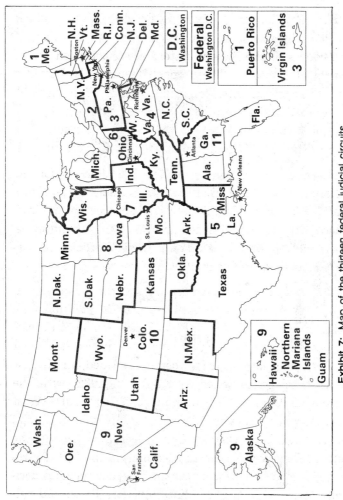

Exhibit 7: Map of the thirteen federal judicial circuits.

Both the *Federal Reporter* and *Federal Supplement* publish thousands of new decisions each year. Unlike Supreme Court decisions, however, not every case considered by the lower federal courts is represented by a decision published in one of the reporter series. Some matters are settled or tried to a jury verdict and do not result in any written opinions. Decisions in many cases are issued as slip opinions but are not published in the reporters. Some of these are available in topical looseleaf services, and many more can be found online, but others can be obtained only from the clerk of the court. The percentage of U.S. Courts of Appeals decisions published varies from circuit to circuit but may average as low as 30%. The percentage of District Court decisions which are published is even lower.

Cases from the lower federal courts before the inception of the *Federal Reporter* are found in a separate West publication called *Federal Cases*. Before 1880 federal court decisions were issued in over a hundred different series of nominative reports. *Federal Cases,* a thirty-volume series published in 1894–97, reports over 20,000 of these decisions. This closed set incorporated virtually all available lower federal court decisions from 1789 to 1880, arranged in alphabetical sequence by case name.

In 1940, West began another series, *Federal Rules Decisions* (F.R.D.), containing a limited number of U.S. District Court decisions (not published in *Federal Supplement*) dealing with procedural issues under the Federal Rules of Civil Procedure and the Federal Rules of Criminal Procedure. *Federal Rules Decisions* also contains proceedings of judicial conferences and occasional speeches or articles dealing with procedural law in the federal courts.

West Publishing Company also issues a number of other reporters in specialized subject fields of federal law. These selective reporters include: *Military Justice Reporter* (1978–date), containing decisions of the U.S. Court of Appeals for the Armed Forces (formerly the U.S. Court of Military Appeals), as well as selected decisions of the Courts of Criminal Appeals; *Bankruptcy Reporter* (1979–date), containing decisions of the U.S. Bankruptcy Courts and bankruptcy decisions from the U.S. District Courts; *United States Federal Claims Reporter* (1982–date), containing decisions of the U.S. Court of Federal Claims (formerly U.S. Claims Court); and *Veterans Appeals Reporter* (1991–date), containing decisions of the U.S. Court of Veterans Appeals. These last three reporters also reprint decisions from the Courts of Appeals and Supreme Court in their subject areas.

Federal court decisions are also printed in a variety of other sources, including commercial topical reporters designed for practitioners in specialized subject areas. Some cases appearing in these sources are not available in West's *Federal Reporter* and *Federal Supplement*, although there is extensive duplication. Lawyers Cooperative publishes two series of cases on procedural issues, *Federal Rules Service* and *Federal Rules of Evidence Service*. Reporters in specialized areas include *American Maritime Cases, Public Utilities Reports Annotated,* and *U.S. Patents Quarterly.* Several topical reporters, such as BNA's *Fair Employment Practice Cases* and CCH's *Trade Cases,* are published as adjuncts to looseleaf services on those topics.

The two computerized legal research services, WEST-LAW and LEXIS, are major sources of lower federal

court decisions. They provide full-text coverage of all federal court cases that appear in print in the various West reporters, back to the earliest decisions in *Federal Cases*. New decisions are available online long before they are published in the *Federal Reporter* or *Federal Supplement*. In addition, the online services also provide access to many decisions which never appear in the reporters, making them the most comprehensive sources for current decisions. Both services include in their databases thousands of decisions not available in any other form, except as slip opinions.

Recent decisions from the Courts of Appeals are also available electronically by modem from the courts themselves, and several circuits have also begun providing new opinions to law schools for access through the Internet.

As with the Supreme Court, both West and Michie publish CD–ROM discs containing decisions of lower federal court decisions. West publishes CD versions of its *Federal Reporter*, *Federal Supplement*, and *Federal Rules Decisions*, with coverage extending back to 1880. Michie's *Federal Law on Disc* consists of separate discs for each circuit, with coverage of most circuits beginning with the court restructuring of 1891.

In an effort to deal with problems created by the increasing number of decisions, some available only through electronic services, each of the U.S. Courts of Appeals has promulgated rules limiting publication and restricting the citation of "unpublished" decisions, or decisions not published in the traditional reporters. Some of the courts prohibit citation of such decisions; some allow citation, but with restrictions; and some limit the precedential value of such decisions. As elec-

tronic dissemination of decisions becomes the norm, these increasingly unworkable attempts to limit access to and use of public decisions are gradually being abandoned.

§ 2–4. STATE COURTS

American state reports are published in two forms: as *official* reports, which are issued under the auspices of the courts themselves as the authoritative text of their decisions, and as *unofficial* reports issued by commercial publishers. The major comprehensive unofficial reporting systems are West Publishing Company's National Reporter System and the online systems LEXIS and WESTLAW. In addition, every state has at least one CD–ROM version of its cases and some state cases appear in specialized reporters of limited subject coverage.

a. Official Reports

Like the *U.S. Reports*, state official reports are the authoritative edition of a court's decisions and must be cited in briefs before that court. Unofficial reports, however, are very widely used and cited, because in most instances they are published more quickly and have superior research aids. In fact, unofficial reports have so surpassed official reports in speed and convenience that many states have ceased publishing official reports series and have designated a commercial reporter as the authoritative source of state case law. Appendix C of this book gives information on the current status of the published reports in each state.

Most official reports contain the decisions of the high court for that state, usually called the supreme court.

Over a dozen states issue more than one series of official reports, in order to cover the decisions of their intermediate appellate courts and in some instances important decisions from their trial courts. In New York, for example, there are three official series of reports (*New York Reports*, covering the Court of Appeals; *Appellate Division Reports*, covering the Appellate Divisions of the Supreme Court; and *Miscellaneous Reports*, covering a selection of the decisions of the various lower courts). Official slip decisions and advance sheets are published for the courts of some states, but not for every state.

Exhibit 8 shows the first page of an opinion of New York's court of last resort, the Court of Appeals, in *New York Reports*. This is the same case that was shown earlier, in Exhibit 1 on page 22, in an unofficial reporter. The text of the opinion is the same in both versions, but instead of four headnotes the official report has just one note summarizing the entire decision.

Even though official reports do not generally tie into a comprehensive digest system like West's, they can provide a valuable perspective on the decisions of a state's appellate courts. If the headnotes are written by lawyers practicing in that state, they may be more attuned to its judicial developments than headnotes written by commercial editors. Some official reports include research leads not mentioned in the West reporters. Exhibit 8, for example, provides "library references" to two legal encyclopedias, *American Jurisprudence 2d* and *New York Jurisprudence 2d*. Official reports are certainly less widely used than West's regional reporters, but they maintain a valuable role in some jurisdictions.

434   **77 NEW YORK REPORTS, 2d SERIES**
Statement of Case

THE PEOPLE OF THE STATE OF NEW YORK, Respondent, v
BERNARD HARRIS, Appellant.

Argued November 16, 1990; decided February 12, 1991

SUMMARY

REARGUMENT of an appeal taken by permission of an Associate Justice of the Appellate Division of the Supreme Court in the First Judicial Department, from an order of that court, entered November 6, 1986, which affirmed a judgment of the Supreme Court (Irving Lang, J.), rendered in Bronx County, convicting defendant after a bench trial of murder in the second degree. Following the reversal by the Court of Appeals upon the original appeal (72 NY2d 614), the United States Supreme Court reversed the judgment and remanded the case to the Court of Appeals "for further proceedings not inconsistent with the opinion of this Court." (495 US —, 110 S Ct 1640.)

People v Harris, 124 AD2d 472, reversed.

HEADNOTE

Crimes — Confession — Confession Obtained after Illegal Arrest —
Attenuation of Causal Connection between Illegality and Statement — State Constitution

Under NY Constitution, article I, § 12, statements obtained from an accused following an arrest made in violation of *Payton v New York* (445 US 573) are not admissible if they are a product of the illegality. In New York police are prohibited from questioning a suspect after an arrest pursuant to a warrant unless counsel is present and, therefore, they have every reason to violate *Payton* because doing so enables them to circumvent the accused's indelible right to counsel. To protect New York citizens from *Payton* violations, NY Constitution, article I, § 12 requires that statements obtained from an accused following an arrest without a warrant in violation of *Payton* must be suppressed unless the taint resulting from the violation has been attenuated. Accordingly, a statement made to police by defendant at the station house to which he was transported after the police arrested him at his apartment in violation of *Payton* must be suppressed under the State Constitution (art I, § 12) where the causal connection between the illegal arrest and defendant's statement was not sufficiently attenuated from the *Payton* wrong because of the temporal proximity of the arrest and the statement, the absence of intervening circumstances and the purpose and flagrancy of the police misconduct.

TOTAL CLIENT-SERVICE LIBRARY® REFERENCES
By the Publisher's Editorial Staff

AM JUR 2d, Evidence, §§ 545, 546, 555-557.
CLS, NY Const, art I, § 12.
NY JUR 2d, Criminal Law, § 112.

Exhibit 8: The first page of a case in the official *New York Reports*.

As with the Supreme Court, the early reports of several of the older states were once cited only by the names of their reporters. Many of these volumes have now been incorporated into numbered series, but it may still be necessary to use a reference work such as *Bieber's Dictionary of Legal Abbreviations* (4th ed. 1993) to decipher a case's citation.

b. National Reporter System

West's National Reporter System includes a series of *regional reporters* publishing the decisions of the appellate courts of the fifty states and the District of Columbia. The National Reporter System divides the country into seven regions, and publishes the decisions of the appellate courts of the states in each region together in one series of volumes. Each of these sets is now in its second series: *Atlantic* (A.2d), *North Eastern* (N.E.2d), *North Western* (N.W.2d), *Pacific* (P.2d), *South Eastern* (S.E.2d), *Southern* (So.2d), and *South Western* (S.W.2d). They are supplemented by separate reporters for the two most litigious states, also in their second series: *California Reporter* (Cal.Rptr.2d) and *New York Supplement* (N.Y.S.2d). (Cases from the highest courts of California and New York appear in both the regional and the state reporter, while lower court cases are not published in the *Pacific* or *North Eastern Reporter*.) These nine reporters, together with West's federal court reporters, comprise a uniform system tied together by the key number indexing and digesting scheme. The map in Exhibit 9 shows which states are included in each region of the reporter system. Appendix B, at the end of the book, gives a complete list of the contents of each reporter and its date of inception.

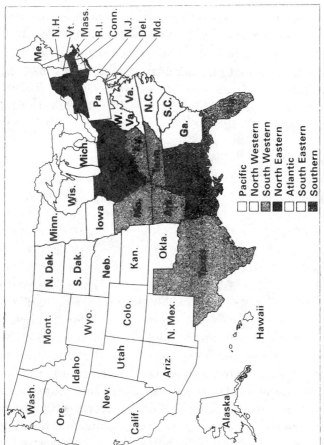

Exhibit 9: National Reporter System map, showing states included in each reporter.

West also publishes individual reporters for over thirty additional states. Unlike the reporters for California and New York, however, the other series simply reprint a state's cases from its regional reporter, including the original regional reporter pagination. These "offprint" reporters are published for practitioners who wish to purchase their state's decisions but rarely need cases from other states.

In most states, cases appear in both official and National Reporter System editions. Cases are traditionally cited to both the official reports and West's regional reporter, with the official reports cited first. The two citations for the same decision are known as *parallel citations*. For example, in *People v. Harris*, 77 N.Y.2d 434, 570 N.E.2d 1051 (1991), the citation to the official *New York Reports* precedes the unofficial *North Eastern Reporter*. The current 15th edition of the *Bluebook* requires parallel citations only for state cases cited in documents submitted to that state's courts; in other documents, only the National Reporter System citation is used.

Frequently a researcher has a citation to only one report of a case and needs to find the other, either to complete the citation in a brief or to examine the other report. Parallel citations can be found in a variety of sources. They often are listed at the beginning of the case itself, as in Exhibit 1 on page 22. *Shepard's Citations,* a service to be discussed in Chapter 3, includes the parallel citation in parentheses at the beginning of its treatment of each case. Tables of cases, which are published for each unit in West's digest system, give both official and unofficial citations to each case listed. The electronic citation checking systems, WESTLAW's *Insta–*

Cite and LEXIS's *Auto–Cite,* to be discussed in Chapter 5, provide a complete list of parallel citations for any case.

One of the simplest sources for finding parallel citations is an annually supplemented West publication called the *National Reporter Blue Book,* which lists the starting page of each case in the official reports and provides cross-references to National Reporter System citations. For about half of the states, West also publishes a *Blue and White Book,* which has two sets of parallel citation tables. The blue pages duplicate the information provided in the *National Reporter Blue Book,* and the white pages provide references from the regional reporter to the official reports. A state's *Blue and White Book* is usually only available in that state.

Some cases appear in only one source, either official or unofficial. Since the National Reporter System was not created until the late nineteenth century, only the official reports exist for many older state cases. On the other hand, over twenty states have discontinued their official reports in recent years. For newer cases from these states, there is no parallel citation to official reports.

c. Electronic Resources

The computer systems of LEXIS and WESTLAW are increasingly comprehensive sources for state court decisions. New decisions from all state appellate courts are added to the databases before they are available in published form, and retrospective coverage of older case law is steadily expanding. WESTLAW, for example, has all state supreme court decisions since 1945, with coverage from some states extending back to the 19th century.

Many state courts have electronic dial-in systems through which new opinions and other information can

be obtained. So far, however, relatively few state court opinions are available on the Internet. On the other hand, every state has at least one CD–ROM version of its opinions. Most have two or more, from West, Michie and other publishers, and many of these products combine court decisions with current statutory codes and other materials.

§ 2–5. CONCLUSION

This chapter has introduced case law as it is published in the United States today, both in print and through a variety of electronic means. Its focus has been on the cases themselves, leaving to subsequent chapters the several complex and powerful methods of finding case law relevant to a research problem. Publication methods are changing rapidly, but the structure of court systems and the nature of judicial decisions remain relatively constant.

In addition to their value as legal precedent and their importance in legal research, court reports constitute a literary form with other values as well. They describe human problems and predicaments—domestic crises, moral failings, economic troubles. They reflect the larger social, political and economic trends and conditions of life in particular periods and places. And they frequently have a unique literary quality which adds to the tone and substance of the prose of their time. Whether brilliant or dull in style, legal writing has always been an influential part of our literature.

CHAPTER 3

CASE RESEARCH: DIGESTS AND SHEPARD'S CITATIONS

---

§ 3–1. INTRODUCTION

For the doctrine of precedent to operate effectively, lawyers must be able to find cases which control or influence a court's decisionmaking. In order to determine the applicable law, lawyers must have some means of locating "cases on point," that is, earlier decisions factually and legally relevant to a dispute at hand. They must then determine whether these decisions are valid law and have not been reversed, overruled, or otherwise discredited. Judicial decisions, however, are published in chronological order, rather than by topic, and are generally not updated once they are published. Other resources are therefore needed to provide subject access to decisions and to verify their current status.

49

This and following chapters discuss a wide variety of tools which perform these functions. Some are resources designed expressly for case research, while others serve several purposes. Statutory codes, looseleaf services, legal treatises, and periodicals are all valuable in case research, but they are discussed in later chapters because case-finding is not their primary function. Annotations and legal encyclopedias, to be discussed in Chapter 4, are important tools designed for case research, although they are not comprehensive enough to be useful in all research situations.

The tools introduced in this chapter, West digests and *Shepard's Citations*, are among the most comprehensive resources in legal research. Each is a thoroughly developed system providing coverage of judicial decisions throughout the country. Both can be quite frustrating for new researchers, because they are complicated tools which are quite different from research materials in most other disciplines. They are nonetheless basic and necessary parts of any case law research.

§ 3–2. WEST KEY–NUMBER DIGESTS

One of the most widely used methods of case-finding is the *digest,* a publication reprinting in a subject arrangement the headnote summaries of each case's points of law. The summaries are grouped under alphabetically arranged topics and then organized into numerical subdivisions within each topic. Digests allow researchers to scan summaries of numerous cases on similar legal issues.

Abridgments and digests were first devised shortly after case reporting began to develop in England. Al-

though early works such as Statham's Abridgment (c. 1490) were prototypes of modern digests, they used only a few broad topics and included a relatively small number of decisions. Gradually these finding tools grew more intensive, employing finer internal subdivisions; and more extensive, covering more areas of law and a larger number of cases.

The most comprehensive digest system in use today is West Publishing Company's *key number system,* based on a comprehensive classification of American legal doctrine and covering every case published in West's National Reporter System. The West digest system consists of over 400 topics, arranged alphabetically from *Abandoned and Lost Property* to *Zoning and Planning.* A partial list of these topics is shown in Exhibit 10. Each topic is divided into numbered sections designating specific points of law. These individual sections are called *key numbers.* Some narrow topics like *Party Walls* employ relatively few key numbers, while broader ones such as *Taxation* or *Trade Regulation* may have thousands. For each topic West provides a scope note and an outline of its classification. Exhibit 11 shows the scope note and the beginning of the outline for the topic *Prisons.*

DIGEST TOPICS

273	Neutrality Laws	321	Rape	367	Subscriptions
274	Newspapers	322	Real Actions	368	Suicide
275	New Trial	323	Receivers	369	Sunday
276	Notaries	324	Receiving Stolen	370	Supersedeas
277	Notice		Goods	371	Taxation
278	Novation	325	Recognizances	372	Telecommunications
279	Nuisance	326	Records	373	Tenancy in Common
280	Oath	327	Reference	374	Tender
281	Obscenity	328	Reformation of	375	Territories
282	Obstructing Justice		Instruments	376	Theaters and Shows
283	Officers and Public	330	Registers of Deeds	378	Time
	Employees	331	Release	379	Torts
284	Pardon and Parole	332	Religious Societies	380	Towage
285	Parent and Child	333	Remainders	381	Towns
286	Parliamentary Law	334	Removal of Cases	382	Trade Regulation
287	Parties	335	Replevin	384	Treason
288	Partition	336	Reports	385	Treaties
289	Partnership	337	Rescue	386	Trespass
290	Party Walls	338	Reversions	387	Trespass to Try Title
291	Patents	339	Review	388	Trial
294	Payment	340	Rewards	389	Trover and
295	Penalties	341	Riot		Conversion
296	Pensions	342	Robbery	390	Trusts
297	Perjury	343	Sales	391	Turnpikes and Toll
298	Perpetuities	344	Salvage		Roads
299	Physicians and	345	Schools	392	Undertakings
	Surgeons	346	Scire Facias	393	United States
300	Pilots	347	Seals	394	United States
302	Pleading	348	Seamen		Magistrates
303	Pledges	349	Searches and Seizures	395	United States
304	Poisons	349A	Secured Transactions		Marshals
305	Possessory Warrant	349B	Securities Regulation	396	Unlawful Assembly
306	Postal Service	350	Seduction	396A	Urban Railroads
307	Powers	351	Sequestration	398	Usury
307A	Pretrial Procedure	352	Set-Off and	399	Vagrancy
308	Principal and Agent		Counterclaim	400	Vendor and Purchaser
309	Principal and Surety	353	Sheriffs and	401	Venue
310	Prisons		Constables	402	War and National
311	Private Roads	354	Shipping		Emergency
313	Process	355	Signatures	403	Warehousemen
313A	Products Liability	356	Slaves	404	Waste
314	Prohibition	356A	Social Security and	405	Waters and Water
315	Property		Public Welfare		Courses
316	Prostitution	357	Sodomy	406	Weapons
316A	Public Contracts	358	Specific Performance	407	Weights and Measures
317	Public Lands	359	Spendthrifts	408	Wharves
317A	Public Utilities	360	States	409	Wills
318	Quieting Title	361	Statutes	410	Witnesses
319	Quo Warranto	362	Steam	411	Woods and Forests
319H	Racketeer Influenced	363	Stipulations	413	Workers'
	and Corrupt	365	Submission of		Compensation
	Organizations		Controversy	414	Zoning and Planning
320	Railroads	366	Subrogation		

Exhibit 10: Part of the list of over 400 West digest topics.

PRISONS

SUBJECTS INCLUDED

Public buildings for confinement of persons held in judicial custody, in either civil or criminal proceedings, and either to secure their production as parties or witnesses in further proceedings, or as punishment by imprisonment, with or without hard labor, whether such buildings be designated as prisons or as jails, penitentiaries, houses of correction, or otherwise

Establishment, maintenance, regulation, and management of such places

Rights, powers, duties and liabilities of wardens, jailers, keepers, and other officers

Custody, care, and maintenance of prisoners in general

SUBJECTS EXCLUDED AND COVERED BY OTHER TOPICS

Arrest and discharge from arrest, jail limits, prison bounds, poor debtors, etc., see ARREST, BAIL, EXECUTION

Convicts, regulation of and their labor, see CONVICTS

Jail breaking, prison breach, etc., see ESCAPE

Reformatory institutions, see INFANTS

Sentences to imprisonment as punishment, see CRIMINAL LAW

For detailed references to other topics, see Descriptive-Word Index

---

Analysis

⟜1. Establishment and maintenance.
   2. Use by United States of state prison or county jail.
   3. Use by city of county jail.
   4. Regulation and supervision.
      (1). In general.
      (2). Judicial supervision.
      (2.1). —— In general.
      (3). —— State prisons.
      (4). Persons held pending trial or on detainer.
      (5). Particular rights, privileges, and restrictions.
      (6). Communications, visitors, privacy, and censorship in general.
      (7). Personal grooming and effects; contraband and searches.
      (8). Access to reading matter.
      (9). Access to mails for correspondence.
      (10). Access to courts.
      (10.1). —— In general.
      (11). —— Access to counsel; paralegal counsel and inmate assistance.
      (12). —— Communication with courts, officers, or counsel.
      (13). —— Law books and law libraries, legal materials, and opportunity for legal work.
      (14). Religious practices and materials.
   5. Officers.

Exhibit 11: The first page of the topic Prisons in a West state digest.

The entries in West's digests come directly from the cases published in the National Reporter System. Editors at West create short abstracts for every significant point of law discussed in each case in the West reporters. Each abstract is classified by topic and key number to designate its subject. These abstracts first appear as headnotes preceding the text of the opinion in the West reporter advance sheet. Exhibit 12 shows the first page of a U.S. District Court decision in *Federal Supplement*, with headnotes assigned to the topics *Federal Civil Procedure, Prisons, Civil Rights*, and *Injunction*.

All headnotes for cases in an advance sheet or reporter volume are reprinted in a Key Number Digest in the front of the advance sheet and at the back of the bound reporter volume. These mini-digests serve as subject indexes to the cases in the advance sheet or volume. West then takes these headnotes, arranged by key number, and reprints them in multivolume digest series to provide subject access to the cases in hundreds of reporter volumes.

This system is the most comprehensive subject approach to case law published. West digests are available for the entire country, for some regions, for individual states, and for a few specific subjects. Choosing the right digest depends on the scope of the inquiry. A researcher may want to find cases from only one jurisdiction, or may be interested in developments throughout the country. A smaller digest obviously covers fewer cases but is usually easier to use.

886 820 FEDERAL SUPPLEMENT

Jorge ACEVEDO, Plaintiff,

v.

James A. FORCINITO, et al., Defendants.

Civ. A. No. 92–0172.

United States District Court,
D. New Jersey.

May 12, 1993.

Prisoner brought § 1983 action in which he alleged that prison officials violated his constitutional right to meaningful access to courts. The District Court, Rodriguez, J., held that providing non-English speaking prisoner with access to law library did not automatically satisfy duty to provide meaningful court access.

Summary judgment motion granted in part and denied in part.

1. Federal Civil Procedure ⊚2470.2

If disputed fact exists that, under controlling substantive law, might affect outcome of suit, entry of summary judgment is precluded. Fed.Rules Civ.Proc.Rule 56(c), 28 U.S.C.A.

2. Federal Civil Procedure ⊚2544

Party seeking summary judgment bears initial responsibility of informing court of basis for motion and must identify portions of pleadings, discovery papers and affidavits which show absence of any genuine issue of material fact. Fed.Rules Civ.Proc.Rule 56(c), 28 U.S.C.A.

3. Federal Civil Procedure ⊚2470

Summary judgment will not be granted if nonmoving party shows there is genuine issue of fact requiring trial. Fed.Rules Civ. Proc.Rule 56(c), 28 U.S.C.A.

4. Prisons ⊚4(10.1)

Prisoners and pretrial detainees have fundamental constitutional right of "access to courts," which encompasses all means that defendant or petitioner might require to get fair hearing from judiciary on all charges

brought against him or grievances alleged by him.

See publication Words and Phrases for other judicial constructions and definitions.

5. Prisons ⊚4(13)

For prisoners who cannot read or understand English, constitutional right of access to courts cannot be determined solely by number of volumes in, or size of, law library; merely making law library available to non-English speaking prisoner does not satisfy duty of prison officials to provide meaningful access.

6. Federal Civil Procedure ⊚2491.5

Triable issues of fact precluded summary judgment for prison officials, as to whether a non-English speaking prisoner was denied meaningful access to courts as result of failure to provide Spanish-speaking legal assistant.

7. Civil Rights ⊚135

Fact of prisoner's filing of complaint against prison officials does not automatically disprove prisoner's claim of denial of access to courts in violation of his civil rights. 42 U.S.C.A. § 1983.

8. Civil Rights ⊚205(1)

Respondeat superior is not available doctrine under § 1983. 42 U.S.C.A. § 1983.

9. Injunction ⊚114(2)

Plaintiff does not have standing to obtain injunctive relief absent showing of real or immediate threat that plaintiff will be wronged again; injunctive relief is wholly prospective, and court must analyze standing to obtain prospective relief separately from standing to obtain retrospective relief.

Jorge Acevedo, pro se.

Ivan M. Sherman, County Counsel, County of Cumberland, Bridgeton, NJ, for defendants.

Exhibit 12: The beginning of a National Reporter System case, showing digest classifications of headnotes.

a. The Comprehensive American Digest System

The *General Digest* collects and publishes headnotes from all West advance sheets. It is the most current component of West's comprehensive series of digests.

The *General Digest* is published about once a month, with each volume covering the entire range of over 400 digest topics. Exhibit 13 shows a page from the *General Digest,* reprinting one of the headnotes, under its topic and key number, from the case shown in Exhibit 12. Note that not every key number is used in this volume.

1081   **PRISONS** ⊱10

prisoner's access to courts is adequate, effective and meaningful.—Oswald v. Graves, 819 F.Supp. 680.

⊱4(12). —— **Communication with courts, officers, or counsel.**

S.D.Cal. 1992. Prison need provide only adequate law library or adequate assistance from persons trained in law, not both, in order to satisfy inmates' constitutional right of access to courts.—U.S. v. Janis, 820 F.Supp. 512.

Preconviction detention facility was required to provide detainee who was representing himself with reasonable opportunity for private consultation with standby counsel, investigator and witnesses; facility would be required to obtain court permission before disclosing taped conversations for any purposes other than internal institution security. 18 U.S.C.A. § 3142(i)(3).—Id.

⊱4(13). —— **Law books and law libraries, legal materials, and opportunity for legal work.**

S.D.Cal. 1992. Prison need provide only adequate law library or adequate assistance from persons trained in law, not both, in order to satisfy inmates' constitutional right of access to courts.—U.S. v. Janis, 820 F.Supp. 512.

Constitution does not guarantee inmates unlimited access to law library.—Id.

Preconviction detention facility was required to provide detainee representing himself at least two hours of law library time five days per week, with additional time preceding his motion and trial dates; although pro se detainee needed more library time than detainees represented by counsel, he did have standby counsel upon whom he could rely for some of his research.—Id.

Prison need not provide its inmates with law library that results in best possible access to courts; typical library holdings need not exceed scope of constitutional concept of access to courts.—Id.

If preconviction detainee reasonably requests research material necessary to litigate civil actions, detention facilities should consider obtaining those materials on temporary basis from another law library, in order to satisfy detainee's constitutional right of access to courts.—Id.

Preconviction detention facility's law library was deficient, in violation of detainee's right of access to courts, to extent federal statutory volumes were incomplete or not up to date, and to extent collection did not include federal defenders manual.—Id.

Preconviction detainee was entitled to have certain materials from his home law library in his cell in order to assist him in representing himself, provided that hard covers were removed and space limitations were not exceeded.—Id.

Preconviction detainee was not entitled to free copies of research materials; as pro se criminal defendant, he could apply to court under Criminal Justice Act for reimbursement for reasonable and necessary photocopy expenses related to his trial. 18 U.S.C.A. § 3006A(d)(1).—Id.

E.D.Mich. 1993. Fundamental right of access to courts requires prison authorities to provide prisoners with either adequate law library or assistance from persons trained in law such that prisoner's access to courts is adequate, effective and meaningful.—Oswald v. Graves, 819 F.Supp. 680.

One-time removal of inmate's name from library call-out list did not deny inmate access to courts, absent showing that denial had caused him any prejudice in pending litigation or actually denied him access to court.—Id.

D.N.J. 1993. For prisoners who cannot read or understand English, constitutional right of access to courts cannot be determined solely by

number of volumes in, or size of, law library; merely making law library available to non-English speaking prisoner does not satisfy duty of prison officials to provide meaningful access.—Acevedo v. Porcinita, 820 F.Supp. 886.

⊱4(14). **Religious practices and materials.**

C.A.10 (Kan.) 1993. Sole specific fact alleged by pro se inmate in connection with his own exercise of religious freedom, that defendants refused to provide member of his faith, could not alone support claim that inmate's right to freedom of religion was denied, so as to state claim under § 1983. U.S.C.A. Const.Amend. 1; 42 U.S.C.A. § 1983.—Sweboda v. Dubach, 992 F.2d 286.

C.A.2 (N.Y.) 1993. Prisoners have constitutional right to participate in congregate religious services, and confinement in keeplock does not deprive prisoners of this right. U.S.C.A. Const. Amend. 1.—Salahuddin v. Coughlin, 993 F.2d 306.

Prisoner's right to practice his religion is not absolute. U.S.C.A. Const.Amend. 1.—Id.

In evaluating constitutionality of restriction on prisoners' free exercise rights, court considers whether there is rational relationship between regulation and legitimate government interests asserted, whether inmates have alternative means to exercise rights, impact that accommodation of rights will have on prison system, and whether ready alternatives exist which accommodate rights and satisfy governmental interests. U.S.C.A. Const.Amend. 1.—Id.

C.A.2 (N.Y.) 1993. Inmate's religious rights were not violated when he was denied congregate religious services while being held in special housing unit for fighting with another inmate.—Salahuddin v. Jones, 992 F.2d 447.

E.D.Mo. 1993. Inmate's exercise of freedom of religion may be restricted by reasonable requirements of prison security. U.S.C.A. Const. Amend. 1.—Childress v. Dole, 820 F.Supp. 458.

Once prison officials have produced evidence that restriction placed on inmate's religious freedom was in response to security concern, burden shifts to inmate claiming First Amendment violation to show by substantial evidence that officials' response was exaggerated. U.S.C.A. Const. Amend. 1.—Id.

Prison officials are accorded much discretion in dealing with security matters in prisons in context of claimed violation of inmate's First Amendment right to freedom of religion. U.S.C.A. Const. Amend. 1.—Id.

Limitations on group religious services and religious materials following excessive altercation between correctional officers and inmates regarding presence of gang colors displayed in dining room were reasonable and did not violate inmate's First Amendment rights; all group activities, not merely religious services, were suspended, there was no indication that security concerns were exaggerated or unwarranted, inmates were permitted to request visits from prison chaplain, and while inmate's hard-bound Koran was confiscated, he could at all times have requested and received soft-back Koran. U.S.C.A. Const.Amend. 1.—Id.

N.Y.A.D. 3 Dept. 1993. Prison did not infringe on inmate's right to freely exercise his religion by denying his request to possess Tarot cards; inmate professed no religious belief pertaining to the use of Tarot cards, but rather simply claimed that he should be allowed to keep them for his edification, recreation, and deep personal interest. McKinney's CPLR 7801 et seq.; U.S.C.A. Const.Amend. 1.—Marcelin v. Coughlin, 598 N.Y.S.2d 354.

Ohio App. 4 Dist. 1992. Statute which required warden of penitentiary to furnish convict with Bible obligated warden to provide inmate

with sacred texts of inmate's Hindu religion. R.C. § 5145.25.—State ex rel. Karmasu v. Tate, 614 N.E.2d 827, 83 Ohio App.3d 199.

⊱5. **Officers.**

⊱7. —— **Appointment, qualification, and tenure.**

W.D.Pa. 1993. Officers of Pennsylvania state police were not authorized agents of Pennsylvania department of corrections and thus did not have authority to promise inmate transfer to another prison in exchange for cooperation in flushing out kidnapping plot.—Fay v. Ryan, 818 F.Supp. 882.

Under Pennsylvania law, state police officers did not have apparent authority to bind department of corrections to agreement to transfer inmate to another prison in exchange for inmate's assistance in helping uncover kidnapping plot within prison, as department of corrections did not in any way convey to inmate that state police were authorized to act for department and department did not fail to indicate to inmate that they did not acquiesce or ratify actions of state police.—Id.

⊱10. —— **Liabilities in general.**

C.A.6 (Ky.) 1993. In order to hold prison official liable for failure to supervise and control his subordinates, prisoner must, at minimum, show that official at least implicitly authorized, approved or knowingly acquiesced in unconstitutional conduct of offending officers; however, liability cannot be based solely on right to control employees.—Hicks v. Frey, 992 F.2d 1450, rehearing denied.

S.D.Ind. 1993. Captain at county jail, at whose direction three-way restraints were used on pretrial detainee following his suicide attempt in absence of medical evaluation, was liable in her individual capacity for compensatory damages to detainee in his § 1983 lawsuit based on deprivation of his due process rights. U.S.C.A. Const. Amend. 7; 42 U.S.C.A. § 1983.—Jones v. Thompson, 818 F.Supp. 1263.

County jail shift commander was liable in his individual capacity for compensatory damages in pretrial detainee's § 1983 civil rights suit, where extended use of three-way restraints on detainee following his suicide attempt in absence of medical review, and denial of even basic amenities such as personal hygiene and toilet usage were made known to commander, commander condoned acts through his lack of intervention, and commander made no effort to have medical evaluation conducted regarding continued need for use of restraints. 42 U.S.C.A. § 1983.—Id.

D.Md. 1992. Prison officials were entitled to qualified immunity in inmate's action challenging alleged violation of his privacy rights resulting from design of prison dormitory's bathroom area; reasonable persons in officials' positions could have failed to appreciate the construction of prison facility and guard assignments would violate inmate's rights.—Arey v. Robinson, 819 F.Supp. 478.

N.C.App. 1993. By expressly providing through a statute for a cause of action against prison officials for negligence in the performance of their official duties, General Assembly abrogated common-law immunity for jail officials in negligence action. G.S. §§ 58-76-5, 153A-224(a).—Slade v. Vernon, 429 S.E.2d 744.

County jail officials were immune from inmate's negligence suit based as public officers they could not be held individually liable for mere negligence in performance of their duties.—Id.

County jail inmate's mere allegations of malice on part of jail officials, without more, were insufficient to overcome jail officials' motion for summary judgment on the ground that they were immune from suit for mere negligence in the performance of their duties.—Id.

Per subsequent case history information see Table of Cases Affirmed, Reversed or Modified

Exhibit 13: A *General Digest* page, showing a headnote reprinted from the case in Exhibit 12.

The *General Digest* provides cumulative tables in every tenth volume indicating which key numbers appear in which volumes, but the entries themselves do not cumulate. After five years one must look through over fifty separate volumes to search for recent cases. At that point, however, West recompiles the headnotes and publishes them in a multivolume set called a *Decennial Digest*. *Decennial Digests* are so named because they used to be published every ten years. The *Eighth Decennial,* for example, covers cases decided between 1966 and 1976. Due to the increased volume of case law, West now compiles these digests every *five* years. The *Ninth Decennial Digest* consists of separate parts for 1976–81 and 1981–86, and the *Tenth Decennial Digest, Part 1* covers cases from 1986 to 1991.

The first unit of the American Digest System, called the *Century Digest,* covers the long period from 1658 to 1896. It was followed by a *First Decennial Digest* for 1897 to 1906, and subsequent Decennials for each decade since. The topics and key numbers used for points of law are generally the same in each unit of the digest system, from the most recent back to the *First Decennial.* The *Century Digest* employs a slightly different numbering system, but the *First Decennial* provides cross-references between the two units. Thus research under a digest key number can turn up cases from the seventeenth century to the present.

The law, of course, has not remained static over these centuries. West attempts to stay abreast of new developments by revising and expanding old topics and by establishing new topics. When new or revised topics are introduced, they are accompanied by tables converting older topics and key numbers into those newly adopted

and vice versa. The digest changes slowly, however, and it may take several years for new areas of legal doctrine to be recognized and to receive adequate coverage. Until 1972, for example, there was no key number for sex discrimination, and cases in this area were classified under a general "Nature of rights protected" key number. For the next seventeen years all sex discrimination headnotes were assigned to just one key number, and finally in 1989 the Civil Rights topic was reorganized and coverage of sex discrimination was expanded to eleven key numbers. Until changes such as these occur, cases in developing areas can be difficult to find in the digests.

The *Decennial* and *General Digests* include alphabetical Tables of Cases, which can be used to find a case's citation if only the names of its parties are known. Tables of Cases provide parallel citations to both official and unofficial reports, and information about a case's later history (whether it was affirmed, reversed, or modified). They also list the key numbers under which a case's headnotes appear, but one should always examine the case itself to determine which headnotes are relevant to a particular inquiry. Every *Decennial Digest* has its own Table of Cases (except the *Century Digest* and the *First Decennial,* which have a combined case table in volumes 21 to 25 of the *First Decennial*). Each *General Digest* volume also has a table listing the cases it covers; like the tables of key numbers, this list cumulates in every tenth volume. Exhibit 14 shows a portion of a *General Digest* table of cases, listing the decision shown in Exhibit 12.

A

A., In Interest of, FlaApp 2 Dist, 618 So2d 336. See F.A., In Interest of.

A., Matter of, Mont, 852 P2d 127. See A.S.A., Matter of.

Abadie v. Poppin, NDCal, 154 BR 36.—Bankr 2052, 2053, 2130, 2187, 3782; Fed Cts 47.

Abate v. Southern Pacific Transp. Co., CA5 (La), 993 F2d 107.—Damag 49.10; States 18.15; Torts 8.5(4); U S 50(1), 50(2), 50.10(4).

Abdel–Sater v. State, TexApp–Hous [14 Dist], 852 SW2d 671.—Crim Law 408, 627.10(1), 627.10(2.1), 627.10(7.1), 627.10(8), 759(1), 795(1.5), 795(2.10), 795(2.70), 1134(1), 1144.-13(2.1), 1159.2(7), 1159.6; Drugs & N 63, 64, 65, 67.

Abellon v. Nyack Hosp., NYAD 3 Dept, 598 NYS2d 393.—Work Comp 828.

ABN Amro Bank N.V., New York Branch v. Carmania Corp., N.V., SDNY, 154 BR 160. See Carmania Corp., N.V., In re.

Abrams v. Communications Workers of America, AFL–CIO, DDC, 818 FSupp 393.— Arbit 1.1; Labor 104, 219, 434.1.

Acacia Nat. Life Ins. Co. v. Hollis, CA2 (Conn), 991 F2d 968. See Ames Dept. Stores, Inc. Note Litigation, In re.

Academy Corp. v. Sunwest N.O.P., Inc., TexApp–Hous [14 Dist], 853 SW2d 833.—Forci E & D 43(7).

A. Cardi Const. Co., Inc., In re, BkrtcyDRI, 154 BR 403.—Bankr 2181, 2182.1, 2187, 3073; Courts 89.

Accu–Sort Systems, Inc. v. Lazerdata Corp., EDPa, 820 FSupp 928.—Fed Civ Proc 2493, 2545; Trade Reg 870(2).

Accu–Weather, Inc. v. Thomas Broadcasting Co., PaSuper, 625 A2d 75.—App & E 927(2); Contracts 16, 22(1), 28(3).

Ace Beverage Co. v. Municipal Court (People), CalApp 2 Dist, 20 CalRptr2d 153.—Crim Law 577.10(8); Mand 28, 61, 168(4), 187.9(2).

Ace Housemovers v. Wilson, FlaApp 2 Dist, 617 So2d 857. See Youngblood v. Wilson.

Acevedo v. Forcinito, DNJ, 820 FSupp 886.— Civil R 135, 205(1); Fed Civ Proc 2470, 2470.2, 2491.5, 2544; Inj 114(2); Prisons 4(10.1), 4(13).

A.C.R. by L.R. v. Vara, NJSuperL, 625 A2d 41, 264 NJSuper 555.—States 112.2(2), 209.

Adam v. Adam, RI, 624 A2d 1093.—Courts 175; Divorce 255, 306, 311.5; Equity 67, 71(1).

Adamo v. State Farm Lloyds Co., TexApp–Hous [14 Dist], 853 SW2d 673.—App & E 863, 934(1), 1073(1); Insurance 146.5(4), 514.-9(1), 514.10(1), 514.10(2), 514.21(1); Judgm 186.

Adams v. Com., Mass, 613 NE2d 897, 415 Mass 360.—Double J 165.

Adams v. Industrial Com'n, IllApp 5 Dist, 185 IllDec 399, 614 NE2d 533.—Work Comp 854, 976, 999, 1637.

Adams v. Keystone Ins. Co., NJSuperAD, 624 A2d 1008, 264 NJSuper 367.—Const Law 55, 154(3), 296(1); Insurance 4(2), 125(1).

Adams v. McPherson, NYAD 3 Dept, 597 NYS2d 505.—Divorce 303(1), 303(8), 305, 402(8).

Adams v. State, GaApp, 430 SE2d 35, 208 GaApp 29, cert den.—Crim Law 273.2(1), 273.3, 304(11), 369.2(5), 374, 736(1), 777.

Adams Outdoor Advertising, Ltd. v. Borough of Coopersburg Zoning Hearing Bd., PaCmwlth, 625 A2d 768.—Zoning 70, 721, 745.1.

Adamson v. City of Provo, Utah, DUtah, 819 FSupp 934.—Civil R 192, 210, 234; Const Law 48(1), 251.3, 277(1), 277(2), 278(1.1); Em Dom 2(1); Fed Civ Proc 2481, 2491.5, 2514, 2721, 2732.1; Fed Cts 430; Lim of Act 43, 46(7), 95(1), 95(14), 104½; Mun Corp 220(9), 728.

Aderhold v. Four Seasons Travel, Inc., Ala, 617 So2d 667.—Corp 243(1), 582, 590(1); Frds St of 20.

Adler v. William Blair & Co., IllApp 1 Dist, 184 IllDec 672, 613 NE2d 1264.—App & E 959(1), 1079; Cons Prot 34; Fraud 3, 20, 23, 46; Partners 366; Plead 236(6); Sec Reg 278.

A.D.R., In Interest of, SD, 499 NW2d 906.— Assault 92(3); Homic 300(2); Infants 68.7(2), 68.7(4); Stip 14(1).

Advanced Micro Devices, Inc. v. Intel Corp., CalApp 6 Dist, 20 CalRptr2d 73, 16 CA4th 346.—Arbit 29.1, 29.6, 73.1, 73.7(4), 73.9.

Advanced Power Systems, Inc. v. Hi–Tech Systems, Inc., EDPa, 148 FRD 138.—Fed Civ Proc 1271, 1855.1.

Ad–Vantage Promotions, Matter of, NYAD 3 Dept, 597 NYS2d 504. See Cobb, Matter of.

Aetna Cas. and Sur. Co. v. Brooks, NYAD 1 Dept, 597 NYS2d 376.—Indem 6.

Aetna Cas. & Sur. Co. v. Compass and Anchor Club, Inc., EDVa, 820 FSupp 240.— Decl Judgm 361.1.

Aetna Cas. and Sur. Co. v. Reisman, NYAD 2 Dept, 598 NYS2d 12. See Reisman v. Coleman.

Aetna Life & Cas. Co. v. Wisconsin Health Care Liability Ins. Plan, WisApp, 500 NW2d 691. See Martin by Scoptur v. Richards.

A.F., In re, Vt, 624 A2d 867.—App & E 842(2), 1008.1(5), 1010.1(4); Evid 584(1), 588; Infants 155, 173.1, 178, 179, 230.1.

AF Property Partnership v. State, Dept. of Revenue, ColoApp, 852 P2d 1267.—Judgm 181(32), 186; Tax 1202, 1261, 1319.

African Bio–Botanica, Inc. v. Ecco Bella, NJSuperAD, 624 A2d 1003, 264 NJSuper 359. See African Bio–Botanica, Inc. v. Leiner.

African Bio–Botanica, Inc. v. Leiner, NJSuperAD, 624 A2d 1003, 264 NJSuper 359.— Corp 325, 397; Interest 47(1); Princ & A 136(1), 138, 146(2).

A.G. v. State, FlaApp 3 Dist, 617 So2d 871.— Infants 254.

Exhibit 14: Part of a Table of Cases in a *General Digest* volume.

Tables of Cases list decisions by the name of the first party, usually the plaintiff or appellant. If only the name of the defendant or appellee is known, it is necessary to use a separate Defendant–Plaintiff Table. These tables provide citations and cross-references to the main Tables of Cases, but they are only published for *Decennial Digests* since 1976. Tables in the earlier *Decennials* and the *General Digests* list cases by plaintiff only.

There is no overall Table of Cases for the entire American Digest System, so the approximate date of decision is needed to find the appropriate *Decennial Digest*. If the jurisdiction of the case is known, it is usually more convenient to use one of the state or federal digests discussed in the next subsection.

b.   Jurisdictional and Regional Digests

The American Digest System covers cases appearing in all of West's reporters, and is therefore a massive, sometimes unwieldy finding tool. West also publishes smaller digests covering the decisions of smaller geographical or jurisdictional units. There are digests for four of the regional reporter series (*Atlantic, North Western, Pacific,* and *South Eastern*), and digests for every state but Delaware, Nevada and Utah. Each state digest is devoted to only one jurisdiction, except for the *Dakota Digest* and the *Virginia–West Virginia Digest*. The state digests include references to all the cases West publishes from the state's courts, as well as federal cases arising from the U.S. District Courts in that state.

One advantage of using a state digest instead of the American Digest System is that one volume can contain all relevant headnotes from a century or more. Instead of being issued in ten-year installments, state digests are

kept up to date through the use of annual *pocket parts,* supplements which fit into flaps inside the back covers of each volume.   Pocket parts are a common method of updating many legal publications, including statutory collections and many secondary materials.   Whenever a volume with a pocket part or other supplement is used, it is essential to check the supplement for current information.   The digest sets are brought further up to date between annual pocket parts by quarterly pamphlets and by the digests in reporter advance sheets.

Exhibit 15 shows a page from a pocket part for *West's New Jersey Digest 2d*, showing the headnote already seen in the *General Digest* in Exhibit 13.   Unlike the *General Digest*, this page covers several years worth of cases, from 1984 through 1993.   It is limited, however, to decisions of New Jersey state courts, the federal district court in New Jersey, and the U.S. Court of Appeals and U.S. Supreme Court reviewing cases arising in New Jersey.   For most purposes, a digest such as this is more effective and saves considerable time.   The *Decennial* and *General Digests* are most useful when a persuasive case from another jurisdiction or a comprehensive survey of the entire country is needed.

Some state digests have begun second or third series, so that one set does not cover the entire history of the state's court reports.   Each set must then be consulted for comprehensive research, but often it is only necessary to check the current set for recent cases on point.

There is also a separate series of digests for federal court decisions, containing headnotes reprinted from the *Supreme Court Reporter, Federal Reporter, Federal Sup-*

mates from sending outgoing correspondence to public officials, government agencies, and media representatives unopened and uncensored; free speech rights of inmates are significant, and, even though outgoing mail could contain dangerous material, i.e., escape plans, plans relating to ongoing criminal activity, and threats of blackmail or extortion, that threat was minimal in light of proposed audience, e.g., legitimate public officials, government agencies, and media members. U.S.C.A. Const.Amend. 1.—Id.

⚖4(13). —— **Law books and law libraries, legal materials, and opportunity for legal work.**

C.A.5 (N.J.) 1988. Central inquiry in determining if proposed legal access program withstands constitutional scrutiny is whether adequate assistance for persons trained in law is made available to prisoners who do not have access to law library.—Valentine v. Beyer, 850 F.2d 951.

D.N.J. 1993. For prisoners who cannot read or understand English, constitutional right of access to courts cannot be determined solely by number of volumes in, or size of, law library; merely making law library available to non-English speaking prisoner does not satisfy duty of prison officials to provide meaningful access.—Acevedo v. Forcinito, 820 F.Supp. 886.

D.N.J. 1992. Confiscation of inmate's legal papers in retaliation for filing lawsuits violates inmate's right of access to the courts.—Caputo v. Fauver, 800 F.Supp. 168, affirmed 995 F.2d 216.

D.N.J. 1990. New Jersey prison regulations governing legal copying services entitled inmate to free copies of his medical file pursuant to discovery request. Fed.Rules Civ.Proc.Rules 34, 78, 28 U.S.C.A.—DeMarco v. Ginn, 137 F.R.D. 214.

⚖4(14). **Religious practices and materials.**

U.S.N.J. 1987. Separate burden should not have been placed on state prison officials to prove that no reasonable method existed by which prisoners' religious rights could be accommodated without creating bona fide security problems, based on prisoners' claim that prison regulations inhibited exercise of their constitutional rights and violated free exercise of religion clause of the First Amendment. U.S.C.A. Const.Amend. 1.—O'Lone v. Estate of Shabazz, 107 S.Ct. 2400, 482 U.S. 342, 96 L.Ed.2d 282, on remand Appeal of Shabazz, 829 F.2d 32, on remand 829 F.2d 32.

State prison officials acted in reasonable manner in precluding prisoners who were members of Islamic faith from attending religious service held on Friday afternoons, and prison regulations to that effect did not violate free exercise of religion clause of the First Amendment; prison policies were related to legitimate security and rehabilitative concerns, alternative means of exercising religious faith with respect to other practices were available, and placing Islamic prisoners into work groups so as to exercise religious rights would have adverse impact. U.S.C.A. Const. Amend. 1.—Id.

C.A.5 (N.J.) 1988. Prohibition against group activity without supervision of prison authorities did not violate free exercise rights of Muslim inmates who engaged in unsupervised, group prayer, known as Du'a; inmates established leadership structure within prison; and authorities had valid, rational reasons for not permitting inmates to establish structure within prison. U.S.C.A. Const. Amend. 1.—Cooper v. Tard, 855 F.2d 125, rehearing denied.

Prohibition against group activity without supervision of prison authorities did not violate equal protection rights of Muslim inmates who engaged in unsupervised, group prayer; there was difference between sporting events in yard and informal discussion of controversial topics on one hand and

organized, functioning, alternative authority structure among Muslim inmates; regulation made no distinction based on religious group or sect; and other religious groups did not engage in unsupervised group activities. U.S.C.A. Const.Amend. 14. —Id.

C.A.5 (N.J.) 1986. State was required to show that prison regulations, which prevented inmates of Islamic faith from attending weekly religious services, were intended to serve, and did serve, the important penological goal of security, and that there was no reasonable method by which the inmates' religious faiths could be accommodated without creating bona fide security problems; modifying St. Claire v. Cuyler, 634 F.2d 109. U.S.C.A. Const.Amend. 1.—Shabazz v. O'Lone, 782 F.2d 416, stay denied 107 S.Ct. 21, 478 U.S. 1033, 92 L.Ed.2d 772, certiorari granted 107 S.Ct. 268, 479 U.S. 881, 93 L.Ed.2d 245, reversed 107 S.Ct. 2400, 482 U.S. 342, 96 L.Ed.2d 282, on remand Appeal of Shabazz, 829 F.2d 32, on remand 829 F.2d 32.

Where it is found that reasonable methods of accommodation can be adopted without sacrificing either the state's interest in security or the prisoners' interest in freely exercising their religious rights, the state's refusal to allow the observance of a central religious practice cannot be justified and violates the prisoner's First Amendment rights; modifying holding of St. Claire v. Cuyler, 634 F.2d 109. U.S.C.A. Const.Amend. 1.—Id.

D.C.N.J. 1984. Shabazz v. O'Lone, 595 F.Supp. 928, vacated 782 F.2d 416, stay denied 107 S.Ct. 21, 478 U.S. 1033, 92 L.Ed.2d 772, certiorari granted 107 S.Ct. 268, 479 U.S. 881, 93 L.Ed.2d 245, reversed 107 S.Ct. 2400, 482 U.S. 342, 96 L.Ed.2d 282, on remand Appeal of Shabazz, 829 F.2d 32, on remand 829 F.2d 32.

⚖7. —— **Appointment, qualification, and tenure.**

N.J. 1989. Determination to impose penalty of suspension, rather than discharge, for prison guard from whose unit escape occurred and who falsely indicated that he had made a required prisoner count was supported by the record.—Matter of Warren, 566 A.2d 534, 117 N.J. 295.

N.J.Super.A.D. 1991. Dismissal was appropriate sanction for refusal by correction officers to submit to mandatory drug testing, even though officers had good records and alleged that they would have complied with testing order had they been given basis for its issuance, where dismissal was penalty for positive test result and any less severe punishment for refusal to take test would create incentive not to comply with test order.—Caldwell v. New Jersey Dept. of Corrections, 595 A.2d 1118, 250 N.J.Super. 592, certification denied 606 A.2d 367, 127 N.J. 555.

Due process rights of corrections officers who were dismissed for failure to comply with mandatory drug test order were violated where no information was provided to officers at pretermination and departmental hearings as to underlying facts which constituted "reasonable individualized suspicion" that officers used or were under influence of controlled dangerous substances where failure to disclose information deprived officers of opportunity to rebut reasons why they had been ordered to submit to drug test and why they refused test; officers were entitled to general statement explaining how assistant commissioner reached his conclusion that sufficient suspicion existed, including fact that unnamed staff and inmate informants had implicated officers.—Id.

Corrections officers who were dismissed for violation of mandatory drug test order were not entitled to award of back pay as remedy for due process violations at pretermination hearings where, after full evidentiary hearing before admin-

Exhibit 15: A page from *West's New Jersey Digest 2d,* showing a headnote from the case in Exhibit 12.

plement, and *Federal Rules Decisions*. The current set is known as the *Federal Practice Digest 4th*. Its volumes are supplemented by annual pocket parts, and the entire set is further updated with bimonthly pamphlets. Earlier cases are covered by four previous sets, the *Federal Digest* (1754–1939), *Modern Federal Practice Digest* (1939–61), *Federal Practice Digest 2d* (1961–75), and *Federal Practice Digest 3d* (1975 to about 1985).

The decisions of the Supreme Court of the United States are also covered by a West digest devoted solely to its decisions, the *United States Supreme Court Digest*. (Note that Lawyers Coop also has a digest for the Supreme Court with a similar name, *United States Supreme Court Digest, Lawyers' Edition*.) Other digests for specialized federal courts include the *Bankruptcy Digest*, *Military Justice Digest*, and *United States Federal Claims Digest*.

All of these regional and jurisdictional digests include Tables of Cases which can be used to find decisions by name. These tables are usually more convenient than the *Decennial Digest* tables since they cover longer time periods and are updated by pocket parts. Except for the regional digests, these sets include Defendant–Plaintiff Tables as well.

c. *Words and Phrases*

West also reprints headnote abstracts in a separate multivolume set, *Words and Phrases*. Headnotes are included in *Words and Phrases* if the court is defining or interpreting a legally significant term, and they are arranged alphabetically rather than by key number. Most researchers do not use *Words and Phrases* very often, but it may be a useful tool when the meaning of a

specific term is in issue. Exhibit 16 shows a page from *Words and Phrases,* including a headnote from the case shown in Exhibit 12 interpreting prisoners' constitutional right of "access to courts." (Note in Exhibit 12 that headnote 4 is followed by a reference to *Words and Phrases* as a source for other judicial definitions of this term.) The current *Words and Phrases* volumes were all published over twenty years ago, so here it is usually most productive to *begin* research in the pocket part.

Words and Phrases covers the entire National Reporter System. Smaller lists of "Words and Phrases" also appear in many West digests and in West reporter volumes and advance sheets. These lists are not quite as convenient because they do not reprint the headnotes themselves. Instead they simply provide names and citations for the defining cases. (You can also find Words and Phrases entries online by using the WP field in WESTLAW.)

ACCESS TO INFORMATION

small fraction of gross business income. Gross v. Zoning Bd. of Adjustment of City of Philadelphia, 227 A.2d 827, 826, 424 Pa. 603.

Township district granted permit for blacktop plant in mining industry of township as an "accessory use" to mining and quarrying operations, where about 95% of blacktop material would come from existing quarrying operation, and blacktop operation would use only small number of employees in comparison to surrounding complex, and some elements of blacktop plant could be utilized both by new operation and existing facilities, and quarrying operations often function in conjunction with blacktop plants. Booth v. Board of Adjustment of Rockaway Tp., 234 A.2d 681, 683, 50 N.J. 302.

Within urban renewal plan permitting office building on particular square "and accessory uses such as employee restaurants and off-street parking necessary to serve the primary uses," and considering the legislative history of the plan and context of entire plan specifying broad range of retail commercial uses for nearby areas, "accessory uses" were limited to restaurants, dining rooms, cafeterias, snack bars, carry-outs, food cart service, food and beverage vending machine facilities, small stands, and off-street parking, all such uses being solely for employees occupying the building and their visitors. L'Enfant Plaza North, Inc. v. District of Columbia Redevelopment Land Agency, D.C.D.C., 345 F.Supp. 508, 515.

ACCESSORY USE DOCTRINE

"Accessory use doctrine" is, in essence, only an acknowledgement that certain general types of real estate usage have a natural and reasonable tendency to lead to certain other more specific uses. Klavon v. Zoning Hearing Bd. of Marlborough Tp., 340 A.2d 631, 634, 20 Pa.Cmwlth. 22.

ACCESSORY USES CUSTOMARILY INCIDENT

Use made of units after purchase, which involved installation of kitchens, bathrooms, and sleeping facilities so as to be suitable for 24-hour occupancy, materially differed from historic nonconforming use of structures as public bathhouses prior thereto and could not be considered "accessory uses customarily incident" to use of premises as a one-family dwelling or detached two-family dwelling permitted by zoning ordinance. Rye Beach Village Dist. v. Beaudoin, 315 A.2d 181, 184, 114 N.H. 1.

ACCESS ROADS

United States was not liable under Federal Tort Claims Act for injuries of automobile passenger and death of his wife on detour being used because of construction of dam and reservoir by United States, on ground that detour was "access road" under Act dealing with flood control, where detour was part of state highway system, was many miles from dam-site, and was not under supervision or control of United States. Spears v. U.S., D.C.Okl., 221 F.Supp. 990, 992.

ACCESS TO

Person with rights of "access to" children may approach them, communicate with them, and visit with them, but may not take possession or control of children away from managing conservator; conversely, person with rights to "possession of" chil-

dren may exercise possession and control to exclusion of all other persons including managing conservator during periods of possession and a person with rights of possession also has rights and responsibility toward children's care and behavior. Hopkins v. Hopkins, Tex.App.–Corpus Christi, 853 S.W.2d 134, 137.

ACCESS TO A CHILD

Within meaning of statute defining term "suit affecting the parent-child relationship", for purpose of statute conferring exclusive continuing jurisdiction upon court which acquires original jurisdiction of such a suit, as a suit for appointment of managing or possessory conservator, for access to or support of a child, or for establishment or termination of parent-child relationship, the term "access to a child" is limited to a suit brought for determination of legal right to access to a child, rather than a proceeding to enforce a right which currently exists under a previous court order. Ex parte Jabara, Tex.Civ.App., 556 S.W.2d 592, 595.

Term "access to a child" in statutes providing that a party affected by a court order setting terms and conditions for possession of or access to a child may file a motion requesting court to modify such order has same meaning as "visitation rights." Howard v. Pullicino, Tex.Civ.App., 519 S.W.2d 254, 257.

ACCESS TO COURTS

Prisoners and pretrial detainees have fundamental constitutional right of "access to courts," which encompasses all means that defendant or petitioner might require to get fair hearing from judiciary on all charges brought against him or grievances alleged by him. Acevedo v. Forcinito, D.N.J., 820 F.Supp. 886, 887.

"Access to courts" to which prisoners are constitutionally entitled encompasses all means defendant or petitioner might require to get fair hearing from judiciary on all charges brought against him for grievances alleged by him. Gilmore v. Lynch, D.C.Cal., 319 F.Supp. 105, 110.

Effective "access to the courts," which encompasses all the means required for a litigant to get a fair hearing from judiciary on charges brought against him or grievances alleged by him, is a constitutional right. O'Conner v. Mowbray, D.C.Nev., 504 F.Supp. 139, 141.

Inmate is entitled to meaningful access to the courts under the Fourteenth Amendment, and prisoner's right to "access to the courts" encompasses right to contact attorney visits. Casey v. Lewis, D.Ariz., 773 F.Supp. 1365, 1367.

ACCESS TO EVIDENCE

See, Area of Constitutionally Guaranteed Access to Evidence.

ACCESS TO INFORMATION

Interpretation of phrase "access to information" in definition of confidential employee for purposes of exclusion from collective bargaining unit to mean access to confidential information or information not available to employee association was in harmony with purpose and policy of exclusion to exclude from collective bargaining only those employees whose inclusion in bargaining unit would prevent

Exhibit 16: A page from *Words and Phrases*, showing an abstract from the case shown in Exhibit 12.

d. Finding Cases in Digests

To use a digest, the researcher must identify the topic and key number relevant to the problem. Digest topics and key numbers can be found in several ways: (1) by using a Descriptive Word Index after analyzing the factual and legal issues involved in a problem; (2) by surveying a relevant legal concept; or (3) from the headnotes of a case known to be on point.

Descriptive Word Method. To find the appropriate key number under which cases are digested, it is usually most productive to begin with a Descriptive Word Index, which lists common words and specific factual terms. These indexes, with tens of thousands of legally significant catchwords and phrases, accompany each digest set.

One can approach a Descriptive Word Index either by looking up legal issues, such as causes of action, defenses, or relief sought; or by looking up factual elements in an action, such as parties, places, or objects involved. For example, in a personal injury suit by a law student who had sustained a back injury from carrying too many heavy casebooks, the researcher might use the index to investigate some of the legal issues (negligence, assumption of risk, damages) or, usually more effectively, some of the specific facts of the case (student, university, books, back injury). Exhibit 17 shows a page from a Descriptive Word Index in a typical West digest, covering the subject matter of prisoner access to law libraries.

PRISONS

42 Md D 2d—456

References are to Digest Topics and Key Numbers

PRISONS—Cont'd
CONSTITUTIONAL and statutory provisions—
Good conduct. **Prisons 15(2)**
Personal and civil rights in general. **Const Law 82(13)**
CONSTITUTIONAL law—
Commitment, vested rights. **Const Law 92**
Control, executive encroachment. **Const Law 74**
Good time, vested rights. **Const Law 104**
Impairment of contracts. **Const Law 121(1)**
CONTROL of prisoners. **Prisons 13**
CONVICTS, see this index Convicts
COUNSEL for prisoner—
Access to. **Prisons 4(11)**
Consultation with. **Prisons 4**
Management proceedings. **Prisons 13(9)**
COUNTY to which prisoner is removed for trial as liable for expenses of removal. **Counties 139**
CUSTODY of prisoners—
Arrest **39**
Prisons 13
Compensation of officers—
Prisons 18
Sheriffs 39
Habeas corpus, see this index Habeas Corpus
Maintenance and care. **Prisons 17**
Sheriff's liability for ill treatment. **Sheriffs 105**
DETAINER against prisoner—
Federal penal institution outside of state, authority of state court judge—
Courts 495
Mand 61
DISCIPLINARY proceedings against prisoners. **Prisons 13**
Double jeopardy considerations. **Double J 24**
Procedure. **Prisons 13**
Review of proceedings. **Prisons 13**
Right to counsel. **Prisons 13**
DISCIPLINE. **Prisons 13**
Pretrial detainee. **Prisons 17**
DUE process in administration. **Const Law 272**
ESCAPE, see this index Escape
ESTABLISHMENT. **Prisons 1**
EXPENSES, incidental. **Prisons 18**
FALSE imprisonment, see this index False Imprisonment
FREEDOM of conscience. **Const Law 84.5(14)**
FREEDOM of speech and press—
Regulations. **Const Law 90.1(1.3)**
GAMBLING, criminal responsibility. **Gaming 72(2)**
HABEAS CORPUS—
Grounds for relief. **Hab Corp 512–515**
INJUNCTIONS—
Preliminary injunctions—
Grounds and objections. **Inj 138.60**
Proceedings. **Inj 139–159½**
INMATE grievances—
Damages—
Authority to award. **Prisons 9**
JAIL fees. **Prisons 18(3)**
JUDICIAL review of prison administration generally. **Prisons 4**
JUDICIAL supervision. **Prisons 4(2, 3), 13(3), 13.5(3)**
LAW libraries and materials. **Prisons 4(13)**
LAW library—
Inadequate library, other legal assistance provided—
Const Law 328
Prisons 4
LETTERS to attorney, state agents refusing to mail, copies sent to prosecutor, fair trial. **Crim Law 641.12(2)**
MAIL for prisoners. **Prisons 4**
MAINTENANCE. **Prisons 17**
Of prisoners. **Prisons 17**
MANAGEMENT. **Prisons 12**
MENTAL hospital, retransfer from. **Prisons 13.5(3)**
MENTALLY ill prisoners, transfer. **Prisons 13**

PRISONS—Cont'd
MUNICIPAL corporations. **Mun Corp 268**
NARCOTICS, transferring by kissing prisoner. **Poisons 9**
OFFICERS. **Prisons 5–11**
Action on sheriff's bond for injuries inflicted on prisoner—
App & E 1144
Sheriffs 168(6)
Appointment. **Prisons 7**
Bonds, see this index Official Bonds
Civil liability. **Prisons 10**
Compensation. **Prisons 8, 18**
Sheriffs and constables. **Sheriffs 38, 39**
Criminal liability. **Prisons 10**
Eligibility. **Prisons 7**
Ill treatment by sheriff. **Sheriffs 105**
Illness, release. **Crim Law 1001**
Powers. **Prisons 9**
Qualification. **Prisons 7**
Tenure. **Prisons 7**
OVERCROWDING, elimination, possible release of certain prisoners. **Prisons 17**
PERSONAL appearance of prisoners. **Prisons 4**
PHYSICIANS, review of compensation. **Cert 26**
PRETRIAL detainee, discipline. **Prisons 17**
RECORDS of prison. **Prisons 12**
REFORMATORIES, see this index Reformatories
REGULATIONS—
Freedom of speech and press, see also, Freedom of speech and press, ante
RELATIVES—
Support liability, generally, post
RELIGION, prisoner's right to practice. **Prisons 4**
RELIGIOUS liberty. **Const Law 84.5(14)**
RESCUE of prisoners, see this index Rescue
RIOTS—
Malicious destruction of property, indictment and conviction. **Mal Mis 1**
RULES for prison generally. **Prisons 4**
SALE of convict products. **Convicts 13**
SEARCHES and seizures, see this index Searches and Seizures
SHERIFFS and constables as jail officers. **Officers**, generally, ante
SHOWERS, male prisoners, female officers. **Prisons 12**
SOLITARY confinement. **Prisons 13(5)**
SUPERVISION. **Prisons 4**
SUPPORT liability. **Paupers 47**
TITLES of laws affecting. **Statut 119(2)**
TORTS—
Municipal establishment and maintenance. **Mun Corp 734**
United States officers, claims against. **U S 50.10(3)**
TRANSFER. **Prisons 13.5**
Retransfer from mental hospital. **Prisons 13.5(3)**
TRANSFER of prisoners. **Prisons 13**
Halfway house arrangement. **Prisons 13**
TRUSTY system in prisons. **Prisons 4**
UNITED States courts, abstention from exercise of jurisdiction. **Fed Cts 50**
USE of county jail by—
City. **Prisons 3**
United States. **Prisons 2**
VISITATION rights. **Prisons 4**
WORK stoppage, general lockup, equal protection—
Const Law 250.3(2), 272(2)
Crim Law 1213
Prisons 13(2)
WORKERS' compensation, fighting, course of employment. **Work Comp 697**
WORKERS' compensation for injuries to prisoners. **Work Comp 387**

Exhibit 17: A typical page from a digest Descriptive Word Index.

The index provides references to key numbers, under which abstracts and citations are then found. This is usually a simple step, but the researcher should be prepared for some frustration. Even the most thorough index cannot list every possible approach to a legal or factual issue. It is often necessary to rethink issues, reframe questions, check synonyms and alternate terms, and follow leads in cross-references. Thesauri can be helpful here.

With patience, you can usually find a reference to an appropriate topic and key number. When turning from the index to the volume of digest abstracts, it is helpful to look first at the outline of the topic to verify that the legal context is indeed appropriate. A researcher looking for cases on the substantive law of burglary, for example, may find that a reference leads instead to a key number dealing with the weight of evidence in criminal cases generally.

Remember that the key number system is the same throughout the West system, and therefore that references in any jurisdictional digest's Descriptive Word Index can be used in any other West digest. The index in each state digest covers the entire system, even if that state has no case law under a particular key number. The indexes in recent *Decennial Digests* are not nearly so comprehensive, so even when searching for cases in those digests it is best to begin with a state Descriptive Word Index if one is available.

Topic Approach. Some researchers use an alternative approach, choosing the West digest topic most relevant to the problem and analyzing its table of contents to select the appropriate key number. (A list of these topics appears in front of each digest volume, and a portion was reproduced above in Exhibit 10 on page 52. The table of contents for the Prisons topic is reproduced in Exhibit 11 on page 53.) This method has the advantage of providing the context of the individual key numbers, offsetting somewhat the lack of explanatory text in the digests. Reading through the outline may help clarify the issues or raise concerns the researcher had not yet considered. However, this approach can be very time-consuming, and a beginning researcher may not have the legal background to choose the right topic. The indexes are a faster and more reliable starting point.

Case Headnotes. The easiest and most foolproof way to use the digest is to begin with the headnotes of a case on point. When you already know of a relevant case, you can find it in the National Reporter System, scan its headnotes for relevant issues, and then use the key numbers accompanying these headnotes in searching the digest. This eliminates the need to search through indexes or to analyze the digest's classification system, and reduces the likelihood of turning to the wrong issue or getting stuck in a dead end. This method, of course, requires that at least one initial case be found through other means, but almost all of the research tools to be discussed in subsequent chapters can serve this purpose.

Despite their unquestioned value as case-finders, digests have several shortcomings. They consist simply of separate unevaluated case abstracts, with no explanatory text. There is no indication that a case is no longer good

law unless it has been directly reversed or modified. The researcher must often wade through many irrelevant entries to find citations to significant authorities.

Digest entries may reflect dicta and may even misstate points of law in the cases they abstract. It is essential to locate and read the cases themselves in order to find and synthesize those which are actually pertinent. Finally, the current status and authority of these cases must be determined. For this purpose it is necessary to turn to a separate set of research tools.

§ 3–3. SHEPARD'S CITATIONS

The body of published American case law contains many decisions which have long since been overruled or limited to specific facts. Before relying on any case, the attorney must verify its current validity. The most commonly used tool for this purpose is a service known as *Shepard's Citations*.

If *Shepard's Citations* only verified the current status of cases, it would still be a useful tool. However, it also lists virtually every subsequent case citing the decision in issue. *Shepard's* thus allows the researcher to trace the development of a legal doctrine from the time a known case was decided forward to the present.

Citation indexes, indicating later citations to a given document, are now used widely in scholarly research. They were first developed in legal research, and legal citators such as *Shepard's* are still the most developed and most extensive tools of their kind.

Shepardizing, as this updating process is commonly known, accomplishes three major purposes:

a. Tracing a case's judicial history, by providing parallel citations for the decision and references to other proceedings in the same case.

b. Verifying the current status of a case to determine whether it is still good law or has been overruled, limited, or otherwise diminished.

c. Providing research leads to later citing cases, as well as periodical articles, attorney general opinions, *ALR* annotations, and other resources.

Shepard's publishes citators for the Supreme Court, the lower federal courts, every state, the District of Columbia, Puerto Rico, and each region of the National Reporter System. These citators are supplemented frequently to provide up-to-date information on the status of cases. Each published set contains one or more maroon bound volumes, and one or more gold, red or blue paperback supplements. To help researchers know which volumes or supplements they need to use, the cover of each supplement includes a list, "What Your Library Should Contain," of the current volumes and pamphlets for the set.

Exhibit 18 shows a page from *Shepard's Maryland Citations,* indicating treatment of *Baltimore v. Silver,* 263 Md. 439 (1971). Note the variety of information Shepard's presents on this case:

(1) After the page number, the name of the case and the date of decision are provided. This feature appears only in newer *Shepard's* volumes. Note that Shepard's does not always follow standard *Bluebook* form in case names; for criminal cases it uses the name of the state instead of the usual *Commonwealth, People,* or *State.*

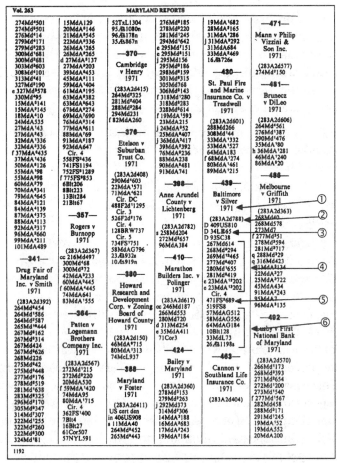

Exhibit 18: A page from *Shepard's Maryland Citations*, showing treatment of a Maryland Court of Appeals case.

(2) The first citation after the name and date is the parallel citation, listed in parentheses. This cross-reference usually appears in the volume or pamphlet in which a case is first listed. Remember that lower federal court cases and recent cases from many state courts do not have parallel citations to official reports.

(3) Next are listed citations of decisions in the same litigation. An appeal in this case was dismissed by the United States Supreme Court. The abbreviation "D" is one of several signals Shepard's uses to indicate a citation's effect, as shown in the list of abbreviations in Exhibit 19.

(4) Then follow citations of later citing decisions in Maryland courts, first in *Maryland Reports* and then in *Maryland Appellate Reports*. This section lists the exact page on which the Shepardized case is cited, rather than the first page of the citing decision. It is essential to check these listings, because the treatment of a case by later decisions may have just as important an effect on its precedential value as a direct reversal or affirmance. This case has been neither overruled nor questioned, and aspects of its holding has been *explained* (e) in a Maryland Court of Special Appeals decision at 23 Md. App. 202. Small raised numbers to the left of the page numbers of the citing cases correspond to the number of the headnote in *Silver* which states the legal principle involved in the citing case. The introductory signals and the raised numbers allow the researcher to focus on those cases which deal specifically with a particular aspect of the case in question.

(5) Decisions from the state's courts are followed by citations to federal court decisions, arranged by circuit.

ABBREVIATIONS—ANALYSIS

CASES

History of Case

a	(affirmed)	Same case affirmed on appeal to higher level court.
cc	(connected case)	The case is related to your case in some way in that it involves either the same parties or arises out of the same subject matter. However, it is not the same action on the merits.
D	(dismissed)	An action which has been appealed from a lower court to a higher court has been discontinued without further hearing.
m	(modified)	The lower court's decision is changed in some way, either during a rehearing or by action of a higher court. For example, if a court of appeals affirms a trial court decision in part and reverses it in part, that trial court decision is shown as modified by the a court of appeals.
r	(reversed)	The lower court is reversed on appeal to a higher court.
s	(same case)	The case is the identical action to your case, although at a different stage of the proceedings. "Same case" refers to many different situations, including motions and opinions that preceded your case. It is important to read these cases if you need to know exactly what occurred.
S	(superseded)	A subsequent opinion has been substituted for your case.
v	(vacated)	The opinion has been rendered void and is no longer of precedential value.
US	cert den	Certiorari has been denied by the U. S. Supreme Court.
US	cert dis	Certiorari has been dismissed by the U. S. Supreme Court.
US	reh den	Rehearing has been denied by the U. S. Supreme Court.
US	reh dis	Rehearing has been dismissed by the U. S. Supreme Court.

Treatment of Case

c	(criticized)	The court is disagreeing with the soundness of your decision, although the court may not have the jurisdiction or the authority to materially affect its precedential value.
d	(distinguished)	The case is different from your case in significant aspects. It involves either a dissimilar fact situation or a different application of the law.
e	(explained)	The court is interpreting your case in a significant way.
f	(followed)	Your case is being relied upon as controlling or persuasive authority.
h	(harmonized)	The cases differ in some way; however, the court finds a way to reconcile the differences.
j	(dissenting opinion)	Your case is cited in the dissent of this opinion.
L	(limited)	The court restricts the application of your opinion. The court usually finds that the reasoning of your opinion applies only in very specific instances.
o	(overruled)	The court has determined that the reasoning in your case is no longer valid, either in part or in its entirety.
p	(parallel)	This letter is usually found in older cases where your case was described as "on all fours" or "parallel" to the citing case.
q	(questioned)	Soundness of decision or reasoning in cited case questioned.

Exhibit 19: List of case history and treatment abbreviations used in *Shepard's Citations.*

Again citations include headnote numbers indicating the subject matter and list the exact page on which the case is mentioned. *Silver* has been cited in two federal district court cases, both from districts within the Fourth Circuit.

(6) Finally, references to the case in Maryland attorney general opinions, law review articles, and *ALR* annotations are noted. The abbreviations used by Shepard's (such as "MdL" for *Maryland Law Review*) may be unfamiliar, since they are not the same as those in the *Bluebook* or other standard sources. Each Shepard's volume, however, contains a table listing the abbreviations it uses.

The format for all Shepard's citators is similar, but the coverage varies among the series. There are several important differences between state Shepard's units and their corresponding regional reporter units. For example, compare the treatment of the same case in *Shepard's Maryland Citations* in Exhibit 18 and *Shepard's Atlantic Reporter Citations* in Exhibit 20. After the parallel citations, both sets provide judicial history citations and references to later Maryland cases. Under the official citation in Exhibit 18, the cases are listed as they appear in Md. and Md. App.; under the regional citation in Exhibit 20, the same cases are listed as published in A.2d. The researcher can thereby find later cases in the same reporter series as the citation being Shepardized. Note that the small raised numbers in the two versions are not the same, since the numbering of headnotes may differ between the two reporters.

Both state and regional citators include references to citing federal cases and to *ALR* annotations, but the

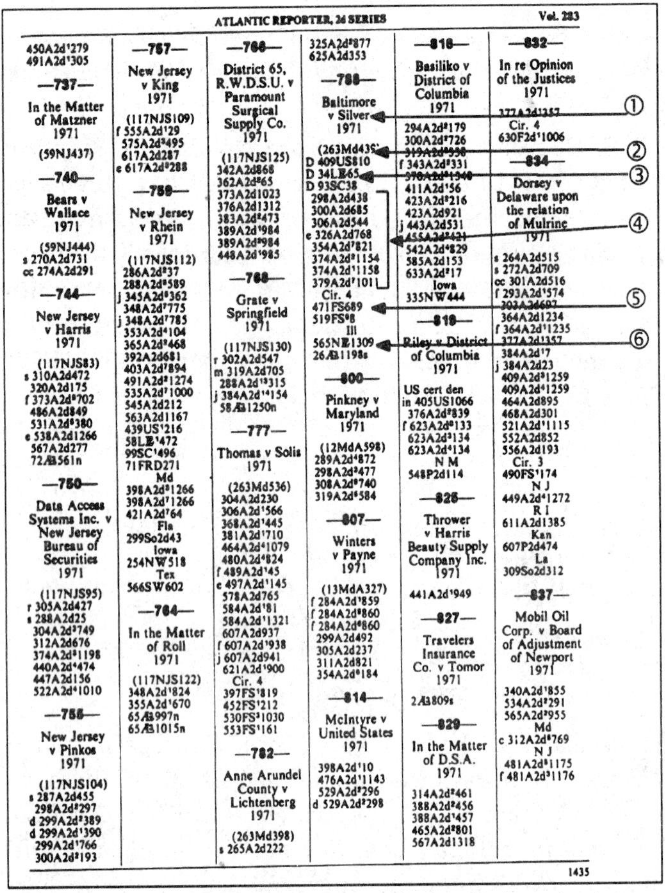

ATLANTIC REPORTER, 2d SERIES Vol. 283

450A2d[1]279
491A2d[1]305

—737—
In the Matter
of Matzner
1971
(59NJ437)

—740—
Bears v
Wallace
1971
(59NJ444)
s 270A2d731
cc 274A2d291

—744—
New Jersey
v Harris
1971
(117NJS83)
s 310A2d472
320A2d175
f 373A2d[8]702
486A2d849
531A2d[8]380
e 538A2d1266
567A2d277
72ALR3d561n

—750—
Data Access
Systems Inc. v
New Jersey
Bureau of
Securities
1971
(117NJS95)
r 305A2d427
s 288A2d25
304A2d[3]749
312A2d676
374A2d[5]1198
440A2d[4]474
447A2d156
522A2d[4]1010

—755—
New Jersey
v Pinkos
1971
(117NJS104)
s 287A2d455
298A2d[2]297
d 299A2d[2]389
d 299A2d[1]390
299A2d[1]766
300A2d[2]193

—757—
New Jersey
v King
1971
(117NJS109)
f 555A2d[1]29
575A2d[3]495
617A2d287
e 617A2d[3]288

—759—
New Jersey
v Rhein
1971
(117NJS112)
286A2d[2]37
288A2d[6]589
j 345A2d[6]362
348A2d[7]775
j 348A2d[7]785
353A2d[4]104
365A2d[3]468
392A2d681
403A2d[7]894
491A2d[2]1274
535A2d[7]1000
545A2d212
563A2d1167
439US[1]216
58LE[1]472
99SC[1]496
71FRD271
Md
398A2d[8]1266
398A2d[7]1266
421A2d[7]64
Fla
299So2d43
Iowa
254NW518
Tex
566SW602

—764—
In the Matter
of Roll
1971
(117NJS122)
348A2d[1]824
355A2d[1]670
65ALR3d997n
65ALR3d1015n

—766—
District 65,
R.W.D.S.U. v
Paramount
Surgical
Supply Co.
1971
(117NJS125)
342A2d868
362A2d[2]65
373A2d1023
376A2d1312
383A2d[2]473
389A2d[1]984
389A2d[2]984
448A2d[1]985

—768—
Grate v
Springfield
1971
(117NJS130)
r 302A2d547
m 319A2d705
288A2d[13]315
j 384A2d[14]154
58ALR3d1250n

—777—
Thomas v Solis
1971
(263Md536)
304A2d230
306A2d[1]566
368A2d[1]445
381A2d[1]710
464A2d[4]1079
480A2d[4]824
f 489A2d[1]45
e 497A2d[1]145
578A2d765
584A2d[1]81
584A2d[1]1321
607A2d937
f 607A2d[1]938
j 607A2d941
621A2d[1]900
Cir. 4
397FS[1]819
452FS[1]212
530FS[3]1030
553FS[1]161

—782—
Anne Arundel
County v
Lichtenberg
1971
(263Md398)
s 265A2d222

325A2d[2]877
625A2d353

—788—
Baltimore
v Silver ← (1)
1971
(263Md439) ← (2)
D 409US810
D 34LE65 ← (3)
D 93SC38
298A2d438
300A2d685
306A2d544
e 326A2d768
354A2d[7]821
374A2d[2]1154
374A2d[1]1158
379A2d[7]101 ← (4)
Cir. 4
471FS689 ← (5)
519FS[6]8
Ill
565NE1309 ← (6)
26ALR3d1198s

—800—
Pinkney v
Maryland
1971
(12MdA598)
289A2d[4]872
298A2d[3]477
308A2d[9]740
319A2d[6]584

—807—
Winters
v Payne
1971
(13MdA327)
f 284A2d[1]859
f 284A2d[8]860
f 284A2d[9]860
299A2d492
305A2d237
311A2d821
354A2d[6]184

—814—
McIntyre v
United States
1971
398A2d[1]10
476A2d[1]1143
529A2d[2]296
d 529A2d[2]298

—816—
Basiliko v
District of
Columbia
1971
294A2d[2]179
300A2d[2]726
319A2d[2]558
f 343A2d[2]331
378A2d[2]1340
411A2d[1]56
423A2d[2]216
423A2d921
j 443A2d531
455A2d[2]421
542A2d[4]829
585A2d153
633A2d[2]17
Iowa
335NW444

—818—
Riley v District
of Columbia
1971
US cert den
in 405US1066
376A2d[2]839
f 623A2d[8]133
623A2d[3]134
623A2d[4]134
N M
548P2d114

—825—
Thrower
v Harris
Beauty Supply
Company Inc.
1971
441A2d[1]949

—827—
Travelers
Insurance
Co. v Tomor
1971
2ALR3d809s

—829—
In the Matter
of D.S.A.
1971
314A2d[2]461
388A2d[2]456
388A2d[1]457
465A2d[2]801
567A2d1318

—832—
In re Opinion
of the Justices
1971
377A2d1357
Cir. 4
630F2d[1]1006

—834—
Dorsey v
Delaware upon
the relation
of Mulrine
1971
s 264A2d515
s 272A2d709
cc 301A2d516
f 293A2d[1]574
303A2d697
364A2d1234
f 364A2d[1]1235
377A2d1357
384A2d[1]7
j 384A2d23
409A2d[3]1259
409A2d[4]1259
464A2d895
468A2d301
521A2d[1]1115
552A2d852
556A2d193
Cir. 3
490FS[1]174
N J
449A2d[4]1272
R I
611A2d1385
Kan
607P2d474
La
309So2d312

—837—
Mobil Oil
Corp. v Board
of Adjustment
of Newport
1971
340A2d[1]855
534A2d[2]291
565A2d[2]955
Md
c 312A2d[6]769
N J
481A2d[8]1175
f 481A2d[3]1176

1435

Exhibit 20: A page from *Shepard's Atlantic Reporter Citations*, showing treatment of the same case as in Exhibit 18.

regional citator omits the attorney general and law review citations found in *Shepard's Maryland Citations.* Instead, however, it is the only source for citations to the case from courts in other states. Note here that the *Silver* case has been cited by one other state court, an Illinois decision in the *North Eastern Reporter*. Compre-

hensive Shepard's research on a state court decision always requires checking *both* state and regional Shepard's units.

U.S. Supreme Court cases are covered in *Shepard's United States Citations,* which is published in three separate sets for the *U.S. Reports, Lawyers' Edition,* and *Supreme Court Reporter.* The coverage of all three sets is the same, providing references to federal and state court cases (under both official and regional reporter citations), as well as annotations and law review articles. In Shepard's supplementary pamphlets new decisions from the U.S. Courts of Appeals which are not yet published in the *Federal Reporter* are listed by docket numbers, and a table in the back of each pamphlet lists the names and dates of these slip opinions. A new feature, "Citation Summaries," provides narrative information on selected citations in each pamphlet.

Lower federal court decisions are covered in a large set of *Shepard's Federal Citations*, with separate parts for decisions in the *Federal Reporter* and *Federal Cases* and for decisions in *Federal Supplement* and specialized reporters. Law review citations are listed in these volumes, but there is also a separate *Shepard's Federal Law Citations in Selected Law Reviews* listing journal references to cases from the Supreme Court and the lower federal courts (as well as to the U.S. Constitution and federal statutes).

Other Shepard's publications include a number of citators covering specialized areas of law, to some extent duplicating the coverage of its comprehensive general sets; a series of *Case Names Citators* for most jurisdictions, which can be used like digest case tables to find citations; and *Shepard's Acts and Cases by Popular*

Names: Federal and State, which provides citations of cases that are known by terms other than the names of their parties, such as the "Slaughterhouse Cases" or the "Steel Seizure Case."

Updating cases through *Shepard's Citations* is an essential part of the legal research process. With its peculiar abbreviations and telegraphic format, Shepardizing can be confusing at first. Each volume, however, includes tables of its abbreviations and introductory pages explaining its format and scope. Shepard's also issues an instructional pamphlet, *How to Use Shepard's Citations,* which is available in most law libraries.

As will be discussed in Chapter 5, *Shepard's Citations* is also available online through WESTLAW and LEXIS, and on CD–ROM, as well as in print. The electronic versions are not available in all research situations, but they have several advantages over their print counterparts. Citing entries are compiled into one listing, eliminating the need to search through multiple volumes and pamphlets. Because page space is no longer a concern, case treatments and names of publications can be spelled out rather than abbreviated. Instead of scanning a list, the researcher can have a computer search for specific treatments or headnote numbers. Finally, the online versions allow the researcher to go directly from a Shepard's display directly to the text of citing cases.

Despite these advantages of electronic Shepardizing, the printed volumes of *Shepard's Citations* remain a useful and quick means to verify the current validity of a decision and to find research leads. In many instances the simplest way to find recent cases in an area is to check the *Shepard's* listing for an older, seminal case and

then turn to the citing decisions to determine the state of the law today.

§ 3–4. CONCLUSION

West digests and *Shepard's Citations* are the two printed case-finding tools that deal most comprehensively with American federal and state judicial decisions. Their exhaustive scope makes them vital resources in many research situations that are not covered by more specialized tools. Both systems are the product of extensive editorial labor to organize case law and to make it accessible to legal researchers. Even when research is done through full-text electronic databases, these elaborate systems can be powerful tools to assist in research.

One feature noticeably lacking in both systems is a narrative text describing and explaining the state of the law. The next chapter introduces two research tools which are less comprehensive but may be easier to use.

CHAPTER 4

CASE RESEARCH: ANNOTATIONS AND ENCYCLOPEDIAS

§ 4–1. INTRODUCTION

This chapter introduces two additional resources useful for finding case law. Annotations and legal encyclopedias are less comprehensive than digests or *Shepard's Citations* because they cover far fewer published decisions. On the other hand, they are usually easier to use because they provide narrative discussions of the cases rather than simply collections of headnotes or lists of citations.

Annotations and encyclopedias also differ from other narrative resources such as treatises and law review articles, which often analyze problems critically. These narrative case-finding tools are specifically designed to

organize varied judicial decisions into a coherent statement of law. They generally do not question these decisions, nor do they attempt to integrate case law into a broader view of society. As the work of publishers' editorial staffs rather than of academic legal scholars, they are best viewed as research tools rather than as secondary authority which may persuade a tribunal. They can be cited as convenient compilations of prevailing judicial doctrine, which is after all their primary purpose.

§ 4–2. AMERICAN LAW REPORTS ANNOTATIONS

At the same time that West was developing its National Reporter System in the late 19th century, other publishers were attempting a different approach to case reporting. These publishers selected "leading cases" for full-text publication, and provided commentaries, or *annotations,* which described other cases with similar facts, holdings, or procedures. Selective publication was not as successful as comprehensive reporting, but the annotations have proved to be valuable case research tools.

Among the early sets of annotated reporters were the "Trinity series" (*American Decisions, American Reports* and *American State Reports*) (1871–1911) and *Lawyers Reports Annotated* (1888–1918). In 1919, Lawyers Cooperative Publishing Company (LCP) began a new series called *American Law Reports (ALR),* which continues to be published in two current series: *ALR5th* for general and state legal issues, and *ALR Federal* for issues of federal law. A few annotations on Supreme Court cases are also published in LCP's *United States Supreme Court Reports, Lawyers' Edition.*

a. Annotation Formats

An *ALR* volume contains from ten to twenty annotations, each analyzing decisions on an issue raised in an illustrative recent case, which is printed in full either before the annotation or at the end of the volume. Each annotation begins with a table of contents, a detailed subject index, and a table listing the jurisdictions of the cases discussed. In new volumes since 1992 (the beginning of *ALR5th*), this introductory material has also included a useful section, Research References, providing leads to encyclopedias, practice aids, digests, and other sources (usually published by LCP), and including sample electronic search queries and relevant West digest key numbers. Exhibits 21 and 22 show pages from the beginning of an *ALR5th* annotation on damages for injury to bridges. Exhibit 21 shows the beginning of the table of contents, and Exhibit 22 shows parts of the index and jurisdictional table.

DAMAGES FOR INJURY TO BRIDGE   31 ALR5th
31 ALR5th 171

Table of Contents

Research References
Index
Jurisdictional Table of Cited Statutes and Cases

ARTICLE OUTLINE

172

Exhibit 21: The beginning of an annotation in *ALR5th*, showing part of the table of contents.

31 ALR5th　　DAMAGES FOR INJURY TO BRIDGE
31 ALR5th 171

Reasonable value less salvage, § 4

Regulations, current, as affecting replacement cost, § 5

Related annotations, § 1[b]

Remaining life expectancy of bridge, § 5, 6, 8, 11[c], 17, 22

Rental value of land, § 14, 26

Repair, restoration, or replacement, cost of, § 3, 5, 7-9, 11-14, 15-18, 28, 29, 31, 32[a]

Retirement funds, charges for, § 27

Revenue losses, § 26

Safety requirements, current, as affecting replacement cost, § 5

Salvage, § 4-6, 11[b], 12[a], 22, 30

Scope of annotation, § 1[a]

Ships and vessels, § 5, 7, 15-17, 19, 25

State funds for repair of damage caused by flood, § 33[a]

Statutes imposing liability for injuries to bridge, § 11-13, 19, 20

Steel company's railroad bridge, § 26

Storage of materials, charges for, § 27

Sufficiency of evidence, § 31, 32

Summary, § 2

Supervisory work, cost of, § 21

Temporary bridges, § 6, 7, 19, 20

Termination of county engineer for destruction of historic bridge, § 24, 32[a]

Toll bridge, § 14, 16, 26

Total destruction of bridge, § 3-6, 11, 14, 15

Town chairman, testimony of, § 29

Train derailment, § 17

Trees and brush carried downstream following rain, § 14

Tugboats, § 15, 17, 23

Undamaged portions of bridge, costs of removing, § 25

Unemployment insurance, charges for, § 27

Unexpected contingencies, allowance for, § 25

Useful life remaining, § 5, 6, 8, 11[c], 17, 22

Vacations, charges for, § 27

Value, actual or real, § 3-5, 11[b], 14, 15, 17, 24, 26, 30, 32

Value, cost of repair greater than, § 8

Value, market, § 3, 5, 10, 11[a, b], 14-18, 29, 30, 32

Wages of thruway authority workers, § 21

Weather as factor, § 14, 17, 19, 25

Wooden bridge, § 3, 19

Jurisdictional Table of Cited Statutes and Cases*

UNITED STATES

28 USCS §§ 1346, 2671 et seq. See § 19

Beaufort & M. R. Co. v The Damyank (1954, DC NC) 122 F Supp 82— § 15

Canal Barge Co., Petition of (1971, ND Miss) 323 F Supp 805—§ 26

* Statutes, rules, regulations, and constitutional provisions bearing on the subject of the annotation are included in this table only to the extent, and in the form, that they are reflected in the court opinions discussed in this annotation. The reader should consult the appropriate statutory or regulatory compilations to ascertain the current status of relevant statutes, rules, regulations, and constitutional provisions.

For federal cases involving state law, see state headings.

Exhibit 22: A page from an *ALR5th* annotation, showing portions of the index and Jurisdictional Table.

The text of the annotation begins with sections describing its scope, listing related *ALR* annotations, and providing a general overview. The annotation then summarizes cases on point from throughout the country, arranged according to their facts and holdings. Exhibit 23 shows a section of the annotation on injury to bridges, discussing cases which use different approaches to determine the appropriate measure of damages.

The annotations range in length from several paragraphs to over a hundred pages. Although *ALR* does not contain an annotation relevant to every legal problem, an annotation directly on point can save considerable time for the researcher. It does the initial time-consuming work of finding relevant cases, and also arranges them according to specific fact patterns and holdings.

Even older annotations can be used to find references to recent case law, because *ALR* volumes are supplemented every year. Volumes in *ALR3d, ALR4th, ALR5th,* and *ALR Federal* are updated through annual pocket parts describing new cases, but *ALR1st* and *ALR2d* use other methods. While these older annotations are not used as often as those in the newer series, many remain current and continue to be updated. *ALR2d* volumes have no pocket parts, so new cases are instead summarized in a separate set of blue *Later Case Service* volumes, which *do* have annual pocket parts. Annotations in *ALR1st* are updated through a set called *ALR1st Blue Book of Supplemental Decisions,* which simply lists the citations of relevant cases.

cost of restoring the bridge to the condition it was in prior to the accident.

In an admiralty action involving two counties seeking damages to a drawbridge as a result of a collision caused by a vessel, which broke the drawbridge in two, and the bridge was never repaired but superseded by another, the court in In re Hibbard (1928, CA2 NY) 27 F2d 686, apparently recognizing the propriety of the measure of damages applied, observed that it became necessary to estimate the cost of the bridge's restoration to its original condition.

In a case where a state highway bridge was completely destroyed when a loaded coal truck attempted to cross it, the court in Commonwealth, Dep't of Highways v Pine Coal Co. (1967, Ky) 414 SW2d 134, stated that if the bridge had not been completely destroyed, then the measure of damages would be the cost of restoration to its original condition.

§ 10. Difference in value

In an action brought by the state to recover damages for, apparently, partial damage to a highway bridge, the court in the following case stated that where there is proof that a bridge does not have a market value, the measure of damages is the difference in value to the plaintiff of the bridge before and after the accident.

Determining that the trial court erroneously instructed the jury in an action by the state to recover damages for, apparently, partial damage to a highway bridge, the court in State ex rel. State Highway Com. v Beaty (1974, Mo App) 505 SW2d 147, noting that a bridge may not have a market value, pointed out that the proper measure of damages where there is proof that a bridge does not have a market value, as in the present case, is the difference in value to the plaintiff of the bridge before and after the accident, citing Gulf, M. & O. R. Co. v Smith-Brennan Pile Co. (1949, Mo App) 223 SW2d 100, § 18. The court recognized that such a measure was more in accord with settled principles of the measure of damages than a list of costs of repairs.

2. Actions Under Statutes Imposing Liability for Injuries to Bridge

§ 11. Statutes imposing liability for "all damages"—bridge totally destroyed[9]

[a] Cost of repair or replacement

In an action brought under a statute imposing liability for "all damages" to a public highway or bridge, the court in the case set forth below concluded that the proper measure of damages was the cost of repairing or replacing the bridge, the bridge having been totally destroyed.

The court in Tuscaloosa County

---

9. While most of the decisions indicate whether a bridge was destroyed or only damaged, sometimes it is not entirely clear. Accordingly, cases where the court speaks of a bridge's collapse, although it may be possible that such a bridge was capable of repair, are treated as involving destroyed bridges in the absence of an indication from the court that repairs were sought or possible.

Exhibit 23: Part of the text of an *ALR5th* annotation.

b. Finding Annotations

The basic tool for subject access to *ALR* is the six-volume *ALR Index,* which provides coverage of annotations in *ALR2d, ALR3d, ALR4th, ALR5th, ALR Federal,*

and *Lawyers' Edition 2d,* and is kept current by quarterly pocket parts. (The annotations in the first series of *ALR* are indexed in a separate *ALR First Series Quick Index*.) There are also two less comprehensive indexes reprinting excerpts from the six-volume index: *ALR Federal Quick Index*, covering *ALR Fed* and *L.Ed.2d* annotations, and *ALR Quick Index*, covering *ALR3d, ALR4th,* and *ALR5th* and published in an annual softcover edition. Exhibit 24 shows a section of the *ALR Quick Index*, including an entry for the annotation shown in Exhibits 21–23.

BRICKS AND BRICKLAYERS

Delay, contractual provision for per diem payments for delay in performance as one for liquidated damages or penalty, 12 ALR4th 891

Earning capacity, sufficiency of evidence, in personal injury action, to prove impairment of earning capacity and to warrant instructions to jury thereon, 18 ALR3d 88

Insurance, continuance or resumption of work as affecting finding of total or permanent disability within insurance coverage, 24 ALR3d 8

Landlord's liability for injury or death due to defects in outside walks, drives, or grounds used in common by tenants, 68 ALR3d 382

Subcontractors, duty and liability of subcontractor to employee of another contractor using equipment or apparatus of former, 55 ALR4th 725

Taxes, what constitutes manufacturing and who is a manufacturer under tax laws, 17 ALR3d 7

Unemployment compensation, eligibility as affected by claimants's refusal to accept employment at compensation less than that of previous job, 94 ALR3d 63

BRIDGES

Accessibility, way of necessity over another's land where a means of access does exist, but is claimed to be inadequate, inconvenient, difficult, or costly, 10 ALR4th 447

Animals, liability for killing or injuring, by motor vehicle, livestock or fowl on highway, 55 ALR4th 822

Annexation of land, what land is contiguous or adjacent to municipality so as to be subject to annexation, 49 ALR3d 589

Building and construction contracts
- bids and bidding, see group Bids and Bidding in this topic
- civil engineer, liability of, 43 ALR4th 911
- government liability for injury or death resulting from design, construction, or failure to warn of narrow bridge, 2 ALR4th 635
- unjust enrichment of landowner based on adjoining landowner's construction, improvement, or repair of commonly used highway, street, or bridge, 22 ALR5th 800

Carriers (this index)

Cemeteries, liability in action based upon negligence, for injury to, or death of, person going upon cemetery premises, 63 ALR3d 1252

Changed conditions clause in public works or construction contract with state or its subdivision, 56 ALR4th 1042

Construction contracts, see group Building and construction contracts in this topic

Damages, measure and elements of damages for injury to bridge, 31 ALR5th 171

Design defects
- architects and engineers, validity and construction, as to claim alleging design defects, of statute imposing time limitations upon action against architect or engineer for injury or death arising out of defective or unsafe condition of improvement to real property, 93 ALR3d 1242
- contractor's liability to contractee for defects or insufficiency of work attributable to the latter's plans and specifications, 6 ALR3d 1394
- governmental entity or public officer, liability for personal injury or damages arising out of vehicular accident due to negligent or defective design of a highway, 45 ALR3d 875

Exhibit 24: An excerpt from the *ALR Quick Index.*

Remember that each *ALR* annotation includes as section 1[b] a list of other annotations on related topics. If a quick check of the index does not turn up an annotation directly on point but does lead to one on a related issue, it may be useful to turn to that annotation and read through its list of related annotations. This list may lead to analogies or concepts the researcher may not have thought to check in the index.

Another means of access to annotations is through the *ALR Digest to 3d, 4th, 5th and Federal*, a multivolume set classifying *ALR*'s annotations and cases in a system similar to West's digests, and including references to the publisher's encyclopedias and formbooks. There are also older digests covering *ALR1st* and *ALR2d*.

Besides the *ALR Index* and *ALR* digests, there are several other ways to find annotations. *Shepard's Citations,* discussed in the previous chapter, includes citations to annotations in its treatment of cases. Any time a case is *Shepardized*, under either official or National Reporter System citation, the citing material includes annotations. Occasionally a citing annotation is on issues unrelated to the point for which the case is being researched, but finding an *ALR* reference in *Shepard's* usually indicates that the relevant case law has already been analyzed and summarized.

Many other sources, including some annotated codes and encyclopedias, also include references to relevant *ALR* annotations. This is particularly true of works from LCP, publisher of *ALR*, which provides links between its various research materials.

A researcher using electronic resources can find annotations in additional ways. Annotations beginning with *ALR2d* are online through LEXIS, and beginning with *ALR3d* are also published on CD–ROM. In either version the full texts of the annotations are searchable for particular combinations of terms. Finally, the citation verification system Auto–Cite (to be discussed in § 5–3) lists citing annotations in addition to providing case history information.

If later cases substantially change the law on a subject covered by an annotation, a new annotation is written to supplement or to supersede the older annotation. The older volume's pocket part or other supplement alerts the researcher to the existence of the newer treatment (another good reason to *always* check the pocket part). Another way to determine whether an annotation has been superseded is to check the "Annotation History Tables" in the last volume of the *ALR Index*. This table functions like a citator, listing all superseding and supplementing annotations.

Unlike digests, annotations contain a narrative text summarizing the cases and attempting to reconcile conflicting decisions. The coverage of *ALR* is not encyclopedic, however, so not every research issue is covered by its annotations.

§ 4–3. LEGAL ENCYCLOPEDIAS

Legal encyclopedias seek to describe systematically the entire body of legal doctrine, through a series of alphabetically arranged articles. They are among the first law library resources consulted by many students, since they are relatively easy to use and they provide straightfor-

ward summaries of the law. Their perspective, however, is often quite limited. They tend to emphasize case law and neglect statutes and regulations, and they rarely consider the historical or societal aspects of the rules discussed.

Legal encyclopedias are generally not viewed as persuasive secondary authority but rather as introductory surveys and as tools for case-finding. Their extensive citations to judicial decisions give encyclopedias their major value in legal research.

a. *Corpus Juris Secundum* and *American Jurisprudence 2d*

The two national legal encyclopedias are *Corpus Juris Secundum* (*C.J.S.*), published by West Publishing Company, and *American Jurisprudence 2d* (*Am. Jur. 2d*), published by Lawyers Cooperative Publishing Company. Both employ an alphabetical arrangement of over four hundred broad legal topics similar to those of the digests. Each article begins with a topical outline of its contents. The text, while tending to be general and simplistic in its analysis, can provide an introduction to an unfamiliar area and explain the basic concepts and terminology that underlie a field of law. Numerous footnotes provide references to court decisions supporting the statements in the text. *C.J.S.* also provides references to West key numbers and *Am. Jur. 2d* includes references to *ALR* annotations, both of which can be used to find more cases. Exhibits 25 and 26 show pages from *C.J.S.* and *Am. Jur. 2d* dealing with issues related to the *ALR* annotation seen earlier in this chapter.

VII. INJURIES TO BRIDGES, APPROACHES, OR APPLIANCES

§ 109. In General

    a. In general

    b. Overloading bridge

    c. Defenses

    a. In General

Persons responsible for negligent or intentional injuries to bridges or approaches may be held liable for damages in a civil action, and under some authority there may be a penal or criminal liability.

Research Note

Right of action for damage to a bridge from improper navigation of vessels generally is considered in C.J.S. Shipping §§ 77, 81, and recovery of damages for injuries to bridges from tugs and tows is discussed in C.J.S. Towage §§ 105, 106.

Library References

Bridges ⬥27.

WESTLAW ELECTRONIC RESEARCH

See WESTLAW Electronic Research Guide following Preface.

Where an injury has been negligently or intentionally done to a bridge or its approaches, the wrongdoer may, in an appropriate action, be held accountable for the same;[24] and, if the injury is intentional, he may, under some authority, incur a criminal liability.[25] If the wrong is a negligent one, an action for damages may be maintained at the instance of the corporate owners or of the individual or municipality whose duty it is to repair the same,[26] and such a claim for negligent destruction of a bridge is unaffected by a subsequent vacation of the road on which the bridge has been constructed and maintained.[27] It has been held that a town cannot recover for such injury until it has incurred some expense in making the repairs occasioned thereby.[28] An action for damage to a bridge which is not based on common-law negligence but on statutory negligence cannot be dismissed on the ground that plaintiff is not entitled to bring an action based on common-law negligence.[29] A statute providing that the driver or owner of a vehicle is responsible for damages which a bridge may sustain as a result of negligent or improper operation of such vehicle,[30] does not impose strict liability but makes liability for damages depend on negligent operation of the vehicle, so that proof of negligence is necessary to a recovery of damages.[31]

Liability of contractor.

Where a contract for the construction of a bridge provides that the contractor shall take ample precaution to protect the work against fire, and requires him to make good all parts of the work damaged in construction, such contract applies to damages for which the contractor was responsible in the construction of the work as a whole, that is, to the entire bridge, and not merely to the particular part of the work which he contracted to perform; nor is such liability affected by the fact that the injury was due to the negligence of a person employed to do a part of the work, where it was expressly agreed that the consent should not constitute an assignment of any part of the contract.[32]

Persons entitled to sue.

No general rule can be laid down as to the party in whose name an action for an injury to a bridge or for a penalty for its destruction must be brought, the statutes being by no means uniform in

---

24. Wis.—State v. Yellow Baggage & Transfer Co., 247 N.W. 310, 211 Wis. 391.

Damage to embankments

Ind.—Vanderburgh County Drainage Bd. v. Clouse, App., 398 N.E.2d 701.

25. D.C.—Smith v. District of Columbia, 12 App.D.C. 33.

26. Cal.—Chico Bridge Co. v. Sacramento Transp. Co., 55 P. 780, 123 C. 178.

Ill.—Chicago v. McGinn, 51 Ill. 266.

Owners of unauthorized private crossing

Ind.—Vanderburgh County Drainage Bd. v. Clouse, App., 398 N.E.2d 701.

27. Iowa—Schmitter v. Kauffman, 274 N.W.2d 723.

28. Me.—Freedom v. Weed, 40 Me. 383.

29. Mo.—State ex rel. State Highway Commission v. Blair, App., 484 S.W.2d 36.

30. **Improper meaning negligent**

Word "improper" in statute providing that driver and owner of vehicle is responsible for all damage which highways, including bridges and other public property thereon, may sustain as result of negligent or improper operation of vehicle has almost the same meaning as "negligent."

Okl.—State ex rel. Dept. of Highways v. Sharpensteen, 538 P.2d 1044.

31. Okl.—State ex rel. Dept. of Highways v. Sharpensteen, 538 P.2d 1044.

32. N.Y.—Lord Electric Co. v. City of New York, 145 N.Y.S. 205, 160 A.D. 344, affirmed 112 N.E. 1063, 217 N.Y. 634.

Exhibit 25: A page from the *Corpus Juris Secundum* article on bridges.

Evidence of the obstruction of the highway at times other than that at which an accident for which suit is brought occurred is inadmissible on the question of negligence.[20]

In some cases, evidence as to the mode of construction of highways, streets, and sidewalks in other municipalities or localities is admissible.[1] In other cases, however, a contrary rule prevails and this class of testimony has been held inadmissible.[2] Testimony that the space between the sidewalk and the street proper is not regarded in other cities and towns as a part of the highway which is required to be kept in repair has been held to be inadmissible, upon the ground that it is merely matter of opinion relative to the duties and liabilities of the public authorities.[3]

X. INJURIES TO HIGHWAYS, STREETS, AND BRIDGES

§ 604. Generally.

The wrongful infliction of injury upon a highway, street, or bridge may give rise to both criminal[4] and civil[5] liability. Public authorities invested with the power to control highways may, by statute or ordinance, prohibit the doing of acts which would cause injury thereto, and may impose suitable penalties for the violation of such prohibitions.[6] The view has also been taken that any extraordinary or unreasonable use which damages the way constitutes a nuisance,[7] which may be enjoined or abated at the instance of the controlling public authority.[8] Also, upon the conviction of one charged with the maintenance of a highway nuisance, the court may require the nuisance to be abated.[9]

§ 605. Civil liability.

It is elementary that persons using a highway, street, or bridge for the purpose of travel or transportation by the ordinary methods, in a reasonable

---

20. Rumpel v Oregon Short Line & U. N. R. Co. 4 Idaho 13, 35 P 700.

1. Raymond v Lowell, 6 Cush (Mass) 524, holding that testimony of witnesses as to the condition of streets in other towns in the vicinity, with respect to the inequalities, elevations, and depressions in the space between the sidewalk and the carriageway, is admissible, as bearing on the question of ordinary care, in an action against a town for an injury from a defect in that part of the street.

2. Hubbard v Concord, 35 NH 52.

3. Raymond v Lowell, 6 Cush (Mass) 524.

4. §§ 608–610, infra.

5. §§ 605–607, infra.

6. Korah v Ottawa, 32 Ill 121; Skaggs v Martinsville, 140 Ind 476, 39 NE 241 (holding that an ordinance to prohibit the flowing of water from an overflowing well or spring upon any street or alley is within the grant of power to control streets and enforce sanitary regulations); Crumpler v Vicksburg, 89 Miss 214, 42 So 673.

7. Commonwealth v Allen, 148 Pa 358, 23 A 1115.

Annotation: 5 ALR 769.

8. Texas & P. R. Co. v Interstate Transp. Co. 155 US 585, 39 L Ed 271, 15 S Ct 228; First Nat. Bank v Tyson, 133 Ala 459, 32 So 144; People ex rel. Bryant v Holladay, 93 Cal 241, 29 P 54, error dismd 159 US 415, 40 L Ed 202, 16 S Ct 53; Burlington v Schwarzman, 52 Conn 181; Augusta v Reynolds, 122 Ga 754, 50 SE 998; Valparaiso v Bozarth, 153 Ind 536, 55 NE 439; Bangor Twp. v Bay City Traction & Electric Co. 147 Mich 165, 110 NW 490; Canton v Canton Cotton Warehouse Co. 84 Miss 268, 36 So 266; New York v Rice, 198 NY 124, 91 NE 283; Haverstraw v Eckerson, 192 NY 54, 84 NE 578; Teass v St. Albans, 38 W Va 1, 17 SE 400, ovrld on another point Ralston v Weston, 46 W Va 544, 33 SE 326; Marshfield v Wisconsin Tel. Co. 102 Wis 604, 78 NW 735.

9. State v Southern Indiana Gas Co. 169 Ind 124, 81 NE 1149; Teass v St. Albans, 38 W Va 1, 17 SE 400, ovrld on another point Ralston v Weston, 46 W Va 544, 33 SE 326.

Exhibit 26: A page from the *American Jurisprudence 2d* article on highways, streets and bridges.

In this instance the *C.J.S.* exhibit is from a new 1995 volume, while the *Am. Jur. 2d* volume dates from 1967 and is updated with an extensive pocket part. In other research situations the reverse may be true, since each encyclopedia publishes several revised volumes each year. *Am. Jur. 2d* also includes a *New Topic Service* binder, covering a few newer areas of law which are not covered in the bound volumes. Both encyclopedias, however, are slow to reflect subtle changes in the law or to cover significant trends in developing areas.

The basic means of access to the encyclopedias are the multivolume softcover indexes published annually for each set. Although it is usually possible in a general encyclopedia to find needed information by browsing a volume, the index is a necessary first step in using a legal encyclopedia. Legal encyclopedias have a relatively small number of articles, which tend to be quite lengthy and to cover extensive areas of legal doctrine, so a pinpoint reference from the index is needed. The indexes are very detailed and extensive, but finding the right section may require patience and flexibility.

Other ways to find relevant encyclopedia sections are through references in other works, such as digests, codes, and formbooks. Generally each encyclopedia publisher provides cross-references among its related publications. West's *United States Code Annotated,* for example, provides *C.J.S.* references, while LCP's *United States Code Service* provides *Am. Jur. 2d* references.

Am. Jur. 2d is often shelved with several related publications. The *Am. Jur. Deskbook* provides a wide range of reference information about the legal system, including outlines of the federal government and its court system, standards of the legal profession, financial

tables, and demographic data of legal interest. There are also several multivolume adjunct sets to *Am. Jur. 2d,* some focusing on trial preparation and practice (*Am. Jur. Trials* and *Am. Jur. Proof of Facts*) and others providing legal forms (*Am. Jur. Legal Forms 2d* and *Am. Jur. Pleading and Practice Forms*).

Federal Procedure, Lawyers' Edition is another LCP encyclopedia, similar in format to *Am. Jur. 2d* but focusing specifically on federal law. It emphasizes procedural issues in civil, criminal and administrative proceedings, but many of its eighty chapters also discuss matters of substantive federal law. Because it deals exclusively with federal law rather than attempting to generalize about fifty state jurisdictions, it is often more precise and useful than *C.J.S.* or *Am. Jur. 2d.*

b.   State Encyclopedias

Several states have multivolume encyclopedias specifically focusing on the law of those jurisdictions. These state encyclopedias often do a better job of tying together statutory and case law than the national encyclopedias. Again, while not generally viewed as authoritative, they can provide both a good general overview of state law and extensive footnotes to primary sources.

Exhibit 27 shows a page from *Michigan Civil Jurisprudence* dealing with the same subject as earlier exhibits in this chapter. Note that the footnotes are limited to Michigan cases and also provide references to Michigan statutes and *ALR* annotations.

Other states with encyclopedias include California, Florida, Georgia, Illinois, Maryland, New York, North

---

BRIDGES   **§ 22**

legal authority does not cut off an existing claim for damages arising from establishment of that bridge.

Maxwell v. Bay City Bridge Co., 46 Mich 278, 9 NW 410 (1881).

§ 22. Injury to bridge.

Tortious injury to a bridge is actionable under general negligence principles,[1] and the recovery in such an action may include consequential damages.[2] A person who through willful misconduct injures any public bridge is liable in treble damages, recoverable in an action by the road commissioner of the township where the damage occurred.[3]

A joint contractor has been held not to be liable for injuries to a bridge caused by the wrongful act of the other contractor.[4]

If the state highway commissioner fails to prove any damage to the bridge it is proper for the court, on defendant's motion, to direct a verdict.[5]

---

[1] Where highway bridge is damaged as result of tortious act, state highway commissioner may recover repair costs if less than bridge's value before tortious act, and may recover bridge's value before tortious act if repair costs equal or exceed bridge's value before tortious act. State Highway Com'r v. Predmore, 341 Mich 639, 68 NW2d 130 (1955).

Liability for damage to highway or bridge caused by size or weight of motor vehicle or load, 53 ALR3d 1035.

Collision of privately owned vessel with bridge, causing property damage, 21 NCCA3d 432.

[2] In determining whether cost of constructing and maintaining temporary detour, needed because automobile collision damaged highway bridge, was recoverable as consequential damages in state highway commissioner's action against colliding motorists, common law prevailed in absence of statute. State Highway Com'r v. Predmore, 341 Mich 639, 68 NW2d 130 (1955).

[3] MSA § 9.337; MCL § 230.7.

Statute allowing treble damages for injuries to highways and bridges applies only to active injuries proceeding directly from unlawful acts, and the single damages are limited to what would have been sufficient at the time of the injury to restore the bridge to its former condition. Shepard v. Gates, 50 Mich 495.

Under statute providing for treble damages for injuries to public bridge a party driving logs on a river is not liable for injuries caused by a jam and freshet after notice, except where the act is willful or the negligence so gross as to amount to culpable and wanton negligence. Overseer of Highways of Road Dist. No. 4 of St. Ignace Tp. v. Pelton, 129 Mich 31, 87 NW 1029 (1901).

501

Exhibit 27: A page from *Michigan Civil Jurisprudence*, a typical state encyclopedia.

Carolina, Ohio, Pennsylvania, Tennessee, Texas, Virginia, and West Virginia. Some of these sets are published by West Publishing and include references to *C.J.S.* and West digests, while others are from Lawyers Cooperative Publishing and provide references to *Am. Jur. 2d, ALR,* and other LCP publications.

Researchers in states without local encyclopedias need not despair. The state digest from West can provide a thorough treatment of its case law, although it lacks the narrative text of the encyclopedia and fails to integrate state statutory law. In addition, most states also have treatises on specialized areas of legal doctrine and practice.

§ 4–4. CONCLUSION

The narrative case research tools discussed in this chapter are relatively clear and straightforward, and provide a wealth of references to case law. They do not cover as many cases as the West digests and Shepard's citators discussed in the previous chapter. Nor do they offer the insights and ideas offered by influential treatises or periodical articles, which will be discussed in Chapter 9. Each source has its purpose.

A number of other research tools are also useful as case-finders. Although each of these will be discussed in more detail in other chapters, they are mentioned briefly here because of their relevance to case-finding. **Annotated statutes** include, following each statutory section, abstracts of relevant judicial decisions and are usually the most comprehensive source for finding case law interpreting a statutory provision. **Looseleaf services** devoted to specific subject areas (e.g., labor law, securi-

ties, taxation) include the full text or abstracts of new judicial decisions, and are invaluable research tools in their subject areas. Finally the **electronic research systems** to be discussed in the following chapter are among the most important case-finding tools available.

No single case-finder is the best for all purposes. Selection of the most useful resource depends upon the nature of the problem at hand. A dispute involving the interpretation of a statute leads one to an annotated code for case-finding, while a problem requiring general background knowledge of a topic suggests beginning with a treatise. Each research problem must be analyzed, the available tools evaluated, and the most appropriate approach chosen. Inevitably personal preference plays a part when two or more case-finding tools seem equally useful. Experimentation and the development of skill in using all of these approaches will enable you to make the most effective choices for each problem encountered.

CHAPTER 5

CASE RESEARCH: ELECTRONIC RESOURCES

---

§ 5–1. INTRODUCTION

There is no doubt that computer-based research has dramatically affected case-finding methods. To date, however, it has just begun to change the basic structure of case law literature, and most electronic resources are still derived from print counterparts. As electronic forms increasingly become the standard mode of publication, the legal system will see more far-reaching changes which may affect the concept of precedent in judicial decisionmaking.

Electronic resources are powerful and effective tools in legal research. Full-text databases allow researchers to

determine their own criteria for each search, so that they need not rely totally on reporters' and editors' indexing decisions. Hypertext links permit researchers to move effortlessly from one document or service to another and back again.

We introduce electronic research methods after describing basic print research, for two reasons. An understanding of the underlying print literature remains essential for successful use of electronic resources. Students who make their initial attempt at legal research online may never comprehend the value of other methods which may appear more cumbersome but which can yield more accurate results. In addition, not all researchers have access to the resources discussed in this chapter. While law schools generally have subscriptions allowing their students unlimited use of WESTLAW and LEXIS, in most other circumstances these online systems are either quite expensive or unavailable. CD–ROM and the Internet have increased access to electronic research methods, but they are not yet as extensive or as widely available as printed resources.

This chapter focuses primarily on the online databases WESTLAW and LEXIS, the most powerful and comprehensive electronic resources. Similar, but less sophisticated, search approaches are used with most CD–ROM products and Internet resources.

Change has been a constant feature in the development of computer-based research during its short twenty-year life, and that undoubtedly will continue in the future. Some aspects of the discussion that follows in this chapter will probably be outdated before too long.

§ 5–2. ONLINE DATABASES

The leading online systems in legal research are WESTLAW, a service of West Publishing Company, and LEXIS, a service of Reed Elsevier Inc. Both provide access to a wide range of documents, including judicial opinions. Through an online search, one can retrieve all cases which contain specified terms or combinations of terms. One can also search the databases in ways impossible in print, such as for opinions written by a particular judge or argued by a particular lawyer.

Both WESTLAW and LEXIS contain full texts of opinions from the federal courts and from all fifty states. Cases are generally available online much sooner than they are published on paper. Decisions of the Supreme Court of the United States are added to the databases the same day they are announced, and most appellate court decisions are available within a few days or weeks. Retrospective coverage varies from jurisdiction to jurisdiction. For the federal courts, all published cases since 1789 are included in the online databases. For some states, on the other hand, coverage extends back only a few decades. Both services publish frequently revised directories indicating the coverage dates of their databases.

Cases available online include those published in official reports and commercial reporters such as West's National Reporter System. In addition, the online systems contain many "slip opinions", particularly from the federal courts, not published in any of the traditional printed reporters. For most jurisdictions, however, online coverage is limited to the same courts for which reports are published. Very few state trial court deci-

sions are available either in print or in online case databases.

Before beginning a search, an online researcher must first choose the appropriate database. Both systems have online directories that list the various options available to the researcher. Databases are presented in slightly different ways by the two systems. WESTLAW users select a single *database* identifier for each search, while LEXIS researchers follow a two-step process by selecting a general or topical *library* and then choosing a specific *file* within that library. Decisions of the Supreme Court, for example, are in the SCT database on WESTLAW, and the US file in the GENFED library on LEXIS. These designations do not necessarily indicate the amount of information available. There are, for example, some LEXIS *files* that are much larger than most LEXIS *libraries*. Exhibits 28 and 29 show the systems' online directory displays listing federal court databases.

In both LEXIS and WESTLAW, one can search the decisions of a particular state or a particular court, or

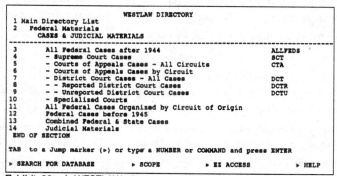

Exhibit 28: A WESTLAW directory screen, showing the identifiers for federal case law databases.

```
Please ENTER, separated by commas, the NAMES of the files you want to search.
You may select as many files as you want, including files that do not appear
below, but you must enter them all at one time.  To see a description of a
file, ENTER its page (PG) number.
          FILES - PAGE 1 of 10 (NEXT PAGE for additional files)

NAME   PG DESCRIP          NAME    PG DESCRIP          NAME   PG DESCRIP

 --COURTS GROUP FILES--    -----SUPREME COURT-----     --SHEPARD'S OVERNIGHT--
MEGA   11 Fed & State Cts  US       1 US Supreme Court FDOVER  3 Overnight Cites
OMNI    1 Fed Cases & ALR  USPLUS  12 US,BRIEFS,PRE-VU ----ADMINISTRATIVE-----
COURTS  1 Fed Cases        BRIEFS  12 Argued from 9/79 ALLREG 17 FEDREG & CFR
CURRNT  1 Cases w/in 2yrs  USLIST  13 Sup.Ct Summaries FEDREG 17 Fed. Register
NEWER   3 Cases from 1944  USLW    13 US Law Week      CFR    17 Code of Fed.Reg
SUPCIR  1 US,USAPP & CAFC  -----LEGISLATIVE------      COMGEN 15 Comp.Gen.Decs.
FED     8 CAFC,CCPA,CIT.   RECORD  27 CongRec frm 1984 ---SECONDARY SOURCES---
 ---U.S. COURT FILES---    BILLS   27 All Bills Files  SSMEGA 40 All Secondary
US      1 US Supreme Ct    PUBLAW  16 US Public Laws   ALR    40 ALR & L.Ed.Annos
USAPP   1 Cts of Appeal    USCODE  16 USCS & PUBLAW    RESTAT 40 Restatements
DIST    1 District Courts  ---------RULES---------     EXTRA  11 In the News...
CLAIMS  2 Ct. Fed. Claims  RULES   32 Federal Rules    PUBS   39 Legal Pubs
To search by Circuits press NEXT PAGE. NOTE: Only court files can be combined.
```

Exhibit 29: A LEXIS ® menu screen, showing case law and other files in the GENFED library.

one can search in databases combining the decisions of several jurisdictions. Generally searches in large databases cost more than searches in more specific databases. Whether to limit research to a particular jurisdiction depends upon a variety of other factors as well, including the purpose of the research and the value of precedent from other jurisdictions. Sometimes the only relevant cases for a research issue are those from the forum state. For other research questions, cases from any federal or state jurisdiction may be useful.

Both systems provide comprehensive databases for searching a broad range of federal and state court decisions. A WESTLAW search among all decisions since 1945 is conducted in the ALLCASES database. All federal cases since 1945 are available in the ALLFEDS database, and appellate decisions from all state courts since 1945 in the ALLSTATES database. (Older decisions are available in separate databases.) On LEXIS, the comprehensive file of court decisions is the MEGA file (in the MEGA, GENFED or STATES libraries). Federal cases since 1789 are found in the GENFED library,

COURTS file; and the file of appellate decisions from all state court systems is the STATES library, COURTS file.

a. Basic Boolean Search Techniques

LEXIS and WESTLAW enable one to search the full text of opinions for words or phrases that may appear in relevant cases. This capability gives researchers a method of searching that is not dependent on predetermined digest classifications or indexing methods. For example, a digest may have several pages of headnotes on prisoner access to legal materials, but a computer search can retrieve those few cases that focus on the needs of prisoners who do not read English. For each computer search, the researcher can create a new set of criteria to frame a research question.

The simplest online search is for a single word, such as *prison.* A one-word search can yield any reference to a particular term, place, or name. The search retrieves only documents using the exact word specified; unlike a digest or printed index, a database has no controlled vocabulary gathering all references to like items in the same place. For most subjects of research, however, more than one word can be used to denote the same concept. One decision may use the word *prison,* another *penitentiary,* and a third *jail.* To search effectively, the researcher must incorporate the various ways of expressing a concept, as in *prison or penitentiary or jail.* The word *or* is one of several "connectors" used in search commands. The connector *or* must actually be typed in a LEXIS search, but WESTLAW understands a space between words to be the same as *or.* On WESTLAW, therefore, the same search could read *prison penitentiary jail.*

Two conventions of computer word searching ease the task of finding relevant words. First, a search for most singular words also finds documents containing their plural and possessive forms. A search for *plaintiff* retrieves not only "plaintiff" but "plaintiffs," "plaintiff's," and "plaintiffs'." Second, both systems have extensive lists of automatically equivalent terms, so that a search for *first* also retrieves documents with the term "1st," and a search for *California* retrieves both "Cal." and "Calif."

A more striking feature is the use of the universal characters * and !. The * character is used in place of one or more letters to retrieve documents with varying spellings. For example, *mari*uana* in a search query retrieves cases using either "marihuana" or "marijuana." The ! character is used with a truncated search term to find a number of related words, giving the researcher even greater flexibility. The term *pris!,* for example, retrieves documents with "prison," "prisoner," or "pristine." It is important not to truncate words too early, however, to avoid retrieving unrelated terms. A search for *pri!* would retrieve not only "prison" words but also "price" and "privacy."

Single-word or synonym searches, even in truncated forms, give the researcher only a fraction of the true power of computerized retrieval. The databases are more than simple concordances of every word in every opinion. A more potent approach is the combination of several terms to retrieve documents matching a highly specific set of criteria tailored to the particular research issue.

One easy way to combine more than one term is to search for a phrase. This is particularly useful when

researching a term of art or when looking for documents citing a particular publication. In LEXIS, simply enter the phrase: *three generations of imbeciles.* Because WESTLAW interprets a blank as *or,* the phrase must be placed within quotation marks: *"three generations of imbeciles".*

Multiple terms can also be combined in a search by using connectors. This combination of terms to retrieve matching documents is known as *Boolean searching,* named after the logician George Boole. One connector, *or,* has already been discussed. The connector *and* is used to find any document containing two or more terms within its text. The search *prison and library* retrieves not only cases involving prison libraries, but also those which use the words "prison" and "library" separately (for example, "library" on the first page and "prison" several pages later). Using the *and* connector permits the database researcher to combine concepts in ways not possible when using most printed resources. For example, an attorney using a digest to research discovery issues in an employment discrimination suit generally must choose between key numbers in the Civil Rights topic and those in the Federal Civil Procedure topic. A case directly on point may be listed under only one of the two topics. Databases circumvent this research problem, since all cases are searched and not just those assigned to a particular topic.

Frequently the most effective way to combine search terms is a *proximity connector,* with which a researcher specifies the maximum number of words that can separate the search terms. This is done by using /*n* in WESTLAW and w/*n* in LEXIS. A search for *prison /5 library* or *prison w/5 library* means *prison* within five

words of *library*. It retrieves documents with phrases such as "prison law library" or "libraries for the prison system," and eliminates many of the false drops that *prison and library* may locate.

In selecting the maximum possible number of words between search terms, the researcher must base the decision on experience and the particular question's context. Another approach is to use the connectors /s and /p in WESTLAW, or *w/s* and *w/p* in LEXIS, to indicate that the search terms appear in the same sentence or in the same paragraph. These connectors eliminate the need to guess a magic number and decrease the retrieval of documents where search terms are physically close but unrelated in use.

These various features and connectors can be combined in a search in any number of ways to create a very detailed and highly focused inquiry. The art of framing successful search requests is learned as you achieve a familiarity with both the legal terminology of a subject area and the available features of an online system.

b. Using Fields and Segments

Another important feature of online searching is the use of document *fields* (in WESTLAW) or *segments* (in LEXIS). Fields or segments are specific parts of a case, such as the names of the parties, the judge writing the opinion, or the date of decision. Limiting a search to a field or segment can produce a much more specific result. The usual process is to identify the field or segment to be searched and to enclose the search terms in parentheses. A search for *miranda* retrieves any cases mentioning Miranda warnings or discussing the testimony of an expert witness named Miranda. A search for *title(mi-*

randa) on WESTLAW or *name(miranda)* on LEXIS, however, retrieves only those cases where one of the parties is named Miranda.

Date searches work in a similar way. Adding *and 1995* to a search would only eliminate cases in which the number "1995" was not mentioned. On the other hand, adding *and date(1995)* to a WESTLAW search or *and date is 1995* to a LEXIS search reduces retrieval to cases decided during that year.

There are numerous searchable fields and segments in online documents. Some allow research that is virtually impossible by other means. For example, it would be a lengthy and tedious process manually to find all opinions written by a particular judge. Online databases can easily retrieve a complete list of a judge's opinions with commands such as *judge(rodriguez)* (on WESTLAW) or *opinionby(rodriguez)* (on LEXIS). The researcher can even examine a judge's decisions on a particular topic by combining this request with other search terms.

In WESTLAW, one can use the *synopsis* and *digest* fields to search only for words in West's introductory summary and headnotes. Limiting the search to words important enough to be mentioned in the synopsis or headnotes retrieves a smaller body of cases more precisely on point. In addition, West digest topics and key numbers can be used in WESTLAW searches, either alone or in combination with other search terms. Each topic is assigned a number, as shown in Exhibit 10 on page 52. WESTLAW key number searches combine the topic number with the key number like this: *310k4(13)*. The topic number for Prisons is 310, and 4(13) is the specific key number covering access to legal materials. The researcher can use topics and key numbers to limit

retrieval to a particular subject matter, and add search terms to specify fact situations within that subject.

c. Natural Language Searching

In 1992 WESTLAW introduced a new method of searching its databases, WIN (*Westlaw Is Natural*). WIN was followed a year later by FREESTYLE on LEXIS. WIN and FREESTYLE use *natural language* searching. A researcher using a natural language method does not combine terms using proximity connectors, but instead enters a phrase or question such as "What is meaningful court access for non-English speaking prisoners? "

Natural language searching does not simply convert this question into a Boolean string of terms. Instead the computer system separates the significant terms from "noise" words such as "what" and "for," and then assigns relative weights to the terms it searches for depending on how often they appear in the database. It then retrieves a specified number of documents which appear most closely to match the query, giving greater weight to the less common terms. LEXIS provides help screens showing how the terms in the search were weighted and which terms appear in each document retrieved.

There are rules for constructing successful natural language searches. WIN can identify phrases, but in FREESTYLE phrases should be entered in quotes so that the computer does not look for the individual words out of context. Both systems have online thesauri to identify synonyms, which are not automatically searched. A natural language search can be limited by using some of the fields and segments employed in Boolean searching, such as date or name of judge. One can also specify certain words that *must* appear in any document retrieved,

known as *control concepts* (in WESTLAW) or *mandatory terms* (in LEXIS).

Natural language searching is easier to learn than Boolean searching, but the searcher gives up some control over the results. This method is generally preferable with very broad searches that might retrieve hundreds or thousands of cases in a Boolean search, since natural language will retrieve the documents that use the key terms most often and thus probably discuss these issues at the greatest length.

One major difference between Boolean and natural language searching is that a Boolean search can retrieve anywhere from nothing to thousands of cases, depending on how well the search is prepared and how commonly the combination of terms is found. Unless a natural language search includes control concepts or mandatory terms, it *always* retrieves a predetermined number of cases (usually 20 or 25). Often the first few cases are right on point, but the degree of relevance can drop off precipitously. In addition, the number of cases retrieved provides no feedback to indicate that the search may have been too broad or too narrow.

Most researchers tend to develop a preference for either the exactness of Boolean searching or the ease of natural language, but it is often fruitful to perform similar searches using both methods. Usually each approach will find some cases that the other misses. Natural language searching is not yet a replacement for Boolean techniques, but it does provide another approach.

d. Reading and Refining Search Results

Once the computer system has found those cases which satisfy a given search request, the researcher has several

options for viewing the retrieved documents. Both systems can display either the full text of cases or only those portions containing the search terms.

The major difference in the presentation of cases between the two systems is that LEXIS provides only the court opinion itself, while WESTLAW includes the synopsis and headnotes for any case published in a West reporter. The synopsis, providing a quick summary of the decision, is particularly useful. Unless the court has provided its own summary or synopsis, it is not always readily apparent in LEXIS what a retrieved case is about.

WESTLAW has two major methods of display, *Term Mode* and *Page Mode*. In Term Mode, one browses the first page of each case (usually containing the synopsis prepared by West editors) plus any pages containing the search terms in the specified relationships. Page Mode permits the researcher to read through the entire document. Entering P or T moves the researcher between these two modes. In addition, a list of retrieved cases is available with the *Cite List* command. WIN provides another display option, *Best Mode*, which picks out the portion of the document which most closely matches the query's terms. Exhibit 30 shows the display in WESTLAW of the Supreme Court case that was seen in Exhibits 2 through 5 in its printed forms.

LEXIS has three basic display options, *Kwic, Full,* and *Cite. Kwic* ("key words in context") displays a window of text of twenty-five words around the appearance of the search terms. (One can also specify a larger or smaller number of words by using the *Var* [for variable] *Kwic* option.) Because LEXIS does not provide editorial synopses, the *Kwic* display includes no initial summary of

```
                    Copr. (C) West 1995 No claim to orig. U.S. govt. works

Citation               Rank(R)          Page(P)           Database        Mode
110 S.Ct. 1640         R 1 OF 5         P 1 OF 42          SCT             TERM
 109 L.Ed.2d 13, 58 USLW 4457
(CITE AS: 495 U.S. 14, 110 S.CT. 1640)
                             NEW YORK, Petitioner
                                       v.
                               Bernard HARRIS.
                                 No. 88-1000.
                             Argued Jan. 10, 1990.
                             Decided April 18, 1990.
   Defendant was convicted in the New York Supreme Court, Bronx County, Lang, J.,
of second-degree murder and he appealed.  The Supreme Court, Appellate
Division, ► 124 A.D.2d 472, 507 N.Y.S.2d 823 (memorandum opinion), affirmed.
On further appeal, the New York Court of Appeals, ► 72 N.Y.2d 614, 536
N.Y.S.2d 1, 532 N.E.2d 1229, reversed.  Certiorari was granted.  The Supreme
Court, Justice White, held that, where the police have probable cause to arrest
a suspect, the exclusionary rule does not bar the State's use of a statement
made by the suspect outside his home, even though the statement is made after a
warrantless and nonconsensual entry into the suspect's home.
   Judgment reversed.
   Justice Marshall filed a dissenting opinion in which Justices Brennan,
Blackmun, and Stevens joined.
```

Exhibit 30: The first screen of a Supreme Court case on WESTLAW, showing the West synopsis.

each case. The *Full* format displays the full text of retrieved cases. The *Cite* format provides a list of case names and citations. A fourth display option in FREE-STYLE, *SuperKwic*, works like WIN's *Best* and focuses on the portion of the document with the highest occurrence of search terms. Exhibit 31 shows the display of the same Supreme Court case in LEXIS.

As part of the screen display of a case, both systems provide citations to published versions, whether in offi-

```
                         LEVEL 1 - 1 OF 5 CASES

                            NEW YORK v. HARRIS

                                No. 88-1000

                     SUPREME COURT OF THE UNITED STATES

            495 U.S. 14; 110 S. Ct. 1640; 1990 U.S. LEXIS 2037; 109 L.
                          Ed. 2d 13; 58 U.S.L.W. 4457

                         January 10, 1990, Argued
                         April 18, 1990, Decided

DISPOSITION:  <=1>  72 N.Y. 2d 614, 532 N.E. 2d 1229, reversed.

OPINION:

    ... [*16] [**1642] warrantless arrest therefore violated Payton even though
there was probable cause.  Applying  <=12>  Brown v. Illinois, 422 U.S. 590
(1975), and its progeny, the court then determined that the station house
statement must be deemed to be the inadmissible fruit of the illegal arrest
because the connection between the statement and the arrest was not sufficiently
attenuated.   [*17]   The court noted that some courts had reasoned ...
```

Exhibit 31: The first screen of a Supreme Court case on the LEXIS ® service, using the *KWIC* format to display the search terms.

cial reports, West reporters, or topical reporters. They also provide "star paging" references showing the exact page in West reporters and in some official reports on which particular text is printed. Note in Exhibit 31 that the text shown is from pages 16–17 of the *U.S. Reports* and page 1642 of the *Supreme Court Reporter*.

If a completed search retrieves too many cases, the researcher can narrow the focus of inquiry in several ways. Both systems allow the researcher to examine the retrieved set of documents for specific terms, whether or not they were included in the initial request. This feature is called *Locate* on WESTLAW and *Focus* on LEXIS. Instead of identifying a new set of cases replacing the original search result, Locate and Focus merely search for and highlight particular terms in the retrieved documents. The researcher can then return to the original request by exiting or canceling this feature.

LEXIS Boolean searching also has a *Modify* feature, which adds new search terms to an existing search. For example, if a search for *prisoner w/10 access* yielded several hundred cases, adding *w/10 legal research* would limit retrieval significantly. The new terms and the original search are combined to create a "Level 2" set of cases satisfying the narrower criteria. This new set can then be modified further for an even more specific "Level 3," and so on. Neither WESTLAW nor LEXIS FREE-STYLE offers "Modify," but the initial search can easily be edited and resubmitted.

One of the most powerful display tools available in WESTLAW and LEXIS is the set of hypertext links embedded in each document. Most judicial opinions cite extensively to other cases, as well as to statutes and other documents. If these cited materials are also avail-

able online, their citations are marked with symbols indicating their availability. When the researcher clicks on a WESTLAW "jump marker" (▶), or types an equal sign and an indicated number on LEXIS, the system immediately displays the document which is cited. From there one can go back to the original document or on to another linked document. This allows researchers to follow leads as they arise rather than making notes for possible future reference. Note in Exhibit 30 the jump markers next to the lower court citations in the West synopsis and in Exhibit 31 the =12 before the citation for *Brown v. Illinois*.

The systems offer a variety of shortcuts and advanced techniques for displaying results, refining searches, and running queries in different databases. One valuable feature which many students overlook is the ability to save a search and have the system automatically run it to check for new material on a daily or weekly basis. This is an excellent way to stay abreast of new developments in a specific case or in an area of interest. This feature is known as WESTCLIP on WESTLAW, and as ECLIPSE on LEXIS.

This discussion of online research methods provides only a brief introduction, of course. Hands-on training and experience are the best ways to achieve the expertise which will help you put your valuable online time to its most effective use. Watch for the inevitable improvements and additions that will be coming!

§ 5–3. RELATED ONLINE TOOLS

Full-text case databases are powerful tools for subject research. WESTLAW and LEXIS also offer a variety of

services to perform more mechanical functions such as document retrieval and citation checking.

Both systems have mechanisms for retrieving a case by typing its citation. Called *Find* on WESTLAW and *Lexsee* on LEXIS, these services do not require use of connectors or field/segment commands. Instead they simply look up a specific citation and display the full text for scanning or printing. *Find* and *Lexsee* are like having entire sets of reporters available, even when researching at home or in a small law office.

A major feature of both online systems is *Shepard's Citations*. The online version of Shepard's is basically the same as the print version described in the preceding chapter. The online Shepard's, however, compiles citing entries into one listing, eliminating the need to search through multiple volumes and pamphlets. Coverage is complete and retrospective, duplicating the "Cases" sections of published Shepard's volumes.

A major advantage of Shepard's online is the ability to limit a display to particular headnotes or treatments. A researcher interested in particular points of law can limit a display to specific headnote numbers, instead of scanning several columns of irrelevant entries in print. By limiting a display to particular treatment symbols, one can retrieve, for example, only those cases that distinguish or limit the holding of the cited decision. Exhibit 32 shows the WESTLAW Shepard's display for the Supreme Court decision in the preceding exhibits, limited to cases which *explain* or *follow* its holding.

The systems allow the researcher to go directly from a case to its Shepard's display with a single keystroke, and

```
                              SHEPARD'S  (Rank 1 of 2)        Page 1 of 3
    CITATIONS TO: 110 S.Ct. 1640
                  New York v Harris 1990

    CITATOR: UNITED STATES CITATIONS
    DIVISION: Supreme Court Reporter
    COVERAGE: First Shepard's volume through Oct. 1995 Supplement
    LOCATED:  E,F
    Retrieval                                          Headnote
      No.     --Analysis--- -------Citation-------       No.
       1       F   Followed   111 S.Ct. at 663

                             Cir. 1
       2       E   Explained  917 F.2d 641, 644            1

                             Cir. 2
       3       F   Followed   760 F.Supp. 997, 1003        2
       4       F   Followed   762 F.Supp. at 55            1
       5       F   Followed   762 F.Supp. at 55            5

      ► Cancel LOCATE request (XLOC) and display complete result
      ► Insta-Cite  ► Shepard's PreView  ► QuickCite  ► Commands  ► SCOPE
      Copyright (C) 1995 McGraw-Hill, Inc.; Copyright (C) 1995 West Publishing Co.
```

Exhibit 32: A Shepard's Citations display in WESTLAW, limited to cases explaining or following the cited case.

then from Shepard's to the text of a citing case. This makes Shepardizing an integral part of the research process, rather than an afterthought too easily neglected.

Because Shepard's online is no more current than Shepard's in print, WESTLAW offers a supplementary service called *Shepard's Preview*. This service provides references to recent cases that have not yet been included in Shepard's print or online coverage.

The full-text case databases of the two systems are even more up to date. A search using a case's name or citation and limited to recent months may find new citing cases well before they have been treated by Shepard's or any other editorial services. In a developing area of law, the latest cases available only through full-text retrieval may be vitally important. WESTLAW has a feature called *QuickCite* which automatically searches the texts of new cases for references to a case being Shepardized. *LexCite*, on LEXIS, operates similarly but is not limited to recent cases.

Both systems also provide services designed to verify the accuracy and validity of citations. *Insta–Cite,* a WESTLAW service, and *Auto–Cite,* available on LEXIS,

focus specifically on later developments in the same litigation and on cases which affect the precedential authority of the case in question. The researcher simply enters the citation of the case. The display includes the name of the case, any parallel citations, and the names and citations of the related cases, with the effect of each subsequent decision noted.

Auto–Cite displays first the citation in question, followed by subsequent and prior decisions in the same litigation. Insta–Cite lists decisions in chronological order, marking the citation in question with an arrow. Auto–Cite also lists annotations in *ALR* or *Lawyers' Edition* that cite any of the cases in its display, while Insta–Cite provides references to any citations in *Corpus Juris Secundum*. Exhibits 33 and 34 show the Insta–Cite and Auto–Cite displays for the case illustrated and Shepardized in earlier exhibits.

Both Insta–Cite and Auto–Cite are rapidly updated and are much more current than either printed or online Shepard's Citations. Particularly for recent cases, it is

```
                                INSTA-CITE
CITATION: 110 S.Ct. 1640
                              DIRECT HISTORY

      1 People v. Harris, 124 A.D.2d 472, 507 N.Y.S.2d 823
           (N.Y.A.D. 1 Dept., Nov 06, 1986) (NO. 26993)
         Order Reversed by
      2 People v. Harris, 72 N.Y.2d 614, 532 N.E.2d 1229, 536 N.Y.S.2d 1
           (N.Y., Oct 20, 1988) (NO. 137)
         Certiorari Granted by
      3 New York v. Harris, 490 U.S. 1018, 109 S.Ct. 1741, 104 L.Ed.2d 178
           (U.S.N.Y., Apr 17, 1989) (NO. 88-1000)
         AND Judgment Reversed by
  => 4 NEW YORK V. HARRIS, 495 U.S. 14, 110 S.Ct. 1640, 109 L.Ed.2d 13,
           58 USLW 4457 (U.S.N.Y., Apr 18, 1990) (NO. 88-1000)
         On Remand to
      5 People v. Harris, 77 N.Y.2d 434, 570 N.E.2d 1051, 568 N.Y.S.2d 702
           (N.Y., Feb 12, 1991) (NO. 269)

                            SECONDARY SOURCES

CORPUS JURIS SECUNDUM (C.J.S.) REFERENCES
      23 C.J.S. Criminal Law Sec.929 Note 64.5 (Pocket Part)

(C) Copyright West Publishing Company 1995
```

Exhibit 33: An Insta–Cite display indicating the history of a Supreme Court decision.

```
Auto-Cite (R) Citation Service, (c) 1995 Lawyers Cooperative Publishing

CITATION YOU ENTERED:

New York v. Harris*1, 495 U.S. 14, 109 L. Ed. 2d 13, 1990 U.S. LEXIS 2037, 110
S. Ct. 1640, 58 U.S.L.W. 4457 (1990)

SUBSEQUENT APPELLATE HISTORY:

    on remand, People v. Harris, 77 N.Y.2d 434, 568 N.Y.S.2d 702, 570
    N.E.2d 1051, 1991 N.Y. LEXIS 210 (1991)

PRIOR HISTORY:

People v. Harris, 124 A.D.2d 472, 507 N.Y.S.2d 823 (1st Dep't 1986)

    rev'd, People v. Harris, 72 N.Y.2d 614, 536 N.Y.S.2d 1, 532 N.E.2d 1229,
    1988 N.Y. LEXIS 2698 (1988)

    and rev'd, (BY CITATION YOU ENTERED)

ANNOTATIONS CITING THE CASE(S) INDICATED ABOVE WITH ASTERISK(S):

*1  When is evidence which is obtained after unconstitutional search or seizure
    sufficiently remote from such search or seizure so as not to be tainted by,
    and not to be inadmissible as fruit of, such search or seizure--Supreme
    Court cases, 109 L. Ed. 2d 787, secs. 3, 7.
```

Exhibit 34: An Auto–Cite display on the same case.

wise to check Auto–Cite or Insta–Cite for any developments since the latest Shepard's supplement.

Finally, the two systems also offer software that performs various citation-checking functions on all citations in a brief or other document. *WestCheck* (from WESTLAW) and *CheckCite* (which uses LEXIS) automatically find the citations in a document, check citation form, dial the host system, access the requested services, and download or print a report for the researcher to peruse.

§ 5–4. CD–ROM MATERIALS

A growing number of court decisions are available in full text on CD–ROM, from a number of publishers. Because CD–ROM products use a variety of software with different methods for searching cases and displaying results, we can only generalize here.

CD–ROM has many of the same advantages of online searching (flexible full-text searching and easy manipulation of retrieved data). Because the information is stored locally on a disc rather than in a remote comput-

er, each search does not incur new charges for connect time and database use. This makes it possible to try several different searches without worrying about the additional cost. The convenience of being able to switch back and forth between CD research and word processing makes it easier to integrate electronic research into drafting memoranda or other documents.

Generally CD search methods are similar to, but not as sophisticated as, online searching. Most CD products do not yet provide natural language software, but they do offer basic Boolean search techniques. The researcher combines terms and finds documents matching requested criteria. One attractive feature with many CD programs is that the exact number of documents with each term is indicated, making it easier to decide how to modify a search to retrieve more or fewer cases. Most CD products also have some features comparable to field or segment searching online, allowing a search to be limited by criteria such as date, jurisdiction, or names of parties.

A CD can store a great deal of information, but it is dwarfed by the massive online files combining all federal or state judicial decisions. A CD library of federal court decisions, for example, occupies dozens of discs, each of which must be searched separately. In such instances CD is better seen as a storage medium for court decisions which would otherwise take up many library shelves. On the other hand, CD excels as a research tool when a more limited number of decisions is needed. It is ideally suited to research in the law of an individual state, a specialized area of practice, or a short time period.

§ 5–5. INTERNET RESOURCES

The Internet has a wide and ever growing body of information. Its main strength in legal research is that it provides materials that are not otherwise widely available, such as administrative documents or legislative information. At this point case law is not very extensively represented on the Internet.

A growing number of recent court decisions are available, however, with coverage beginning in 1990 for the Supreme Court and in 1995 for selected U.S. Courts of Appeals and a few state courts. Most of these cases can be searched for keywords, but the Internet's limitation to very recent decisions means that it is not yet an effective medium for case research. On the other hand, it can be a handy, low-cost way to monitor developments and to get copies of new decisions.

Because judicial decisions are in the public domain, an increasing amount of case law is sure to be added to the Internet in the coming years. It will take some time, however, for Internet databases to be as comprehensive as those available commercially, and for their search software to become as sophisticated as that used by WESTLAW or LEXIS.

§ 5–6. CONCLUSION

The electronic resources discussed in this chapter can save enormous amounts of time and can perform tasks impossible with print resources. As with any research, effective use comes from training and practice. The database companies and CD–ROM publishers offer classes and publish a variety of introductory guides and reference materials.

Many students tend to rely very heavily on electronic resources for all research problems. Only when they leave law school do they learn that computerized research can be very expensive. Yet financial constraints are only one reason not to rely exclusively on a method that is so dependent on the researcher knowing exactly how to phrase a search request. If the language of a decision does not precisely match the request, it will remain undiscovered unless other research methods are also used. The database systems are most effective as part of a research strategy integrating a number of different approaches.

Often the benefit of an author or editor's work in organizing and analyzing cases is indispensable. Treatises and law review articles analyze the leading cases in a subject area, while digests and annotations sort and index cases by precise facts or issues. A computer, on the other hand, can neither decide which cases are most important nor distinguish between holding and dictum. There are times when printed tools can achieve results with greater speed and precision than online research.

The uses of electronic resources in case research are only a small part of their applications in legal research. The rest of this book will include discussion of other kinds of information available online, in CD–ROM, and on the Internet.

CHAPTER 6

STATUTES AND CONSTITUTIONS

---

§ 6–1. INTRODUCTION

Thus far we have focused our attention on case law, because of the importance of appellate decisions in the common law system and in American legal education. Legislative enactments, however, frequently play at least as central a role as cases in legal research. The vast majority of appellate decisions today involve the application or interpretation of statutes, rather than consideration of common law principles.

It is important to determine whether statutes are involved in a specific problem early in the research

process, since that affects the direction of your research
and can save considerable time. Introductory commentaries and cases generally provide references to the relevant statutes, and it is often prudent to check statutory
indexes as well. Experienced researchers develop a
sense of which issues are likely to be governed by statute
and whether these issues are matters of federal or state
law. Problems involving public law will certainly require
statutory research.

Statutes have been used through the ages to formulate
new rules as well as to codify existing custom and judicial
pronouncements. There are very significant differences
today among the statutory forms of different legal systems. The modern codes of the civil law system differ
markedly from Anglo–American statutes and codes.
While the Continental codes legislate general rules in
broad provisions of simple and concise language, British
and American statutes are usually written in considerable detail in order to anticipate every foreseeable application or contingency. American statutory law is constantly growing, as we strive optimistically for legislative
solutions to increasingly complex social and economic
problems.

The nature of legal authority assigned to legislation is
different from that of case law. Statutes have binding or
mandatory authority within their own jurisdiction. In
other jurisdictions they have no effect and are not even
persuasive authority. One state's laws may influence
another state's legislature considering similar legislation,
and judicial decisions applying or construing a statute
may persuade other courts confronting similar issues,
but the statutory language itself carries no authority
outside its own jurisdiction.

American statutes are published in three forms. The first version of a newly enacted statute is the *slip law*. Each law is issued by itself on a single sheet or as a pamphlet with separate pagination. Neither federal nor state slip laws are widely distributed, and their texts reach the public largely through a variety of commercial publications and electronic services.

Next are the *session laws*. The statutes are arranged by date of passage and published in separate volumes for each session of the legislature. The official session laws are generally published in bound volumes after the end of each session, but commercial *advance session law services* provide the texts of new laws in pamphlet form during each legislative session. Each session law volume is indexed, but those indexes are not cumulated, making subject access for more than one session difficult.

In most jurisdictions, the session laws constitute the *positive law* form of legislation, *i.e.,* the authoritative, binding text of the laws. Other forms (such as codes) are only *prima facie* evidence of the statutory language, unless they have been designated as positive law by the legislature.

Although the chronologically arranged session laws contain the official text of legislative enactments, their use as research tools is limited. Researchers usually need the laws currently in force, rather than the laws passed during a specific legislative term. They also need convenient access to amendments and related legislation. Statutory compilations, known generally as *codes,* collect current statutes of general and permanent application and arrange them by subject. The statutes are grouped into broad subject topics, or *titles,* and within each title they are divided into numbered sections. Instead of

appearing together as in the session laws, the parts of a single legislative act may be scattered by subject through several different titles. A detailed index for the whole compilation enables the researcher to find the code sections dealing with particular problems or topics.

In many jurisdictions there are both official and unofficial code publications. If an official edition is published, it is usually the authoritative text and should be cited in briefs and pleadings. However, the commercially published unofficial editions provide additional research material which makes them more useful than the official versions. Most are *annotated* to include references to court decisions which interpret, construe, or apply each statutory section. The annotations, similar to reporter headnotes and digest entries, consist of brief abstracts of legal principles and citations to the cases from which they were taken. The annotated codes also provide fuller editorial notes, historical comments, and cross references to their publishers' other publications.

Codes must be updated regularly to include the numerous statutory changes which occur every time a legislature meets. An outdated code is virtually useless for current research. Some official codes are updated only by the publication of revised volumes every few years. Most annotated codes, on the other hand, are frequently supplemented, usually by annual pocket parts and quarterly pamphlets.

Statutory research is particularly well suited to using printed resources, since code volumes make it convenient to place a section in context and to survey a number of related provisions. Nonetheless a wide range of electronic resources are available. Federal and state codes are online through WESTLAW and LEXIS, and almost all of

these are also available on CD–ROM. The number of codes accessible through the Internet is less extensive but growing each year. These sources can be used to find statutory provisions by citation and through keyword searches. Most of them allow researchers to gain some sense of a code section's context by viewing adjacent sections and by seeing its place in the code's table of contents.

§ 6–2. FEDERAL STATUTES

The United States Congress meets in two-year terms, consisting of two annual sessions. It enacts several hundred statutes each term, either as *acts* or *joint resolutions*. These statutes range from simple designations of commemorative days to complex environmental or tax legislation spanning hundreds of pages. Each law is designated as either a *public law* or a *private law,* and assigned a number indicating the order in which it was passed. Public Law 101–131, for example, is the 131st public law passed during the 101st Congress.

Public laws are designed to affect the general public, while private laws are passed to meet special needs of an individual or small group. The distinction between the two is sometimes blurred, as when a special interest group promotes "public" legislation that actually affects very few people. Both types are passed in the same way and both appear in the session laws, but in separate numerical series. Only *public* laws, however, become part of the statutory code.

a. Slip Laws and Session Laws

The slip law, the first official text of a new statute, is available from Congress itself or from the U.S. Govern-

ment Printing Office. There is often, however, a frustrating time lag between enactment and distribution of slip laws by the government.

Commercial publications provide the texts of federal enactments more quickly than the official sources. Looseleaf services in fields such as tax or trade regulation are excellent sources for new legislation, and are usually supplemented on a weekly basis.

New public laws are also available rapidly online through WESTLAW's US–PL database and the LEXIS's PUBLAW file. Beginning with the 104th Congress in 1995, the Government Printing Office's GPO Access provides the text of public laws through the Internet.

After the end of each session of Congress, the public and private slip laws are cumulated, corrected, and issued in bound volumes as the official *Statutes at Large* for the session. They are cited by volume and page. Pub. L. 101–131, 103 Stat. 777 (1989), shown in Exhibit 35, is published on page 777 of volume 103 of the *Statutes at Large*. The *Statutes at Large* supersede the slip laws as the positive law text of federal laws and remain authoritative for all but those titles of the *U.S. Code* which have been reenacted as positive law. *Statutes at Large* volumes also contain Presidential proclamations, proposed and ratified constitutional amendments, and indexes for each session.

There are also two unofficial session law services providing the texts of public laws during the congressional session, long before the official *Statutes at Large* volume

PUBLIC LAW 101-131—OCT. 28, 1989   103 STAT. 777

Public Law 101-131
101st Congress

An Act

To amend section 700 of title 18, United States Code, to protect the physical integrity of the flag

Oct. 28, 1989
[H.R. 2978]

Be it enacted by the Senate and House of Representatives of the United States of America in Congress assembled,

Flag Protection
Act of 1989
18 USC 700 note.

SECTION 1. SHORT TITLE.

This Act may be cited as the "Flag Protection Act of 1989".

SEC. 2. CRIMINAL PENALTIES WITH RESPECT TO THE PHYSICAL INTEGRITY OF THE UNITED STATES FLAG.

(a) In General.—Subsection (a) of section 700 of title 18, United States Code, is amended to read as follows:

"(a)(1) Whoever knowingly mutilates, defaces, physically defiles, burns, maintains on the floor or ground, or tramples upon any flag of the United States shall be fined under this title or imprisoned for not more than one year, or both.

"(2) This subsection does not prohibit any conduct consisting of the disposal of a flag when it has become worn or soiled.".

(b) Definition.—Section 700(b) of title 18, United States Code, is amended to read as follows:

"(b) As used in this section, the term 'flag of the United States' means any flag of the United States, or any part thereof, made of any substance, of any size, in a form that is commonly displayed.".

SEC. 3. EXPEDITED REVIEW OF CONSTITUTIONAL ISSUES.

Section 700 of title 18, United States Code, is amended by adding at the end the following:

"(d)(1) An appeal may be taken directly to the Supreme Court of the United States from any interlocutory or final judgment, decree, or order issued by a United States district court ruling upon the constitutionality of subsection (a).

"(2) The Supreme Court shall, if it has not previously ruled on the question, accept jurisdiction over the appeal and advance on the docket and expedite to the greatest extent possible.".

[Note by the Office of the Federal Register: The foregoing Act, having been presented to the President of the United States on Monday, October 16, 1989, and not having been returned by him to the House of Congress in which it originated within the time prescribed by the Constitution of the United States, has become law without his signature on October 28, 1989.]

LEGISLATIVE HISTORY—H.R. 2978 (S. 607) (S. 1338):

HOUSE REPORTS: No. 101-231 (Comm. on the Judiciary).
SENATE REPORTS: No. 101-152 accompanying S. 1338 (Comm. on the Judiciary)
CONGRESSIONAL RECORD, Vol. 135 (1989):
    Mar. 16, S. 607 considered and passed Senate.
    Sept. 12, H.R. 2978 considered and passed House.
    Oct. 4, 5, considered and passed Senate, amended.
    Oct. 12, House concurred in Senate amendments.
WEEKLY COMPILATION OF PRESIDENTIAL DOCUMENTS, Vol. 25 (1989)
    Oct. 26, Presidential statement.   [G10252]

Exhibit 35: A Public Law from the United States Congress, as published in *Statutes at Large*.

is published.   Both include the official pagination that will eventually appear in the *Statutes at Large*.

United States Code Congressional and Administrative News (*USCCAN*), published by West, appears first in a monthly advance sheet edition and is recompiled into permanent bound volumes at the end of each session. *USCCAN* contains the complete text of all public laws, and reprints selected congressional committee reports (usually considered the most important sources for legislative history, to be discussed in Chapter 7).   It also includes selected administrative regulations, executive documents, amendments to court rules, and several tables and indexes.

As a supplement to its subject compilation of federal statutes, *United States Code Service,* Lawyers Coop publishes *USCS Advance,* a monthly advance sheet service with the texts of new public laws.   *USCS Advance* also contains new court rules, executive documents, and selected administrative regulations.   Unlike *USCCAN, USCS Advance* does not contain legislative history documents and is not reissued in bound volumes.   Neither *USCCAN* nor *USCS Advance* include *private* laws, which are published only in the official *Statutes at Large*.

b.   The *United States Code*

The first official subject compilations of federal statutes were the *U.S. Revised Statutes* of 1873 and its second edition of 1878.   The *Revised Statutes* of 1873 was reenacted as positive law in its entirety, expressly repealing the original *Statutes at Large* versions of its contents.   It is therefore the authoritative text for most laws enacted before 1873, and is still needed occasionally in modern research.

Although the *Revised Statutes* rapidly became outdated, no other official compilation was prepared for almost fifty years.   Finally, in 1926, the first edition of the *United States Code* was published, arranging the laws by subject into fifty titles.   The *U.S. Code* is published in a completely revised edition of about thirty volumes every six years, with an annual supplement of one or more bound volumes.   These supplements are cumulative, so it is necessary only to consult the main set and its latest supplement.   Twenty-two titles of the Code have been reenacted as positive law, and for them the Code has become the authoritative text.   For the others, the *Statutes at Large* is authoritative and the Code is prima facie evidence of the law.   A list of all Code titles, indicating which titles have been reenacted, appears in the front of each Code volume and is reproduced here as Exhibit 36.

Unlike citations to the *Statutes at Large* or to cases, citations to the *U.S. Code* refer to title and section rather than to volume and page.   For example, 18 U.S.C. § 700 (1994), shown in Exhibit 37, is the citation for section 700 of Title 18 (Crimes and Criminal Procedure).

TITLES OF UNITED STATES CODE

*1. General Provisions.
2. The Congress.
*3. The President.
*4. Flag and Seal, Seat of Government, and the States.
*5. Government Organization and Employees; and Appendix.
†6. [Surety Bonds.]
7. Agriculture.
8. Aliens and Nationality.
*9. Arbitration.
*10. Armed Forces; and Appendix.
*11. Bankruptcy; and Appendix.
12. Banks and Banking.
*13. Census.
*14. Coast Guard.
15. Commerce and Trade.
16. Conservation.
*17. Copyrights.
*18. Crimes and Criminal Procedure; and Appendix.
19. Customs Duties.
20. Education.
21. Food and Drugs.
22. Foreign Relations and Intercourse.
*23. Highways.
24. Hospitals and Asylums.
25. Indians.
26. Internal Revenue Code.

27. Intoxicating Liquors.
*28. Judiciary and Judicial Procedure; and Appendix.
29. Labor.
30. Mineral Lands and Mining.
*31. Money and Finance.
*32. National Guard.
33. Navigation and Navigable Waters.
‡34. [Navy.]
*35. Patents.
36. Patriotic Societies and Observances.
*37. Pay and Allowances of the Uniformed Services.
*38. Veterans' Benefits.
*39. Postal Service.
40. Public Buildings, Property, and Works.
41. Public Contracts.
42. The Public Health and Welfare.
43. Public Lands.
*44. Public Printing and Documents.
45. Railroads.
*46. Shipping; and Appendix.
47. Telegraphs, Telephones, and Radiotelegraphs.
48. Territories and Insular Possessions.
*49. Transportation; and Appendix.
50. War and National Defense; and Appendix

*This title has been enacted as law. However, any Appendix to this title has not been enacted as law.
†This title was enacted as law and has been repealed by the enactment of Title 31.
‡This title has been eliminated by the enactment of Title 10

[G10253]

Exhibit 36: The list of titles in the front of each *United States Code* volume, showing which titles have been reenacted into law.

title XXXIII, §§ 330009(b), 330016(1)(L), Sept. 13, 1994, 108 Stat. 2143, 2147.)

AMENDMENTS

1994—Pub. L. 103–322 substituted "fined under this title" for "fined not more than $10,000" and inserted at end "The term 'livestock' has the meaning set forth in section 2311 of this title."

 # 668. Theft of major artwork

(a) DEFINITIONS.—In this section—

"museum" means an organized and permanent institution, the activities of which affect interstate or foreign commerce, that—

(A) is situated in the United States;

(B) is established for an essentially educational or aesthetic purpose;

(C) has a professional staff; and

(D) owns, utilizes, and cares for tangible objects that are exhibited to the public on a regular schedule.

"object of cultural heritage" means an object that is—

(A) over 100 years old and worth in excess of $5,000; or

(B) worth at least $100,000.

(b) OFFENSES.—A person who—

(1) steals or obtains by fraud from the care, custody, or control of a museum any object of cultural heritage; or

(2) knowing that an object of cultural heritage has been stolen or obtained by fraud, if in fact the object was stolen or obtained from the care, custody, or control of a museum (whether or not that fact is known to the person), receives, conceals, exhibits, or disposes of the object,

shall be fined under this title, imprisoned not more than 10 years, or both.

(Added Pub. L. 103–322, title XXXII, § 320902(a), Sept. 13, 1994, 108 Stat. 2123.)

SECTION REFERRED TO IN OTHER SECTIONS

This section is referred to in section 3294 of this title.

CHAPTER 33—EMBLEMS, INSIGNIA, AND NAMES

[1] So in original. Does not conform to section catchline.

AMENDMENTS

1991—Pub. L. 102–229, title II, § 210(e), Dec. 12, 1991, 105 Stat. 1717, substituted "Use of likenesses of the great seal of the United States, the seals of the President and Vice President, and the seal of the United States Senate." for "Use of likenesses of the great seal of the United States, and of the seals of the President and Vice President." in item 713.

1990—Pub. L. 101–647, title XXXV, § 3518, Nov. 29, 1990, 104 Stat. 4923, inserted a comma after "INSIGNIA" in chapter heading.

1982—Pub. L. 97–258, § 2(d)(1)(A), Sept. 13, 1982, 96 Stat. 1058, struck out item 714 relating to "Johnny Horizon" character or name.

1974—Pub. L. 93–318, § 8, June 22, 1974, 88 Stat. 245, added item 711a.

1973—Pub. L. 93–147, § 1(b), Nov. 3, 1973, 87 Stat. 555, substituted "Misuse of names, words, emblems, or insignia" for "Misuse of names by collecting agencies to indicate Federal agency" in item 712.

1972—Pub. L. 92–347, § 3(c), July 11, 1972, 86 Stat. 462, added item 715.

1971—Pub. L. 91–651, § 2, Jan. 5, 1971, 84 Stat. 1941, inserted ", and of the seals of the President and Vice President" after "United States" in item 713.

1970—Pub. L. 91–419, § 4, Sept. 25, 1970, 84 Stat. 871, added item 714.

1968—Pub. L. 90–381, § 2, July 5, 1968, 82 Stat. 291, added item 700.

1966—Pub. L. 89–807, § 1(b), Nov. 11, 1966, 80 Stat. 1525, added item 713.

1959—Pub. L. 86–291, § 3, Sept. 21, 1959, 73 Stat. 570, added item 712.

1952—Act May 23, 1952, ch. 327, § 2, 66 Stat. 92, added item 711.

1950—Act Sept. 28, 1950, ch. 1092, § 1(a), 64 Stat. 1077, added item 710.

1949—Act May 24, 1949, ch. 139, § 14, 63 Stat. 91, inserted "Uniform of armed forces and Public Health Service" in lieu of enumerating the specific branches in item 702.

 # 700. Desecration of the flag of the United States; penalties

(a)(1) Whoever knowingly mutilates, defaces, physically defiles, burns, maintains on the floor or ground, or tramples upon any flag of the United States shall be fined under this title or imprisoned for not more than one year, or both.

(2) This subsection does not prohibit any conduct consisting of the disposal of a flag when it has become worn or soiled.

(b) As used in this section, the term "flag of the United States" means any flag of the United States, or any part thereof, made of any substance, of any size, in a form that is commonly displayed.

(c) Nothing in this section shall be construed as indicating an intent on the part of Congress to deprive any State, territory, possession, or

In addition to the actual text of statutes, the *U.S. Code* also includes historical notes, cross references, and other research aids. Each section is followed by a parenthetical reference to its source in the *Statutes at Large,* including sources for any amendments. This reference leads to the original text, which may be the positive law form, and from there to legislative history documents relating to the law's enactment.

Often a case or other document refers to a statutory provision by its session law cite rather than a code section. It is then necessary to determine whether a law is still in force and where it is codified. One of the simplest ways to do this is to use a *parallel reference table* at the end of the *U.S. Code.* The example shown in Exhibit 38 converts the Public Law number and *Statutes at Large* citation of Pub. L. 101–131 to its U.S. Code citation, 18 U.S.C. § 700. Other parallel reference tables provide access from the *Revised Statutes* to the *U.S. Code,* and from the former numbering of revised titles to current section numbers.

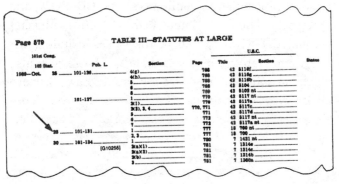

Exhibit 38: Excerpt from a parallel reference table in the *United States Code.*

Another table, of "Acts Cited by Popular Name," can be used to find acts known by name rather than citation. It lists laws alphabetically under either short titles assigned by Congress or names by which they have become commonly known, and provides citations to the laws in both the *Statutes at Large* and the *U.S. Code*. Exhibit 39 shows a page from this table in a *U.S. Code* supplement. *Shepard's Acts and Cases by Popular Names: Federal and State* provides similar information, although each table contains some names not found in the other.

Without a reference to a specific statute, the place to begin research in the *U.S. Code* is its general index. This basic tool for finding federal statutes by subject consists of several volumes, and it is updated in the latest annual supplement. Exhibit 40 shows a page from the index providing references to a variety of provisions under the heading "Flag."

There are several electronic sources for the *United States Code*, including the online systems, CD–ROM, and the Internet. The Government Printing Office publishes an annual CD–ROM edition of the Code, including the popular name table and general index. The Code is also available on the Internet from Cornell Law School's Legal Information Institute, GPO Access, and the House of Representatives Internet Law Library. These versions vary in currency, and are not necessarily more up-to-date than the most recent printed edition. It is necessary to check the date of *either* print or electronic sources consulted and then check the session laws or online databases for recent legislation.

ACTS CITED BY POPULAR NAME   Page 1192

Federally Supported Health Centers Assistance Act of 1992
Pub. L. 102-501, Oct. 24, 1992, 106 Stat. 3268

Fertility Clinic Success Rate and Certification Act of 1992
Pub. L. 102-493, Oct. 24, 1992, 106 Stat. 3146
(Title 42, § 263a-1 et seq.)

Financial Institutions Anti-Fraud Enforcement Act of 1990
Pub. L. 101-647, title XXV, subtitle H, §§ 2560-2594, Nov. 29, 1990, 104 Stat. 4893-4906 (Title 12, § 4201 et seq.)

Financial Institutions Reform, Recovery, and Enforcement Act of 1989
Pub. L. 101-73, Aug. 9, 1989, 103 Stat. 183 (See Tables for classifications)
Pub. L. 101-647, title XXV, §§ 2533, 2559(a), (c), 2596(d), Nov. 29, 1990, 104 Stat. 4882, 4893, 4908
Pub. L. 102-233, title III, § 313, title VII, Dec. 12, 1991, 105 Stat. 1770, 1792
Pub. L. 102-242, title I, §§ 121(b), 161(f), title IV, §§ 422, 472(a), (b), Dec. 19, 1991, 105 Stat. 2251, 2286, 2377, 2386
Pub. L. 102-485, § 2, Oct. 23, 1992, 106 Stat. 2771
Pub. L. 102-550, title IX, § 954, Oct. 28, 1992, 106 Stat. 3894

Financial Institutions Regulatory and Interest Rate Control Act of 1978
Pub. L. 102-242, title II, § 212(f), title IV, § 411, Dec. 19, 1991, 105 Stat. 2301, 2375
Pub. L. 102-550, title XV, §§ 1516, 1532, title XVI, § 1606(b), Oct. 28, 1992, 106 Stat. 4059, 4066, 4087
Pub. L. 102-568, title VI, § 603(a), Oct. 29, 1992, 106 Stat. 4342

Fire Administration Authorization Act of 1992
Pub. L. 102-522, Oct. 26, 1992, 106 Stat. 3410

Fire Safe Cigarette Act of 1990
Pub. L. 101-352, Aug. 10, 1990, 104 Stat. 405 (Title 15, § 2054 note)

Firefighters' Safety Study Act
Pub. L. 101-446, Oct. 22, 1990, 104 Stat. 1045 (Title 15, § 2223a et seq.)

First Deficiency Appropriations Act, fiscal year 1936
Aug. 9, 1989, Pub. L. 101-73, title VII, § 741, 103 Stat. 436

Fiscal year 1990 Dire Emergency Supplemental to Meet the Needs of Natural Disasters of National Significance
Pub. L. 101-100, Sept. 29, 1989, § 108, as added Pub. L. 101-130, Oct. 26, 1989, 103 Stat. 775

Fish and Seafood Promotion Act of 1986
Pub. L. 101-627, title VII, §§ 701, 702, 704(c), Nov. 28, 1990, 104 Stat. 4463, 4464

Fish and Wildlife Conservation Act of 1980
Pub. L. 101-233, § 16(b), Dec. 13, 1989, 103 Stat. 1977
Pub. L. 101-593, title I, § 106, Nov. 16, 1990, 104 Stat. 2955
Pub. L. 102-440, title III, § 301, Oct. 23, 1992, 106 Stat. 2234

Fish Restoration and Management Projects Act
See Federal Aid in Fish Restoration Act

Fishermen's Protective Act of 1967
Nov. 28, 1990, Pub. L. 101-627, title III, 104 Stat. 4462
Nov. 2, 1992, Pub. L. 102-582, title II, § 201, 106 Stat. 4904

Fishery Conservation Amendments of 1990
Pub. L. 101-627, Nov. 28, 1990, 104 Stat. 4436

Fishlake National Forest Enlargement Act
Pub. L. 102-292, May 26, 1992, 106 Stat. 181

Flag Protection Act of 1989
Pub. L. 101-131, Oct. 28, 1989 (Title 18, § 700)

Flammable Fabrics Act
Nov. 16, 1990, Pub. L. 101-608, title I, §§ 107(c), 108(c), 110(c), 115(c), 118(b), 104 Stat. 3112, 3113, 3114, 3120, 3122

Flood Control Act of 1941
Nov. 28, 1990, Pub. L. 101-640, title III, § 302, 104 Stat. 4633
Oct. 24, 1992, Pub. L. 102-486, title XXV, § 2506(c), 106 Stat. 3107

Flood Control Act of 1944
Nov. 28, 1990, Pub. L. 101-640, title I, § 102(u), 104 Stat. 4614

Flood Control Act of 1946
Nov. 28, 1990, Pub. L. 101-640, title I, § 102(y), 104 Stat. 4617

Flood Control Act of 1960
Pub. L. 101-640, title III, § 321, Nov. 28, 1990, 104 Stat. 4643

Flood Control Act of 1968
Pub. L. 103-66, title V, § 5001(a), Aug. 10, 1993, 107 Stat. 378

Flood Control Act of 1970
Pub. L. 101-514, title I, § 105, Nov. 5, 1990, 104 Stat. 2082

Florida Keys National Marine Sanctuary and Protection Act
Pub. L. 101-605, Nov. 16, 1990, 104 Stat. 3089 (Title 16, § 1433 note)
Pub. L. 102-587, title II, §§ 2206(a), 2209, Nov. 4, 1992, 106 Stat. 5053, 5054

Fluid Milk Promotion Act of 1990
Pub. L. 101-624, title XIX, subtitle H, §§ 1999A-1999R, Nov. 28, 1990, 104 Stat. 3914-3926 (Title 7, § 6401 et seq.)
Pub. L. 102-237, title VIII, § 809, Dec. 13, 1991, 105 Stat. 1883
Pub. L. 103-72, § 2, Aug. 11, 1993, 107 Stat. 717

Fluid Milk Promotion Amendments of 1993
Pub. L. 103-72, Aug. 11, 1993, 107 Stat. 717

Follow Through Act
Pub. L. 97-35, title VI, subtitle A, ch. 8, subch. D, formerly C, §§ 661-670, Aug. 13, 1981, 95 Stat. 508-511, as redesignated by Pub. L. 101-508, title V, § 5082(1), Nov. 5,

Exhibit 39: A page from the "Acts Cited By Popular Name" table in the *United States Code.*

GENERAL INDEX Page 630

[G10257]

Exhibit 40: A page from the *United States Code* general index.

c. Annotated Codes

Two commercially published, annotated editions of the
Code are more current and more useful in research than
the official edition. These are the *United States Code
Annotated* (*USCA*), published by West, and the *United
States Code Service* (*USCS*), published by Lawyers Coop.
Both compilations reproduce the title, section numbers
and text of the official edition. The *U.S. Code* and
USCA both make minor technical changes in integrating
Statutes at Large provisions into the Code format.
USCS, on the other hand, preserves the original lan-
guage as published in the *Statutes at Large*.

Besides the text of the statutes, the annotated codes
include extensive indexes, parallel reference tables, and
popular name tables similar to those in the *U.S. Code*.
In addition, they provide the following features:

(1) Notes of court decisions interpreting, construing,
and applying code sections;

(2) Editorial notes and analytical discussions on particular statutes or provisions; and

(3) References to legislative history, administrative
regulations, and various secondary sources.

These various features have made the annotated codes
the most widely used sources of federal statutes. Exhibits 41 and 42 show the same section of Title 18 that was
shown in Exhibit 37, as published in *USCS* and *USCA*.
Exhibit 41 shows the beginning of the section in *USCS*,
followed by cross-references to other Code sections and a
research guide to the publisher's other tools (*Lawyers
Edition* and *ALR* annotations). Exhibit 42 begins in the
middle of the statutory text in *USCA*, and includes
references to West digests and *C.J.S.* Annotations of

cases are arranged by subject, preceded by an alphabetical index.

The unofficial editions are far more current than the official *U.S. Code,* with supplementation by annual pocket parts, quarterly pamphlets, and revised volumes as necessary. When using a *USCA* or *USCS* volume, *always* check its pocket part for recent amendments and notes of new decisions. Exhibit 43 shows these two features in the pocket part for *USCA,* showing the 1989 amendment to the statute and a reference to the 1990 Supreme Court decision declaring the amendment unconstitutional.

EMBLEMS, INSIGNIA AND NAMES   **18 USCS § 700**

1972. Act July 11, 1972, P. L. 92-347, § 3(c), 86 Stat. 459, added item 715.

1973. Act Nov. 3, 1973, P. L. 93-147, § 1(b), 87 Stat. 555, substituted item 712 for former item 712, which read: "Misuse of names by collecting agencies or private detective agencies to indicate Federal agency".

1974. Act June 22, 1974, P. L. 93-318, § 8, 88 Stat. 245, added item 711a.

---

§ 700. Desecration of the flag of the United States; penalties

(a) Whoever knowingly casts contempt upon any flag of the United States by publicly mutilating, defacing, defiling, burning, or trampling upon it shall be fined not more than $1,000 or imprisoned for not more than one year, or both.

(b) The term "flag of the United States" as used in this section, shall include any flag, standard, colors, ensign, or any picture or representation of either, or of any part or parts of either, made of any substance or represented on any substance, of any size evidently purporting to be either of said flag, standard, colors, or ensign of the United States of America, or a picture or a representation of either, upon which shall be shown the colors, the stars and the stripes, in any number of either thereof, or of any part or parts of either, by which the average person seeing the same without deliberation may believe the same to represent the flag, standards, colors, or ensign of the United States of America.

(c) Nothing in this section shall be construed as indicating an intent on the part of Congress to deprive any State, territory, possession, or the Commonwealth of Puerto Rico of jurisdiction over any offense over which it would have jurisdiction in the absence of this section. CR
(Added July 5, 1968, P. L. 90-381, § 1, 82 Stat. 291.)

CROSS REFERENCES

Penalty for mutilation or use of flag for advertising purposes, 4 USCS § 3.
United States defined, 18 USCS § 5.
Use of official insignia, 18 USCS § 701.
Use of great seal of the United States, 18 USCS § 713.

RESEARCH GUIDE

Annotations:
Constitutionality of statutes, ordinances, or administrative provisions prohibiting definance, disrespect, mutilation, or misuse of American flag. 22 L Ed 2d 972.
What constitutes violation of flag desecration statutes. 41 ALR3d 502.
[G10258]

Exhibit 41: A *United States Code Service*, showing the text of 18 U.S.C.S. § 700 (Law.Co-op.1979).

Ch. 33   EMBLEMS, INSIGNIA AND NAMES   **18 § 700**
Note 1

(b) The term "flag of the United States" as used in this section, shall include any flag, standard, colors, ensign, or any picture or representation of either, or of any part or parts of either, made of any substance or represented on any substance, of any size evidently purporting to be either of said flag, standard, colors, or ensign of the United States of America, or a picture or a representation of either, upon which shall be shown the colors, the stars and the stripes, in any number of either thereof, or of any part or parts of either, by which the average person seeing the same without deliberation may believe the same to represent the flag, standards, colors, or ensign of the United States of America.

(c) Nothing in this section shall be construed as indicating an intent on the part of Congress to deprive any State, territory, possession, or the Commonwealth of Puerto Rico of jurisdiction over any offense over which it would have jurisdiction in the absence of this section.

Added Pub.L. 90–381, § 1, July 5, 1968, 82 Stat. 291.

Historical Note

Legislative History. For legislative 1968 U.S.Code Cong. and Adm.News, p. history and purpose of Pub.L. 90–381, see 2507.

Cross References

Penalty for mutilation or use of flag for advertising purposes, see section 3 of Title 4, Flag and Seal, Seat of Government, and the States.

Library References

United States ⊂⟹5½.   C.J.S. Flags § 2.
                                 C.J.S. United States § 8.

Notes of Decisions

Constitutionality 1
Construction 2
Contempt defined 5
Double jeopardy 9
Evidence 12
Flags within section 6
Indictment or information 8
Offenses 7
Power of
  Congress 3
  States 4
Presumptions 11
Selection of jury 10
Sentence 13
Voir dire examination of jurors 10

---

1. Constitutionality
This section is not an attempt to interfere with free speech and does not place any restriction on U.S.C.A.Const. Amend. 1 freedoms greater than is essential to the furtherance of the national interest. U. S. v. Crosson, C.A.Ariz.1972, 462 F.2d

96, certiorari denied 93 S.Ct. 569, 409 U.S. 1064, 34 L.Ed.2d 517.

This section is not unconstitutionally vague. Id.

This section is not unconstitutionally vague or unconstitutional on theory that it invites irrational and selective patterns of enforcement. Joyce v. U. S., 1971, 454 F.2d 971, 147 U.S.App.D.C. 128, certiorari denied 92 S.Ct. 1188, 405 U.S. 969, 31 L. Ed.2d 242.

Fact that situations were bound to exist in which there would be some difficulty in determining whether specific activity was, or could constitutionally be, within sweep of prohibitions of this section did not serve to make this section unconstitutional. Id.

The United States has a substantial genuine and important interest in protecting the American flag from public desecration, and as this section placed only the smallest, if any, obstacle in the

---

Exhibit 42: A *United States Code Annotated* page, showing part of 18 U.S.C.A. § 700 (West 1976) and annotations of cases.

§ 700. Desecration of the flag of the United States; penalties

(a)(1) Whoever knowingly mutilates, defaces, physically defiles, burns, maintains on the floor or ground, or tramples upon any flag of the United States shall be fined under this title or imprisoned for not more than one year, or both.

(2) This subsection does not prohibit any conduct consisting of the disposal of a flag when it has become worn or soiled.

(b) As used in this section, the term "flag of the United States" means any flag of the United States, or any part thereof. made of any substance, of any size, in a form that is commonly displayed.

[See main volume for text of (c)]

(d)(1) An appeal may be taken directly to the Supreme Court of the United States from any interlocutory or final judgment, decree, or order issued by a United States district court ruling upon the constitutionality of subsection (a).

(2) The Supreme Court shall, if it has not previously ruled on the question, accept jurisdiction over the appeal and advance on the docket and expedite to the greatest extent possible.

(As amended Pub.L. 101-131, §§ 2, 3, Oct. 28, 1989, 103 Stat. 777.)

LAW REVIEW COMMENTARIES

This is not a flag: The aesthetics of desecration. Steven G. Gey, Wis.L.Rev. 1549 (1990).

NOTES OF DECISIONS

Review 12a

1. Constitutionality

Flag Protection Act violates First Amendment free speech protections. U.S. v. Eichman, D.D.C.1990, 731 F.Supp. 1123, affirmed 110 S.Ct. 2404, 496 U.S. 310, 110 L.Ed.2d 287.

Government's interest in enacting Flag Protection Act of protecting symbolic value of flag was not sufficiently compelling to satisfy strict scrutiny test, and thus, Act violated First Amendment as applied to defendants charged with violating Act by burning flag during demonstration protesting enactment of Act. U.S. v. Haggerty, W.D.Wash.1990, 731 F.Supp. 415, affirmed 110 S.Ct. 2404, 496 U.S. 310, 110 L.Ed.2d 287.

7. Offenses

Government's interest in protecting physical integrity of United States flag to preserve its symbolic value was not sufficiently compelling to justify convicting defendants for burning United States flags in violation of Flag Protection Act. U.S. v. Eichman, D.D.C.1990, 731 F.Supp. 1123, affirmed 110 S.Ct. 2404, 496 U.S. 310, 110 L.Ed.2d 287.

12a. Review

Strict scrutiny standard applied in determining whether Flag Protection Act violated First Amendment free speech protections; although Act purported to protect physical integrity of flag, its underlying purpose was to preserve the flag's symbolic value. U.S. v. Eichman, D.D.C. 1990, 731 F.Supp. 1123, affirmed 110 S.Ct. 2404, 496 U.S. 310, 110 L.Ed.2d 287.

Exhibit 43: Excerpts from a *United States Code Annotated* pocket part supplement.

Both annotated editions of the Code are available in CD–ROM and online (*USCA* on WESTLAW and *USCS* on LEXIS). WESTLAW has the code in both unannotated (USC) and annotated (USCA) forms, allowing the researcher to decide whether or not to include the extensive case annotations in a search. In some instances searching keywords in the annotations may retrieve far too many documents, but at other times the wording of the annotations may lead the researcher to sections that might not appear relevant at first glance. WESTLAW also has a separate database of the USCA index (USCA–IDX), which may help to clarify statutory language. LEXIS's USCS file contains the Code text, research references, and case annotations from *United States Code Service*. The online Code databases are updated to include laws from the current session of Congress; a note at the beginning of each section indicates the latest public law to be included in Code coverage.

Looseleaf services provide another source for current, annotated statutes in some subject fields. Most services include federal statutes affecting their fields, accompanied by abstracts of judicial and administrative decisions, relevant administrative regulations, and explanatory text. Major tax services such as the CCH *Standard Federal Tax Reporter* are basically heavily annotated editions of the Internal Revenue Code (26 U.S.C.).

§ 6–3. THE UNITED STATES CONSTITUTION

The Constitution is the basic law of the country, defining political relationships, enumerating the rights and liberties of citizens, and creating the framework of national government.

Statutes are often written in extreme detail and specificity. The Constitution, on the other hand, is a concise and spare document that has been applied by the courts to situations unforeseen by its drafters. The constitutional text may be less important in legal research than the Supreme Court's interpretation and application of constitutional principles.

The text of the Constitution appears in numerous publications ranging from simple pamphlets to large annotated texts. It is included in most online and CD–ROM collections of federal statutes and is available on the Internet from the Library of Congress THOMAS system. It is also printed at the beginning of the *U.S. Code, USCA* and *USCS.* The versions in *USCA* and *USCS* are heavily annotated with case abstracts, arranged by subject and thoroughly indexed. Some important provisions have thousands of case abstracts in several hundred subject divisions.

Of the many commentaries on the Constitution, one of the most extensive and authoritative is *The Constitution of the United States of America, Analysis and Interpretation,* currently edited by Johnny H. Killian and most recently published in 1987 by the Congressional Research Service. Pocket part supplementation is provided, but it is neither frequent nor current. Complete revisions are made about every ten years. Many scholars

find this edition the most useful starting point for constitutional research.

Another helpful background source is the *Encyclopedia of the American Constitution* (4 vols. 1986 & Supp. 1992), edited by Leonard W. Levy, Kenneth L. Karst, and Dennis J. Mahoney. Arranged alphabetically, it includes articles on constitutional doctrines as well as on specific decisions, people, and historical periods. Shorter works providing similar treatment of constitutional doctrines include Kermit L. Hall, ed., *The Oxford Companion to the Supreme Court* (1992), and Jethro K. Lieberman, *The Evolving Constitution* (1992).

For further historical research, one can turn to the documents prepared by those who drafted, adopted and ratified the Constitution. The standard source for the proceedings of the constitutional convention is Max Farrand's *The Records of the Federal Convention of 1787* in five volumes (1911, with 1987 supplement). *The Documentary History of the Ratification of the Constitution* (1976–date) provides similar treatment of the ratification debates in the states. *The Founders' Constitution* (1987), a five-volume set edited by Philip B. Kurland and Ralph Lerner, is a useful collection of excerpts from source documents arranged by specific constitutional provision. The constitutional debates, the *Federalist Papers*, and other documents are also available online in WESTLAW's BICENT database.

§ 6-4. STATE STATUTES

State statutory law appears in many of the same forms as federal law. There are slip laws; session laws; annotated codes; and constitutions. The same problems ex-

ist: providing for subject access to chronologically published laws, and keeping up-to-date an ever-changing
mass of legislation. Some state annotated codes are less
well developed than the annotated editions of the *U.S.
Code*, but most are thorough and excellent research tools.
New session laws and codes are available online for all
states; almost every state now has an annotated code
available on CD–ROM; and an increasing number of
states are making statutory materials available through
the Internet.

a. State Session Laws

Slip laws are issued in many of the states, but they are
rarely distributed to the public. Every state, however,
has a publication of the laws enacted at each sitting of its
legislature, similar to the *U.S. Statutes at Large*, usually
with an index for each volume or session. Publication is
often delayed until long after the end of the session, even
though in most states the session laws are the authoritative positive law text of the statutes. The names of the
session law publications vary from state to state (*e.g.,
Acts of Alabama, Statutes of California, Laws of Delaware*); the *Bluebook* lists the current publication for each
state and its citation form.

Commercially published "legislative services" in most
states give access to new laws while the legislature is still
sitting, very much as *USCCAN* and *USCS Advance* do
for congressional enactments. The online systems provide the texts of new legislation in legislative service
databases for every state as well as for the District of
Columbia, Puerto Rico, and the Virgin Islands. WEST-
LAW's databases are identified by the state's postal code
followed by -LEGIS, and LEXIS's files by the postal code
followed by ALS. (Wyoming's session laws are thus in

WY–LEGIS on WESTLAW, and in WYALS on LEXIS.) Multistate searches for new laws can be performed in WESTLAW's LEGIS–ALL database and LEXIS's AL-LALS file.

b. State Codes

All states have subject compilations of their statutes similar to the *U.S. Code*. Some states publish unannotated official codes, but most researchers rely on commercially published collections, annotated with notes of relevant court decisions and other references. Every state has at least one annotated code, and several of the larger states have two competing code publications. The authority of unofficial codes varies from state to state, but they are usually accepted as at least *prima facie* evidence of the statutory law. The *Bluebook* provides a listing by state of the names and citations of current official and commercially published codes. State legal research guides (listed in Appendix A on page 342) provide information about earlier codes and statutory revisions, official and unofficial editions, and statutory indexes for individual states.

Annotated state codes are edited and supplemented in much the same way as federal statutes. The best of the codes contain not only judicial annotations but analytical notes and references to historical sources, secondary material, and attorney general opinions. Exhibit 44 shows a state statute as it appears in a typical annotated code.

State codes usually provide references to the original session laws in parenthetical notes following each section, and most also include tables with cross references

publication. Utilization by the contracting person, firm, or corporation of the cover of the publication, with the state emblem thereon, for advertising purposes shall not constitute a violation of subsection (a) of this Code section. (Ga. L. 1960, p. 985, § 1; Ga. L. 1982, p. 3, § 50.)

Cross references. — Enactment of official Code, § 1-1-1. Offenses against public order and safety, T. 16, Ch. 11.

OPINIONS OF THE ATTORNEY GENERAL

Replica of state flag may not be printed upon packets or envelopes containing sugar in order to promote the image of this state in the minds of the people who use the product. 1967 Op. Att'y Gen. No. 67-323.

"Public service" advertisement bearing name of private sponsor. — A proposed "public service" advertisement which prints, publishes, or otherwise uses the flag of the State of Georgia and bears the name of a private corporate sponsor would be in violation of this section. 1992 Op. Att'y Gen. No. 92-14.

RESEARCH REFERENCES

Am. Jur. 2d. — 3 Am. Jur. 2d, Advertising, § 5. 35 Am. Jur. 2d, Flag, §§ 3, 4. 74 Am. Jur. 2d, Trademarks and Tradenames, § 45.

C.J.S. — 36A C.J.S., Flags, § 2. 81A C.J.S., States, § 39. 87 C.J.S., Trademarks, Trade-names and Unfair Competition, § 147.

50-3-9. Abuse of federal, state, or Confederate flag unlawful.

It shall be unlawful for any person, firm, or corporation to mutilate, deface, defile, or abuse contemptuously the flag of the United States, the flag, coat of arms, or emblem of the State of Georgia, or the flag or emblem of the Confederate States of America by any act whatever. (Ga. L. 1960, p. 985, § 2.)

Cross references. — Offenses against public order and safety, Ch. 11, T. 16.

JUDICIAL DECISIONS

Editor's notes. — These annotations were based on cases decided prior to the U.S. Supreme Court decisions as to burning of the flag of the United States (See Texas v. Johnson, U.S. , 109 S. Ct. 2533, 105 L. Ed. 2d 342 (1989) and United States v. Eichman, 495 U.S. 841, 110 S. Ct. 2404, 110 L. Ed. 2d 287 (1990)).

In light of the similarity of the provisions, decisions under former Code 1933, § 26-2803 are included in the annotations for this section.

This section is not unconstitutional. — The language of this section making it unlawful to mutilate, deface, defile, or contemptuously abuse the flags by any act is not vague, uncertain, or indefinite, and this section is accordingly not unconstitutional. Hinton v. State, 223 Ga. 174, 154 S.E.2d 246 (1967), rev'd on other grounds sub nom. Anderson v. Georgia, 390 U.S. 206, 88 S. Ct. 902, 19 L. Ed. 2d 1039 (1968).

Freedom of speech not involved in prohibitions in section. — The conduct sought to

Exhibit 44: A page from the *Official Code of Georgia Annotated.*

from session law citations and earlier codifications to the current code. Each state code has a substantial general index of one or more volumes. Supplementation is generally by pocket part or looseleaf insertions, updated in many states by quarterly pamphlets and session law services.

LEXIS and WESTLAW provide access to state codes from all fifty states, as well as the District of Columbia, Puerto Rico, and the Virgin Islands. Most of the state code databases include the case notes and other references from the annotated codes. This broadens the search base from the bare statutory language, but it may make it more difficult to weed out sections that are only marginally relevant. WESTLAW users can choose between annotated (XX–ST–ANN) and unannotated (XX–ST) versions of codes; LEXIS users can use a TEXT segment search to limit queries to the statutory language. If these approaches still yield too many code sections, WESTLAW offers databases of code indexes and both systems have databases of code tables of contents.

CD–ROM publication of state statutes is almost as comprehensive as online coverage. A state CD–ROM is a convenient and relatively inexpensive means of access to a particular state's laws. Some CD–ROM publications include both statutes and cases, while others contain simply the annotated code. Both keyword searching and code indexes are generally available. A few state codes (in unannotated form) are now available through the Internet, with more surely to follow in the near future.

Multistate surveys of state laws can be a frustrating and time-consuming process, since each state code may use different terminology and indexing approaches. Several resources are available to help. Both online systems

offer the capability to search combined databases of all available state codes (STAT–ALL or ST–ANN–ALL in WESTLAW, ALLCDE in LEXIS). Topical looseleaf services often collect state laws in their subject areas, and *Martindale–Hubbell Law Digest* summarizes state law on a variety of subjects and provides references to the state codes. Other collections and lists of state statutes (including fifty-state surveys in law review footnotes) are described in a useful series of bibliographies called *Subject Compilations of State Laws* (8 vols., 1981–date).

c. State Constitutions

States cannot deprive citizens of federal constitutional rights, but state constitutions can guarantee rights beyond those provided under the U.S. Constitution. As state constitutional law becomes an increasingly important field of study, the literature of state constitutions is becoming more sophisticated and comprehensive.

The best source for a state constitution is usually the annotated state code, which provides both the latest text and annotations of court decisions interpreting and construing constitutional provisions. Pamphlet texts are also published in many states, and state constitutions are available through the online databases and as part of many state CD–ROM products.

A new series of monographs, *Reference Guides to the State Constitutions of the United States* (1990–date), now covers close to half the states. Each volume includes a summary of the state's constitutional history, a detailed section-by-section analysis of the constitution with background information and discussion of judicial interpretations, and a brief bibliographical essay providing references for further research.

For comparative research, current state constitutions are compiled in *Constitutions of the United States: National and State* (7 vols., 2d ed. 1974–date). William F. Swindler's *Sources and Documents of United States Constitutions* (11 vols., 1973–79) also includes previous state constitutions, with background notes, editorial comments, and a selected bibliography for each state.

Journals and proceedings published for most state constitutional conventions can provide some insight into framers' intent, although the lack of indexing in many older volumes can make for difficult research. These documents are available on microfiche in *State Constitutional Conventions, Commissions, and Amendments,* covering all fifty states from 1776 through 1988, and listed in a series of bibliographies beginning with Cynthia E. Browne's *State Constitutional Conventions from Independence to the Completion of the Present Union, 1776–1959: A Bibliography* (1973).

§ 6–5. SHEPARDIZING STATUTES

Finding statutes through tables, indexes or computer systems is just the first step of statutory research. Before relying on a statute as authority, one must verify that it is still in force and ascertain how it has been affected by subsequent legislation and by judicial decisions. An annotated code usually provides this information, since it is regularly updated with legislative changes and notes of new decisions. Statutes are generally easier to update than cases, since the code editors have already done much of the work.

Another means for updating statutes is *Shepard's Citations*, which enables researchers to find session laws

amending or repealing particular statutes as well as cases citing these statutes. Shepard's also lists other materials that may not be mentioned in an annotated code, such as attorney general opinions and legal periodical articles citing a statute.

Shepard's statutory citators cover virtually all forms of legislative material, including current codes, repealed provisions, session laws, and constitutions. Shepard's lists citing sources under the exact provision or provisions cited; a case citing a specific subsection is listed under that subsection, while one citing a range of sections is listed under an entry indicating the entire range. It may therefore be necessary to scan a number of entries to find relevant citations.

For federal statutes, *Shepard's United States Citations* includes entries for constitutional provisions, U.S. Code sections, and acts in the *Statutes at Large* which have not been incorporated into the Code. It provides citations to these items in cases and *ALR* annotations. (Shepard's has recently discontinued listing amending statutory provisions in *U.S. Citations*, but it is not yet clear whether this change is permanent.) Citations in state cases and law reviews are *not* included in *Shepard's U.S. Citations*. State court decisions citing federal laws are listed in Shepard's state citators, and citing articles in several law reviews are listed in *Shepard's Federal Law Citations in Selected Law Reviews*.

In addition to state cases citing the U.S. Constitution or federal statutes, *Shepard's Citations* for each state provides extensive coverage of state constitutions and statutes. These statutes are usually listed as cited, so it may be necessary to check references under both a

current code section and its predecessors to find relevant material. Shepard's provides references to legislative and judicial developments, as well as citing law review articles and annotations.

As it does for cases, Shepard's uses signals to indicate significant judicial and legislative actions affecting a cited statute. A list of these signals is shown in Exhibit 45. Exhibit 46 shows the treatment of Georgia statutes, indicating that the section shown in Exhibit 44 was cited in a U.S. Supreme Court case and a *Mercer Law Review* article. Note also that § 50–5–3 was amended (A) in 1982 and then repealed (R) in 1993.

ABBREVIATIONS—ANALYSIS

Form of Statute

Amend.	Amendment	Proc.	Proclamation
App.	Appendix	Pt.	Part
Art.	Article	Res.	Resolution
Ch.	Chapter	§	Section
Cl.	Clause	St.	Statutes at Large
Ex. Ord.	Executive Order	Subch.	Subchapter
H.C.R.	House Concurrent	Subcl.	Subclause
	Resolution	Subd.	Subdivision
No.	Number	Sub ¶	Subparagraph
¶	Paragraph	Subsec.	Subsection
P.L.	Public Law	Vet. Reg.	Veterans' Regulations
Pr.L.	Private Law		

Operation of Statute

Legislative

A	(amended)	Statute amended.
Ad	(added)	New section added.
E	(extended)	Provisions of an existing statute extended in their application to a later statute, or allowance of additional time for performance of duties required by a statute within a limited time.
L	(limited)	Provisions of an existing statute declared not to be extended in their application to a later statute.
R	(repealed)	Abrogation of an existing statute.
Re-en	(re-enacted)	Statute re-enacted.
Rn	(renumbered)	Renumbering of existing sections.
Rp	(repealed in part)	Abrogation of part of an existing statute.
Rs	(repealed and superseded)	Abrogation of an existing statute and substitution of new legislation therefor.
Rv	(revised)	Statute revised.
S	(superseded)	Substitution of new legislation for an existing statute not expressly abrogated.
Sd	(suspended)	Statute suspended.
Sdp	(suspended in part)	Statute suspended in part.
Sg	(supplementing)	New matter added to an existing statute.
Sp	(superseded in part)	Substitution of new legislation for part of an existing statute not expressly abrogated.
Va	(validated)	

Judicial

C	Constitutional.	V	Void or invalid.
U	Unconstitutional.	Va	Valid.
Up	Unconstitutional in part.	Vp	Void or invalid in part.

[G10108]

Exhibit 45: List of abbreviations used in statutes sections of *Shepard's Citations*.

Exhibit 46: Treatment of Georgia code sections in *Shepard's Georgia Citations.*

Each state Shepard's citator includes a "Table of Acts by Popular Names or Short Titles," providing the citations of listed acts. Statutes from all jurisdictions are covered, in one alphabetical listing, in *Shepard's Acts and Cases by Popular Names: Federal and State*. This set is most useful when the title but not the state of an act is known, or when similar acts from several states are sought.

Shepard's statutory citators are gradually being added to LEXIS and WESTLAW, but most can only be used in printed form and are not yet available online. Citations to statutes in court decisions and periodical articles can be found online, however, by searching the full-text databases for references to the title or citation of a statute. Such a search may find very recent references that have not yet been covered by either the annotated codes or Shepard's.

Although Shepard's is the only comprehensive citator system, other citators may be useful in specialized areas. Looseleaf services frequently include citators for statutes in their fields, often providing information of changes more quickly than Shepard's. Looseleaf services are available for only some subjects, however, and even in those areas they may not offer coverage as comprehensive as Shepard's.

§ 6–6. UNIFORM LAWS AND MODEL ACTS

A good deal of confusion is caused by widely different state statutes on the same subject. Sometimes the differing treatment is a necessary reflection of a state's history or customs, but in many cases there is no need

for provisions to conflict with each other. The National Conference of Commissioners on Uniform State Laws was created to prepare legislation which would decrease unnecessary variations. The Commissioners have prepared almost 150 laws that are in force in at least one state, and another thirty or so are available for consideration. Among the most widely known is the Uniform Commercial Code, which has been adopted by virtually every state.

Uniform Laws Annotated, published by West (and available online from WESTLAW), contains every uniform law approved by the National Conference, lists of adopting states, Commissioners' notes, and annotations to court decisions from any adopting jurisdiction. These annotations allow researchers in one state to study the case law developed in other states with the same uniform law. The set is supplemented annually by pocket parts and by the *Handbook of the National Conference of Commissioners on Uniform State Laws,* which provides information about recent adoptions and newly proposed legislation. Exhibit 47 shows a section of the Uniform Post–Conviction Procedure Act in *Uniform Laws Annotated*, including a state variation from the official text and annotations of decisions. Since the set is published by West, it also carries citations to the American Digest System, WESTLAW, and other West publications.

§ 14   **POST-CONVICTION PROCEDURE (1980)**

§ 14. [Review].

A final judgment entered under this Act may be reviewed by the [designate appellate court] upon [appeal, writ of error] filed either by the applicant within [___] days or by the state within [___] days after the entry of judgment.

Comment

This section contemplates that the ordinary processes of appellate review will be followed in post-conviction proceedings.

Action in Adopting Jurisdictions

Variations from Official Text:

North Dakota. Section reads: "A final judgment entered under this chapter may be reviewed by the supreme court of this state upon appeal filed either by the applicant within ten days or by the state within thirty days after the entry of judgment."

Library References

American Digest System

Scope and extent of review of criminal proceedings: questions considered in general, see Criminal Law ⬥1134(3).

Encyclopedias

Scope and extent of review in criminal proceedings, see C.J.S. Criminal Law § 1703 et seq.

WESTLAW Electronic Research

Criminal law cases: 110k[add key number].
See, also, WESTLAW Electronic Research Guide following the Explanation.

Notes of Decisions

Excusable neglect   2
Final judgment or order   1

1. Final judgment or order

Denial of postconviction relief was "final order" within meaning of rule permitting extension of time for appeal until final order, if application for postconviction relief was filed before expiration of time for appeal from conviction or sentence; although order did not contain findings and conclusions, no evidence was presented to trial court. State v. Rathjen, N.D.1990, 455 N.W.2d 845.

County court's order, denying defendant's petition for postconviction relief, was clear from circumstances to have effect of final judgment; thus, Supreme Court would treat appeal as appeal from final judgment and hear it. Kaiser v. State, N.D.1987, 417 N.W.2d 175.

2. Excusable neglect

Determination of whether excusable neglect existed to extend time for filing notice of appeal from denial of application for postconviction relief was required; jurisdiction was lacking in absence of excusable neglect. DeCoteau v. State, N.D.1993, 499 N.W.2d 894.

§ 15. [Uniformity of Application and Construction].

This Act shall be applied and construed to effectuate its general purpose to make uniform the law with respect to the subject of this Act among states enacting it.

Exhibit 47: A page from *Uniform Laws Annotated*.

The text of each uniform law can, of course, also be found in the statutory code of each adopting state, accompanied by annotations from that state's courts. The state code contains the law as actually adopted and in force, rather than the text as proposed by the Commissioners.

§ 6–7. LOCAL CHARTERS AND ORDINANCES

Legislation is enacted not only by federal and state jurisdictions, but by counties, towns and cities as well. Unfortunately, many local charters and ordinances are poorly published, rarely annotated, and infrequently supplemented.

Most large cities and counties publish collections of their charters and ordinances, with some attempt at regular supplementation. In recent years, there has been a significant improvement in the publication of municipal ordinances of smaller jurisdictions by specialized legal publishers. For many cities and counties, however, there is still no accessible, up-to-date compilation, and individual ordinances must be obtained from the local clerk's office.

The practicing lawyer must become familiar with what local law sources are published and what steps are necessary to locate further information. With the increasing importance of local law in many fields, such as construction, environmental protection, welfare, housing, and transportation, better access to local ordinances is badly needed. The unavailability of these sources is a serious impediment to the proper administration of justice.

Shepard's provides coverage of local laws in some state citators. Older volumes list municipal charters and ordi-

nances by jurisdiction, with citing references in judicial opinions, state legislation, and law review articles, and also include subject indexes of these charters and ordinances. This feature has been discontinued in newly revised state citators, although in a few states coverage of codified local legislation is still provided.

Shepard's also publishes a subject digest of judicial decisions involving local ordinances, entitled *Ordinance Law Annotations* (1969–date). Like other digests, this set provides brief abstracts of decisions under alphabetically arranged subject headings divided into specific subtopics.

§ 6–8. CONCLUSION

In some respects statutory research is easier than case research, because the major resources are more accessible and more regularly updated. In many situations a good annotated code provides most of the necessary research leads. This convenience is undercut, however, by the opacity of statutory language. Most judicial prose is a model of clarity when compared to the texts of many federal and state statutes.

In researching statutory or constitutional law, the resources discussed in this chapter provide only a first step. Besides finding a relevant provision and updating it through code supplements, *Shepard's Citations,* and online research, it is usually necessary to read judicial decisions applying or construing its language. Attorney general opinions on the meaning of the provision may also be available. A further understanding may be gained from treatises or law review articles.

Finally, ambiguities and vagueness in statutes often lead to difficulties in interpretation. Some statutory

ambiguities stem from poor draftsmanship, but many are the inevitable result of negotiation and compromise in the legislative process. Lawyers frequently study legislative documents to develop an argument for or against a particular interpretation of the statutory text. This research in legislative history is the focus of the next chapter.

CHAPTER 7

LEGISLATIVE HISTORY

---

§ 7–1. INTRODUCTION

The ambiguities so common in the language of statutes require lawyers and scholars to locate legislative documents from which they can learn the intended purpose of an act or the meaning of particular statutory language. Researchers also need to investigate the current status of a proposed law under consideration by the legislature.

These processes—determining the meaning or intent of an enacted law, and ascertaining the status of a pending bill—comprise legislative history research.

Research in legislative history requires an understanding of the legislative process. Each stage of law-making may result in a significant document of legislative history. The following are the most significant steps in the enactment of a law, and their related documents.

Action	Document
Preliminary inquiry	Hearings on the subject of the proposed legislation
Executive recommendation	Presidential message proposing an administration bill
Introduction of bill	Slip bill as introduced
Referred to committee	Committee print of bill
Hearings on bill	Transcript of testimony and exhibits
Reported out of committee	Committee report, including committee's version of bill
Legislative debates	*Congressional Record,* sometimes including texts of bill in amended forms
Passage by first house	Final House or Senate version of the proposed legislation
Other house	Generally same procedure and documents as above
Referred to conference committee (if texts passed by houses differ)	Conference committee version of bill; conference committee report
Passage by one or both houses of revised bill	Enrolled bill sent to President (not available to public)
Approval by President	Presidential signing statement; slip law (also *USCCAN* and *USCS Advance* pamphlets);

> subsequently published in
> *Statutes at Large* and classi-
> fied by subject in the *U.S.
> Code*

§ 7–2. FEDERAL LEGISLATIVE HISTORY SOURCES

Of the many types of documents issued by Congress, a few are particularly important for legislative history research. *Bills* are the major source for the texts of pending or unenacted legislation. *Hearings* can provide useful background on the purpose of an act. *Committee reports* analyze and describe bills and are usually considered the most authoritative sources of congressional intent. *Floor debates* may contain a sponsor's interpretation of a bill or the only explanation of last-minute amendments.

a. Congressional Bills

The texts of bills are needed by researchers interested in pending or failed legislation, and may also help in interpreting an enacted law. Variations among the bills that led to a law can aid in determining the intended meaning of the act. Each deletion or addition made during the legislative process implies a deliberate choice of language by the legislators.

Bills are individually numbered in separate series for each house, and retain their identifying numbers through both sessions of a Congress. At the end of the two-year term, pending bills lapse and must be reintroduced and renumbered if they are to be considered. The bill number is the key to tracing legislative action on a proposed law. It appears on an enacted law both in its slip form and in the *Statutes at Large*.

An individual bill can be obtained from its sponsor, the clerk of the House or Senate, or the appropriate congressional committee. Bills are received by many large law libraries in a slip form or on microfiche from the Government Printing Office, and are also issued commercially on microfiche by Congressional Information Service (CIS). Texts of bills are also available online from WESTLAW, LEXIS, and other electronic services, including the Washington Post's LEGI–SLATE and Congressional Quarterly's Washington Alert. Beginning with the 103d Congress in 1993, bills are available on the Internet from the Government Printing Office's GPO Access and the Library of Congress's THOMAS system.

Exhibit 48 shows the bill H.R. 4924 as introduced in the House of Representatives. This bill, as amended, became the Rhinoceros and Tiger Conservation Act of 1994, Pub. L. 103–391, 108 Stat. 4094.

103D CONGRESS
2D SESSION

H. R. 4924

To assist in the conservation of rhinoceros and tigers by supporting and providing financial resources for the conservation programs of nations whose activities directly or indirectly affect rhinoceros and tiger populations, and of the CITES Secretariat.

IN THE HOUSE OF REPRESENTATIVES

AUGUST 9, 1994

Mr. FIELDS of Texas (for himself, Mr. STUDDS, and Mr. BEILENSON) introduced the following bill; which was referred to the Committee on Merchant Marine and Fisheries

---

A BILL

To assist in the conservation of rhinoceros and tigers by supporting and providing financial resources for the conservation programs of nations whose activities directly or indirectly affect rhinoceros and tiger populations, and of the CITES Secretariat.

1   *Be it enacted by the Senate and House of Representa-*

2 *tives of the United States of America in Congress assembled,*

3 **SECTION 1. SHORT TITLE.**

4   This Act may be cited as the "Rhinoceros and Tiger

5 Conservation Act of 1994".

6 **SEC. 2. FINDINGS.**

7   The Congress finds the following:

Exhibit 48: A congressional bill, as introduced in the House of Representatives.

b. Hearings

Senate and House committees hear testimony on proposed legislation and on other subjects under congressional investigation. The transcripts of most of these hearings are published, accompanied by exhibits (such as statements or statistical material) contributed by interested individuals or groups. The purpose of a hearing is to determine the need for new legislation or to bring before Congress information relevant to its preparation and enactment. Hearings are not held for all legislation, however, nor are all hearings published.

Hearings are available from the particular committee or the Government Printing Office, and are issued on microfiche by CIS. They can provide valuable information on congressional concerns in considering legislation, as well as useful analysis or commentary by witnesses. Their importance as evidence of legislative intent, however, is limited, since they focus more on the views of interested parties rather than those of the lawmakers themselves. Transcripts of hearing testimony are available online from WESTLAW, LEXIS, and LEGI–SLATE.

A search for relevant hearings should not be limited to the session in which a particular law is enacted, because hearings may extend over more than one session and be issued in several parts and volumes. Hearings are generally identified by the *title* which appears on the cover, the *bill number,* the *name of the subcommittee and committee,* the *term* and *session* of Congress, and the *year.* Exhibit 49 shows the first page of *The Rhinoceros and Tiger Conservation Act of 1994: Hearing Before the Subcomm. on Environment and Natural Resources of the House Comm. on Merchant Marine and Fisheries,* 103d Cong., 2d Sess. (1994).

THE RHINOCEROS AND TIGER CONSERVATION ACT OF 1994

TUESDAY, MAY 17, 1994

HOUSE OF REPRESENTATIVES, SUBCOMMITTEE ON ENVI-
RONMENT AND NATURAL RESOURCES, COMMITTEE ON
MERCHANT MARINE AND FISHERIES,

Washington, DC.

The Subcommittee met, pursuant to call, at 2:00 p.m., in room
1334, Longworth House Office Building, Hon. Gerry E. Studds
[chairman of the Subcommittee] presiding.

Present: Representatives Studds, Pallone, and Fields.

Staff Present: Sue Waldron, Press Secretary; Dan Ashe, Sub-
committee Staff Director; Marvadell Zeeb, Subcommittee Clerk;
David Hoskins, Subcommittee Counsel; Harry Burroughs, Minority
Staff Director; Cynthia Wilkinson, Minority Chief Counsel; Tom
Melius, Minority Professional Staff; Margherita Woods, Minority
Clerk; and Sharon McKenna, Minority Counsel.

OPENING STATEMENT OF HON. GERRY E. STUDDS, A U.S. REP-
RESENTATIVE FROM MASSACHUSETTS, AND CHAIRMAN,

Exhibit 49: A page from a congressional hearing on endangered species issues.

Mr. STUDDS. The Subcommittee meets this afternoon to discuss
measures to conserve the remaining populations of rhinos and tigers. In order to satisfy the demand for rhino and tiger parts in
oriental medicines and aphrodisiacs, these magnificent creatures
are being slaughtered by poachers who see tigers only for the value
of their bones, and rhinos only for the value of their horns. Now
threatened with extinction, less than 11,000 rhinos and 6,000 tigers are believed to exist in the wild.

Last fall, the Administration certified that China and Taiwan
were diminishing the effectiveness of an international wildlife conservation treaty and, in April, President Clinton imposed trade
sanctions on wildlife products from Taiwan for that nation's failure
to implement measures to end the illegal trade of rhino and tiger
parts. Although the President did not impose a similar ban on
China, he indicated that the Administration would continue to
monitor China's progress.

Congressmen Fields, Beilenson, and I have introduced the Rhinoceros and Tiger Conservation Act to provide financial assistance
for rhino and tiger conservation projects and to impose a moratorium on the importation of fish and wildlife products from countries which continue to be involved in the rhino or tiger trade.

(1)

Exhibit 49: A page from a congressional hearing on endangered species issues.

c. Committee Reports

Reports are generally the most important source of legislative history. They are issued by the committees of each house on bills reported out of committee (*i.e.*, sent to the whole house for consideration) and by conference committees of the two houses to reconcile differences between House and Senate versions of a bill. Reports usually include the text of the bill, describe its contents and purposes, and give reasons for the committee's recommendations, sometimes with minority views. Committees also issue reports on various investigations, studies and hearings not related to pending legislation.

Committee reports are published in numbered series which indicate house, Congress, and report number, with conference committee reports included in the series of House reports. Exhibit 50 shows the first page of H.R. Rep. No. 748, 103d Cong., 2d Sess. (1994), reporting the House Committee on Merchant Marine and Fisheries' views on H.R. 2978.

Committee reports are issued by the Government Printing Office, and are sometimes available from the committee or from the House or Senate clerk. All the reports for a session are published, along with House and Senate Documents, in the bound official compilation called the *Serial Set*. Selected reports are also reprinted in *USCCAN,* and all reports are available on microfiche from CIS. WESTLAW's LH database and the CMTRPT file in LEXIS contain all committee reports beginning in 1990, with selected earlier coverage.

103D CONGRESS 2d Session	HOUSE OF REPRESENTATIVES	REPORT 103–748

RHINOCEROS AND TIGER CONSERVATION ACT OF 1994

SEPTEMBER 26, 1994.—Committed to the Committee of the Whole House on the State of the Union and ordered to be printed

Mr. STUDDS, from the Committee on Merchant Marine and Fisheries, submitted the following

REPORT

[To accompany H.R. 4924]

[Including cost estimate of the Congressional Budget Office]

The Committee on Merchant Marine and Fisheries, to whom was referred the bill (H.R. 4924) to assist in the conservation of rhinoceros and tigers by supporting and providing financial resources for the conservation programs of nations whose activities directly or indirectly affect rhinoceros and tiger populations, and of the CITES Secretariat, having considered the same, report favorably thereon without amendment and recommend that the bill do pass.

SUMMARY OF THE REPORTED BILL

H.R. 4924 authorizes appropriations of $10 million per year in fiscal years 1996–2000 for a Rhinoceros and Tiger Conservation Fund to provide financial assistance for projects to conserve rhinoceros and tigers. Conservation is broadly defined as all methods and procedures necessary to bring rhinoceros and tigers to the point at which there are sufficient populations to ensure that those species do not become extinct. To receive funding, a country whose activities directly or indirectly affect rhinoceros or tiger populations, the CITES Secretariat, or any other person may submit a project proposal to the Secretary of the Interior. Within 6 months of receiving a final proposal, the Secretary must approve or disapprove the proposal based on criteria established by the bill.

PURPOSE OF THE BILL

The purposes of H.R. 4924 are to assist in the conservation of rhinoceros and tigers by supporting and providing financial resources for conservation programs of nations whose activities di-

79–006

Exhibit 50: A House committee report.

d. Debates

The *Congressional Record* is a nearly verbatim transcript of legislative debates and proceedings, published each day that either house is in session. In addition, the *Record* includes extensions of floor remarks and any other material a Senator or Representative wishes to have printed.

Each issue contains a Daily Digest which summarizes the day's activities, including news of legislation introduced, reported on, or passed, and any committee actions taken. An index to the *Record* is published every two weeks.

The *Congressional Record* is available through various online and CD–ROM databases. Coverage in WESTLAW (CR database) and LEXIS (RECORD file) begins in 1985, with the 99th Congress. Internet coverage through GPO Access and THOMAS begins in 1994.

Several years after the session, a bound edition of over thirty volumes is published. That compilation includes a cumulative index, a cumulation of the Daily Digest, and a cumulative "History of Bills and Resolutions" table listing all bills introduced during the session and summarizing their legislative history. The bound edition also contains a "History of Bills Enacted into Public Law," arranged by public law number and providing bill numbers, committee report numbers, and dates and pages of consideration of each bill in the *Congressional Record*.

The *Congressional Record* never contains hearings and only rarely includes committee reports. Bills are sometimes read into the *Record*, particularly if they have been amended on the floor or in conference committee. The

Congressional Record's primary role, however, is as a report of debates and actions taken. An excerpt from the *Record,* showing House consideration of H.R. 2978, is shown in Exhibit 51.

September 27, 1994   CONGRESSIONAL RECORD — HOUSE   H9869

[Two columns of member names list]

NOT VOTING—11

□ 1650

The Clerk announced the following pairs:

On this vote:

Mr. Dicks and Mr. Fazio for, with Mr. Armey against.

Mr. DE LA GARZA, Mr. LEHMAN, Mrs. THURMAN, Mr. HILLIARD, and Mr. CUNNINGHAM changed their vote from "yea" to "nay."

Mr. QUILLEN, Mr. LIPINSKI, Mrs. VUCANOVICH, and Messrs. SKEEN, LIVINGSTON, COSTELLO, POSHARD, SWETT, MYERS of Indiana, ROSE and POMEROY changed their vote from "may" to "yea."

So (two-thirds not having voted in favor thereof) the motion was rejected.

The result of the vote was announced as above recorded.

ANNOUNCEMENT BY THE SPEAKER PRO TEMPORE

Mr. FIELDS of Louisiana. Pursuant to the provision of clause 5 of rule I, the Chair announces that he will postpone further proceedings today on the remaining motions to suspend the rules on which a recorded vote or the yeas and nays are ordered, or on which the vote is objected to under clause 4 of rule XV. Such rollcall votes, if post-

poned, will be taken on Wednesday, September 28, 1994.

ANNOUNCEMENT OF INTENTION TO OFFER A MOTION TO INSTRUCT CONFEREES ON H.R. 820, NATIONAL COMPETITIVENESS ACT OF 1993

Mr. WALKER. Mr. Speaker, pursuant to clause 1(c), rule XXVIII, I am announcing that tomorrow I intend to offer a motion to instruct conferees on the bill (H.R. 820) to amend the Stevenson-Wydler Technology Innovation Act of 1980 to enhance manufacturing technology development and transfer, to authorize appropriations for the Technology Administration of the Department of Commerce, including the National Institute of Standards and Technology, and for other purposes:

Mr. WALKER moves that the managers on the part of the House at the conference on the disagreeing votes of the 2 Houses on the Senate amendment to the bill, H.R. 820, be instructed to insist on a provision that requires a regulatory impact analysis and unfunded mandate estimate for each bill or joint resolution reported by any committees of the House or Representatives or the Senate, or considered on the floor of either House, and for every Federal department or executive branch agency regulatory action.

RHINOCEROS AND TIGER CONSERVATION ACT OF 1994

Mr. STUDDS. Mr. Speaker, I ask unanimous consent that the Committee on Merchant Marine and Fisheries be discharged from further consideration of the bill (H.R. 4864) to assist in the conservation of rhinoceros and tigers by supporting and providing financial resources for the conservation programs of nations whose activities directly or indirectly affect rhinoceros and tiger populations, and of the CITES Secretariat, and ask for its immediate consideration.

The Clerk read the title of the bill.

The SPEAKER pro tempore. Is there objection to the request of the gentleman from Massachusetts?

Mr. FIELDS of Texas. Mr. Speaker, reserving the right to object, this is an extremely important piece of legislation, and I rise in support of H.R. 4864, the Rhinoceros and Tiger Conservation Act of 1994. I am pleased to have been joined by Chairman STUDDS and my good friend, TONY BEILENSON, in introducing this bill.

I was prompted to introduce this legislation because the populations of rhinos and tigers continue to plummet despite their protected status under the Convention on International trade in Endangered Species of Wild Flora and Fauna [CITES]. For example, approximately 1 million rhinos existed at the turn of the century. In 1987, the population had dwindled to 11,000, or half of the number that experts consider necessary for the species to survive. The statue of tigers is not any better. At the beginning of this century, there may have been as many as

100,000 tigers in the wild; today, the total is probably fewer than 6,000.

Habitat destruction is partially responsible for the decline, but the predominant cause is the senseless slaughter of the animals by unscrupulous international poachers. Although agricultural activities and commercial logging are destroying large blocks of tiger habitat, poaching is by far having the most dramatic impact. Tigers are killed for their fur and certain body parts are used in medicines. In China, Korea, and Taiwan, rhino horn is used as a fever-reducing agent, and in Yemen it is used to make decorative handles for ceremonial daggers. The trade in rhino and tiger parts is so lucrative that outlaws will go to extraordinary lengths to kill the animals.

It has also been brought to my attention that one reason for the sharp decline in the population of the black rhino in Africa is due in principal because of the disappearing votes of the... In a large number of instances, poaching has been carried out by nationals of Zambia who cross into Zimbabwe to kill rhinos. The Zambian authorities have consistently declined to provide meaningful cooperation with Zimbabwe's antipoaching units stationed along the border. Thus, Zambian poachers unite stationed along the border. Thus, Zambian poachers who kill rhinos escape back into their country and remain free because their government authorities choose not to extradite them.

Unless immediate steps are taken, these magnificent animals will cease to exist throughout most, if not all, of their range. That would be a monumental tragedy.

I am encouraged by President Clinton's announcement on April 11, that for the first time in history, trade sanctions under the Pelly amendment would be imposed on wildlife products from Taiwan. This action should send a clear message to Taiwan and other nations that the United States will not tolerate the wanton annihilation of these species.

While the People's Republic of China [PRC] was also certified under the Pelly amendment, I am pleased that the administration did not place any sanctions on that country. I am aware that they are continuing to make significant progress to stop any illegal trade of rhino and tiger products. I am sure this will be factored into any further certification actions.

Part of the problem in the conservation of these species is that range states do not have sufficient money or manpower to stop poachers. In recognition of this problem, our bill authorizes $10 million per year for a Rhinoceros and Tiger Conservation Fund. The Secretary of the Interior would be tasked with administering the fund and providing financial assistance for rhino and tiger conservation projects. The committee amendment provides the Administrator of the Agency for Inter-

---

Exhibit 51: An excerpt from the *Congressional Record.*

House and *Senate Journals* are also published, but unlike the *Congressional Record,* they do not include the verbatim debates. The journals merely outline the proceedings, indicate whether there was debate, and report the resulting action and votes taken.

The predecessors of the *Congressional Record,* which began in 1873, are: the *Annals of Congress* (1789–1824); the *Register of Debates* (1824–37); and the *Congressional Globe* (1833–73).

e. Other Congressional Publications

Congress also produces a variety of other publications which are less frequently consulted in legislative history research. These publications can, however, be important sources of other information.

Committee prints contain a variety of material prepared specifically for the use of a committee, ranging from studies by the committee staff or outside experts to compilations of earlier legislative history documents. Some prints contain statements by committee members on a pending bill.

House and Senate documents include reports of some congressional investigations not found in the regular committee reports, special studies or exhibits prepared for Congress, presidential messages, and communications from executive departments or agencies. They are published in a numbered series for each house, and appear in the official *Serial Set.* Presidential documents, including messages accompanying proposed legislation and state-

ments issued when signing or vetoing bills, also appear in the *Congressional Record* and the *Weekly Compilation of Presidential Documents*.

The Senate issues two series of publications in the process of treaty ratification. *Treaty documents* contain the texts of treaties before the Senate for its advice and consent, and *Senate executive reports* from the Foreign Relations Committee contain its recommendations on pending treaties. These publications are discussed more fully in Chapter 12. Other Senate committees also issue executive reports, containing their recommendations on presidential nominations to the executive and judicial branches.

§ 7–3. RESEARCHING THE HISTORY OF ENACTED LAWS

Legislative history research of enacted laws is usually undertaken to determine congressional meaning or to clarify ambiguous language. The most important documents for these purposes are the committee reports, which are written by the staff of the committee considering a bill to explain its provisions to other legislators.

The *bill number* is usually the key to finding congressional documents. Researchers beginning with a *Statutes at Large* citation or a Public Law number can find the bill number in several ways. Since 1903, the *Statutes at Large* has included this number at the head of the text, as shown in Exhibit 35 on page 127. Numerous tables providing this cross-reference are also available, including the *Congressional Record* Daily Digest's History of Bills Enacted into Public Law, CCH's *Congressional Index*, USCCAN's Table of Public Laws, and *CIS/Index*.

This section focuses on a few major resources that are most often used for historical research. Most of the materials to be discussed in § 7–4 can also serve this function, but their primary purpose is to provide information about current developments. Electronic resources, for example, are discussed in the next section because their retrospective coverage is limited.

a. *Statutes at Large* and *USCCAN*

Committee reports are usually easy to find if the text of the act is available. The *Statutes at Large* includes a legislative history summary at the end of each public law. This summary provides citations of committee reports, lists the dates of consideration and passage in each house, and includes references to presidential statements. These features can be seen at the bottom of Exhibit 35. Summaries have appeared at the end of each law passed since 1975, and earlier *Statutes at Large* volumes include separate "Guide to Legislative History" tables.

U.S. Code Congressional and Administrative News (*USCCAN*), published by West, has already been discussed as a source of the texts of enacted laws. In addition, it reprints selected committee reports on many acts. Because *USCCAN* contains both the acts and the reports, it is a convenient compilation of the major documents necessary for basic research. *USCCAN* also provides references to those committee reports it does not reprint.

Exhibit 52 shows the beginning of the House report on the Rhinoceros and Tiger Conservation Act of 1994, as set out in *USCCAN*. Note that the report is preceded by references to steps in the passage of the legislation,

RHINOCEROS AND TIGER CONSERVATION ACT OF 1994

P.L. 103–391, see page 108 Stat. 4094

DATES OF CONSIDERATION AND PASSAGE

House: September 27, 1994

Senate: October 7, 1994

Cong. Record Vol. 140 (1994)

House Report (Merchant Marine and Fisheries Committee)
No. 103–748, Sept. 26, 1994
[To accompany H.R. 4924]

No Senate Report was submitted with this legislation.

HOUSE REPORT NO. 103–748

[page 1]

The Committee on Merchant Marine and Fisheries, to whom was referred the bill (H.R. 4924) to assist in the conservation of rhinoceros and tigers by supporting and providing financial resources for the conservation programs of nations whose activities directly or indirectly affect rhinoceros and tiger populations, and of the CITES Secretariat, having considered the same, report favorably thereon without amendment and recommend that the bill do pass.

SUMMARY OF THE REPORTED BILL

H.R. 4924 authorizes appropriations of $10 million per year in fiscal years 1996–2000 for a Rhinoceros and Tiger Conservation Fund to provide financial assistance for projects to conserve rhinoceros and tigers. Conservation is broadly defined as all methods and procedures necessary to bring rhinoceros and tigers to the point at which there are sufficient populations to ensure that those species do not become extinct. To receive funding, a country whose activities directly or indirectly affect rhinoceros or tiger populations, the CITES Secretariat, or any other person may submit a project proposal to the Secretary of the Interior. Within 6 months of receiving a final proposal, the Secretary must approve or disapprove the proposal based on criteria established by the bill.

PURPOSE OF THE BILL

The purposes of H.R. 4924 are to assist in the conservation of rhinoceros and tigers by supporting and providing financial resources for conservation programs of nations whose activities di-

[page 2]

rectly or indirectly affect rhinoceros and tiger populations and of the CITES Secretariat.

Exhibit 52: A page from the Legislative History section of *United States Code Congressional and Administrative News.*

including dates of consideration and passage in each house.

Both the monthly advance sheets of *USCCAN* and the annual bound volumes also include legislative history tables. For each public law, the tables list the date approved, the *Statutes at Large* citation, the bill and report numbers, the committees that recommended the legislation, and the dates of consideration and passage. The monthly issues also include a table of "Major Bills Pending," arranged by subject and showing the progress of current legislation.

b. Congressional Information Service (CIS)

The major means of subject access to congressional publications is the *CIS/Index,* published by the Congressional Information Service. The index began in 1970, and covers nearly all congressional publications except the *Congressional Record.* It indexes hearings, reports, prints, and documents, by subject and name (corporate and individual), with supplementary indexes by title, bill number, and other identifying numbers. The indexes provide references to abstracts summarizing the contents of these documents. Exhibit 53 shows an excerpt from the subject index in the 1994 volume of *CIS/Index.* Exhibit 54 shows a page of abstracts, including coverage of the hearing shown earlier in Exhibit 49 on page 166.

Index of Subjects and Names

Exhibit 53: An excerpt from the subject index in *CIS/Index*.

Merchant Marine and Fisheries   H561-57

CRIMMINS, Sean T., Vice President and General Tax Counsel, Ashland Oil Co.; representing Chemical Manufacturers Association.
MARTIN, Dawn M., Political Director and Director, D.C. Office, American Oceans Campaign; also representing Friends of the Earth and U.S. Public Interest Research Group.
REEDER, Clinton B., representing National Association of Wheat Growers.
ZWICK, David, President, Clean Water Action.

Statements and Discussion: Views on clean water funding options; factors contributing to increased clean water funding needs; opposition to H.R. 2199, with objections to new excise taxes; need to strengthen the CWA; support for "polluter pays" concept, with concern about various bill provisions.

Unfairness to agriculture interests of H.R. 2199 taxes on fertilizers and pesticides (related graphs, p. 201-211); recommendations regarding clean water policy; support for bill; perspectives on water quality issues.

Insertions:

a. Barnes, George D., Jr. (WEF), water quality research, statement prepared for House Science, Space, and Technology Committee *Subcom on Technology, Environment, and Aviation*, Sept. 23, 1993 (p. 120-125).

b. Rubin, A. Robert (NC State Univ), wastewater treatment in small and rural communities, statement prepared for House Public Works and Transportation Committee *Subcom on Water Resources and Environment*, Feb. 23, 1993 (p. 128-149).

c. Rasmussen, Paul E. (et al.), "Biological and Economic Sustainability of Wheat/Fallow Agriculture" from 1993 Columbia Basin Agricultural Research Annual Report (p. 212-222).

H561-53   U.S. PASSENGER VESSEL DEVELOPMENT ACT.
June 14, 1994.   103-2.
iii+28 p.   GPO $1.50
S/N 552-070-16786-2.
CIS/MF/3
•Item 1021-B; 1021-C.
•Y4.M53:103-99.
MC 94-27417.

Committee Serial No. 103-99. Hearing before the *Subcom on Coast Guard and Navigation* to consider H.R. 3821 (dept rpts. text, p. 15-28), the U.S. Passenger Vessel Development Act, to amend the Shipping Act and the Merchant Marine Act to allow foreign-built passenger cruise ships that meet International Convention for the Safety of Life at Sea (SOLAS) standards to operate temporarily in the U.S. if a replacement ship is ordered to be built in the U.S. within three years.

Supplementary material (p. 15-28 includes departmental reports.

H561-53.1: June 14, 1994. p. 3-14.

Witness: McGOWAN, John F. (Capt.), Deputy Chief, Office of Marine Safety, Security, and Environmental Protection, Coast Guard.

Statement and Discussion: Safety concerns about H.R. 3821 SOLAS provision; merits of Coast Guard inspection of foreign ships prior to operation in the U.S.

Volume 25, Number 1-12

H561-54   REAUTHORIZATION OF THE ATLANTIC STRIPED BASS CONSERVATION ACT.
May 4, 1994.   103-2.
iii+62 p.   GPO $2.50
S/N 552-070-16839-7.
CIS/MF/3
•Item 1021-B; 1021-C.
•Y4.M53:103-102.

Committee Serial No. 103-102. Hearing before the *Subcom on Fisheries Management* to examine Atlantic striped bass conservation programs in connection with Atlantic Striped Bass Conservation Act of 1984 (ASBCA) reauthorization (Subcom background memo, p. 57-59).

Supplementary material (p. 23-62) includes witnesses' written statements and correspondence.

H561-54.1: May 4, 1994. p. 3-10.

Witness: SHAEFER, Richard H., Director, Office of Fisheries Conservation and Management, National Marine Fisheries Service, NOAA.
EDWARDS, Gary B., Assistant Director, Fisheries, Fish and Wildlife Service.

Statements and Discussion: Importance of ASBCA, with support for reauthorization.

H561-54.2: May 4, 1994. p. 11-22.

Witness: DUNNIGAN, John H., Executive Director, Atlantic States Marine Fisheries Commission.
COLVIN, Gordon C., Director, Marine Resources, New York State Department of Environmental Conservation.
CAPUTI, Gary, Vice President, Jersey Coast Anglers Association.

Statements and Discussion: Support for ASBCA reauthorization; review of striped bass conservation management issues.

H561-55   RHINOCEROS AND TIGER CONSERVATION ACT OF 1994.
May 17, 1994.   103-2.
iii+58 p.   GPO $2.50
S/N 552-070-16837-1.
CIS/MF/3
•Item 1021-B; 1021-C.
•Y4.M53:103-104.

Committee Serial No. 103-104. Hearing before the *Subcom on Environment and Natural Resources* to consider H.R. 3987 (text, p. 47-56), the Rhinoceros and Tiger Conservation Act of 1994, to establish a Rhinoceros and Tiger Conservation Fund to provide financial aid to conservation projects for endangered rhinoceros and tiger species in Africa and Asia.

Supplementary material (p. 18-58) includes witnesses' written statements and correspondence.

H561-55.1: May 17, 1994. p. 2-6.

Witness: BEILENSON, Anthony C., (Rep, D-Calif)

Statement and Discussion: Merits of sponsored H.R. 3987.

H561-55.2: May 17, 1994. p. 6-17.

Witness: BEATTIE, Mollie H., Director, Fish and Wildlife Service, Department of Interior.
HEMLEY, Ginette, Director, TRAFFIC USA, World Wildlife Fund.

BOLZE, Dorene, Policy Analyst, Wildlife Conservation Society.

Statements and Discussion: Status of and efforts to protect endangered rhinoceros and tiger species; general support for H.R. 3987.

H561-56   NMFS, FWS, AND NBS BUDGETS FOR FY96.
Apr. 12, 1994.   103-2.
v+145 p.   GPO $5.50
S/N 552-070-16872-9.
CIS/MF/4
•Item 1021-B; 1021-C.
•Y4.M53:103-105.

Committee Serial No. 103-105. Hearing before the *Subcom on Environment and Natural Resources* and the *Subcom on Fisheries Management* to review National Marine Fisheries Service (NMFS), Fish and Wildlife Service (FWS), and National Biological Survey (NBS) FY95 budget requests (Subcom background memo, p. 117-123).

Supplementary material (p. 38-145) includes witnesses' written statements and replies to Subcom questions and correspondence.

H561-56.1: Apr. 12, 1994. p. 7-116.

Witness: FRAMPTON, George T., Jr., Assistant Secretary, Fish and Wildlife and Parks, Department of Interior.
BEATTIE, Mollie H., Director, FWS.
HESTER, F. Eugene, Deputy Director, NBS.
SCHMITTEN, Rolland A., Assistant Administrator, Fisheries, NOAA; Director, NMFS.
ENO, Amos S., Director, National Fish and Wildlife Foundation.

Statements and Discussion: Summary of FWS FY95 budget request (related tables, p. 48-61 passim); overview of NBS mission and FY95 budget request; highlights of NMFS FY95 budget request (related tables, p. 99-104); recommendations on fish and wildlife policies and FY95 budget requests.

H561-57   IMPACT OF THE OCEAN DUMPING ACT AND FEDERAL DREDGING POLICY ON REGIONAL DREDGING ISSUES.
June 14, 1994.   103-2.
iv+304 p.   GPO $12.00
S/N 552-070-16974-1.
CIS/MF/6
•Item 1021-B; 1021-C.
•Y4.M53:103-107.

Committee Serial No. 103-107. Hearing before the *Subcom on Oceanography, Gulf of Mexico, and the Outer Continental Shelf* to examine the impact on port dredging projects of EPA environmental regulation and Army Corps of Engineers (COE) permitting process under Title I of the Marine Protection, Research, and Sanctuaries Act, known as the Ocean Dumping Act (ODA), which restricts ocean disposal of contaminated sediments dredged from ports (Subcom background memo, p. 282-291).

Supplementary material (p. 49-304) includes witnesses' prepared statements and written replies to Subcom questions, articles, correspondence, and:

- H.R. 3821, the U.S. Passenger Vessel Development Act, to amend the Shipping Act of

CIS/INDEX   301

Exhibit 54: Abstracts of hearings in *CIS/Index*.

CIS/Index is published monthly, with quarterly cumulations and annual bound volumes (*CIS/Annual*). The annual volumes also include comprehensive legislative histories of enacted laws, with references to bills, hearings, reports, debates, presidential documents and all legislative actions. These summaries were included in the *Abstracts* volumes until 1983, and since 1984 have been published in separate *Legislative Histories* volumes. Rather than limiting coverage to a single term of Congress, they include references to earlier hearings and other documents on related bills from *prior* Congressional sessions. These are probably the most complete and descriptive summaries of the legislative history of federal enactments. Exhibit 55 shows the CIS legislative history of the Rhinoceros and Tiger Conservation Act of 1994.

CIS publishes several other indexes to congressional documents before 1970: *CIS US Serial Set Index* (covering reports and documents), *CIS Index to US Senate Executive Documents and Reports, CIS US Congressional Committee Hearings Index, CIS Index to Unpublished US Senate Committee Hearings, CIS Index to Unpublished US House of Representatives Committee Hearings,* and *CIS US Congressional Committee Prints Index.*

Comprehensive coverage of both earlier materials and current documents is provided on CD–ROM through the *CIS Congressional Masterfile. CIS/Index* is also available online through DIALOG Information Systems and on WESTLAW, and microfiche collections of all publications listed in the various indexes are available from CIS.

Public Law 103-391 108 Stat. 4094

Rhinoceros and Tiger Conservation Act of 1994

October 22, 1994

Public Law

1.1 Public Law 103-391, approved Oct. 22, 1994. (H.R. 4924)

(CIS94:PL103-391 4 p.)

"To assist in the conservation of rhinoceros and tigers by supporting and providing financial resources for the conservation programs of nations whose activities directly or indirectly affect rhinoceros and tiger populations, and of the CITES Secretariat."

Establishes a Rhinoceros and Tiger Conservation Fund to provide financial aid to conservation projects for endangered rhinoceros and tiger species, as proposed by African and Asian nations whose activities affect rhinoceros and tiger populations or by the secretariat of the Convention on International Trade in Endangered Species of Wild Fauna and Flora (CITES).

P.L. 103-391 Reports

103rd Congress

2.1 H. Rpt. 103-748 on H.R. 4924, "Rhinoceros and Tiger Conservation Act of 1994," Sept. 26, 1994.

(CIS94:H563-18 9 p.)
(Y1.1/8:103-748.)

Recommends passage of H.R. 4924, the Rhinoceros and Tiger Conservation Act of 1994, to establish a Rhinoceros and Tiger Conservation Fund to provide financial aid to conservation projects for endangered rhinoceros and tiger species in African and Asian nations.
H.R. 4924 is related to H.R. 3987.

P.L. 103-391 Debate

140 Congressional Record
103rd Congress, 2nd Session - 1994

4.1 Sept. 27, House consideration and passage of H.R. 4924.

4.2 Oct. 7, Senate consideration and passage of H.R. 4924.

P.L. 103-391 Hearings

99th Congress

5.1 "Conservation of Species and the Endangered Rhinoceros," hearings before the Subcommittee on Natural Resources, Agriculture Research, and Environment, House Science, Space, and Technology Committee, Sept. 25, 1986.

(CIS87:H701-22 iii + 170 p.)
(Y4.Sci2:99/156.)

100th Congress

5.2 "Technologies for Conserving Species: Saving the Endangered Rhinoceros," hearings before the Subcommittee on Natural Resources, Agriculture Research, and Environment, House Science, Space, and Technology Committee, June 22, 1988.

(CIS89:H701-23 iii + 188 p. il.)
(Y4.Sci2:100/133.)

103rd Congress

5.3 "Conservation of Rhinos and Reauthorization of the Sikes Act," hearings before the Subcommittee on Environment and Natural Resources, House Merchant Marine and Fisheries Committee, Nov. 3, 1993.

(CIS94:H561-23 iv + 216 p.)
(Y4.M53:103-76.)

5.4 "Rhinoceros and Tiger Conservation Act of 1994," hearings before the Subcommittee on Environment and Natural Resources, House Merchant Marine and Fisheries Committee, May 17, 1994.

(CIS94:H561-55 iii + 58 p.)
(Y4.M53:103-104.)

P.L. 103-391 Documents

103rd Congress

7.1 H. Doc. 103-162, "Violations Relating to Endangered Species, Message from the President," Nov. 8, 1993.

(CIS93:H560-8 i + 2 p.)
(Y1.1/7:103-162.)

Exhibit 55: A CIS legislative history for the Rhinoceros and Tiger Conservation Act of 1994.

c. Compiled Legislative Histories

Gathering a complete legislative history can be a very time-consuming process, since the documents are scattered among many publications and may be difficult to obtain. For some major enactments, however, convenient access is provided by publications which reprint the important bills, debates, committee reports, and hearings. These compiled histories can save the researcher the considerable time and trouble involved in finding relevant references and documents. They are published both by government agencies (particularly the Congressional Research Service of the Library of Congress) and by commercial publishers. Compilations issued by the government are listed and indexed in Bernard D. Reams, Jr., *Federal Legislative Histories: An Annotated Bibliography and Index to Officially Published Sources* (1994). Compiled legislative histories, including bills and committee reports, are available online for several statutes, including major bankruptcy, tax, securities, and environmental acts.

The basic tool for identifying and locating published compiled legislative histories is Nancy P. Johnson's *Sources of Compiled Legislative Histories* (1993). Arranged chronologically by Congress and Public Law number, it provides a checklist of all available compiled legislative histories from 1789 through the 101st Congress, and includes an index by name of act.

§ 7–4. DETERMINING THE STATUS
OF PENDING BILLS

A number of resources, both printed and electronic, are available for researching bills currently before the Congress. Most of these can also be used to research the history of enacted laws as well, but their major strength is that they are frequently updated to provide current information.

Status tables are among the most useful tools for locating and tracing congressional bills. These tables list pending bills by number, indicate actions taken, and provide references to relevant documents. Many status tables include a short summary of each bill.

a. *Congressional Index*

CCH's *Congressional Index* is one of the most useful and current sources of congressional information. Issued in two looseleaf volumes for each Congress, it provides extensive coverage of pending legislation, including an index of bills by subject and author, a digest of each bill, and a status table of actions taken on each bill. This status table contains references to hearings, a feature lacking in many other legislative research aids.

Exhibit 56 shows excerpts from the subject index, bill digest, and status table sections of *Congressional Index*, indicating information on rhinoceros and tiger conservation. Note in the subject index that there are three bills listed on the same topic. Often several similar bills are introduced, and status tables can be used to determine which of these bills is proceeding to consideration and enactment (and which is languishing without attention).

Animal Medicinal Drug Use Clarification Act
   of 1994...S 340
Animals and wildlife
 . endangered species
 . . amendments, economic and property
       rights...H 3978
 . . habitat acquisition, state and local...
       S 2553
 . . private property rights...S 1915; 2451;
       H 3875; 3997; 5073
 . . reauthorization...H 5144
 . . rhinoceros and tigers...S 1925; H 3987; 4924
 . experimentation
 . . Defense Department...H 4971
 . Fish and Wildlife Service
 . . appropriations, FY 1995...H 4602
 . Flower Garden Banks National Marine
       Sanctuary, TX
 . . boundaries...H 3886
 . horses
 . . thoroughbred promotion...S 2512
 . . transportation, humane treatment...
       S 2522

H 4923—Agriculture—dairy products—milk
       marketing orders
   By Barca.
   To equalize the minimum adjustments to
prices for fluid milk under milk marketing orders and to require the Secretary of Agriculture to conduct a study regarding the solids
content of beverage milk. (To Agriculture.)
H 4924—Animals and wildlife—endangered
       species—rhinoceros and tigers
   By Fields (TX), Studds and Bellenson.
   To assist in the conservation of rhinoceros
and tigers by supporting and providing financial
resources for the conservation programs of
nations whose activities directly or indirectly
affect rhinoceros and tiger populations, and of
the CITES Secretariat. (To Merchant Marine
and Fisheries.)
H 4925—Public works—water resources
       projects—reclamation, Redwood Valley
       Water District, CA
   By Hamburg.
   To extend for 1 year the authority of the
Bureau of Reclamation to sell certain loans to
the Redwood Valley Water District. (To Natural
Resources.)

                        * 4924
Introduced..........................8/9/94
Ref to H Merchant Marine Com 8/9/94
Ordered reptd w/o amdts by Com 8/11/94
Reptd w/o amdts, H Rept 103-748, by Com .....
....................................9/26/94
Passed by H (Voice) 9/27/94
Placed on S calendar 9/28/94
Passed by S (Voice) 10/7/94
Signed by President.................10/22/94
Public Law 103-391 (108 Stat 4094) ...10/22/94

                         4925
Introduced..........................8/9/94
Ref to H Natural Resources Com 8/9/94
Ordered reptd w/o amdts by Com 9/28/94
Reptd w/o amdts, H Rept 103-795, by Com .....
....................................10/3/94

Exhibit 56: Excerpts from the subject index, bill digests, and House
Bills status table in CCH's *Congressional Index*.

Congressional Index also provides a wide range of other information on Congress, including lists of members and committee assignments; an index of enactments and vetoes; lists of pending treaties, reorganization plans, and nominations; a table of voting records; and a weekly newsletter on developments in Congress. It does not, however, contain the actual texts of bills or reports.

b. Congressional Quarterly Publications

Congressional Quarterly (CQ) publishes several services on congressional activity. The *Congressional Quarterly Weekly Report* summarizes activity on major legislation, and is most useful for its coverage of new developments and background discussion of pending legislation. It contains tables of House and Senate votes, a status table for major legislation, and a legislative history table for new public laws. The annual *Congressional Quarterly Almanac* cumulates much of the information in the Weekly Report into a useful summary of the congressional session. Exhibit 57 shows a page from the *CQ Weekly Report* summarizing action by the House committee considering H.R. 4924.

CQ also publishes the daily *Congressional Monitor,* which summarizes each day's activities and provides schedules of upcoming actions. It is somewhat similar to the *Congressional Record*'s Daily Digest, but also contains forecasts of expected activity, brief excerpts of important congressional documents, a weekly list of printed hearings, reports and other legislative documents, and a weekly status table of active bills arranged

by broad subject categories. It is not as complete a status table as those discussed previously, and is therefore most useful for quick daily information on major legislative activity.

GOVERNMENT & COMMERCE

ENVIRONMENT

Panel Moves To Stem Poaching Of Rhinos and Tigers

Trying to halt the poaching of rhinoceroses and tigers, the House Merchant Marine and Fisheries Committee approved by voice vote Aug. 11 a bill aimed at protecting these rare animals.

The panel quickly adopted the measure (HR 4924) by ranking Republican Jack Fields of Texas instead of marking up a tougher bill (HR 3987) that would have imposed a moratorium on importing wildlife products from foreign countries that engage in activities harmful to rhinos and tigers.

Fields and Chairman Gerry E. Studds, D-Mass., said they changed markup vehicles to avoid a turf battle with the Ways and Means Committee, which oversees trade issues.

The bill would create a fund to be administered by the Interior secretary for rhino and tiger conservation programs in the animals' home countries. It is modeled after a fund created by Congress in 1988 to protect African elephants as part of the Endangered Species Act reauthorization (PL 100-478).

The measure would authorize $10 million annually for the rhino and tiger fund from fiscal 1996 through fiscal 2000.

Scientists estimate that there were about 1 million rhinos and 100,000 tigers in the world at the turn of the century. Because of poaching and destruction of their habitat, it is estimated that there are now fewer than 11,000 rhinos and 6,000 tigers in the wild.

The trading of rhino and tiger body parts and exportation of products made from them are lucrative businesses. Ground rhinoceros horns, for example, are used to treat headaches and control fevers and are worth as much as $60,000 per kilogram.

Tigers are primarily killed for their fur, but parts of the animal's body are ground and used in medicines to treat pain, kidney and liver problems, and some heart ailments. A pelt is worth up to $14,000, and tiger bone can sell for $900 to $1,300 per kilogram.

The rhino and tiger populations continue to decline even though the animals are protected under an international treaty, the Convention on International Trade in Endangered Species, signed by more than 120 countries.

Last September, Interior Secretary Bruce Babbitt and the treaty's governing body found that China and Taiwan were not doing enough to stem illegal trade of rhino and tiger body parts. In response, President Clinton imposed trade sanctions on Taiwan in April and put China on notice that it could face a similar ban. China avoided sanctions because it has taken limited steps to control illegal trade.

Fields said he still supports tougher sanctions on countries that illegally trade these animal parts even though it is not reflected in his bill. "It should not be viewed as a step back in our leadership position," he said.

By Catalina Camia

ENVIRONMENT

Senate Passes Bill On Waste Hauling

The Senate on Aug. 11 quickly approved by voice vote legislation reauthorizing federal programs for transporting hazardous materials.

Before passing the bill (HR 2178), the Senate backed an unrelated bipartisan amendment aimed at providing regulatory reform for the nation's trucking industry.

That amendment — modeled after a separate bill sponsored by Sens. Jim Exon, D-Neb., and Bob Packwood, R-Ore., (S 2275) to shrink the Interstate Commerce Commission (ICC) by removing some of its trucking duties — also was approved by voice vote. (*Background, Weekly Report, p. 2236*)

The portion of the bill covering the

By Carroll J. Doherty

transport of hazardous materials included the text of an amended version of S 1640, the Senate's hazardous materials reauthorization bill.

The revised bill, sponsored by Exon, would provide $75.3 million from fiscal year 1994 through fiscal year 1997 for programs established by the Hazardous Materials Transportation Act.

Exon said in a statement that the substitute also would implement significant safety changes. It would require the Transportation Department to study the use of new highway technologies to promote safe transport of hazardous materials.

Exon added that the Senate bill made only modest changes in the House version of hazardous materials legislation. The House approved HR 2178 last Nov. 21. (*1993 Almanac, p. 221*)

The amendment proposing changes in regulations for the trucking industry would broaden provisions to clear the way for new entrants to the trucking

industry. That could stimulate greater competition, according to the amendment's proponents.

The Exon-Packwood amendment also would eliminate an existing requirement that most interstate trucking companies file their rates with the ICC, which regulates interstate trucking.

The House has yet to address the issue of regulatory reform for the trucking industry. But it did cut off funding for the ICC in the fiscal 1995 transportation appropriations bill (HR 4556).

Packwood indicated that his amendment would take a more moderate approach by eliminating most of the ICC's role in overseeing interstate trucking. It also would require the ICC to devote more resources to administration of the rail industry.

Packwood said in a statement that the proposal was aimed at avoiding the "uncertainty, confusion and potential chaos that could ensue if we simply eliminate the ICC without a larger strategy."

Exhibit 57: A page from the *CQ Weekly Report.*

Bill-tracking information, daily schedules, information on committee markups and votes, and the text of bills and debates are also available from CQ in its online service, Washington Alert (which is available through WESTLAW). Finally, CQ is the publisher of several reference works on Congress, the most comprehensive of which is *Congressional Quarterly's Guide to Congress* (4th ed. 1991).

c. Electronic Resources

CQ's Washington Alert is just one of several online services providing information on current legislation. LEGI–SLATE, a service of the Washington Post Company, includes the text of bills, committee reports, and the *Congressional Record* from the current Congress. LEGI–SLATE tracks action on each bill day-by-day, providing information such as committee referrals, committee markups, and recorded floor votes. Coverage begins with the 96th Congress in 1979.

The LEXIS file BLTRCK and the WESTLAW database US–BILLTRK also provide up-to-date information on the progress of a bill through Congress. Billcast, a service of George Mason University available through both LEXIS and WESTLAW, attempts to forecast each bill's chances of passage. As noted earlier, the online systems also have databases containing the texts of bills, committee reports, and the *Congressional Record,* as well as a wide range of other information on Congress and its members. Exhibit 58 shows information from a bill-tracking report on LEXIS.

```
                    Copyright (c) 1995 LEXIS-NEXIS,
            a division of Reed Elsevier Inc. All rights reserved.

                          Bill Tracking Report
                              103rd Congress
                                2nd Session

                        U. S. House of Representatives
           103 Bill Tracking H.R. 4924; 1994 Bill Tracking H.R. 4924;

              RHINOCEROS AND TIGER CONSERVATION ACT OF 1994

DATE-INTRO: August 9, 1994

LAST-ACTION-DATE: October 22, 1994

STATUS: Became public law (P.L. 103-391)

SPONSOR: Representative Jack Fields R-TX

TOTAL-COSPONSORS:  2 Cosponsors: 2 Democrats / 0 Republicans

SYNOPSIS:  A bill to assist in the conservation of rhinoceros and tigers by
supporting and providing financial resources for the conservation programs of
nations whose activities directly or indirectly affect rhinoceros and tiger
populations, and of the CITES Secretariat.

ACTIONS: Committee Referrals:
08/09/94 House Merchant Marine and Fisheries Committee

Legislative Chronology:

08/09/94 140 Cong Rec H 7298    Referred to the House Merchant Marine and
                                Fisheries Committee
08/11/94 140 Cong Rec D 986     House Merchant Marine and Fisheries Committee
                                ordered reported
09/26/94 140 Cong Rec H 9761    Reported in the House (H. Rept. 748)
09/27/94 140 Cong Rec H 9873    Passed in the House by voice vote
09/27/94 140 Cong Rec H 9872    House agreed to the committee amendment in the
                                nature of a substitute, by voice vote
09/28/94 140 Cong Rec S 13579   House requested the concurrence of the Senate
09/28/94 140 Cong Rec S 13579   Read the first and second time by unanimous
                                consent, ordered placed on the calendar in the
                                Senate
09/28/94 140 Cong Rec E 1973    Remarks by Rep. Sabo MN
10/07/94 140 Cong Rec S 14960   Passed in the Senate by voice vote -- clearing
                                the measure for the President
10/22/94 140 Cong Rec D 1254    Signed by the President on October 22, 1994
                                (P.L. 103-391)

BILL-DIGEST: (from the CONGRESSIONAL RESEARCH SERVICE)

     Rhinoceros and Tiger Conservation Act of 1994 - Requires the
Secretary of the Interior (Secretary) to provide financial assistance
for conservation of rhinoceros and tiger projects.

     Authorizes the Convention of International Trade Endangered
Species on Wild Fauna and Flora (CITES) Secretariat, or any other
person, to submit to the Secretary a project proposal for the conservation
of such animals.
```

Exhibit 58: An online bill-tracking report on LEXIS.

Through the Internet, GPO Access and THOMAS provide the text of bills, the *Congressional Record*, bill summaries, status information, and news on major bills. Their scope of coverage will undoubtedly expand in the coming years.

d. *Congressional Record* Status Tables

As discussed earlier, the *Congressional Record* includes status tables which can be useful for current and retrospective research. A "History of Bills and Resolutions" table is published in the fortnightly index and cumulated for each session in the bound index volume. It includes a brief summary of each bill, the committee investigating the proposed legislation, and any actions taken on the legislation to date, including amendments and passage. It is the best source of page references to debates within the *Record,* and includes House and Senate Report numbers, if any, and the Public Law numbers of measures enacted. It does not, however, include any references to hearings.

The final cumulative table is not issued for several years after the end of a session, and it is less complete than commercial sources such as *CIS/Index* or *Congressional Index.* The *Congressional Record* has included history tables since 1873, however, and the older tables can be invaluable for retrospective research.

The fortnightly table is available on a more timely basis, but it lists only those bills and resolutions acted upon within the preceding two week period. It may therefore be necessary to consult more than one index to find references to a particular bill. If a bill is listed, however, the information is complete from date of introduction to the present. An entry from this table is illustrated in Exhibit 59.

H.B. 36   CONGRESSIONAL RECORD INDEX

H.R. 4880—Continued
   Cosponsors added. H10007 [28SE]
H.R. 4887—A bill to amend the Nuclear Waste Policy
   Act of 1982 to reaffirm the obligation of the
   Secretary of Energy to provide for the safe disposal
   of spent nuclear fuel beginning not later than January
   31, 1998, and for other purposes; jointly, to the
   Committees on Energy and Commerce; Natural Re-
   sources.
   By Mr. GRAMS, H6698 [2AU]
   Cosponsors added. H6984 [4AU], H8755 [19AU],
   H8770 [20AU], H9087 [12SE], H9351 [20SE],
   H10007 [28SE], H10727 [4OC]
H.R. 4896—A bill to grant the consent of the Congress
   to the Kansas and Missouri Metropolitan Culture
   District Compact; to the Committee on the Judiciary.
   By Mr. WHEAT (for himself and Mrs. Meyers of
   Kansas), H6763 [3AU]
   Debated, H10467 [3OC]
   Text, H10467 [3OC]
   Reported (H. Rept. 103–774), H10536 [3OC]
   Rules suspended. Passed House, H10611 [3OC]
   Passed Senate, S15031 [8OC]

Passed Senate, S14660 [7OC]
H.R. 4924—A bill to assist in the conservation of
   rhinoceros and tigers by supporting and providing
   financial resources for the conservation programs
   of nations whose activities directly or indirectly
   affect rhinoceros and tiger populations, and of the
   CITES Secretariat; to the Committee on Merchant
   Marine and Fisheries.
   By Mr. FIELDS of Texas (for himself, Mr. Studds,
   and Mr. Beilenson), H7298 [9AU]
   Reported (H. Rept. 103–748), H9761 [26SE]
   Committee discharged. Passed House amended, H9869
   [27SE]
   Text, H9870, H9871 [27SE]
   Amendments, H9871 [27SE]
   Placed on the calendar, S13579, S13623 [28SE]
   Passed Senate, S14960 [7OC]
H.R. 4925—A bill to extend for 1 year the authority
   of the Bureau of Reclamation to sell certain loans
   to the Redwood Valley Water District; to the Com-
   mittee on Natural Resources.
   By Mr. HAMBURG, H7298 [9AU]
   Reported (H. Rept. 103–795), H10537 [3OC]

Exhibit 59: Excerpt from a *Congressional Record* "History of Bills and Resolutions" table.

e. Legislative Calendars

Both houses and most committees issue calendars of pending business for the use of their members. Perhaps the most valuable is the House of Representatives' *Numerical Order of Bills and Resolutions Which Have Passed Either or Both Houses, and Bills Now Pending on the Calendar,* which is issued *daily.* Each issue is cumulative and includes all bills in either House or Senate that have been reported out of committee. Committee calendars are also excellent sources of information on upcoming hearings. House and Senate calendars for the current Congress are available on the Internet through GPO Access.

f. Directories and Guides

One of the fastest and simplest ways to find information on pending legislation is to call a congressional staff member responsible for drafting or monitoring the bill.

The *Official Congressional Directory* is published biennially and provides information about individuals, offices
and the organizational structure of Congress. Two commercial directories issued more frequently, with more
extensive lists of phone numbers for staff members, are
Congressional Staff Directory (three times per year) and
Congressional Yellow Book (quarterly). The *Congressional Staff Directory* is available on LEXIS (CONDIR),
and the *Congressional Yellow Book* on WESTLAW (CON-
GYB).

For further information on researching the congres-
sional process, see Judith Manion, Joseph Meringolo &
Robert Oaks, *A Research Guide to Congress: How to
Make Congress Work for You* (2d ed. 1991); or Robert U.
Goehlert & Fenton S. Martin, *Congress and Law–Mak-
ing: Researching the Legislative Process* (2d ed. 1989).
How Our Laws Are Made, by Edward F. Willett, Jr.,
House Law Revision Counsel, is available in print as
House Document 101–139 and online through THOMAS.

§ 7–5. STATE LEGISLATIVE HISTORY

The search for legislative history documents on the
state level can be very difficult. Although almost every
state has a legislative journal, very few of these actually
include transcripts of the debates. Bills are usually
available from the state legislatures on request, but they
are not widely distributed and are hard to locate after
enactment. Only a few states publish committee reports,
and even fewer publish hearings.

Status information on pending bills in state legislatures, on the other hand, is available through a number
of online databases. WESTLAW and LEXIS both have
files for all fifty states to provide the texts of pending

bills and to report on their progress. A number of states have official bill-tracking services or publish digests of current bills, and most have services providing bill status information by telephone.

Many states have official agencies for the recommendation and drafting of new legislation. These groups, including law revision commissions, judicial councils, and legislative councils, recommend new rules or legislation and prepare drafts of bills designed to implement their proposals. Their recommendations are often enacted into law. If so, the published report of the commission or council may provide an invaluable source of legislative history for the resulting enactment. Sources for finding such documents include the *State Government Research Checklist* (Council of State Governments).

Two useful sources for identifying the legislative resources available for each state are Mary L. Fisher's *Guide to State Legislative and Administrative Materials* (4th ed. 1988), and Lynn Hellebust's *State Legislative Sourcebook: A Resource Guide to Legislative Information in the Fifty States* (annual). These publications provide information on the legislative processes in each state and include references to published and online sources.

Directory information on state legislatures, including organization, members, committees, and staffs, is contained in official state manuals (sometimes called *Bluebooks* or *Redbooks*), published annually or biennially by most states. A list of these directories, *State Reference Publications*, is published annually. The Council of State Governments' biennial *Book of the States* is a useful source of varied information on state legislative trends and developments.

§ 7–6. CONCLUSION

Legislative history is sometimes viewed as an arcane and complex field, but it is a basic legal research process. A grasp of the major resources is necessary for any lawyer. Legislative materials are essential tools both in interpreting statutes and in monitoring current legal developments.

In many instances, a review of material reprinted in *USCCAN* may be sufficient to determine whether a further inquiry in legislative resources in necessary. From there a fuller picture may be obtained from *CIS/Index* or other tools. The electronic resources available from the online databases and from the government itself are steadily making information on pending legislation more easily accessible.

CHAPTER 8

ADMINISTRATIVE LAW

----

§ 8–1. INTRODUCTION

Although administrative and executive agencies have existed in this country since its creation, their real growth began with the Industrial Revolution in the late nineteenth century. Increasingly complex problems of society and economy led to an expansion of the traditional functions of executive departments and to the creation of many new administrative agencies.

In this century, two World Wars and an economic depression hastened this development. Congress created new regulatory agencies to carry out its economic legislation when it became apparent that the legislative branch

lacked the expertise and personnel to handle the task. Congress gave the agencies power to promulgate regulations in order to perform their statutory functions, and to hold quasi-judicial hearings to enforce their regulations.   Administrative regulations and decisions have continued to proliferate to this day.

Administrative agencies exist on all levels of our political system: in the federal government, where access to regulations and decisions is achieved with relative ease; in the states, where administrative materials are often difficult to locate; and on the local level, where published texts of regulations and agency decisions are virtually nonexistent.

§ 8–2. BACKGROUND REFERENCE MATERIALS

Research in administrative law requires a preliminary understanding of the structure and functions of the agency under consideration. The most comprehensive source for such information is the *United States Government Manual,* an annual directory of the federal government, with primary emphasis upon the executive branch and regulatory agencies. Each executive department and agency is described with the following coverage:

Citations to statutes creating and affecting the agency

Descriptions of the agency's functions and authority

Information about subsidiary units and predecessor agencies

Names and functions of major officials

Organizational charts

Sources of information available from the agency

The *Manual* is one of the most important reference books of the federal government, and can often save a researcher considerable time by providing quick answers to questions which might otherwise require extensive research. The *Manual* is also available through LEXIS (USGM file) or WESTLAW (US–GOVMAN database), and on the Internet from GPO Access. Exhibit 60 shows parts of the *Government Manual*'s entry for the Consumer Product Safety Commission.

The *Federal Regulatory Directory* (7th ed. 1994) is another useful source of information on activities and personnel, with more extensive entries on the major regulatory agencies than the *Government Manual*. The *Federal Staff Directory* (semiannual) and *Federal Yellow Book* (quarterly) both contain extensive listings of agency personnel and telephone numbers. (Both are also available online—the *Federal Staff Directory* in the FEDDIR file on LEXIS, and the *Federal Yellow Book* in the FEDYB database on WESTLAW.) The *Washington Information Directory* (annual) includes descriptions, addresses and phone numbers for both governmental and nongovernmental agencies in the capital.

The Consumer Product Safety Commission protects the public against unreasonable risks of injury from consumer products; assists consumers in evaluating the comparative safety of consumer products; develops uniform safety standards for consumer products and minimizes conflicting State and local regulations; and promotes research and investigation into the causes and prevention of product-related deaths, illnesses, and injuries.

The Consumer Product Safety Commission is an independent Federal regulatory agency established by the Consumer Product Safety Act (15 U.S.C. 2051 et seq.). The Commission consists of five Commissioners, appointed by the President with the advice and consent of the Senate, one of whom is appointed Chairman.

In addition to the authority created by the Consumer Product Safety Act, the Commission has responsibility for implementing provisions of the Flammable Fabrics Act (15 U.S.C. 1191), the Poison Prevention Packaging Act of 1970 (15 U.S.C. 1471), the Federal Hazardous Substances Act (15 U.S.C. 1261), and the act of August 2, 1956 (15 U.S.C. 1211), which prohibits the transportation of refrigerators without door safety devices.

Activities

To help protect the public from unreasonable risks of injury associated with consumer products, the Commission:

—requires manufacturers to report defects in products that could create substantial hazards;

—requires, where appropriate, corrective action with respect to specific substantially hazardous consumer products already in commerce;

—collects information on consumer product-related injuries and maintains a comprehensive Injury Information Clearinghouse;

—conducts research on consumer product hazards;

—encourages and assists in the development of voluntary standards related to the safety of consumer products;

—establishes, where appropriate, mandatory consumer product standards;

—bans, where appropriate, hazardous consumer products; and

—conducts outreach programs for consumers, industry, and local governments.

Offices

The Commission's headquarters is located at East West Towers, 4330 East West Highway, Bethesda, MD 20814. Regional offices are located in Chicago, IL; New York, NY; and San Francisco, CA. Field offices are maintained in various cities.

Sources of Information

Consumer Information The Commission operates a toll-free Consumer Product Safety Hotline, 800–638–CPSC; and a teletypewriter for the hearing-impaired, 800–638–8270 (or in Maryland only, 800–492–8140).
General Inquiries Information on Commission activities may be obtained from the Office of Information and Public Affairs, Consumer Product Safety Commission, Washington, DC 20207. Phone, 301–504–0580.
Reading Room A public information room is maintained at the Commission.

For further information, contact the Office of Information and Public Affairs, Consumer Product Safety Commission, East West Towers, 4330 East West Highway, Bethesda, MD 20814. Phone, 301–504–0580.

Exhibit 60: Excerpts from an entry in the *United States Government Manual.*

§ 8–3. PUBLICATION OF FEDERAL REGULATIONS

To some extent federal regulations follow the publication paradigm of statutes; they are first issued chronologically and then codified by subject. Because there are so many agencies issuing such a large body of regulations, however, administrative law has developed its own distinct system. This system is based on a *daily* publication which serves as the counterpart to session laws and also provides notices of proposed regulatory actions and explanations of actions taken.

a. *Federal Register*

As more and more executive and administrative orders and regulations were promulgated in the early New Deal period, locating regulations and determining which were in effect became increasingly difficult. There was no requirement that regulations be published or centrally filed. Two important cases reached the U.S. Supreme Court before it was discovered that the administrative regulations on which they were based were no longer in effect. The press and opponents of the New Deal criticized the government for prosecuting people under nonexistent laws.

This furor led Congress in 1935 to establish the *Federal Register* as a daily gazette for executive and administrative promulgations. The *Register* began publication on March 14, 1936 as a chronological source for administrative documents, similar to a session law text. As with statutes, however, chronological publication by itself was

insufficient to provide access to current regulations by subject. A 1937 amendment to the Federal Register Act created the *Code of Federal Regulations,* with provisions for indexing and supplementation.

To have general legal effect, executive orders and administrative regulations must be published in the *Federal Register.* A regulation which is not published in the *Register* is not binding unless one can be shown to have had *actual* and *timely* notice of the regulation.

In addition to new regulations, the *Federal Register* also contains *proposed rules,* affording the public an opportunity to comment on the regulations which agencies plan to adopt; *presidential documents*; and *notices* of meetings and other regulatory activities. The *Register* generally provides agencies' explanations of proposed rules, and their responses to comments received from interested parties. Exhibits 61 and 62 show a new regulation of the Consumer Product Safety Commission, and part of the agency's explanation of the reason for the regulation, as published in the *Federal Register.*

Each daily *Federal Register* begins with a table of contents and a list noting the *Code of Federal Regulations* citations of new or proposed regulations in the issue. The table of contents is organized alphabetically by agency, so researchers with specialized interests can easily monitor an agency's activity. A portion of the table of contents for the issue containing the regulation in the previous exhibits is shown in Exhibit 63. Exhibit 64 shows part of the list of *CFR* parts affected in the same *Federal Register* issue.

2. *General Software Note.* General License GTDR, without written assurance, is available to all destinations, except Country Groups S and Z, Iran, and Syria, for release of software that is generally available to the public by being:

*   *   *   *   *

Supplement No. 1 to § 799.2 [Amended]

3. In Supplement No. 1 to §799.2 (Interpretations), Interpretations Nos. 24, 25, and 26 are removed.

Dated: October 12, 1995.

Sue E. Eckert,
Assistant Secretary for Export Administration.

[FR Doc. 95-25742 Filed 10-16-95; 8:45 am]
BILLING CODE 3610-DT-P

CONSUMER PRODUCT SAFETY COMMISSION

16 CFR Part 1700

Poison Prevention Packaging Requirements; Exemption of Certain Iron Containing Dietary Supplement Powders

AGENCY: Consumer Product Safety Commission.

ACTION: Final rule.

SUMMARY: The Commission is amending its regulations to exempt from child-resistant packaging requirements those dietary supplement powders that have no more than the equivalent of 0.12 percent weight-to-weight elemental iron. The Commission issues this exemption because there are no known poisoning incidents with these products, and the dry powdered form deters children from ingesting them in harmful amounts.

DATES: The exemption is effective on October 17, 1995.

FOR FURTHER INFORMATION CONTACT:
Michael Bogumill, Division of Regulatory Management, Consumer Product Safety Commission, Washington, DC 20207; telephone (301) 504-0400 ext. 1368.

SUPPLEMENTARY INFORMATION:

A. Background

In 1978, the Consumer Product Safety Commission ("the Commission") required child-resistant packaging ("CRP") for drugs and dietary supplements that contain iron. 16 CFR 1700.14(a) (12) and (13). The Commission issued these rules under the Poison Prevention Packaging Act ("PPPA"), 15 U.S.C. 1471–1476, which authorizes the Commission to require CRP to protect children under 5 years of age from poisoning hazards posed by harmful household substances.

Specifically, CRP is required for dietary supplements "that contain an equivalent of 250 milligrams or more of elemental iron, from any source, in a single package in concentrations of 0.025 percent or more on a weight-to-volume basis for liquids and 0.05 percent or more on a weight-to-weight basis for nonliquids." 16 CFR 1700.14(a)(13). This requirement does not apply if iron is present only as a colorant. *Id.*

On May 11, 1994, Nutritech, Inc. ("Nutritech"), petitioned the Commission to exempt unflavored, unsweetened iron powders from CRP requirements for dietary supplements containing iron. Nutritech manufactures an unsweetened, unflavored vitamin, mineral, and amino acid powder intended to be mixed with fruit juice. The petitioner stated several reasons why CRP is unnecessary for this dietary supplement. (1) [1] The Commission published a notice in the Federal Register on August 4, 1994, soliciting comments on the petition, 59 FR 39747, and received no responses.

B. Proposed Rule and Comment

On April 7, 1995, the Commission published a notice granting Nutritech's petition to initiate rulemaking and proposing to exempt certain powdered iron-containing dietary supplements from CRP requirements. 60 FR 17660. The Commission proposed that the exemption would apply to dietary supplement powders, both flavored and unflavored, with no more than the equivalent of 0.12 percent w/w elemental iron.

In response to the proposed rule, the Commission received one comment. The comment, submitted on behalf of an organization called SI Metric, objected that the proposed regulation did not use proper SI metric terminology. The Commission has considered the comment and has made some changes in the preamble to ensure that measurements are presented in metric terminology. However, the Commission declines to make some changes suggested by the commenter—for example, using the term mass rather than weight. The Commission also believes that its expression of the percentage of concentration of iron for liquids and non-liquids as weight-to-volume ("w/v") or weight-to-weight ("w/w") measurements is appropriate. Based on the United States Pharmacopeia guidelines, the percent

w/v refers to the number of grams of a constituent in 100 milliliters of solution, and the percent w/w is the number of grams of a constituent in 100 grams of solution or mixture. The Commission believes that its use of terminology is consistent with throughout the Federal government. Moreover, the terminology is consistent with other regulations under the PPPA.

C. Toxicity Data

The minimum toxic and lethal doses of iron are not well defined. Generally, doses of elemental iron from 20 to 60 milligrams per kilogram of body weight ("mg/kg") may produce mild symptoms of poisoning, 60 mg/kg is the minimal dose for serious toxicity, and approximately 180 to 250 mg/kg is considered a lethal dose. However, fatalities of young children have been reported at lower doses. (2)(3)

According to the relevant scientific and medical literature, where information on the formulation was available, the majority of pediatric poisoning incidents involved solid iron—in the form of tablets or capsules—with the remaining cases involving liquid preparations. Among the reported ingestion incidents, fatalities and serious cases of toxicity usually involve ingestion of adult preparations (such as prenatal vitamins) that contain 60 mg or more of elemental iron per tablet. The literature search did not identify a single case of pediatric poisoning involving powdered iron formulations. (2)(3)(5)

When the Food and Drug Administration ("FDA") published proposed labeling and packaging requirements for iron-containing dietary supplements and drugs, 59 FR 51030 (October 6, 1994), it decided to limit the proposed rules to products in solid oral dosage forms (tablets and capsules) and not include liquid or powder products. (2)

The Commission's own 1994 study of pediatric iron poisonings and fatalities found that the majority of serious outcomes involved products in solid or capsule form. The report showed that all 38 of the in-depth investigations of iron ingestion deaths of children under 5 years old occurring between 1988 and 1993 involved solid capsule or tablet formulations. In 1993, 57 hospital emergency room cases documented through NEISS involved ingestion of iron capsules or tablets by children under 5 years old, and one involved liquid iron. As noted, there were no known pediatric poisonings that involved powdered formulations. This study was based on data from the Commission's National Electronic Injury

---

[1] Numbers in parentheses identify documents listed at the end of this notice.

Exhibit 61: *Federal Register* page, showing background information on new regulation.

availability of dietary supplement powders with no more than the equivalent of 0.12 percent weight-to-weight elemental iron are such that special packaging is not required to protect children from serious personal injury or serious illness resulting from handling, or ingesting such substance. Accordingly, the Commission voted to grant the petition and proposed to amend 16 CFR 1700.14(a)(13) to exempt from requirements for child resistant packaging those dietary supplement powders with no more than the equivalent of 0.12 percent weight-to-weight elemental iron. 60 FR 17660 (April 7, 1995).

After considering all available and relevant information, the Commission determines to issue the proposed exemption on a final basis.

G. Regulatory Flexibility Certification

Under the Regulatory Flexibility Act (Pub. L. 96–354, 5 U.S.C. 601 *et seq.*), when an agency issues proposed and final rules, it must examine the rules' potential impact on small businesses. The Act requires agencies to prepare and make available for public comment an initial regulatory flexibility analysis if a proposed rule would have a significant impact on a substantial number of small businesses, small organizations, and small governmental jurisdictions.

When the Commission proposed to exempt powdered iron-containing dietary supplements from CRP requirements, it found that the exemption would not have any significant economic impact on a substantial number of small entities. The exemption will give manufacturers of these products the option of packaging products using any packaging they choose. As far as CPSC is aware, powdered iron-containing dietary supplements are not currently packaged in CRP. The Commission's Compliance staff is exercising its enforcement discretion regarding these products pending completion of this rulemaking. Thus, the exemption will bring no change in the current packaging of products subject to the exemption. The Commission is not aware of any information that would alter its conclusion that this exemption will not have any significant economic effect on a substantial number of small entities.

H. Environmental Considerations

The Commission's regulations at 16 CFR 1021.5(c)(3) state that rules exempting products from child-resistant packaging requirements under the PPPA normally have little or no potential for affecting the human environment. The Commission did not foresee any special or unusual circumstances surrounding the proposed rule and found that exempting these products from the PPPA requirements would have little or no effect on the human environment. For this reason, when the Commission issued the proposed exemption, it concluded that no environmental assessment or impact statement is required in this proceeding. That conclusion remains unchanged.

I. Effective Date

Because this rule provides for an exemption, no delay in the effective date is required. 5 U.S.C. 553(d)(1). Accordingly, the rule shall become effective upon publication of the final rule in the **Federal Register**.

List of Subjects in 16 CFR Part 1700

Consumer protection, Infants and children, Packaging and containers, Poison prevention, Toxic substances.

Conclusion

For the reasons given above, the Commission amends Title 16 of the Code of Federal Regulations to read as follows:

PART 1700—[AMENDED]

1. The authority citation for part 1700 continues to read as follows:

Authority: 15 U.S.C. 1471–1476. Secs. 1700.1 and 1700.14 also issued under 15 U.S.C. 2079(a)

2. Section 1700.14(a)(13) is revised to read as follows:

§ 1700.14 Substances requiring special packaging.

(a) * * *

(13) *Dietary supplements containing iron.* Dietary supplements, as defined in § 1700.1(a)(3), that contain an equivalent of 250 mg or more of elemental iron, from any source, in a single package in concentrations of 0.025 percent or more on a weight-to-volume basis for liquids and 0.05 percent or more on a weight-to-weight basis for nonliquids (e.g., powders, granules, tablets, capsules, wafers, gels, viscous products, such as pastes and ointments, etc.) shall be packaged in accordance with the provisions of § 1700.15 (a), (b), and (c), except for the following:

(i) Preparations in which iron is present solely as a colorant; and

(ii) Powdered preparations with no more than the equivalent of 0.12 percent weight-to-weight elemental iron.

* * * * *

Dated: October 6, 1995.

Sadye E. Dunn,

Secretary, Consumer Product Safety Commission.

Reference Documents

The following documents contain information relevant to this rulemaking proceeding and are available for inspection at the Office of the Secretary, Consumer Product Safety Commission, Washington, Room 502, 4330 East-West Highway, Bethesda, Maryland 20814.

1. Briefing Memorandum with attached briefing package, March 14, 1995.

2. Memorandum from Sandra E. Inkster, Ph.D., HSPS, to Jacqueline N. Ferrante, Ph.D., HSPS, "Review of Iron Toxicity: Relevance to a Petition Requesting Exemption for Powdered, Iron-Containing Dietary Supplements," February 15, 1995.

3. Memorandum from Catherine A. Sedney, EPHF, to Jacqueline N. Ferrante, Ph.D., HSPS, "Petition to Exempt Iron-Containing Supplement Powders from PPPA Requirements," February 16, 1995.

4. Memorandum from Marcia P. Robins, EPSS, to Jacqueline N. Ferrante, Ph.D., HSPS, "Preliminary Market Information: Petition for Exemption from Child-Resistant Packaging Requirements for Powdered Iron-Containing Dietary Supplements," March 10, 1995.

5. Briefing Memorandum with attached briefing package, September 19, 1995.

6. Memorandum from Marcia P. Robins, EPSS, to Jacqueline N. Ferrante, Ph.D., HSPS, Final Regulatory Flexibility Act Issues: Petition for Exemption from Child-Resistant Packaging Requirements for Powdered Iron-Containing Dietary Supplements," July 5, 1995.

[FR Doc. 95–25322 Filed 10–16–95: 8:45 am]

BILLING CODE 6355-01-P

DEPARTMENT OF HEALTH AND HUMAN SERVICES

Food and Drug Administration

21 CFR Part 558

New Animal Drugs For Use In Animal Feeds; Decoquinate

AGENCY: Food and Drug Administration, HHS.

ACTION: Final rule.

SUMMARY: The Food and Drug Administration (FDA) is amending the animal drug regulations to reflect approval of a supplemental new animal drug application (NADA) filed by Rhone-Poulenc, Inc. The supplemental NADA provides for use of decoquinate Type A medicated articles to make Type C medicated feeds for young sheep for the prevention of certain forms of coccidiosis.

EFFECTIVE DATE: October 17, 1995.

FOR FURTHER INFORMATION CONTACT: Melanie R. Berson, Center for Veterinary

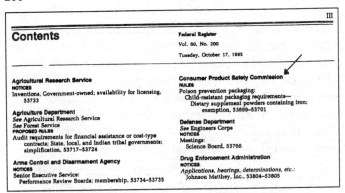

Exhibit 63: Portion of *Federal Register* table of contents.

Exhibit 64: List of CFR Parts Affected in a daily issue of the *Federal Register.*

Several readers' aids are provided in the back of each issue, including telephone numbers for information and assistance, a listing of *Federal Register* pages and dates for the month, and a list of new public laws. The most important of these readers' aids is a cumulative list of *CFR* parts affected since the beginning of the month. This list is one of the basic tools for determining the current status of federal regulations.

An index to the *Federal Register,* arranged by agency rather than by subject, is published monthly. Each index cumulates references since the beginning of the year. More detailed indexing and more current coverage are provided by the *CIS Federal Register Index,* which is issued weekly with bound semiannual volumes.

The *Federal Register* is also available online through the major database systems. Coverage begins in the summer of 1980, with new issues online within a week of publication. The *Register* is in WESTLAW's FR database, and on LEXIS it is in the FEDREG file of the CODES or GENFED library. Free access over the Internet is available through GPO Access, beginning with volume 59 (1994).

The *Register* has permanent reference value because it includes some material which never appears in the *Code of Federal Regulations.* It provides the only complete history of regulations with the text of all changes, and includes the following documents which may not be carried over to the *CFR*: descriptions of agency organization and reorganization, proposed rules, policy statements relating to the adoption of new rules, and rules which have been repealed. Researching the histories of administrative agency regulations would be impossible without access to the *Federal Register.*

A detailed explanation of the *Federal Register* is provided in the Office of the Federal Register's *The Federal Register: What It Is and How to Use It* (rev. ed. 1992).

b. *Code of Federal Regulations*

The first *Code of Federal Regulations* was published in 1938. The set now consists of over two hundred paperback volumes which are revised and reissued each year. The regulations in the *CFR* are collected from the *Federal Register* and arranged in a subject scheme of fifty titles, similar to that of the *U.S. Code*. The titles are divided into chapters, each containing the regulations of a specific agency. The back of every *CFR* volume contains an alphabetical list of federal agencies indicating the title and chapter of each agency's regulations.

CFR chapters are divided into parts, each of which covers a particular topic. Finally parts are divided into sections, the basic unit of the *CFR*. Exhibit 65 shows a sample page of the *CFR* from Title 16 (Commercial Practices), Chapter II (Consumer Product Safety Commission), Part 1700 (Poison Prevention Packaging). A citation to the *CFR* provides the title, section, and year of publication: 16 C.F.R. § 1700.1 (1995).

Consumer Product Safety Commission   § 1700.1

SUBCHAPTER E—POISON PREVENTION PACKAGING ACT OF 1970 REGULATIONS

PART 1700—POISON PREVENTION PACKAGING

Sec.
1700.1 Definitions.
1700.2 Authority.
1700.3 Establishment of standards for special packaging.
1700.4 Effective date of standards.
1700.5 Noncomplying package requirements.
1700.14 Substances requiring special packaging.
1700.15 Poison prevention packaging standards.
1700.20 Testing procedure for special packaging.

AUTHORITY: Pub. L. 91–601, secs. 1–9, 84 Stat. 1670–74, 15 U.S.C. 1471–76. Secs. 1700.1 and 1700.14 also issued under Pub. L. 92–573, sec. 30(a), 88 Stat. 1231, 15 U.S.C. 2079(a).

SOURCE: 38 FR 21247, Aug. 7, 1973, unless otherwise noted.

§ 1700.1 Definitions.

(a) As used in this part:

(1) *Act* means the Poison Prevention Packaging Act of 1970 (Pub. L. 91–601, 84 Stat. 1670–74; 15 U.S.C. 1471–75), enacted December 30, 1970.

(2) *Commission* means the Consumer Product Safety Commission established by section 4 of the Consumer Product Safety Act (86 Stat. 1210; 15 U.S.C. 2053).

(3) *Dietary supplement* means any vitamin and/or mineral preparation offered in tablet, capsule, wafer, or other similar uniform unit form; in powder, granule, flake, or liquid form; or in the physical form of a conventional food but which is not a conventional food; and which purports or is represented to be for special dietary use by humans to supplement their diets by increasing the total dietary intake of one or more of the essential vitamins and/or minerals.

(b) Except for the definition of "Secretary," which is obsolete, the definitions given in section 2 of the act are applicable to this part and are repeated herein for convenience as follows:

(1) [Reserved]

(2) *Household substance* means any substance which is customarily produced or distributed for sale for consumption or use, or customarily stored, by individuals in or about the household and which is:

(i) A hazardous substance as that term is defined in section 2(f) of the Federal Hazardous Substances Act (15 U.S.C. 1261(f));

(ii) A food, drug, or cosmetic as those terms are defined in section 201 of the Federal Food, Drug, and Cosmetic Act (21 U.S.C. 321); or

(iii) A substance intended for use as fuel when stored in a portable container and used in the heating, cooking, or refrigeration system of a house.

(3) *Package* means the immediate container or wrapping in which any household substance is contained for consumption, use, or storage by individuals in or about the household and, for purposes of section 4(a)(2) of the act, also means any outer container or wrapping used in the retail display of any such substance to consumers. "Package" does not include:

(i) Any shipping container or wrapping used solely for the transportation of any household substance in bulk or in quantity to manufacturers, packers, or processors, or to wholesale or retail distributors thereof; or

(ii) Any shipping container or outer wrapping used by retailers to ship or deliver any household substance to consumers unless it is the only such container or wrapping.

(4) *Special packaging* means packaging that is designed or constructed to be significantly difficult for children under 5 years of age to open or obtain a toxic or harmful amount of the substance contained therein within a reasonable time and not difficult for normal adults to use properly, but does not mean packaging which all such children cannot open or obtain a toxic or harmful amount within a reasonable time.

(5) *Labeling* means all labels and other written, printed, or graphic matter upon any household substance or

669

Exhibit 65: Federal agency regulation as compiled in the *Code of Federal Regulations*.

At the beginning of each *CFR* part there is an *authority note* showing the statutory authority under which the regulations have been issued. After this note, or at the end of each section, there is a *source note,* providing the citation and date of the *Federal Register* in which the regulation was last published in full. This reference is very useful for finding background information and comments explaining the regulations. In Exhibit 65, note that the regulations are issued under the authority of 15 U.S.C. § 1471–76, and that the source for Part 1700 generally is 38 FR 21247, Aug. 7, 1973.

CFR volumes are updated and replaced on a rotating cycle throughout the year. The revisions of the various titles are issued on a quarterly basis—Titles 1–16 with regulations in force as of January 1; titles 17–27 as of April 1; titles 28–41 as of July 1; and titles 42–50 as of October 1.

The *CFR* is accompanied by monthly pamphlets entitled *LSA: List of CFR Sections Affected,* which cumulate references to all changes since the latest annual revision of the titles in the *Code of Federal Regulations.* *LSA* lists *Federal Register* pages of any new or proposed rules affecting *CFR* sections, and indicates the nature of the change with notes such as "amended," "removed," or "revised." Exhibit 66 shows a page from the October 1995 *LSA,* indicating that several sections of 16 *CFR* were revised, removed, or added in 1995, and referring to the *Federal Register* issue shown in Exhibits 61 and 62.

68　　　LSA—LIST OF CFR SECTIONS AFFECTED

CHANGES JANUARY 3, 1995 THROUGH OCTOBER 31, 1995

Exhibit 66: Notice of new regulations in *LSA: List of CFR Sections Affected.*

Each *LSA* issue cumulates all changes since the latest *CFR* edition. Unless the *CFR* volume is more than a year old, it is only necessary to examine the most recent monthly issue. *LSA* brings a search for current regulations up to date within a month or two. The very latest changes can then be found by using the cumulative List of CFR Parts Affected in the last *Federal Register* issue for each month not covered in *LSA*. These lists in the *Register* thus serve as a daily supplement to the *CFR* and *LSA*.

The *CFR* pamphlets may not reflect all of the changes made during the year if sections were modified more than once. As noted above, the *Federal Register* therefore remains the only source for obtaining *all* of the different versions which may have been in effect, even briefly, during the year.

In the back of each *CFR* volume there is a list of sections that have been repealed, transferred, or otherwise changed since 1986. Changes from 1949 to 1985 are listed in a separate series of *List of CFR Sections Affected* volumes for the entire *CFR*. These lists are useful in researching the history of a regulation or in tracking down a reference to an older *CFR* section no longer appearing in the current annual edition.

The *CFR* includes an annually revised "Index and Finding Aids" volume providing access by agency name and subject. Exhibit 67 shows a sample page from this index. In addition, much more detailed subject access is provided in CIS's multivolume *Index to the Code of Federal Regulations* (annual).

The current edition of the *CFR* is also available online from LEXIS and WESTLAW. Both systems also have

---

Plutonium   **CFR Index**

Pears, plums, and peaches grown in
  California, 7 CFR 917
Prunes grown in designated counties in
  Washington and in Umatilla County,
  Oregon, 7 CFR 924

Plutonium
Air transportation of plutonium, 10 CFR 871

Pneumoconiosis
See Black lung benefits

Poison prevention
See also Lead poisoning
Federal Caustic Poison Act, 21 CFR 1230
Formal evidentiary public hearing
  procedures, 16 CFR 1502
Poison prevention packaging, 16 CFR 1700
  Applications for exemption from
    preemption of State and local
    requirements, 16 CFR 1061
  Exemption petitions procedures and
    requirements, 16 CFR 1702
  Policy and interpretation statements, 16
    CFR 1701
Public Health Service, requests for health
  hazard evaluations, 42 CFR 85
Toxic substances control, administrative
  assessment of civil penalties and
  revocation or suspension of permits,
  consolidated practice rules, 40 CFR 22

Police
See Law enforcement officers

**Political activities (Government
employees)**
ACTION, prohibitions on electoral and
  lobbying activities, 45 CFR 1226
Civil service
  Political activity of Federal employees, 5
    CFR 734
    Residing in designated localities, 5 CFR
      733
  Prohibited practices, 5 CFR 4
Community Services Office, grantee
  personnel management, 45 CFR 1069
General Accounting Office, 4 CFR 7
Legal Services Corporation, 45 CFR 1608
State or local officers or employees, 5 CFR
  151

Political affiliation discrimination
ACTION, 45 CFR 1225

Job Training Partnership Act,
  nondiscrimination and equal opportunity
  requirements, 29 CFR 34
Prisons Bureau, 28 CFR 551

Political candidates
See also Campaign funds
Air carriers, credit extension to political
  candidates, 14 CFR 374a
Aircraft operators, carriage of candidates in
  Federal elections, 14 CFR 91
Cable television service, 47 CFR 76
Candidate status and designations for Federal
  office, 11 CFR 101
Communications common carriers,
  miscellaneous rules, 47 CFR 64
Debts owed by candidates and political
  committees, 11 CFR 116
Election campaign documents, filing, 11
  CFR 105
Federal office candidates or their
  representatives, credit extension for
  transportation, 49 CFR 1325
Radio broadcast services, 47 CFR 73

Political committees and parties
Campaign fund allocations of candidate and
  committee activities, 11 CFR 106
Campaign fund reports by political
  committees, 11 CFR 104
Debts owed by candidates and political
  committees, 11 CFR 116
Depositaries for campaign funds, 11 CFR
  103
Election campaign documents, filing, 11
  CFR 105
Income taxes, exempt organizations, political
  organizations, 26 CFR 1 (1.527-1—
  1.527-9)
Political committees registration,
  organization, and recordkeeping, 11
  CFR 102
Presidential election campaign financing,
  contribution and expenditure limitations
  and prohibitions, 11 CFR 110
Presidential nominating conventions
  Federal financing, 11 CFR 9008
  Registration, and reports, 11 CFR 107

552

Exhibit 67: A page from the subject index in the "Index and Finding
Aids" volume of *CFR*.

databases containing prior editions of CFR, and LEXIS has a combined file of both Register and CFR, called ALLREG. Internet access to the CFR is available through the House of Representative's Internet Law Library.

§ 8–4. RESEARCH IN FEDERAL REGULATIONS

There are several methods of finding federal regulations. In addition to the official and commercial indexes for the *Federal Register* and the *Code of Federal Regulations,* and online access through the database systems, numerous other sources provide references to relevant regulations.

Both annotated editions of the United States Code contain cross-references to regulations in the notes following specific sections. In addition, the "Index and Finding Aids" volume of the *Code of Federal Regulations* contains a "Parallel Table of Authorities and Rules," allowing a researcher with a statute or presidential document to find regulations enacted under its authority.

Administrative regulations on selected subjects, such as taxation, labor relations, and securities, also appear in commercially published looseleaf services. The regulations are well indexed and frequently supplemented, usually on a weekly basis. For that reason and also because of their integration with other relevant primary sources and interpretive material, researchers often turn to looseleaf services, if available, for convenient and current access to administrative regulations.

Both WESTLAW and LEXIS provide comprehensive access to federal regulations, and both include special-

ized databases in a number of federal regulatory fields. These topical "libraries" contain relevant regulations and administrative decisions, as well as statutes and judicial decisions. Online searches can often retrieve a variety of legal documents with greater speed and effectiveness than traditional methods.

Shepard's Code of Federal Regulations Citations provides citations to federal and state court decisions and to articles in selected law journals which have cited or discussed sections of the *Code of Federal Regulations*. Because the *CFR* itself is not annotated, this is the only published source with comprehensive coverage of judicial treatment of regulations. *Shepard's CFR Citations* does not, however, indicate amendments or other changes in the regulations themselves. Shepard's indicates the year of the *CFR* edition cited (with an asterisk), or the year of the citing reference if no *CFR* edition is specified (with a delta). As in Shepard's statutory citators, alphabetical symbols indicate significant impact of court decisions on cited regulations. Exhibit 68 shows a page from this citator, listing decisions under regulations in Title 16 of *CFR*. Note that various sections in Part 1700 have been cited in several court decisions, *ALR* annotations, and a *Northwestern University Law Review* article. No published decisions have addressed the validity of Part 1700, but various sections in Part 1615 have been found constitutional (C) and others void and invalid (V).

In order to make a complete search for a current regulation, the researcher should follow these steps:

(a) Consult the subject index in the "Index and Finding Aids" volume of the *Code of Federal Regula-*

CODE OF FEDERAL REGULATIONS			TITLE 17

§ 1512.18(d)(2)(v)
Cir. DC
C559F2d791°1976

§ 1512.18(d)(2)(vi)
Cir. DC
C559F2d791°1976

§ 1512.18(j)
Cir. DC
C559F2d796°1976

§ 1512.18(k)(1)
Cir. DC
C559F2d796°1976

§ 1512.18(k)(2)
Cir. DC
C559F2d796°1976

§ 1512.18(m)
Cir. DC
C559F2d797°1976

§ 1512.18(n)
Cir. DC
C559F2d797°1976

§ 1512.19
Cir. DC
Up559F2d786°1976

Part 1602
Cir. 2
614FS233°1984
Md
481A2d253△1984

§ 1602.1
et seq.
Cir. 8
532FS919°1977

§ 1602.2(e)
Cir. 5
632F2d1260°1979

Part 1605
55NYL370°1980

§ 1610.3
Cir. 8
532FS920°1977

§ 1610.3(a)(2)
Minn
297NW733°1977

§ 1610.4
Cir. 8
532FS919°1977
Minn
297NW733°1977
N Y
414NYS2d331△1979

§§ 1613.211 to 1613.282
Cir. 9
780FS1280△1991

Part 1615
Cir. 2
725F2d186°1983
Cir. 4
Vp666F2d84°1980
434FS418°1971
Cir. DC
721F2d387°1983

§ 1615.1(a)
Cir. 2
C725F2d187△1984
C564FS1404△1983
Cir. 4
666F2d84°1980

§ 1615.1(c)
Cir. 2
C564FS1404°1982
Cir. 4
666F2d84°1980
Cir. 8
488FS894△1980

§ 1615.2(b)
Cir. 2
C564FS1404°1982

§ 1615.3
et seq.
Cir. 2
564FS1403°1982

§ 1615.31(a)(3)
Cir. 8
488FS894△1980

§ 1615.31(b)(4)
Cir. 8
488FS893△1980

§ 1615.31(b)(5)
Cir. 8
488FS893△1980

§ 1615.31(b)(6)
Cir. 8
488FS893△1980

§ 1615.64
Cir. 2
725F2d187°1982
564FS1404°1982
Cir. 4
V666F2d84°1980

§ 1615.65
Cir. 4
V666F2d84°1980

Part 1616
Cir. DC
721F2d387°1983

§ 1616.2(a)
Cir. 4
666F2d84△1981

§§ 1630.1 to 1630.5
Cir. 4
635F2d300△1980
Cir. 11
737F2d990△1984

§ 1630.4
Cir. 11
737F2d991°1984

§ 1630.31(a)
Cir. 11
737F2d990△1984

§ 1630.31(a)(6)
Cir. 11
737F2d991△1984

§ 1630.31(c)
Cir. 11
737F2d990△1984 ←

Part 1700
Ill
483NE941△1985

§ 1700.1
et seq.
Cir. 5
695F2d160△1983

§ 1700.1(b)(2)(i)
Cir. 7
778FS1431°1991
14△66n△1993

§ 1700.14
Cir. 2
539FS353°1981
87△RF604n

§ 1700.14(a)(7)
Cir. 6
778FS1431°1990
Cir. 7
778FS1431°1990
14△66n△1993

§ 1700.14(a)(10)
Cir. 7
759FS455△1991
Cir. 8
766F2d1193△1985
75NwL985°1980
87△RF637n

§ 1700.15
Cir. 2
539FS353°1981
87△RF604n△1988

§ 1700.15(a)
Cir. 7
778FS1431°1990
Cir. 7
778FS1431°1990
14△66n△1993

§ 1700.15(b)
Cir. 6
778FS1431°1990
Cir. 7
778FS1431°1990
14△66n△1993

T.16Appendix

Part 438
Appendix A
Cir. 2
612F2d644°1979
Appendix B
Cir. 2
612F2d644°1979
Appendix C
Cir. 2
612F2d644°1979
Part 600
Cir. 5
975F2d1096°1991
987F2d292°1992
9F3d1173°1993

§ 600.2
Cir. 5
777FS491△1991

TITLE 17

Cir. 2
131FRD419△1990
Cir. 7
724FS551△1989

Parts 0 to 199
Cir. 2
577FS855△1984

§ 0.3
409US299△1973
34LE533△1973
93SC579△1973
Cir. 7
447F2d719△1971

§ 0.3(a)
409US311△1973
34LE541△1973
93SC585△1973

§ 0.3(b)
409US311△1973
34LE541△1973
93SC585△1973

§ 0.3(c)
Cir. 2
466FS1358°1971

§ 0.7
Cir. 7
547F2d48°1975

§ 0.7(d)
Cir. 7
547F2d50°1975

§ 0.8
409US299△1973
34LE533△1973
93SC579△1973
Cir. 7
447F2d719△1971

§ 0.12
Cir. 7
547F2d48°1975

§ 0.12(a)
Cir. 7
547F2d50°1975

§ 0.12(b)
Cir. 7
547F2d50°1975

§ 0.13
Cir. 7
547F2d48°1975

§ 0.13(a)
Cir. 7
547F2d50°1975

§ 0.13(b)
Cir. 7
547F2d48°1975

397

Exhibit 68: A page from *Shepard's Code of Federal Regulations Citations*.

tions to ascertain the relevant title and section of the *CFR*, or find a *CFR* reference in an annotated code or other source.

(b) Locate the regulation in the current annual edition of its *CFR* title, noting the date of the latest revision.

(c) Check the latest monthly pamphlet of *LSA* to determine if changes in the section have occurred since the last revision.

(d) Use the cumulative List of CFR Parts Affected in the most recent issue of the *Federal Register*. This list updates the *LSA* pamphlet by indicating any changes made within the current month. Depending on the dates covered in the most recent *LSA*, it may be necessary to check the last *Federal Register* in the preceding month as well.

(e) Locate the changes that have occurred by consulting the pages in daily issues of the *Federal Register* referred to in the lists in steps (c) and (d).

(f) Shepardize the regulation in Shepard's *Code of Federal Regulations Citations* to obtain citations to decisions interpreting it.

Some of these steps can be avoided by using electronic resources or a looseleaf service, if available. Because computer databases or looseleaf services may not contain the latest text of a regulation or may not provide references to all the cases listed in Shepard's, steps (d), (e) and (f) should still be employed to ensure that the regulation in question is current and valid.

§ 8–5. ADMINISTRATIVE DECISIONS
AND RULINGS

Besides promulgating regulations of general application, administrative agencies also have quasi-judicial
functions in which they hold hearings and issue decisions
involving specific parties. Over twenty federal agencies,
including the major regulatory commissions, publish
those decisions in a form similar to official state reports
of court decisions. These reports are usually published
first in advance sheets or slip decisions and then cumulated, though not promptly, into bound volumes. Depending on the agency, the volumes of decisions may
include indexes, digests and tables. However, because
most of these aids are noncumulative, applying only to
the decisions in one volume, they are of limited utility.
Subject access to the decisions of most agencies is effectively provided only by the privately published looseleaf
services or by online databases.

Many looseleaf services and topical reporters publish
decisions of administrative agencies in their subject fields
(e.g., CCH *Trade Regulation Reporter,* which includes
decisions of the Federal Trade Commission). These services usually contain better indexing than the official
reports, appear more promptly, and provide other useful
research material, such as related statutes, court decisions, regulations and news developments. Some of the
services, however, offer decisions only in a digested form.

Pike & Fischer's *Administrative Law,* now in its third
series, is devoted to *procedural* aspects of administrative
law and contains both court decisions and agency decisions on issues such as agency jurisdiction, freedom of
information, and judicial review. The decisions are published in looseleaf binders and are accompanied by a

cumulative digest and a deskbook including legislative history documents for major procedural statutes.

Computer services, such as LEXIS and WESTLAW, include decisions of the major agencies in their specialized regulatory databases. Online coverage includes many administrative decisions that are not published in either official reports or looseleaf services.

Shepard's covers the decisions of federal agencies in *Shepard's United States Administrative Citations,* which lists citations to the decisions and orders of over a dozen major administrative tribunals, and in several of its topical citators. These citators provide citations to agency decisions in court decisions and law review articles as well as in later agency decisions. Decisions of the Federal Energy Regulatory Commission, for example, can be Shepardized in *Shepard's Federal Energy Law Citations.* Other topical citators containing coverage of administrative decisions include *Federal Labor Law Citations, Federal Tax Citations, Immigration and Naturalization Citations,* and *Occupational Safety and Health Citations.*

§ 8–6. EXECUTIVE DOCUMENTS

In addition to supervising the executive departments and the independent agencies, the President of the United States also functions as a lawmaker in his own right. In that capacity, he issues a variety of legally significant documents, most of which (since 1965) appear promptly in an official publication, the *Weekly Compilation of Presidential Documents.* Each issue of the *Weekly Compilation* contains an index to all material in the current quarter, and there are cumulative annual indexes.

Public Papers of the Presidents is an official Federal Register publication cumulating the contents of the

Weekly Compilation of Presidential Documents. Series of
annual volumes have been published for Herbert Hoover
and for all presidents after Franklin D. Roosevelt. Cumulated indexes for the papers of each administration
have also been published. Papers of most of the earlier
presidents are generally available in commercially published editions.

a. Executive Orders and Proclamations

The distinction between executive orders and proclamations is blurred, but orders usually involve an exercise
of presidential authority related to government business,
while proclamations are announcements of policy or of
matters requiring public notice. Orders and proclamations are numbered in separate series and published in
the *Federal Register.* All orders and proclamations appearing in the *Register* are also reprinted in *USCCAN*
and *USCS Advance.* WESTLAW has a database of executive orders since 1936 and other presidential documents
since 1984, and LEXIS has all presidential documents
since 1981. Exhibit 69 shows a presidential proclamation as printed in the *Federal Register.*

Each year's orders and proclamations are compiled in
Title 3 of the *Code of Federal Regulations.* The annual
compilation includes a subject index as well as tables
listing the year's presidential documents, indicating older
executive orders and proclamations affected during the
year, and listing statutes cited as authority for presidential documents. Proclamations, but *not* executive orders,
also appear in the *Statutes at Large.*

9593

Federal Register
Vol. 60, No. 33
Friday, February 17, 1995

Presidential Documents

Title 3—

The President

Proclamation 6770 of February 15, 1995

National Poison Prevention Week, 1995

By the President of the United States of America

A Proclamation

Children are the future of our country, and protecting them is America's most sacred responsibility. All of us—government leaders, citizens, parents—are bound to do whatever we can to keep them safe and healthy. Simple safety measures—such as using child-resistant packaging correctly, locking cupboards, keeping prescriptions and cleaning supplies out of the reach of a child's hands—all can protect our most precious resource from the dangers of poison and other hazardous substances.

The U.S. Consumer Product Safety Commission (CPSC) has made great progress in safeguarding our young people by mandating child-resistant packaging for medicine and dangerous chemicals. And the invaluable work of the Nation's poison control centers has saved countless lives, both young and old. These public health efforts have reduced childhood poisoning deaths from 450 in 1961 to 62 in 1991.

However, according to the American Association of Poison Control Centers, nearly 1 million children each year are exposed to potentially poisonous medicines and household chemicals. Every year we lose children to poisoning—and almost all of these poisonings are preventable. This week—and every week—we must rededicate ourselves to informing everyone of the importance of prevention and to educating all caregivers about ways to prevent childhood poisonings.

To encourage the American people to learn more about the dangers of accidental poisonings and to take more preventive measures, the Congress, by Public Law 87–319 (75 Stat. 681), has authorized and requested the President to issue a proclamation designating the third week of March of each year as "National Poison Prevention Week."

NOW, THEREFORE, I, WILLIAM J. CLINTON, President of the United States of America, do hereby proclaim the week beginning March 19, 1995, as National Poison Prevention Week. I call upon all Americans to observe this week by participating in appropriate ceremonies and activities.

IN WITNESS WHEREOF, I have hereunto set my hand this fifteenth day of February, in the year of our Lord nineteen hundred and ninety-five, and of the Independence of the United States of America the two hundred and nineteenth.

William J Clinton

[FR Doc. 95–4274
Filed 2-16-95, 11:17 am]
Billing code 3195-01-P

Exhibit 69: A proclamation, as published in the *Federal Register*.

The Office of the Federal Register has periodically published a *Codification of Presidential Proclamations and Executive Orders.* Arranged by subject in fifty chap-

ters similar to the titles in the *U.S. Code* and *CFR*, it reprints all proclamations and executive orders issued since 1961 which have continuing effect. The volume also includes tables indicating the status of *every* proclamation and order issued since 1961. No new edition, however, has been published since 1989.

Presidential documents since 1984 are indexed in the *CIS Federal Register Index,* as well as in the official *Federal Register* index. Earlier presidential documents are indexed by subject, name, and date in the *CIS Index to Presidential Executive Orders and Proclamations,* which covers from 1787 through 1983. A reference bibliography describes the documents, which are available from CIS on microfiche.

Coverage of proclamations and executive orders is included in *Shepard's Code of Federal Regulations Citations.* The presidential documents are listed by number, with references to citing court decisions and law review articles.

b. Other Presidential Documents

A variety of other documents are printed in the *Federal Register* along with executive orders and proclamations, but are not included in either numbered series. These documents, such as memoranda, notices, letters, and presidential determinations, are also reprinted in the annual *CFR* cumulation of Title 3. Some, but not all, are reprinted in *USCCAN* and *USCS Advance. Reorganization plans,* another form of presidential action, are little used today, but older plans were published in the *Federal Register, CFR,* and *Statutes at Large,* and citations to plans are listed in *Shepard's Code of Federal Regulations Citations.*

Presidential messages from the President to Congress explain proposed legislation or vetoes, report on the state of the nation, and serve other functions. These messages are published in the *Congressional Record,* in the *House* and *Senate Journals,* as *House* and *Senate Documents,* and in the *Weekly Compilation of Presidential Documents.*

Executive agreements are diplomatic arrangements with other nations made under the President's power to conduct foreign affairs. Unlike treaties, these executive agreements do not require the advice and consent of the Senate. Since 1950, agreements have appeared in the official bound series, *U.S. Treaties and Other International Agreements (UST).* Prior to that date, they were published in the *Statutes at Large.* Executive agreements are discussed with other international agreements in Chapter 12.

§ 8–7. STATE AND LOCAL ADMINISTRATIVE LAW

Like the federal government, state governments have experienced a dramatic increase in the number and activity of their administrative agencies. In many states, however, publication of agency rules and decisions is far less systematic than that of the federal government.

Nearly all states publish official manuals paralleling the *United States Government Manual* and providing quick access to information about government agencies and officials. *The Book of the States,* issued biennially by the Council of State Governments, provides in one volume basic information on government operations in each of the fifty states.

About forty states issue subject compilations of their administrative regulations, and most supplement these with weekly or monthly registers. The *Bluebook* indicates what is published in its list of basic primary sources for each state. For those states without compilations or registers, a researcher must apply to the Secretary of State or to the particular agency for a copy of a specific regulation. The online systems provide access to administrative codes and registers for a small but growing number of states.

Decisions of some state agencies, especially those dealing with banking, insurance, public utilities, taxation, and workers' compensation, may be published in official form in chronological series. A few looseleaf services also include state administrative decisions, and a growing number of state agency decisions are included in the online databases.

On the municipal and local level, administrative decisions are almost never published, and regulations, if published, are rarely kept up to date. When a specific regulation is known to exist, it must be obtained by request from a town clerk or particular agency. It is difficult, however, to determine the existence of local regulations since they are not available to the public in a compiled or current text, and are rarely indexed in official files.

§ 8–8. OPINIONS OF THE ATTORNEYS GENERAL

The opinions of the U.S. Attorney General and the state attorneys general can have considerable significance in legal research. These officials render formal and informal opinions of law in response to questions

from government officials. Although their decisions are advisory in nature and do not have binding authority, they are given considerable weight by the courts in interpreting statutes and regulations.

Traditionally the U.S. Attorney General published opinions in a series entitled *Opinions of the Attorneys General of the United States,* but very few opinions are issued these days. This function has been delegated to the Department of Justice's Office of Legal Counsel, which has issued *Opinions of the Office of Legal Counsel* beginning in 1977. Opinions of both the Attorney General and OLC are also available online through the database systems. References to opinions citing statutory provisions are included in the annotations to *USCA* and *USCS,* but are not listed in *Shepard's U.S. Citations.*

Most states also publish attorney general opinions in slip opinions and bound volumes. Some states publish the opinions every year, but in others there is a long time lag between the date an opinion is issued and the date of its publication. Each volume of opinions usually contains an index, but these rarely cumulate. State attorney general opinions are also available online in LEXIS and WESTLAW, with coverage in most states beginning in 1977.

Many of the annotated state codes provide references to attorney general opinions construing particular statutes, and several of Shepard's state citators include citing attorney general opinions in their treatment of cases and statutes.

Source information for state attorneys general opinions is provided in Mary L. Fisher's *Guide to State Legislative and Administrative Materials* (4th ed. 1988).

The looseleaf *Pimsleur's Checklists of Basic American Legal Publications,* issued by the American Association of Law Libraries, includes a listing of all published volumes of attorney general opinions.

§ 8–9. CONCLUSION

From its early days as one of the most bibliographically inaccessible areas of law, federal administrative law has developed a highly sophisticated research framework. This development stemmed from four separate publishing innovations: the looseleaf services; the improvements brought by the Federal Register System; the expanded Shepard's coverage of administrative materials; and the development of specialized computer databases. Access to state administrative law is less advanced but is improving steadily.

It is important to remember that administrative agency actions are governed by statutes and reviewable by the courts. Administrative procedure acts and judicial decisions have established many important procedural safeguards of agency rulemaking and adjudication. Administrative law research is not limited to the specialized publications discussed in this chapter, since much of the governing law is found in statutes and case law.

CHAPTER 9

SECONDARY MATERIALS

---

§ 9–1. INTRODUCTION

From the primary sources of law, we now turn to the vast literature of unofficial, non-authoritative, *secondary* materials. The law is a dynamic, evolving body of principles rather than a mechanical application of fixed rules, and any material which persuades or influences a tribunal carries some degree of authority. Primary sources of law may be more authoritative than secondary materials, but the difference is relative, not absolute. Legal research can be a wide-ranging and creative inquiry.

Traditional legal secondary materials set forth and analyze established legal doctrine. Some works describe the context or background of legal matters, while others illuminate the possible consequences of proposed legal actions. Secondary materials can directly affect the de-

velopment of the law by shaping law reform or stimulating new legislation. The creative insights of some published writings can reveal trends and patterns in unsettled areas or expose incipient strains and shifts in apparently settled law.

Although secondary materials are as old as legal research, only in this century have the courts considered them to be persuasive authority. The extension of legal concern into many new areas of human activity and the growing willingness of the courts to re-examine traditional rules have increased the importance of scholarly commentaries and empirical studies. A greater interest in the social and economic consequences of legal actions has led judges and lawyers to turn to nonlegal scholarship to address new and complex legal problems.

Secondary materials also perform several basic functions in legal research. They can refresh the reader's recollection of a familiar area or provide an introduction to a developing field of law. They provide guidelines and forms to simplify daily law practice. They serve as finding aids by providing citations to primary sources and other secondary material.

§ 9–2. TEXTS AND TREATISES

Thousands of texts and treatises written by legal scholars and practitioners address many topics of substantive and procedural law. These range from multivolume topical encyclopedias and detailed surveys to short monographs on specific issues or limited aspects of practice in particular jurisdictions.

Legal treatises first appeared in the twelfth century, shortly after the earliest English reports in the *Plea*

Rolls. They analyzed the developing common law and contributed their own influence to this development. By restating and synthesizing decisions and statutes, texts and treatises have continued to impose order on the chaos of individual precedents. Although they lack legal authority and effect, some are written by scholars of outstanding reputation and receive considerable judicial respect. Other texts offer convenient guides by which practitioners can familiarize themselves with particular fields of law, and often contain practice checklists and sample forms. The inclusion of case tables, indexes, and other research aids can facilitate the use of treatises as finding tools.

Among the varied types of texts, the following groups can be noted: multivolume scholarly surveys of particular fields in depth (e.g., *Corbin on Contracts,* Wright & Miller's *Federal Practice and Procedure*); hornbooks and student texts (e.g., *Prosser and Keeton on Torts* and West's Nutshell Series); practitioners' handbooks in particular fields, many of which are published by groups such as the American Law Institute–American Bar Association (ALI–ABA) Joint Committee on Continuing Legal Education or the Practising Law Institute (PLI); procedural manuals, ranging from one-volume compendia like the *New York Standard Civil Practice Service Desk Book* to multivolume sets like *American Jurisprudence Proof of Facts*; specialized monographs on relatively narrow topics; and self-help publications such as those published by Nolo Press (e.g., *How to File for Bankruptcy* and *The Power of Attorney Book*).

The everchanging nature of law requires a literature capable of reflecting change promptly and accurately. Some form of updating, whether by looseleaf inserts,

pocket parts or periodic revision, is essential to preserve a treatise or text's value for current law coverage. The bypaths of legal bibliography are cluttered with the debris of outdated and unrevised texts.

There are several ways to find relevant and useful texts and treatises. The most reliable method is to follow research leads provided by cases or periodical articles. Treatises are often cited in these sources, and such references are likely to lead to works which are considered well-reasoned and reputable.

Your local law library's catalog is a valuable resource, particularly because it indicates books that are immediately available. A subject search may turn up a large number of publications, but most catalogs allow searches to be limited to recent publications or to books kept in a library reserve collection. Even online catalogs from remote libraries can be helpful in identifying what resources are available, for purchase or interlibrary loan. Even the largest law libraries do not have every possible text, so research limited to one library's holdings may miss important works.

There are several printed guides listing legal publications by subject. Most, however, do not differentiate between major treatises and obscure monographs, and few are updated regularly. Two useful resources are James A. McDermott, ed., *Recommended Law Books* (2d ed. 1986), a rather dated list of basic materials in over fifty subject areas, annotated with practitioners' and reviewers' comments; and *Encyclopedia of Legal Information Sources* (2d ed. 1993), which lists texts, periodicals and looseleaf services in over four hundred law-related subjects. Most state legal research guides (listed in Appendix A at page 342) describe or list the treatises

and practice materials focusing on the law of particular jurisdictions.

It is often difficult for the researcher to evaluate texts, but the following considerations may aid in selection: the purpose of the particular publication; the reputation of the author and publisher, and the standing of their previous books; the organization and scope of the work; the clarity, comprehensiveness and usefulness of its scholarly apparatus (footnotes, tables, index, bibliography, etc.); and the adequacy of supplementation and present timeliness.

Although printed texts remain the norm, some are available electronically and more will undoubtedly follow. WESTLAW now provides access to several dozen treatises, including *Appleman on Insurance Law and Practice,* Wright & Miller's *Federal Practice and Procedure,* and LaFave & Scott's *Substantive Criminal Law.* Treatises are also available on some CD–ROM products. *Moore's Federal Practice* and Gordon & Mailman's *Immigration Law and Procedure*, for example, are both included in topical CD libraries from Matthew Bender. Perhaps the most significant change in treatise format created by electronic information retrieval methods has been the inclusion of hypertext features, allowing the researcher to move from one part of a text to another or from a secondary source to a primary source cited in a footnote. This can save considerable time, particularly in eliminating irrelevant research leads.

§ 9–3. RESTATEMENTS OF THE LAW

Some of the most important commentaries on American law are found in the series called *Restatements of the Law.* Prepared under the auspices of the American Law

Institute, these texts attempt to organize and articulate the rules of American common law. Their comprehensive coverage of selected subject fields can be seen as an unofficial, common-law emulation of the codes of the civil law system. The Restatements' reporters and advisors are well-known scholars and jurists, and their work is often persuasive in the courts—perhaps more so than any other secondary material.

To date, the Restatements cover eleven specific fields: agency, conflict of laws, contracts, foreign relations law, judgments, property, restitution, security, torts, trusts, and unfair competition. The process of drafting a Restatement is a long one, which may involve the publication of several tentative drafts. The first series of nine Restatements was published between 1932 and 1946, and after several years a second series (of all the original topics except restitution and security) was issued to reflect new developments or later thinking. Three components of the *Restatement of the Law (Third)* have been published: Foreign Relations Law (1987), Trusts—Prudent Investor Rule (1992), and Unfair Competition (1995).

The Restatements are divided into sections, each of which contains a basic "black letter" statement of law, followed by explanatory comments and illustrations of particular examples and variations on the general proposition. These comments are followed in recent Restatements by Reporter's Notes providing background information on the development of the section. In the three earliest *Restatements (Second),* for agency, torts, and trusts, the Reporter's Notes are not printed after each section but appear in separate appendix volumes. Exhibit 70 shows a typical page from a Restatement.

Ch. 4   APPROPRIATION OF TRADE VALUES   § 43

employer); GTI Corp. v. Calhoun, 309 F.Supp. 762 (S.D.Ohio 1969) (five-year "hold-over" agreement unenforceable as an unreasonable restraint on the employee's use of general skill and training). See also, e.g., Dorr–Oliver, Inc. v. United States, 432 F.2d 447 (Ct.Cl.1970).

§ 43. Improper Acquisition of Trade Secrets

"Improper" means of acquiring another's trade secret under the rule stated in § 40 include theft, fraud, unauthorized interception of communications, inducement of or knowing participation in a breach of confidence, and other means either wrongful in themselves or wrongful under the circumstances of the case. Independent discovery and analysis of publicly available products or information are not improper means of acquisition.

Comment:

a. *Scope of protection.* The owner of a trade secret does not have an exclusive right to possession or use of the secret information. Protection is available only against a wrongful acquisition, use, or disclosure of the trade secret. See § 40. Use or disclosure of a trade secret in breach of a duty of confidence is treated in §§ 41 and 42. This Section considers the acquisition, use, and disclosure of trade secrets by persons who have not obtained the secret through a confidential disclosure.

b. *Proper means of acquisition.* Unless a trade secret has been acquired under circumstances giving rise to a duty of confidence, a person who obtains the trade secret by proper means is free to use or disclose the information without liability. Unlike the holder of a patent, the owner of a trade secret has no claim against another who independently discovers the secret. Similarly, others remain free to analyze products publicly marketed by the trade secret owner and, absent protection under a patent or copyright, to exploit any information acquired through such "reverse engineering." A person may also acquire a trade secret through an analysis of published materials or through observation of objects or events that are in public view or otherwise accessible by proper means.

Illustrations:

1. *A* sells a drug compounded from a secret formula. *B*, a competing drug manufacturer, purchases a quantity of *A* 's drug on the open market and learns the formula through scientific analysis. *B* then begins to market a similar product. *B* has not acquired *A* 's trade secret by improper means.

493

Exhibit 70: A page from the *Restatement of the Law (Third), Unfair Competition.*

A general index volume was published for all of the Restatements in the first series. Although there is no general index for the second or third series, each Restatement includes its own index and the current editions of all Restatements are accessible online through WEST-LAW (REST database) and LEXIS (RESTAT file).

Appendices to each Restatement in the second and third series provide annotations to court decisions which have applied or interpreted its provisions. Another way to find cases and law review articles citing a Restatement section is to use *Shepard's Restatement of the Law Citations*.

§ 9–4. PERIODICALS

Legal periodicals are among the most highly influential secondary sources in American law. Some articles have led directly to major changes in legal doctrine. However, the number of periodicals has proliferated beyond need or reason, so it is necessary to learn several means of access and to evaluate articles carefully.

a. Types of Legal Periodicals

The most serious and highly reputed legal periodicals are the academic law reviews produced at the major American law schools. Student-edited law reviews are published by virtually all accredited law schools, and contain both articles by established scholars and student comments and case notes. These articles and comments are marked by extensive footnotes citing to primary sources and other secondary sources. These footnotes make law review articles very useful research tools.

In addition to general law reviews, there is an ever growing number of specialized academic journals, focus-

ing on topics from ecology to industrial relations. Most of these are student-edited, but a few specialized scholarly journals, such as the *American Journal of Legal History* and the *Journal of Legal Studies,* are edited by faculty.

Numerous periodicals are published by the American Bar Association and other professional groups. Bar journals tend to feature articles of a shorter, more popular nature than the law reviews and contain more news of current legal developments. Most ABA sections issue their own publications, including several respected, scholarly journals. Several state and local bar associations and specialized bar groups also publish journals, usually of more limited scope and quality.

For current awareness purposes, the most useful periodicals may be the many topical legal newsletters focusing on narrow practice areas. Newsletters are often expensive, but they are effective means for busy specialized practitioners to keep up to date on new developments. Issued weekly or monthly, newsletters often summarize and provide brief abstracts of recent judicial, administrative and legislative actions. They may be among the few sources reporting on new, relatively limited fields of practice. *Legal Newsletters in Print* (annual) lists well over a thousand newsletters, with descriptions, subscription information, and a subject index.

Daily legal newspapers providing local court calendars and announcements are published in many cities, and some include lower court decisions not reported elsewhere. Several, such as the *New York Law Journal* or the *Los Angeles Daily Journal,* also contain useful articles on prominent attorneys and current legal developments. Two weekly newspapers, the *National Law Jour-*

nal and *Legal Times,* are national in scope and report on a wide range of legal news issues.

b. Periodical Indexes

Articles in periodicals and journals can be found through a variety of means. Several indexes provide subject access to articles; a growing number of journals are available online in full-text databases; and citators provide references to articles citing cases and other documents.

There are two general indexes to English-language legal periodical literature. Both are available in published volumes with monthly updating pamphlets, on CD–ROM, and online through WESTLAW and LEXIS.

The older of the two indexes is *Index to Legal Periodicals and Books* (*ILP*), which began publication in 1908. It indexes almost 700 legal periodicals by subject and author, in a format similar to the *Readers Guide to Periodical Literature.* (Books were only added to *ILP*'s coverage, and to its title, in 1994.) Since 1983 articles have been indexed under both subject and author. Before that, however, bibliographic information appeared only under the subject entries, with the author entries providing cross-references to the subject headings. *ILP* also includes tables of cases and statutes that are the focus of articles, and a book review section. Exhibit 71 shows a page from its subject/author index. For the period preceding the *ILP,* one can use the Jones–Chipman *Index to Legal Periodical Literature,* which covers the years 1803 to 1937.

SUBJECT AND AUTHOR INDEX 873

Trade regulation—*cont.*
Consolidation, coordination, competition, and coherence: in search of a forward looking communications policy. M. D. Director, M. Botein. 47 *Fed. Comm. L.J.* 229-36 D '94
Free speech and unfree markets. K. M. Sullivan. 42 *UCLA L. Rev.* 949-65 Ap '95
Health care reform: perspectives from the economic theory of regulation and the economic theory of statutory interpretation. H. N. Butler, J. R. Macey. 79 *Cornell L. Rev.* 1434-58 S '94
The market for loyalties: electronic media and the global competition for allegiances. M. E. Price. 104 *Yale L.J.* 667-705 D '94
Missed connections: one failed attempt to ease restrictions on Bell Operating Companies. J. R. Walker, student author. 47 *Fed. Comm. L.J.* 439-55 D '94
Vertical integration and program access in the cable television industry. D. Waterman. 47 *Fed. Comm. L.J.* 511-34 Ap '95

See/See also the following book(s):
The ABA guide to international business negotiations; a comparison of cross-cultural issues and successful approaches; editors, James R. Silkenat, Jeffrey M. Aresty. American Bar Assn. Section of Law Practice Mgt.; American Bar Assn. Section of Int. Law & Practice 1994 237p
Counseling emerging companies in going international; Alan S. Gutterman, editor. American Bar Assn. Section of Int. Law & Practice 1994 663p il
Cross, F. B. and Miller, R. L. West's Legal environment of business; text, cases, ethical, regulatory and international issues. West 1994 xxiv,643p
Export practice; customs and international trade law; edited by Terence P. Stewart. Practising Law Inst. 1994 xxxii,853p
The Regulated economy; a historical approach to political economy; edited by Claudia Goldin and Gary D. Libecap. University of Chicago Press 1994 312p il
Schwab, S. C. Trade-offs; negotiating the Omnibus Trade and Competitiveness Act. Harvard Business School Press 1994 275p

Australia
Causation and reliance in misleading and deceptive conduct law. W. Pengilley. 2 *Competition & Consumer L.J.* 134-54 N '94
Economists in the [Trade Practices] Act. N. R. Norman. 1 *Competition & Consumer L.J.* 49-63 Ag '93
Section 82 and damages for lost commercial opportunity. A. Finlay. 2 *Competition & Consumer L.J.* 82-7 Ag '94
Silence as misleading conduct: reasonable expectations in the wake of Demagogue Pty Ltd v Ramensky [[1992] 110 A.L.R. 608] A. J. Robertson. 2 *Competition & Consumer L.J.* 1-15 Ag '94
The Trade Practices Act 1974—twenty years on. A. Fels. 2 *Competition & Consumer L.J.* 89-97 N '94

See/See also the following book(s):
Business regulation and Australia's future; edited by Peter Grabosky and John Braithwaite. Australian Inst. of Criminology 1993 274p il

Great Britain

See/See also the following book(s):
Ogus, A. I. Regulation; legal form and economic theory. Clarendon Press; Oxford Univ. Press 1994 xxiv,355p

Hungary

See/See also the following book(s):
Legal aspects of doing business in Hungary; [by] Dewey Ballantine, Theodore Goddard—Hungary. Longman 1994 129p

Kansas
Judicial regulation in Kansas: the rise and fall of the court of visitation and the industrial court. B. J. Moline. 63 *J. Kan. B.A.* 28-36 D '94

Massachusetts
Telecommunications and the competitive advantage of Massachusetts. W. F. Weld. 47 *Fed. Comm. L.J.* 395-400 D '94

Vietnam

See/See also the following book(s):
Stults, T. J. and Massa, P. J. How to do business in Vietnam. Indochina 2000 1994 292p

Trade secrets
See also
Unfair competition
The copyright and trade secret protection of communication software: placing a lock on interoperability. S. N. Dupont. 13 *J. Marshall J. Computer & Info. L.* 17-41 O '94
Discovery of trade secrets. J. R. McKown. 10 *Santa Clara Computer & High Tech. L.J.* 35-67 Je '94
Government seizures of trade secrets: what protection does the takings clause provide? I. S. Matsil, student author. 48 *SMU L. Rev.* 687-721 Mr/Ap '95
Keeping trade secrets secret. R. N. Coe. 76 *J. Pat. & Trademark Off. Soc'y* 833-9 N '94
Protecting biotechnology trade secrets in university and industrial research. C. S. McDaniel. 16 *Hous. J. Int'l L.* 565-90 Spr '94
Section 301 of the Omnibus Trade and Competitiveness Act of 1988: a formidable weapon in the war against economic espionage. M. A. Moyer, student author. 15 *Nw. J. Int'l L. & Bus.* 178-205 Fall '94
Trade secret protection for mass distributed software. R. L. Johnston, A. R. Grogan. 11 *Computer Law.* 1-13 N '94

See/See also the following book(s):
Worldwide trade secrets law; Terrence F. MacLaren, editor. Clark Boardman Callaghan 1993

Czech Republic
The secrets of success: confidential business information in the Czech and Slovak Republics. J. F. Swiller, student author. 7 *Transnat'l Law.* 497-521 Fall '94

Iowa
Brown v. Iowa Legislative Council [490 N.W.2d 551 (Iowa 1992)]: struggling with the application of the Freedom of Information Act to computerized government records. E. M. Dillon, student author. 13 *J. Marshall J. Computer & Info. L.* 123-43 O '94

New York (State)
The New York law of trade secrets: a practical guide. V. A. Cundiff. 67 *N.Y. St. B.J.* 32-5+ My/Je '95

New Zealand
Techniques for effective information management—what can be protected and how do you do it? J. G. Robertson. 1994 *N.Z. L.J.* 336-43 S '94

Quebec (Province)
Protecting ideas and information in common law Canada and Quebec. M. Goudreau. 8 *Intell. Prop. J.* 189-216 Jl '94

Slovakia
The secrets of success: confidential business information in the Czech and Slovak Republics. J. F. Swiller, student author. 7 *Transnat'l Law.* 497-521 Fall '94

West Virginia
West Virginia trade secrets in the 21st century: West Virginia's Uniform Trade Secrets Act. L. A. Jarr, student author. 97 *W. Va. L. Rev.* 525-52 Wint '95

Trade unions *See* Unions

Trademarks
See also
Gray market goods
Passing off
Annual review. 84 *Trademark Rep.* 635-1042 N/D '94
Antidilution laws: the unresolved dilemma of preemption under the Lanham Act. R. A. de Sevo. 84 *Trademark Rep.* 300-24 My/Je '94
Application of the Lanham Act to extraterritorial activities: trend toward universality or imperialism? P. E. Kraver, R. E. Purcell. 77 *J. Pat. & Trademark Off. Soc'y* 115-37 F '95
Atlanta '96: Olympic countdown to ambush Armageddon? S. M. McKelvey. 4 *Seton Hall J. Sport L.* 397-445 '94
A call to improve trademark survey evidence. P. J. Welter. 85 *Trademark Rep.* 205-10 Mr/Ap '95
Cancellation under section 14(3) for registrant misrepresentation of source. T. H. Davis, Jr. 85 *Trademark Rep.* 67-88 Ja/F '95
The changing landscape of international trademark law. J. M. Samuels, L. B. Samuels. 27 *Geo. Wash. J. Int'l L. & Econ.* 433-55 '93/'94
Color as a trademark under the Lanham Act: confusion in the circuits and the need for uniformity. J. C. Carraway, student author. 57 *Law & Contemp. Probs.* 243-79 Aut '94
The color conundrum continues: Master Distributors v. Pako [986 F.2d 219 (1993)] and Qualitex v. Jacobson Products [1994 WL 669 (Jan. 3, 1994)] W. F. Coppersmith, III, student author. 24 *Cumb. L. Rev.* 299-323 '93/'94

Exhibit 71: A page from the 1994–95 *Index to Legal Periodicals and Books* subject/author index.

The newer index, which began publication in 1980, is issued in several formats under various names: *Current Law Index (CLI), LegalTrac,* and *Legal Resource Index (LRI).* It provides access to more than 800 legal and law-related periodicals, using detailed Library of Congress subject headings with extensive subheadings and cross-references. The printed version, *Current Law Index,* has separate indexes for subjects and authors, as well as case and statute tables. Exhibit 72 shows an excerpt from its subject section.

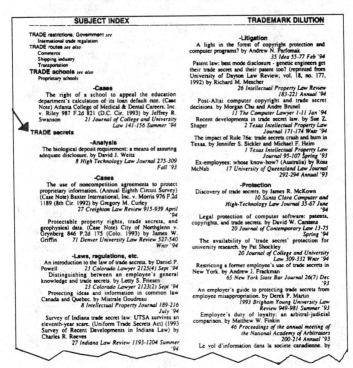

Exhibit 72: Excerpts from the 1994 *Current Law Index* subject index.

The information in both indexes is also available on CD–ROM and online, combining several annual volumes in a single electronic index. *ILP* on CD–ROM is part of the Wilsondisc program, and the CD–ROM version of *CLI* is called *LegalTrac*. *LegalTrac* is somewhat broader in scope than *CLI*, including citations to several legal newspapers and to relevant articles in non-law periodicals. Both systems allow the researcher either to use the subject headings assigned by the indexers or to create keyword searches impossible with printed sources.

The online version of *ILP* is part of the Wilsonline system, and *LRI* is available through several database systems. WESTLAW and LEXIS have databases for both *ILP* and *LRI*, although they are not available under all subscription plans. The search procedures summarized in Chapter 5 can be used to find any document that includes particular combinations of words in the authors' names, article titles, and subject headings.

For articles before 1980, the published *Index to Legal Periodicals* remains the only general access method. To find articles published since 1980, however, there may be several available approaches. For some searches, the printed volumes and pamphlets may be as quick and effective as a CD–ROM or online search. For others, a computer can pinpoint information that might otherwise take hours to find.

The most recent articles, too new to be covered in either *ILP* or *LRI*, are indexed in the *Current Index to Legal Periodicals*, a weekly subject guide to the contents of over 300 law reviews. This index fills the gap between publication of current periodical issues and their coverage by the permanent, more comprehensive indexes. Current issues are also online in WESTLAW.

The *Index to Foreign Legal Periodicals* provides comprehensive access to more than 300 periodicals and selected collections of essays, primarily from countries outside the common law system. It also indexes articles in selected American and Commonwealth journals on international law, comparative law, or the domestic law of other countries, so it can be useful in any international or foreign law research. It is divided into four sections: subject, geographic, book review and author indexes. *IFLP* is available electronically on CD–ROM and through WESTLAW and RLIN.

The *Index to Periodical Articles Related to Law* indexes law-related articles in journals and periodicals outside the legal field. It excludes any articles covered in *ILP*, *LRI*, or the *Index to Foreign Legal Periodicals*. The index consists of four cumulative volumes covering 1958 to 1988, supplemented by quarterly issues.

Indexes from other disciplines can be as valuable in many legal research situations as the strictly legal indexes. Major indexes such as *Index Medicus, PAIS International in Print*, and the *Social Sciences Index* can expand the parameters of a legal research inquiry into an interdisciplinary investigation. There are hundreds of specialized indexing and abstracting services covering current writing and developments in particular disciplines, such as *Psychological Abstracts* and *Sociological Abstracts*.

Like the legal periodical indexes, most of these indexes are accessible on CD–ROM or through online database systems. WESTLAW provides access to many databases from DIALOG Information Systems, including PAIS, MEDLINE (the online version of *Index Medicus*), and

PSYCINFO (the online version of *Psychological Abstracts*).

c. Online Full–Text Databases

While periodical indexes and abstracts are valuable sources of research leads, an ever growing body of periodical literature is also available online in full text. These databases allow researchers to create their own search terms and examine parts of articles rather than relying on a standardized indexing perspective. Instead of a few subject headings and title words, every word in the text and footnotes can be used in a search request.

Both WESTLAW and LEXIS provide databases containing the text of thousands of legal periodical articles. The LAWREV library on LEXIS and the JLR database on WESTLAW provide comprehensive access to hundreds of law reviews, and there are numerous smaller databases for journals in specialized subject areas.

There are several advantages to full-text searching. Articles discussing a topic briefly can be found, as well as those focusing fully on the topic. New and developing areas that do not yet have standardized subject headings can be found using keyword searches. Perhaps most importantly, even if no article in the online database is quite on point, footnote references matching a search query can often lead to numerous relevant articles in other journals, in volumes predating online coverage, and in monographs or journals outside the legal field.

Despite the ease and benefits of full-text searching, no search for law review articles is complete without also checking the periodical indexes as well (either online or in the printed volumes). While the indexes do not provide immediate access to the text of the articles, they

include coverage of several hundred journals that are not available electronically in full text.

d. Periodical Citators

As noted in earlier chapters, Shepard's citators include references to law review articles which cite federal and state court decisions and statutes. Each of Shepard's state citators includes coverage of law reviews and bar journals published within the state, as well as twenty national law reviews. *Shepard's Federal Law Citations in Selected Law Reviews* indexes law review citations to federal court decisions, the U.S. Constitution, and statutory material.

One can also Shepardize a law review article to find both primary sources and other articles in which *it* is cited, tracing an article's influence on the courts and on other scholars. *Shepard's Law Review Citations* covers articles in over 180 legal periodicals, indicating citations both in later law review articles and in federal or state court decisions. Like Shepard's state case law citators and *Federal Law Citations in Selected Law Reviews,* it is accessible online through WESTLAW and LEXIS as well as in print.

There are several citation indexes which function like Shepard's for periodicals in other academic disciplines. *Science Citation Index* (coverage since 1955), *Social Sciences Citation Index* (coverage since 1966), and *Arts & Humanities Citation Index* (coverage since 1976) allow a researcher to find later publications citing earlier books and articles. These indexes cover several thousand journals, and can also be used to find articles by subject or author. They are available online on DIALOG (as *Scisearch, Social Scisearch,* and *Arts & Humanities Search*)

and through WESTLAW, enhancing their flexibility and value as comprehensive index systems. The *Social Sciences Citation Index /Social Scisearch* includes many legal periodicals in its coverage, so it can be used to find both legal periodical articles citing other works and articles from other disciplines citing legal literature.

§ 9–5. CONCLUSION

This very brief survey of secondary materials does not reflect their full impact on the judicial process and on legal research in general. Legal authority is a broad spectrum of many sources reflecting a multitude of influences on judicial decision making, rather than a simple hierarchy of sources. Increasing attention has focused on the role of secondary sources in legal thinking and their relative influence on the courts. In addition, secondary materials serve more basic functions of explaining the law and simplifying the work of practicing lawyers and researchers. For all of these reasons, secondary sources both in law and in other disciplines play a large role in any legal research strategy.

CHAPTER 10

SPECIALIZED AND PRACTICE
MATERIALS

----

§ 10–1. INTRODUCTION

The resources many lawyers turn to most often are not the general codes, digests, and indexes we have discussed thus far, but instead tools specifically designed for use in specialized areas of law or in everyday practice. Some of the materials discussed in this chapter make lawyers' lives considerably easier, by compiling primary sources in convenient formats or by providing checklists and forms for routine matters. Others provide access to the important rules that govern how courts operate and how lawyers behave. These are essential tools for any well-prepared legal researcher.

§ 10–2. LOOSELEAF SERVICES

Looseleaf services, one of the unique inventions of legal bibliography, are frequently supplemented tools which focus on specific subject areas and contain primary legal sources, finding aids, and secondary material. These publications provide *comprehensive* and *current* access to selected fields of legal literature.

The first looseleaf services were issued just before World War I, and were designed to facilitate research in the new federal income tax law. Other services began in public law areas where government regulation was the central focus of legal development, such as labor, antitrust, securities, and regulated industries such as banking, communication, transportation, and utilities. Services are now also published in such varied areas as criminal law, environmental protection, health care, and housing. For many lawyers specializing in these fields, looseleaf services are their primary research tools. They are also popular because they provide prompt notice of new legal developments and they integrate a diverse collection of sources and documents.

There are several ways to determine whether a service is published on a particular topic of interest. References to looseleaf services frequently appear in law review articles and cases. Lawyers or professors specializing in a field can provide useful leads, and law librarians can explain what services are available. *Legal Looseleafs in Print* is an annual directory of looseleaf publications, including (but not limited to) regularly supplemented services. At the end of this volume, Appendix D provides a selected list of looseleaf services and CD–ROMs in fields of major interest.

a. Formats and Features

There are two basic types of looseleaf services: *cumulating* and *interfiling*. In a cumulating service, new material updating the service is usually filed as a unit at the end of the set. This material *supplements* the existing compilation and does not replace pages already filed. Cumulating services are very useful in areas where it is necessary to monitor new information from a variety of sources. *The United States Law Week,* published by the Bureau of National Affairs (BNA), is a typical cumulating service. Other cumulating BNA services, such as *Antitrust and Trade Regulation Report, Criminal Law Reporter, Family Law Reporter,* and *Securities Regulation & Law Report,* serve as excellent current awareness tools in their fields.

Interfiling services, on the other hand, are updated by replacing superseded pages with revised pages. New pages are inserted where appropriate within the service, rather than simply added at the end. The insertion of new pages means that page numbers cannot simply be numbered sequentially (page 1 may be followed by pages 1a and 1a–1). In order to provide a consistent numbering system, many interfiling services refer instead to material by *paragraph number.* A "paragraph" in this sense can range from a few sentences to several pages. Each court decision, for example, may be designated by one paragraph number.

Interfiling services are well suited to areas in which it is essential to apply recent legal developments to a large body of primary sources such as statutes or regulations. CCH (formerly Commerce Clearing House) publishes a wide variety of interfiling services, such as *Congressional*

Index, Federal Securities Law Reports, Standard Federal Tax Reports, and *Trade Regulation Reports.*

Some services have the attributes of both cumulating and interfiling services, with current awareness newsletters and regularly updated compilations of primary sources. Whether cumulating or interfiling, or both, a looseleaf service must be frequently supplemented if it is to be a trustworthy resource. Most of the major services are updated weekly or biweekly. Many treatises are also published in looseleaf format, but they are not looseleaf *services* if they are only updated once or twice a year.

Looseleaf services cover a wide range of subjects, and no two services are exactly alike. The methods of access and organization vary according to the nature of the primary sources, the characteristics of the legal field, and the editorial approach. In areas where one major statute dominates the legal order, the service may be arranged by statutory sections or divisions. Taxation services, for example, are structured according to the sections of the Internal Revenue Code. If several statutes are significant, the service can be divided into areas by the relevant statutes. Labor law services, for example, offer separate treatment of the Labor Management Relations Act, Title VII of the Civil Rights Act of 1964, and the Wage and Hour Act. In other fields where common law or judicial rules predominate, or where there is a mixture of case and statutory law (such as family law, trusts and estates, or corporations), the service may follow a logical arrangement by subject. Despite these marked differences, looseleaf services share several common features.

A looseleaf service presents *all* relevant primary authority in one place, regardless of its original form of publication. This may include decisions of federal and

state courts; statutes, both federal and state; regulations of administrative agencies in the field; and decisions and other documents from those administrative
agencies. Much of this material is available elsewhere in
the law library, but some may not be published other
than in looseleaf services.

Looseleaf services also summarize and analyze these
primary sources. Some contain detailed analytical notes
by topic, which function like a case digest in explaining
and providing access to the primary sources. Exhibit 73
shows a page from CCH's *Food Drug Cosmetic Law
Reports,* a typical interfiling service. This page explains
application of federal food laws to animal products and
alcoholic beverages. Note the references to relevant
statutes and cases found elsewhere in the service.

One of the most valuable functions of a looseleaf
service is that it provides coverage of proposed legislation, pending litigation, and other developments in its
area. *Food Drug Cosmetic Law Reports* does this in a
New Developments section included in each weekly update. Exhibit 74 shows a page of new developments,
including a notice in ¶ 41,110 about a petition filed to
require nutrition labeling for beer and wine. Note that
the entry includes a *back reference* to the textual discussion in Exhibit 73, allowing the researcher to place a
document in context and to find other relevant sources.

Note that Exhibits 73 and 74 have both page numbers
(at the top) and paragraph numbers (at the bottom).
Remember that the paragraph number is the point of
reference to the material, while the page number is used

50,410   Labeling—Adulteration   1622   11-1-93

and that there is no FDA regulation governing that subject. *U.S. v. Ener-B Nasal Gel* (DC ED NY 1991) 1989-92 FDC LRept Dev Trans Bind ¶ 38,253.

.92 Boric acid.—A product consisting of 100 percent boric acid is both a food and a drug under the provisions of the Act, and products consisting of approximately 95 percent boric acid and 5 percent sodium chloride (salt) are foods. These products were offered for the conservation, preservation, and sterilization of food, and their shipment in interstate commerce was enjoined because of the harmful potentialities of boric acid when taken internally in indiscriminate doses. *U.S. v. Price* (DC Minn 1943) Notices of Judgment, Foods, No. 5759.

.93 Vitamin capsules.—Because the labeling of vitamin capsules represented them to be of value as a dietary and nutritional supplement, they were

food within the meaning of the FDC Act. Also, because the labeling represented the capsules to be of value as a curative or preventative of disease conditions in man affecting the structure and function of the body, they were drugs within the meaning of the Act. *U.S. v. Vitasafe Formula M* (DC NJ 1964) 1963-67 FDC LRept Dev Trans Bind ¶ 40,151, 226 FSupp 266; rev'd on other grounds (CA-3 1965) 1963-67 FDC LRept Dev Trans Bind ¶ 40,195, 345 F2d 864; cert den (US SCt 1965) 382 US 918.

.935 Inasmuch as the 12th Revision of the Pharmacopoeia recognized vitamins A, B_1, C, D, D_2, D_3, and G, vitamin capsules were considered drugs and not food. *U.S. v. Hain* (DC SD Calif. 1943) Notices of Judgment, Foods, No. 5770.

¶ 50,028   Human Food and Animal Food

The food provisions of the Federal Food, Drug, and Cosmetic Act are equally applicable to food for humans and food for animals. Decisions and rulings compiled in this division, therefore, apply as well to the material discussed in the "Animal Feed ● Pet Food" division. There are additional considerations involved in the safety, purity, and labeling of animal feeds, however, primarily because of the frequent use of animal drugs and medicated premixes in animal feed. Also, the Delaney Clause, which is discussed in detail at ¶ 56,056 in the "Food Additives ● GRAS Substances ● Prior Sanctions" division, has particular reference to animal feed, because additives shown to cause cancer in test animals can only be permitted in animal feed for food-producing animals if no residues of the additives would remain in the food product (.01). The adulteration provisions discussed in this division apply to animal feed that is in violation of this special provision.

The Food and Drug Administration has codified its regulations in such a way that, although the statute treats human and animal food together, the regulations are discrete. Many of the animal food regulations are identical to the corresponding regulations concerning human food appearing in this and other divisions, but all of the FDA's animal food regulations appear in the "Animal Feed ● Pet Food" division.

Citations

.01 FDC Act § 409(c)(3)(A), 21 U.S.C. 348(c)(3)(A), see ¶ 198.

¶ 50,031   Status of Alcoholic Beverages

The FDA has the authority to take action with respect to adulterated food products, including alcoholic beverages. The Bureau of Alcohol, Tobacco, and Firearms has authority over distilled spirits, wines, and malt beverages; in particular, the Federal Alcohol Administration Act gives the BATF the authority to promulgate regulations with regard to the labeling and advertising of alcoholic beverages to ensure that they provide adequate information regarding the identity and quality of the products.

The FDA and the BATF have agreed that the BATF is responsible for the promulgation and enforcement of regulations regarding the labeling of alcoholic beverages. If the FDA determines that the presence of an ingredient in an alcoholic beverage poses a recognized public health problem, and that the substance must be identified on

¶ 50,028   ©1993, Commerce Clearing House, Inc.

Exhibit 73: A page from the CCH *Food Drug Cosmetic Law Reports.*

41,500

cyclophosphamide and etoposide could be toxic to normal, healthy subjects. Because of this concern, the FDA requires the submission of INDs for in vivo bioavailability or bioequivalence studies of cytotoxic drugs at 21 CFR 320.31(a)(3). The petition stated that the FDA should not allow such INDs to go into effect unless they provide that the studies will be conducted only in patients with susceptible malignancies. The petition also asked the agency to issue guidance specifying that bioavailability or bioequivalence studies of cyclophosphamide or etoposide in humans should be conducted only in patients with susceptible malignancies. Such guidance would serve to counter the statement at 21 CFR 320.25(a)(2) that in vivo bioavailability studies should "ordinarily" be done in normal subjects.

Back reference: ¶71,015.

¶ 41,109   PETITION CRITICIZES FDA TOBACCO PROPOSAL

Citizen Petition No. 95P-0354, filed with the Food and Drug Administration October 31, 1995.

Caffeine Beverages—Regulation as Drugs—Petition.—The reasons the FDA asserted for its proposed regulation of tobacco products as drugs and/ or devices could also lead the agency to regulate caffeine-containing beverages in a similar manner, according to a petition submitted by the Competitive Enterprise Institute. Although purporting to request the regulation of caffeine, the petition states that its real purpose is to generate a public discussion of whether FDA regulation does more harm than good. According to the petition, the FDA's proposal to regulate tobacco is based on regulatory criteria that are open-ended and could greatly expand the agency's reach. The FDA has failed to engage in the cost/ benefit analysis that would provide a clearer indication of how to advance the public interest. Regulating caffeine would be the same as regulating tobacco, an unnecessary restriction of consumer choice, and would divert resources from the FDA's critical task of approving health-enhancing drugs and medical devices, the petition suggests.

Back reference: ¶70,065.

¶ 41,110   NUTRITION LABELING FOR BEER AND WINE SOUGHT

Citizen Petition No. 95P-0353, filed with the Food and Drug Administration October 31, 1995.

Nutrition Labeling—Beer and Wine—Petition.—Nutrition labeling requirements for beer and wine have been requested in a petition filed with the FDA by Paul W. Mason. According to the petitioner, some beers contain up to 250 mg/ L of magnesium and some wines contain up to 245 mg/ L of magnesium. The petitioner is concerned that consumers who take magnesium supplements could experience an unwanted laxative effect from drinking unlabeled beverages with high magnesium levels. On the other hand, consumers who do not take supplements could avoid magnesium deficiencies by choosing magnesium-rich beers. The petitioner contended that the FDA and the Bureau of Alcohol, Tobacco, and Firearms have prohibited brewers from adding nutrition labels, using the rationale that alcoholic beverages should not be seen as sources of nutrition. The agencies' stance prevents consumers from making informed decisions, the petitioner argued.

Back references: ¶ 50,031; 50,176.

¶ 41,111   STAY ON ASTAXANTHIN REGULATION LIFTED

Food and Drug Administration Order, published at 60 FR 55446, November 1, 1995.

Color Additives—Stay—Removed.—A stay on two paragraphs of the regulation permitting the use of astaxanthin as a color additive in salmonid fish feed has been lifted by the FDA. The stay was issued in response to a color additive manufacturer's objection and hearing request concerning the two paragraphs, which address label declarations on fish that

¶ **41,109**

Exhibit 74: A page of new developments in CCH's *Food Drug Cosmetic Law Reports.*

only for filing purposes. Many researchers are misled by the page numbers, particularly when (as in these exhibits) they are similar to the paragraph numbers.

Detailed, regularly updated indexes provide fast and convenient access to looseleaf services. A typical service includes several kinds of indexes.

The general or *topical index* provides a detailed subject approach to the subject area. In many services, an additional index known as a "Current Topical Index" or "Latest Additions to Topical Index" provides access to new materials. Exhibit 75 shows a reference to ¶ 41,110 in the *Food Drug Cosmetic Law Reports* "Current Topical Index to New Matters." A much more comprehensive "Topical Index—Food" provides references to the discussion in ¶ 50,031 shown in Exhibit 73.

Finding lists provide direct references to particular statutes, regulations, or cases by their citations. These can be particularly useful in searching for agency materials, such as IRS rulings or SEC releases. Some of these lists also include information on the current validity of materials listed.

Cumulative indexes, used in some services, are designed so that researchers who have already found the paragraph number of the relevant topic do not need to consult further topical indexes to find current material. Under listings by paragraph number, cumulative indexes update each topic by providing references to new materials which have not yet been incorporated into the main discussion. Exhibit 76 shows a page from the Current Cumulative Index in the *Food Drug Cosmetic Law Reports,* including a reference under ¶ 50,031 to the labeling petition shown in Exhibit 74.

1733 11-13-95   **36,601**

Current Topical Index to New Matters

See also "Topical Index to New Matters" at page 36,651.

References are to paragraph (¶) numbers.

A

Acquired immune deficiency syndrome (AIDS)
. therapies
. . protease inhibitor drug, open label protocol . . . 40,896
. vaccine
. . development, issues, OTA report . . . 41,044

Adulteration, food
. injunction
. . cheese, filth, unsanitary conditions . . . 38,412
. live animals
. . applicability . . . 38,409
. release to claimant
. . other violations, appropriateness . . . 38,416
. shrimp, decomposition
. . compliance policy guide, revocation . . . 40,918
. tolerances, regulatory limits, and action levels, petitions
. . regulation revocation, proposal . . . 45,745

Adulteration, veterinary drugs
. injectable products
. . sterilization, policy, revision . . . 40,908

Advisory committees
. annual reports
. . availability . . . 41,078
. Creutzfeldt-Jakob disease
. . establishment . . . 40,879
. veterinary medicine
. . request for nominations . . . 40,869

Analgesic drug products, external, OTC
. reopening of administrative record
. . patch products, petition . . . 40,971
. . petition . . . 40,940
. waiver of testing requirements
. . petition . . . 41,021

Animal feed
. additives, safety factors
. . regulation revocation, proposal . . . 45,745
. canned, thermally processed low-acid
. . revocation of subparts, proposal . . . 45,745
. clinical investigations
. . financial disclosure, comment opportunity . . . 40,865
. dietary supplement law, applicability . . . 40,858

Antibiotic drugs, generally
. abbreviated applications
. . requirements, standing to sue . . . 38,425

Anticaries drug products, OTC
. final monograph . . . 41,074

Antiemetic drug products, OTC
. ingredients
. . petition . . . 40,861

Approved drugs, list
. equivalence to conditionally approved drug
. . alternative listing methods, petition . . . 41,026

B

Beverages, alcoholic
. nutrition labeling
. . petition . . . 41,110

Bioequivalence, drugs
. definitions and procedures
. . validity . . . 38,419
. veterinary drugs
. . definitions and procedures, validity . . . 38,419

Biological products
. adverse experience reporting
. . electronic submissions, pilot project . . . 40,873
. clinical investigators
. . financial disclosure, comment opportunity . . . 40,865
. facilities, pilot or small-scale
. . guidance . . . 40,923
. licensing applications
. . refusals to file, oversight committee . . . 40,827
. . revocation . . . 41,104
. regulations
. . obsolete, revocation, proposal . . . 45,745

Blood and blood products
. computer software
. . premarket submissions, deadline extension . . . 41,073
. donor suitability
. . prisoners, CBER recommendation . . . 40,872
. licenses
. . suspension . . . 41,028
. safety and quality
. . quality assurance guideline . . . 40,927
. . recommendations, response . . . 41,081
. . regulatory approach, recommendations . . . 40,928

Bronchodilator drug products, OTC
. ephedrine ingredients, removal
. . proposal . . . 45,719

Butter
. labeling
. . color additive declaration, proposal . . . 45,716

C

Cacao products
. food standards
. . revocation, proposal . . . 45,745

Cheese
. adulteration
. . injunction . . . 38,412
. labeling
. . color additive declaration, proposal . . . 45,716

Civil monetary penalties—see Enforcement

Cocoa beans
. tolerances

Exhibit 75: References to new materials in a CCH *Food Drug Cosmetic Law Reports* topical index.

Current Cumulative Index

See also Cumulative Index at page 36,921.

The Cumulative Index coordinates the latest developments
with the basic explanations of the Reporter. After consulting a
paragraph in the Reporter, refer to the same paragraph number
(left column) in this Index, where you will find a summary of
related new matters with references (right column) to the full
report in the "Food and Drug Decisions," "New Developments,"
or "Proposed Regulations" division. If the paragraph is not listed,
there have been no new developments.

Exhibit 76: A page from the Current Cumulative Index in the CCH *Food Drug Cosmetic Law Reports.*

Detailed instructions, often entitled "How to use this reporter," are frequently provided at the beginning of the first volume of a looseleaf service. Services can vary considerably, and a particular service may include features that appear confusing at first but are very useful to the experienced researcher. These instructions are often neglected, but a few moments of orientation can save considerable time and frustration.

b. Research Approaches

Because looseleaf services differ depending on the subject matter and the publisher's approach, it is difficult to generalize about the best research procedures. The following steps, however, are applicable to most services:

1. Determine whether a looseleaf service is available for the subject matter to be researched.

2. Peruse the instructions at the front of the service, in order to obtain an adequate working orientation.

3. Use the service's various indexes to locate the specific material needed. Most often this means beginning in the Topical Index by subject. A Finding List can be used if you already have a reference to a specific relevant document (such as an order, regulation, or ruling).

4. Study the texts of the relevant primary sources, as well as the service's explanations and commentary.

5. Follow research leads suggested by cross-references to cases and other documents.

6. Update your research results by checking the cumulative or "latest additions" indexes for recent materials, and by using a citator if available.

§ 10–3.　TOPICAL ELECTRONIC RESOURCES

While looseleaf services remain the preferred research tools of many specialists, a growing number of lawyers are turning to computerized services to perform similar functions.　Like looseleaf services, topical CD–ROM systems provide both explanatory or analytical material and the texts of primary sources under discussion.　Keyword searching allows more flexibility than looseleaf indexes, and hypertext links allow researchers to move conveniently back and forth between different types of documents.　Examples of these tools include West Publishing's *CD–ROM Libraries* in bankruptcy, federal securities, federal taxation, and government contracts; or *CCH Access* CD–ROMs in several areas of taxation as well as federal securities and Medicare and Medicaid. The annual *Directory of Law–Related CD–ROMs* provides an extensive listing of these resources, and Appendix D in this volume covers both looseleaf and CD–ROM services which are now available.　As with most current bibliographic lists in law, new sources will undoubtedly be available by the time this book is published.

CD–ROM services eliminate the need for laborious filing of replacement pages, but new discs are generally not issued as frequently as looseleaf supplements.　It is usually necessary to finish updating research, therefore, through the online systems or other means.

The online databases also provide topical electronic libraries, simply by providing different combinations of material in specialized databases or libraries.　The online services are usually the most up-to-date sources for current information and new documents.　Many of BNA's major weekly services are also available through both

WESTLAW and LEXIS. Other online databases are even more frequently updated, including daily reports in areas such as banking, international trade, labor, securities, and taxation.

The Internet is still developing as a force in specialized legal research. In some areas it is possible to find news reports and discussions, as well as some otherwise hard-to-find documents. Coverage of primary sources, however, is sparse and unpredictable. The Net can be a good way to save some money and find contacts, but it is not yet a reliable place to find the full range of information needed in legal practice. James Evans's *Law on the Net* (1995) provides a directory of resources in over 40 subject areas.

§ 10–4. PRACTICE AND PROCEDURE

This section covers a range of other materials needed in legal practice. The first two subsections, on *rules governing court proceedings* and *legal ethics*, are primary sources with which any lawyer must be familiar. *Records and briefs* can clarify the holdings in decided cases or offer research leads on the issues discussed. Like *formbooks*, they can also be used as models in drafting documents.

a. Court Rules

Rules for the regulation of court proceedings are enacted in a variety of ways. Some are promulgated by statute, and others by the courts themselves or by conferences of judges. Most major court rules are available in a number of sources, including some which provide annotations of cases in which they are applied or construed.

The Federal Rules of Civil Procedure, the Federal Rules of Criminal Procedure, and Federal Rules of Appellate Procedure were drafted by judicial Advisory Committees pursuant to congressional authorization. The Federal Rules of Evidence were enacted by Congress itself. All of these rules are included in the three major editions of the U.S. Code, accompanied by Advisory Committee comments. *USCA* and *USCS* also include extensive case annotations and other research aids. The major rules sets also appear in a variety of pamphlets and reference publications, as well as online from both WESTLAW and LEXIS. Major treatises such as Wright & Miller's *Federal Practice and Procedure* and *Moore's Federal Practice* are organized rule-by-rule, providing the texts and official comments accompanied by very extensive discussions.

Rules of the Supreme Court and of the individual U.S. Courts of Appeals are also included in each edition of the U.S. Code. Local U.S. District Court rules are usually available in court rules pamphlets published for individual states, and lower federal court rules from the entire country are published in *Federal Local Court Rules,* a five-volume looseleaf set from the Lawyers Cooperative Publishing Company.

Amendments to the major federal rules are printed by Congress as House Documents and are reproduced in the advance sheets for each of West's federal court reporters as well as in *Lawyers' Edition, USCCAN* and *USCS Advance.* New Supreme Court rules also appear in the official *U.S. Reports*.

Most federal court rules, including those for individual circuits and districts, are covered in *Shepard's United States Citations.* *Shepard's* provides references to rule

amendments and to citations in federal court decisions and *ALR* annotations. Citing law review articles are listed separately in *Shepard's Federal Law Citations in Selected Law Reviews,* and state cases citing federal rules are listed in each Shepard's *state* statutory unit.

The rules governing proceedings in state courts are usually included in the annotated state codes, accompanied by notes of relevant cases. For most states there are also annual softcover volumes providing convenient access to rules and procedural statutes. Many of these publications are unannotated, but some contain useful annotations and commentary. More elaborate practice sets in many jurisdictions include all of these features, as well as legal forms for each rule and section.

Court rules are fully covered in each of Shepard's state citators. Changes in rules are noted, as well as citations in federal and state court decisions, selected law reviews, *ALR* annotations, and (in some states) attorney general opinions.

b. Legal Ethics

The law governing the professional activities of lawyers is found in a distinct body of literature consisting of codified rules of conduct, ethics opinions of bar committees, and disciplinary decisions of courts.

While rules vary from state to state, most jurisdictions have adopted some form of the Model Rules of Professional Conduct, promulgated by the ABA in 1983. A few states still have rules based on the ABA's older Model Code of Professional Responsibility (1969). The rules in force in a particular state are usually found in the volumes containing the state's court rules, although they can sometimes be difficult to find. Only a few of these

sources are annotated with notes of decisions under the rules. The *National Reporter on Legal Ethics and Professional Responsibility*, a looseleaf service, reprints the unannotated rules from every state as well as the District of Columbia and Puerto Rico.

Annotated Model Rules of Professional Conduct (2d ed. 1992) provides the text of the ABA rules with comments, legal background, and notes of decisions from various jurisdictions. Although it contains the ABA's rules rather than those adopted in any specific jurisdiction, it is a useful source for comparative analysis and commentary. The annotated rules are online in WESTLAW's ABA–AMRPC database; the ETHICS library in LEXIS has a CODES file containing the Model Rules and the Code of Judicial Conduct, including official comments but no background notes or annotations. The leading treatise on the Model Rules is Hazard & Hodes, *The Law of Lawyering* (2d ed. 1990-date).

Opinions on legal ethics are issued by the courts, the American Bar Association, and state bar associations. Court decisions and ABA opinions are available on WESTLAW and LEXIS, but very few state bar opinions are online. Some can be found in the *National Reporter on Legal Ethics and Professional Responsibility*, and most state bars have some sort of publication providing information about their ethics opinions, either summarizing them or reprinting them in full text.

The *ABA/BNA Lawyers' Manual on Professional Conduct* is often a good place to begin research. This looseleaf service includes an extensive commentary with background and practical tips, as well as news of developments and abstracts of new decisions. It is available both in print and on WESTLAW (ABA–BNA file).

c. Records and Briefs

The printed records and briefs of the parties in cases before appellate courts are often available for research use. The record is a transcript of proceedings in the lower court, including the trial testimony, pleadings, motions, and judgments. The briefs consist of the written arguments and authorities cited by the attorneys for the parties on appeal. These documents enable attorneys and other researchers to study in detail the arguments and facts of significant cases decided by appellate courts.

The records and briefs of the Supreme Court of the United States go to several libraries around the country, while many more libraries subscribe to microform editions. Briefs since 1979 are available online through LEXIS (GENFED library, BRIEFS file), and WESTLAW coverage begins in 1990 (SCT–BRIEF database). Records and briefs of the U.S. Courts of Appeals and state appellate courts have a more limited distribution, but many are distributed to local law libraries within the circuit or state and some are also available in microform.

These documents are usually filed by the report citation or docket number of the case in which they were submitted. The researcher typically begins with an interest in a particular decision and then seeks this additional source of material on that case. There is no direct subject access to appellate records and briefs.

Unlike appellate cases, trial court litigation generally does not produce a set of "briefs." Some cases go to trial without any written submissions on points of law; others produce a variety of memoranda or briefs submitted to support or oppose motions before, during and after trial. These documents are kept on file at the courthouse and

may become part of the record if a case is appealed, but at the trial court level there is no single set of "briefs" as there is in most appellate proceedings.

d. Formbooks

In the course of legal practice, there are many basic transactions and court filings that occur with regularity. Rather than redraft these documents each time the need arises, attorneys frequently work from sample versions of standard legal documents and instruments. Model forms are available from a variety of sources, in both printed collections and electronic products. Some sets of forms are annotated with discussion of the underlying laws, checklists of steps in completing the forms, and citations to cases in which the forms were in issue.

Both Lawyers Coop and West publish multivolume compilations of forms in an encyclopedic format with extensive indexing, notes and cross-references. Lawyers Coop has two sets: *Am. Jur. Legal Forms 2d* provides forms of instruments such as contracts, leases, and wills, and *Am. Jur. Pleading and Practice Forms* focuses on litigation and other practice before courts and administrative agencies. *West's Legal Forms* (2d ed.) includes in one set both practice forms and instruments.

Both companies also issue sets devoted to forms used in federal practice, *Federal Procedural Forms, Lawyers' Edition* and *West's Federal Forms*. There are specialized sets or volumes for most states and for particular subject areas. In addition, manuals of practice for virtually every state contain sample forms, and compilations of statutory forms are often issued in conjunction with state codes.

Several sets of forms are available on CD–ROM, streamlining further the drafting process by eliminating the need to retype each new form. These CD–ROM publications include *AmJur Legal Forms 2d on LawDesk, Michie's Forms on Disc,* and *Nichols New Electronic Cyclopedia of Legal Forms.* In addition, most law firms have electronic libraries of forms and pleadings for in-house use.

Most jurisdictions have published sets of *model* or *pattern jury instructions* designed for judges to explain the applicable law to jurors before they weigh the evidence and reach their decision. Model jury instructions can be useful as forms, and they can also provide a concise summary of a jurisdiction's ruling law on the issues covered. Some of these sets of instructions are published by state court systems, and others by bar associations. Still others are unofficial but highly respected, such as E.J. Devitt et al., *Federal Jury Practice and Instructions* (4th ed. 1987–92), which is available on WESTLAW as well as in print. *Michie's Jury Instructions on CD–ROM* contains over 7,000 model instructions, for both federal and state jurisdictions.

§ 10–5. CONCLUSION

Specialized looseleaf and electronic services, court rules, and other practice materials are some of the most important resources in the arsenal of practicing lawyers. Research skill in finding substantive law may be futile without a similar understanding of research in procedural law. Therefore, a solid grasp of the publication forms is a necessary part of legal practice.

CHAPTER 11

REFERENCE RESOURCES

---

§ 11–1. INTRODUCTION

This chapter provides a brief look at materials designed to provide quick answers to relatively simple questions. These are not places to find lengthy legal analysis, but instead sources for facts, background data, statistics, telephone numbers, and addresses. Knowing how to find this information quickly can save valuable time for other aspects of legal research.

One group of reference materials, dictionaries and related research aids, has been discussed in Chapter 1, at pages 8-9. In addition there are several other types of material with which you should become familiar.

§ 11–2. HANDBOOKS

Legal researchers often need quick access to factual information or a legal summary. A variety of reference publications satisfy this need. While they are no substi-

257

tute for more extensive legal research, these works can answer questions and save considerable time. They are the legal counterparts to general reference works such as the *World Almanac.*

Martindale–Hubbell Law Digest is an annual three-volume set containing brief digests of the law of every state and many foreign countries on specific substantive and procedural legal topics, as well as federal intellectual property law digests, uniform acts, and A.B.A. codes. The law digests generally provide citations to the primary sources on which they are based. Too limited for serious research, these digests are useful for a brief statement of law on a particular point or for a reference from which further research can be undertaken. LEXIS provides online access to these digests in the MHDIG file. Exhibit 77 shows an excerpt from a state law digest. Note that the digest provides references to the state code and explains which uniform acts the state has adopted.

Unlike the legal encyclopedias discussed earlier, which attempt to summarize legal doctrines, *West's Guide to American Law: Everyone's Legal Encyclopedia* (1983–85, with bound supplements) is a handy reference tool with brief articles on many American legal issues and institutions. It is written for a lay audience and provides basic background information. A more scholarly encyclopedic work, with shorter articles but broader coverage, is the one-volume *Oxford Companion to Law* (1980), by David M. Walker. Although written from a British perspective, this useful and lively volume offers extensive coverage of American, European, and comparative law.

NEW MEXICO LAW DIGEST

FACTORS . . . *continued*

Consignment Agreements.—Artists' consignments governed by 56-11-1 et seq. No other statutory provisions except as such agreements may be covered by Uniform Commercial Code. (55-9-114). See topic Commercial Code.

Qualifying Nonresident Liquor Wholesalers or Manufacturers.—May obtain nonresident licenses in this state. (60-6A-7). Nonresident licensees may sell only to licensed manufacturers and wholesalers. (60-6A-7).

FILING FEES:

See topics Commercial Code; Corporations; Deeds; Mortgages of Real Property.

FOOD, DRUGS, AND COSMETICS:

Essentially the same as the Federal Food, Drug, and Cosmetic Act. As to food control provisions see The New Mexico Food Act, 25-2-1 et seq., New Mexico Dairy Product Act (25-7A-1 et seq.). As to drugs, devices, and cosmetics see The New Mexico Drug, Device and Cosmetic Act, 26-1-1 et seq. Pharmacists permitted to substitute certain lower cost drugs for those prescribed.

Uniform Controlled Substances Act, 1970 version adopted. (30-31-1 et seq.).

FORECLOSURE:

See topics Liens; Mortgages of Real Property.

FOREIGN CORPORATIONS: See Corporations.

FRANCHISES:

Uniform Franchise and Business Opportunities Act not adopted.

Alcoholic Beverages.—Failure of supplier to act in good faith in complying with terms or terminating franchise violates Liquor Control Act. Wholesaler may bring action against supplier for violation. (60-8A-7 to -11).

Franchise Tax.—Imposed on every domestic or foreign corporation having or exercising corporate franchise in N.M. except: Insurance companies paying premium tax, tax exempt trusts and tax exempt organizations. (7-2A-1 et seq.). Rate is $50 per taxable year. (7-2A-5.1). Credit given for solar or wind energy equipment and installation (7-2A-8.1), for geothermic investment (7-2A-8.5), for preservation of cultural property (7-2A-8.6), and corporate-supported child care (7-2A-14).

Motion Pictures.—Contracts restricting franchise to product of any producer or distributor for more than one year unlawful. (57-5-9).

Motor Vehicle Dealers.—Franchising governed by 57-16-1 et seq. Manufacturers and distributors must not place unreasonable restrictions on or fail to renew on generally available terms, or unreasonably prohibit transfer of franchise. (57-16-8, -9).

Municipalities.—Action questioning privilege or franchise granted by municipal corporation must be brought within six years of grant. (37-1-26).

Public Utilities.—Franchise ordinance not effective for at least 30 days; must be published at least twice; voters may petition for vote on granting franchise; expense of vote born by applicant; contract limited to 25 years. (3-42-1).

Constitutional Restriction on Franchise Grant.—Legislature must not grant exclusive franchises. (N.M. Const. Art. IV, §26).

FRAUDS, STATUTE OF:

English Statute of Frauds adopted as part of common law of New Mexico. (110 N.M. 559, 798 P.2d 160; 4 N.M. 336, 16 P. 275). See also topic Commercial Code.

Contracts of Sale.—Common law applies, no special statutory provisions. See, however, topic Commercial Code.

Part Performance.—Common law applies, no special statutory provisions. See, however, topic Commercial Code.

FRAUDULENT SALES AND CONVEYANCES:

Uniform Fraudulent Conveyances Act repealed, effective June 16, 1989.

Uniform Fraudulent Transfer Act adopted without substantive revision. (56-10-14 et seq.).

Exhibit 77: An excerpt from the New Mexico Law Digest in the *Martindale-Hubbell Law Digest.*

The *Am. Jur. 2d Deskbook,* discussed above on page 93, is one of several compendia of addresses, digests, and statistical information. Similar works include *The Lawyer's Almanac* (annual); *The Legal Researcher's Desk Reference* (biennial); and *West's Legal Desk Reference* (1991). These helpful volumes, each with somewhat different contents, provide convenient and quick access to material that might otherwise be difficult to collect.

§ 11–3. STATISTICS

Lawyers frequently need statistics for many purposes, such as to support an argument, counsel a client, or prepare for trial. The handbooks and compendia just discussed include a variety of statistics useful in legal practice. There are also major resources devoted specifically to statistical information.

The *Statistical Abstract of the United States,* published annually by the Bureau of the Census in print and on CD–ROM, is a general reference source with which any legal researcher should be familiar. It covers a wide range of economic and demographic statistics, and is particularly useful because it gives sources for each of its tables. It thus serves as a convenient lead to agencies and sources providing more extensive coverage of specific areas. Exhibit 78 shows a page from the *Statistical Abstract,* providing statistics on prisoner populations in the United States. Note that both tables provide references to more detailed publications from the U.S. Bureau of Justice Statistics.

Adults on Probation, in Prison, on Parole—Death Sentence   219

No. 353. Adults on Probation, in Jail or Prison, or on Parole: 1980 to 1992

[As of December 31, except jail counts as of June 30]

ITEM	Total [1]	Probation	Jail	Prison	Parole
1980	1,840,400	1,118,097	[2]182,288	319,598	220,438
1981	2,006,600	1,225,934	[2]195,085	360,029	225,539
1982	2,192,600	1,357,264	207,853	402,914	224,604
1983	2,475,100	1,582,947	221,815	423,898	246,440
1984	2,689,200	1,740,948	233,018	448,264	266,992
1985	3,011,400	1,968,712	254,986	487,593	300,203
1986	3,239,400	2,114,621	272,735	526,436	325,638
1987	3,459,600	2,247,158	294,092	562,814	355,505
1988	3,714,100	2,356,483	341,893	607,766	407,977
1989	4,055,600	2,522,125	393,303	683,367	456,803
1990	4,348,100	2,670,234	403,019	743,382	531,407
1991	4,536,200	2,729,322	424,129	792,535	590,198
1992	4,763,200	2,811,611	441,781	851,205	658,601
Sex:					
Male	4,050,900	2,257,900	401,100	804,200	587,700
Female	712,300	553,700	40,700	47,100	70,800
Race:					
White	2,682,200	1,689,500	233,000	411,800	347,800
Black	1,781,700	857,100	195,200	427,700	301,600

[1] Totals may not add due to individuals having multiple correctional statuses.   [2] Estimated.

Source: U.S. Bureau of Justice Statistics, *Correctional Populations in the United States, 1992.*

No. 354. Prisoners Under Sentence of Death: 1980 to 1993

[As of December 31. Excludes prisoners under sentence of death who remained within local correction systems pending exhaustion of appellate process or who had not been committed to prison]

CHARACTERISTIC	1980	1990	1991	1992	1993	CHARACTERISTIC	1980	1990	1991	1992	1993
Total [1]	688	2,346	2,466	2,575	2,716	Unknown	163	279	313	315	332
						Marital status:					
White	418	1,368	1,450	1,506	1,566	Never married	268	996	1,071	1,132	1,222
Black and other	270	978	1,016	1,067	1,150	Married [2]	229	632	663	671	671
						Divorced [2]	217	726	746	780	823
Under 20 years	11	8	14	12	13						
20 to 24 years	173	168	179	188	211	Time elapsed since					
25 to 34 years	334	1,110	1,087	1,078	1,066	sentencing:					
35 to 54 years	166	1,006	1,129	1,212	1,330	Less than 12 months	185	231	252	265	262
55 years and over	10	64	73	85	96	12 to 47 months	389	753	718	720	716
						48 to 71 months	102	436	441	444	422
Years of school						72 months and over	38	934	1,071	1,146	1,316
completed:											
7 years or less	68	178	173	181	185	Legal status at arrest:					
8 years	74	186	181	180	183	Not under sentence	384	1,345	1,415	1,476	1,562
9 to 11 years	204	775	810	836	885	Parole or probation [3]	115	578	615	702	754
12 years	162	729	783	831	887	Prison or escaped	45	128	102	101	102
More than 12 years	43	209	222	232	244	Unknown	170	305	321	296	298

[1] For 1980 to 1991, revisions to the total number of prisoners were not carried to the characteristics except for race.   [2] Includes persons married but separated, widows, widowers, and unknown.   [3] Includes prisoners on mandatory conditional release, work release, leave, AWOL, or bail. Covers 24 prisoners in 1989, 26 in 1990, and 29 in 1991 and 1992.

Source: U.S. Bureau of Justice Statistics, *Capital Punishment,* annual.

Exhibit 78: A page from the *Statistical Abstract of the United States.*

Each year the U.S. Department of Justice publishes two major sources for criminal justice statistics. *Uniform Crime Reports* (also known as *Crime in the United States*) focuses on criminal activities, and *Sourcebook of Criminal Justice Statistics* provides a broader range of statistics on the social and economic impacts of crime.

Information on court caseloads can be found in the *Annual Report* of the Administrative Office of the United States Courts and *State Court Caseload Statistics* (National Center for State Courts, annual). Data on the composition of the U.S. legal profession is found in *The Lawyer Statistical Report*, published periodically by the American Bar Foundation; the most recent report, published in 1994, covers the profession as of 1991.

Yearbooks and annual reports of trade associations, labor unions, financial institutions, public interest groups, and both federal and state government agencies generally contain statistical data relating to the work and interests of those organizations. Access to these sources can be obtained through the following comprehensive indexes: *American Statistics Index* (1973–date), covering U.S. government sources; *Statistical Reference Index* (1980–date), covering state governmental and private sources; and *Statistics Sources* (2 vols., annual) covering a wide range of sources. *American Statistics Index* is also available on WESTLAW.

§ 11–4. NEWS SOURCES

While a general encyclopedia or almanac may provide background information on historical persons and events, for recent information there are few sources that can rival the coverage of major daily newspapers such as the *New York Times* or *Washington Post*. Access to these papers is available through extensive indexes published in annual volumes, but a far more convenient and powerful method of finding information is searching online full-text newspaper databases such as those available through WESTLAW and LEXIS–NEXIS.

WESTLAW provides access to hundreds of newspapers, as well as wire services and several hundred business publications, by arrangement with Dow Jones News/Retrieval. One can search in a specific publication, in NP for all newspapers, and ALLNEWS for all news sources. LEXIS–NEXIS has a NEWS library with the text of newspapers, magazines, trade journals, newsletters, and wire services. There is considerable overlap in coverage between WESTLAW and LEXIS–NEXIS, with the major exceptions being the *Wall Street Journal* (available only on WESTLAW) and the *New York Times* (retrospective coverage available only on LEXIS–NEXIS). Other online systems with extensive news databases include DIALOG and DataTimes (both available through WESTLAW under some subscription plans).

In legal practice, these online news databases may be as valuable as the databases with case law or statutes. Through them, an attorney can find current information on people, corporate or government activities, or international developments.

§ 11-5. DIRECTORIES

Access to names and contact information is vital in legal practice and in legal research. Lawyers often need to file documents with courts and agencies, find background information on clients or opposing counsel, and establish contacts within the profession. One well-placed telephone call can sometimes yield more information than hours of research in books or databases.

Several directories provide addresses, telephone numbers, and biographical information for lawyers, judges, and courts throughout the country. Directories of prac-

ticing lawyers are also published for individual states and for particular fields of professional specialization.

The annual *Martindale–Hubbell Law Directory* provides the most comprehensive listing of lawyers in all U.S. states and some foreign countries. The main seventeen-volume set contains listings of lawyers by state and city. At the beginning of each volume, every lawyer has a one-line entry indicating date of birth, date of admission to practice, college, law school, and address or affiliation. The rest of the volume contains fuller descriptions of those lawyers and law firms who purchase space beyond the simple alphabetical listings. The set is accompanied by an alphabetical index and an areas of practice index. A separate *Martindale–Hubbell International Law Directory* provides selective coverage for other countries. *Martindale–Hubbell* is available on CD–ROM and online through LEXIS.

There are many other national directories of lawyers and law firms. Several are available through WEST-LAW, including the National Association for Law Placement's *Directory of Legal Employers* (NALP–DIR) and *West's Legal Directory* (WLD). *Who's Who in American Law* (biennial) is a useful source of biographical information on prominent attorneys and legal scholars. The *Law Firms Yellow Book* (semiannual) provides information on the management and recruiting personnel of major law firms, and includes an index by law school. Several specialized directories are published with the title *Law & Business Directory of . . .*, covering corporate counsel, litigators, and attorneys practicing bankruptcy or environmental law.

Federal courts and judges are covered in a number of directories. A two-volume looseleaf publication, *Alma-*

nac of the Federal Judiciary, provides information on federal judges, including noteworthy rulings, media coverage, and lawyers' evaluations of the judge's ability and temperament. The *Judicial Staff Directory* (annual) also provides basic biographical information, as well as extensive listings of court personnel; it is available as the JUDDIR file on LEXIS. The official *United States Court Directory* (semiannual) provides names, addresses and telephone numbers.

The American Bench (biennial) is a biographical directory of both federal and state courts, covering almost every judge in the United States. Addresses and telephone numbers, but not biographical data, are also available in *BNA's Directory of State and Federal Courts, Judges, and Clerks* (biennial) and *Want's Federal–State Court Directory* (annual). All three books also include basic information on each state's court system.

Federal government offices in Washington can be a major source of information. Directories of Congress and the federal agencies have been described earlier, on pages 188-89 and 193-94 respectively. Without a specific branch or agency in mind, the best place to start may be the *Washington Information Directory* (annual), which is organized by subject and lists congressional committees, government agencies, and private organizations.

Interest groups, professional organizations and trade associations can be invaluable sources of information in the areas of their concern. Many welcome inquiries from researchers and can provide press releases and documents not available in print or online. The standard directory of these organizations is the *Encyclopedia of Associations* (3 vols., annual), which provides addresses, telephone and fax numbers, as well as information

about the organization's activities and publications. Exhibit 79 shows entries for just a few of the listed organizations of attorneys. The *Encyclopedia of Associations* is also available in CD–ROM and online through both WESTLAW (ENASSC) and LEXIS (EOA). *National Trade and Professional Associations of the United States* (annual) is a less extensive directory useful for finding addresses and telephone numbers of business-related organizations.

★4962★ Attorneys

★4962★ NATIONAL LAWYERS CLUB (NLC)
c/o Federal Bar Association
1815 H St. NW, Ste. 408
Washington, DC 20006
John G. Blanche III, Exec. Staff Dir.
PH: (202)638-0252   FX: (202)775-0295
Founded: 1959. **Members:** 1,825. Private legal club. Presently inactive.

★4963★ NATIONAL LAWYERS GUILD (NLG)
55 6th Ave.
New York, NY 10013
Rick Bent, Exec.Dir.
PH: (212)966-5000
Founded: 1937. **Members:** 9,000. **Budget:** $270,000. **Regional Groups:** 120. Lawyers, law students, legal workers, and jailhouse lawyers dedicated to seeking economic justice, social equality, and the right to political dissent. Serves as national center for progressive legal work providing training programs to both members and nonmembers. Sponsors skills seminars in different areas of law. Maintains speakers' bureau; offers legal referrals. **Committees:** Affirmative Action/Anti-Discrimination; Civil Liberties; Criminal Law; International; Labor; Law Students in Action; Rural Justice; Summer Projects; Theoretical Studies. **Projects:** Central American Refugee Defense Fund; Grand Jury; National Immigration; Visa Denial. **Subcommittees:** AIDS Network; Cuba; Disinformation and Information Restriction; Faculty Network; Gay Rights; IADL Representative; International Law; Middle East; Peace and Disarmament; Philippines; Puerto Rico; Relations-International Organization; Southern Africa. **Task Forces:** Anti-Repression; Anti-Sexism; Central America; Chile; Economic Rights; Ireland; Military Law; Movement Support Network. **Publications:** *National Lawyers Guild—Guild Notes*, quarterly. Newsletter. Price: $50.00/year. Circulation: 10,000 ● *National Lawyers Guild—Guild Practitioner*, quarterly. Price: $15.00/year ● *National Lawyers Guild—Referral Directory*, biennial. Geographically arranged directory of guild lawyers and their legal services. Price: $15.00/copy. Advertising: not accepted. **Conventions/Meetings:** annual meeting.

★4964★ SERBIAN-AMERICAN BAR ASSOCIATION (SABA)
c/o Deyon Ranko Brashich
1040 6th Ave., 23rd fl.
New York, NY 10018
Deyon Ranko Brashich, Pres.
PH: (212)575-1778   TX: 42357 Brfin
Founded: 1984. **Members:** 12. Attorneys, judges, and legal professionals of Serbian origin. (Serbia is a region in present-day Yugoslavia, but has existed in the past as an autonomous nation.) Seeks to provide educational services; takes positions on national and international issues that are consistent with Serbian heritage. Bestows Man (or Woman) of the Year Award. **Conventions/Meetings:** annual meeting.

Exhibit 79: Entries on professional associations in the *Encyclopedia of Associations.*

§ 11–6. CONCLUSION

This chapter's introductory survey of legal reference sources presents just a small fraction of the valuable literature of reference materials. Legal research is rarely confined to the insular world of legal materials, and it is important for researchers to be able to find information in a wide variety of disciplines. The standard, comprehensive source for determining what reference materials are available is the American Library Association's *Guide to Reference Books* (11th ed. 1996). The Guide describes basic resources in hundreds of disciplines, including dictionaries, encyclopedias, bibliographies, research guides, directories, and periodical indexes. It provides the necessary background to enable the legal researcher to work in other disciplines.

CHAPTER 12

INTERNATIONAL LAW:
U.S. SOURCES

---

§ 12–1. INTRODUCTION

International law is that body of law which governs relations among nations. It can be distinguished from *foreign law,* which refers to the domestic, internal law of other nations. There is a further distinction between *public* international law and *private* international law. Public international law concerns the rules, treaties, customs and procedures that regulate national states in their relations with each other. Private international law (or conflict of laws) determines where, and by whose law, controversies involving more than one jurisdiction are resolved. Private international law also determines how foreign judgments are enforced.

A transnational or multinational legal practice often requires knowledge of each of these areas of law. Law-

yers representing an American firm investing in another country, for example, must be aware of treaties between the two nations as well as the investment and trade laws of both the United States and the other country. They may also need to examine jurisdictional issues in resolving disputes or in determining the application of one country's rules in the other's courts. The next two chapters focus on international law, while research in the law of foreign countries is the subject of Chapters 14 and 15.

The sources of United States international law and practice are important both for transnational practice and for their impact on domestic law. This material includes treaties, foreign relations documentation, and other primary and secondary sources of international scope. Because they have significance both externally and internally, these publications are essential to research in American law and are discussed separately in this chapter. The next chapter will cover more general sources of international law.

Unless the issue to be researched involves a known document (such as a court decision, statute or treaty) as a starting point, then background reading in a secondary source is recommended as an initial step. Preliminary study in a treatise or law review article can help clarify complex issues of international law and usually leads to relevant primary sources. The methods discussed in Chapter 9 for finding secondary materials can be used to find relevant works on most issues in international law.

§ 12–2. TREATIES AND EXECUTIVE AGREEMENTS

Treaties are formal agreements between countries, and have legal significance for both domestic and international purposes. Treaties between two governments are called *bilateral*; those entered into by more than two governments are called *multilateral*. Since Article VI of the Constitution provides that treaties are part of the supreme law of the land and shall bind all judges, they have the same legal effect and status as federal statutes. Treaties can thus supersede prior statutes, and statutes can supersede treaties as the controlling law within the United States. A treaty no longer valid as the law of the land may still be binding between the United States and another country, unless it has been formally abrogated.

Treaties of the United States are negotiated and drafted by the executive branch of the government, but require approval by two-thirds of the Senate. After Senate approval, treaties are ratified and proclaimed by the President. *Executive agreements* are made with other countries by the President and generally do not require Senate consent. They may, however, be submitted to the Senate for approval if the President so decides. Most of the sources discussed here cover both treaties and executive agreements.

The effective date of a treaty may be different for international and domestic purposes. For international implementation, the effective date is that specified in the treaty itself. Most modern treaties do designate an effective date, usually in the final clause. If a date is not so indicated, the effective date is considered to be the date on which ratifications are exchanged between the signatories. For the purposes of domestic law, treaties

generally become effective when proclaimed by the President. Executive agreements become effective on the date specified in the agreement.

Research on a United States treaty typically involves the following steps: (1) finding its text in an authoritative source; (2) determining whether it is in force and with what parties and reservations; and (3) interpreting its provisions, with the aid of judicial decisions and legislative history.

a. Sources

The treaties of the United States are published in a variety of forms—official and unofficial, national and international, current and retrospective.

Official sources. Until 1949, treaties were published in the *Statutes at Large* for each session of Congress. Beginning in 1950, a separate chronological publication, *United States Treaties and Other International Agreements (UST)*, has been the permanent form of official treaty publication. Several volumes of *UST* are published annually, containing all treaties and executive agreements to which the United States is a party. *UST* volumes are published after a long delay, unfortunately, and most treaties do not appear until eight or ten years after they are signed.

Treaties and agreements are issued first in a slip format in the preliminary series, *Treaties and Other International Acts Series (TIAS)*. *TIAS* has been published since 1945 as the successor to two earlier series: *Treaty Series* (1908–45) and *Executive Agreement Series* (1929–45). Slip treaties are consecutively numbered and issued in separately paginated pamphlets, each containing the text of one treaty or agreement, first in English

and then in the languages of the other parties. *TIAS* publication is more current than *UST*, but still involves a time lag of several years.

Treaties and executive agreements are generally cited by the date on which they are signed by representatives of the United States and the other signatory countries. Exhibit 80 shows the first page of the Agreement for the Interdiction of Narcotic Trafficking, Aug. 28, 1981, U.S.–Haiti, 34 U.S.T. 4321.

After signing but before approval, treaties are transmitted to the Senate for its consideration in the form of *Treaty Documents* (formerly called *Senate Executive Documents*). These pamphlets, which usually include transmittal messages from the President and the Secretary of State, provide early access to the texts of treaties.

Current sources. Because of the long delays in the publication of treaties in *TIAS* and in the bound volumes of *UST*, two commercial services are important sources for current access to treaties.

UST Current Service (1990–date), published by William S. Hein & Co., offers bimonthly delivery of the full texts of U.S. treaties and executive agreements on microfiche. *UST Current Service* assigns numbers to the new agreements and provides indexing by country and subject, on looseleaf pages and as part of Hein's CD-ROM treaty index.

Consolidated Treaties & International Agreements: Current Document Service (1990–date), from Oceana Publications, is a quarterly print publication containing

HAITI

Narcotic Drugs: Interdiction of Trafficking

Agreement signed at Port-au-Prince August 28, 1981;
Entered into force August 28, 1981.
And amending and extending agreements;
Effected by exchange of notes.
Signed at Port-au-Prince December 18 and 21, 1981;
Entered into force December 21, 1981.
And exchange of notes.
Signed at Port-au-Prince February 18, 1982;
Entered into force February 18, 1982.
And exchange of notes.
Signed at Port-au-Prince October. 15 and 22, 1982;
Entered into force October 22, 1982.

AGREEMENT BETWEEN THE GOVERNMENT OF THE UNITED STATES OF AMERICA AND THE GOVERNMENT OF HAITI FOR THE INTERDICTION OF NARCOTICS TRAFFICKING

This is an agreement for the interdiction of narcotics made in accordance with the general agreement for technical cooperation (reached through an exchange of notes in Port-au-Prince on May 2, 1951)[1] between the Secretary of State for Foreign Affairs of the Republic of Haiti, Edouard Francisque, as representative of the Government of Haiti, and the Ambassador of the United States, Ernest H. Preeg, as a representative of the Bureau of International Narcotics Matters of the Department of State of the United States of America.

ITEM I. The Government of Haiti agrees that the Haitian Navy will patrol the Windward Passage in areas coordinated with the United States Coast Guard until on or about December 31, 1981. As part of their coastal patrol mission, they will locate and report to the U.S. Coast Guard the location, direction of travel and description of vessels suspected of narcotics trafficking activities.

ITEM II. The Bureau of International Narcotics Matters of the Department of State agrees to provide petroleum, oil, lubricants and necessary routine maintenance for Haitian naval vessels on narcot-

---

[1] TIAS 2414, 2635; 3 UST 545, 4731.

Exhibit 80: The first page of an agreement in *United States Treaties and Other International Agreements.*

new treaties and agreements. Each issue of *CTIA* includes appendices indexing treaties by country and by subject.

International Legal Materials, published bimonthly since 1962 by the American Society of International Law, contains the texts of treaties of major significance and sometimes provides drafts before final agreement. Although selective, it provides access to many recent documents reflecting U.S. international law developments. Treaties in *ILM* are available on both WESTLAW (ILM) and LEXIS (ILMTY).

The WESTLAW database USTREATIES provides access to treaties beginning in 1979, and the CD–ROM *TIARA (Treaties & International Agreements Researchers' Archive)* contains the text of over 7,000 treaties currently in force.

Retrospective sources. The best historical source for U.S. treaties and agreements is the definitive, official compilation, *Bevans' Treaties and Other International Agreements of the United States of America 1776–1949* (13 vols., 1968–75). Including all ratified treaties and agreements up to the beginning of *UST,* the set contains four volumes of multilateral treaties (arranged chronologically) and eight of bilateral treaties (arranged alphabetically by country). Volume 13 provides indexes by country and subject.

Treaties which were never approved by the Senate, or which for some other reason did not become effective, are collected in *Unperfected Treaties of the United States of America 1776–1976* (7 vols., 1976–94), edited by Christian Wiktor. Each treaty is prefaced by an historical note, and volume 7 includes a general index to the set.

Other sources. There are a few compilations of United States treaties on specific subjects. These include looseleaf collections of tax treaties from both CCH and Warren, Gorham & Lamont, and *Extradition Laws and Treaties* (1979–date), compiled by Igor I. Kavass and Adolf Sprudzs. The *United States Code* includes the texts of a few important treaties which substantially affect related statutory provisions (such as the Universal Copyright Convention in Title 17). *USCCAN* also publishes a few selected treaties after ratification.

United States treaties also appear in a variety of multinational compilations, including the *League of Nations Treaty Series,* the *United Nations Treaty Series,* and the *Consolidated Treaty Series.* These are discussed with other general international law sources in Chapter 13.

b. Indexes, Guides and Citators

Treaties are generally published chronologically rather than by subject. Several finding tools and indexes are available, however, to provide subject access.

Treaties in Force, an annual publication of the Department of State, is the official index to current United States treaties and agreements. It offers citations to all of the major treaty publications, including *Statutes at Large, TIAS, UST, Bevans, League of Nations Treaty Series,* and *U.N. Treaty Series.* The first part of the index lists bilateral treaties by country and then, under each country, by subject. The second section indexes multilateral treaties by subject. This index is usually the starting point for searching current treaties. Its two sections are illustrated in Exhibit 81.

HAITI

AGRICULTURAL COMMODITIES

Agricultural commodities agreement. Signed at Port-au-Prince March 20, 1975; entered into force March 20, 1975.
28 UST 4462; TIAS 8600.

Related agreements:
March 22, 1976 (28 UST 4483; TIAS 8601).
May 14 and 17, 1976 (28 UST 4490; TIAS 8601).
November 30, 1976.
April 13, 1977.
June 23, 1978.

Agricultural commodities agreement, with memorandum of understanding. Signed at Port-au-Prince June 8, 1979; entered into force June 8, 1979.
TIAS

Related agreements:
June 24, 1980.
May 25, 1981.
May 28, 1982.
August 17 and 18, 1982.
June 8, 1983.
June 12, 1984.

Agricultural commodities agreement, with annexes and memorandum of understanding. Signed at Port-au-Prince May 30, 1985; entered into force May 30, 1985.
TIAS

Amendments:
June 2 and 5, 1986.
June 19, 1987.

COPYRIGHT (See APPENDIX)

CUSTOMS

Agreement relating to reciprocal customs privileges for consular officers and clerks. Exchange of notes at Port-au-Prince August 14 and 24, 1945; entered into force August 24, 1945.
59 Stat. 1868; EAS 503; 8 Bevans 791; 139 UNTS 311.

FISHERIES

(See also CONSERVATION; WHALING)

Convention on fishing and conservation of living resources of the high seas. Done at Geneva April 29, 1958; entered into force March 20, 1966.
17 UST 138; TIAS 5969; 559 UNTS 285.
States which are parties:
Australia
Belgium
Bosnia-Herzegovina
Burkina Faso
Cambodia
Colombia
Denmark [1]
Dominican Rep.
Fiji
Finland
France
Haiti
Jamaica
Kenya
Lesotho
Madagascar
Malawi
Malaysia
Mauritius
Mexico
Netherlands [2]
Nigeria
Portugal
Sierra Leone
Solomon Is.
South Africa
Spain [3]
Switzerland
Thailand
Tonga
Trinidad & Tobago
Uganda
United Kingdom [3]
United States [4]
Venezuela
Yugoslavia [5]

NOTES:
[1] With reservation.
[2] Applicable to Netherlands Antilles and Aruba.
[3] With a statement.
[4] With an understanding.
[5] See note under YUGOSLAVIA in bilateral section.

Exhibit 81: Excerpts from *Treaties in Force*, showing treatment of bilateral treaties (left) and multilateral treaties (right).

A *Guide to the United States Treaties in Force,* edited by Igor I. Kavass and Adolf Sprudzs, is also issued annually and provides several additional means of access to current treaties. Part I includes numerical lists of all treaties in force. Part II contains subject and country indexes to both bilateral and multilateral treaties. Part III focuses on multilateral treaties, with a chronological index and a directory of countries indicating the agreements to which each is a party.

US Department of State Dispatch, an official weekly magazine which replaced the monthly *Department of State Bulletin* in 1990, includes in one issue each month a "Treaty Actions" section reporting on current treaty developments and supplementing the annual *Treaties in Force.* Special supplements to *Dispatch* are occasionally issued with the texts of major treaties. Online access to *Dispatch* is available in WESTLAW's USDPTSTDIS database and LEXIS's DSTATE file. Exhibit 82 shows part of a "Treaty Actions" feature in an issue of *Dispatch.*

A bimonthly journal, *Foreign Policy Bulletin: The Documentary Record of United States Foreign Policy,* also reports on treaty developments in a section entitled "Treaties—Current Actions," and includes the texts of selected major treaties. Both *Dispatch* and *Foreign Policy Bulletin* are useful sources for current information on U.S. practice in international law.

The major collections and series of U.S. treaties and international agreements are indexed in the *United States Treaty Index: 1776–1990 Consolidation,* edited by Igor I. Kavass and published by Hein. This multivolume work includes a numerical guide to treaties and agree-

Treaty Actions

Treaty Actions

Multilateral

Chemical Weapons
Convention on the prohibition of the development, production, stockpiling, and use of chemical weapons and on their destruction, with annexes. Done at Paris Jan. 13, 1993. [Senate] Treaty Doc. 103-21[1].
Ratifications: Denmark, July 13, 1995; Peru, July 20, 1995.

Children
Convention on protection of children and cooperation in respect of intercountry adoption. Done at The Hague May 29, 1993. Entered into force May 1, 1995[5].
Signatures: Luxembourg, June 6, 1995; Poland, June 12, 1995. *Ratifications:* Poland, June 12, 1995.

Convention on the rights of the child. Done at New York Nov. 20, 1989. Entered into force Sept. 2, 1990[2].
Accessions: Botswana, Mar. 14, 1995; Solomon Islands, Apr. 10, 1995; Palau, Aug. 4, 1995. *Ratifications:* Qatar, Apr. 3, 1995; Turkey, Apr. 4, 1995; South Africa, June 16, 1995.

Copyrights
Berne convention for the protection of literary and artistic works of Sept. 9, 1886, as revised. Done at Paris July 24, 1971, amended in 1979. Entered into force Mar. 1, 1989 for the U.S.
Accessions: Moldova, Aug. 1, 1995[1]; Ukraine, July 25, 1995[2].

Genocide
Convention on the prevention and punishment of the crime of genocide. Adopted by the UN General Assembly at Paris Dec. 9, 1948. Entered into force Jan. 12, 1951; for the U.S. Feb. 23, 1989. *Accession:* Singapore, Aug. 18, 1995.

Patents
Patent cooperation treaty, with regulations. Done at Washington June 19, 1970. Entered into force Jan. 24, 1978. TIAS 8733; 28 UST 7645.
Accession: Lesotho, July 21, 1995.

Strasbourg agreement concerning the international patent classification. Done at Strasbourg Mar. 24, 1971. Entered into force Oct. 7, 1975. TIAS 8140; 26 UST 1793.
Accession: Malawi, July 24, 1995.

Property
Convention of Paris for the protection of industrial property of Mar. 20, 1883, as revised. Done at Stockholm July 14, 1967. Entered into force Apr. 26, 1970; for the U.S. Sept. 5, 1970; except for Articles 1-12 which entered into force May 19, 1970; for the U.S. Aug. 25, 1973. TIAS 8923, 7727; 21 UST 1583, 24 UST 2140.
Accession: Costa Rica, July 28, 1995.

Nice agreement concerning the international classification of goods and services for purposes of the registration of marks of June 15, 1957, as revised. Done at Geneva May 13, 1977. Entered into force Feb. 6, 1979; for the U.S. Feb. 29, 1984.
Accession: Malawi, July 24, 1995.

Terrorism
Convention on the safety of the United Nations and associated personnel. Done at New York Dec. 9, 1994[1].
Ratification: Norway, July 3, 1995.

Weapons, Conventional
Convention on prohibitions or restrictions on the use of certain conventional weapons which may be deemed to be excessively injurious or to have indiscriminate effects, with annexed protocols. Adopted at Geneva Oct. 10, 1980. Entered into force Dec. 2, 1983.

Protocol on non-detectable fragments (Protocol I) to the convention on prohibitions or restrictions on the use of certain conventional weapons which may be deemed to be excessively injurious or to have indiscriminate effects. Adopted at Geneva Oct. 10, 1980. Entered into force Dec. 2, 1983.

Protocol on prohibitions or restrictions on the use of mines, booby-traps, and other devices (Protocol II) to the convention on prohibitions or restrictions on the use of certain conventional weapons which may be deemed to be excessively injurious or to have indiscriminate effects. Adopted at Geneva Oct. 10, 1980. Entered into force Dec. 2, 1983.
Accession: Malta, June 26, 1995.
Enters into force for the U.S.: Sept. 24, 1995.

Protocol on prohibitions or restrictions on the use of incendiary weapons (Protocol III) to the convention on prohibitions or restrictions on the use of certain conventional weapons which may be deemed to be excessively injurious or to have indiscriminate effects. Adopted at Geneva Oct. 10, 1980. Entered into force Dec. 2, 1983[4].
Accession: Malta, June 26, 1995.

Women
Convention on the elimination of all forms of discrimination against women. Adopted by the UN General Assembly Dec. 18, 1979. Entered into force Sept. 3, 1981[1]. [Senate] Ex. R, 96th Cong., 2d Sess.
Accession: Azerbaijan, July 10, 1995.

Bilateral

Argentina
Agreement amending the air transport services agreement of Oct. 22, 1985, as amended and extended. Effected by exchange of notes at Buenos Aires Apr. 11 and July 3, 1995. Entered into force July 3, 1995.

Agreement for cooperation in the Global Learning and Observations to Benefit the Environment (GLOBE) program, with appendices. Signed at Buenos Aires June 28, 1995. Entered into force June 28, 1995.

Armenia
Postal money order agreement. Signed at Yerevan and Washington June 26 and Aug. 3, 1995. Entered into force Sept. 1, 1995.

Austria
Agreement amending the air services agreement of Mar. 16, 1989. Effected by exchange of notes at Vienna June 14, 1995. Entered into force Aug. 1, 1995.

Canada
Memorandum of understanding concerning counterterrorism research and development, with annex. Signed at Washington and Ottawa June 12 and 23, 1995. Entered into force June 23, 1995.

Dominican Republic
Postal money order agreement. Signed at Washington and Santo Domingo Aug. 6 and 14, 1995. Entered into force Sept. 1, 1995.

Egypt
Grant agreement for private sector import program. Signed at Cairo Aug. 12, 1995. Entered into force Aug. 12, 1995.

Hungary
Agreement extending the annex to the air transport agreement of July 12, 1989, as extended. Effected by exchange of notes at Washington July 6 and 12, 1995. Entered into force July 12, 1995.

Kazakstan
Agreement amending the agreement of Dec. 13, 1993, concerning the provision to the Republic of Kazakstan of material and services for the establishment of a government-to-government communications link. Signed at Almaty June 30, 1995. Entered into force June 30, 1995.

Agreement amending the agreement of Dec. 13, 1993, concerning the provision of material, services, and related training to the Republic of Kazakstan in connection with the destruction of silo launchers of intercontinental ballistic missiles and associated equipment and components. Signed at Almaty July 1, 1995. Entered into force July 1, 1995.

Exhibit 82: "Treaty Actions" in an issue of the *US Department of State Dispatch.*

ments, and indexes by date, country, and subject. The consolidated index is updated annually by the *Current Treaty Index*, and cumulative electronic access to both publications is available through *Hein's United States Treaty Index on CD–ROM*.

A major part of determining the current status of a treaty is checking sources such as *Treaties in Force* and *Dispatch* to see whether its validity has been affected by later diplomatic action. Treaties can also be affected, however, by judicial or legislative action, so relevant cases and statutes must also be examined. Court decisions interpreting a treaty can also provide authoritative material for the researcher who seeks information on its meaning or effect.

Shepard's United States Citations—Statutes Edition covers treaties, including references to citing federal court decisions and (through 1990) to later treaty action or legislation affecting a cited treaty. For treaties up to 1949, citations are included in the *Statutes at Large* section. After 1950, a separate section lists treaties by *UST* citation or *TIAS* number. *Shepard's U.S. Citations* does not include citations to treaties in state court decisions, but there are similar sections for *Statutes at Large* and *UST* in the statutes volumes of every state Shepard's citator.

The *United States Code Service* includes a volume of *International Agreements* containing the texts of about two dozen major conventions and treaties, accompanied by research references and annotations of federal and state court decisions. Another volume, *Annotations to Uncodified Laws and Treaties*, has no treaty texts but provides broader coverage of decisions interpreting U.S. treaties, including sections for treaties with Native

American nations, multilateral treaties (listed by date), and bilateral treaties (listed by country).

As with other documents, a treaty title or citation can also be used as a search term in online databases. The researcher can find cases or periodical articles which have cited the treaty, perhaps including some too recent to be included in *Shepard's* or *USCS*.

c. Legislative History

Treaties often contain ambiguities which can lead to controversies in interpretation and application. The documents produced during congressional deliberation and action on a treaty can be useful sources for understanding its text. When sent to the Senate for its advice and consent, a treaty is referred to the Senate Foreign Relations Committee. The committee may hold hearings, which may or may not be published. The committee then refers the treaty to the full Senate with its recommendation.

Treaty Documents contain the text of treaties as they are transmitted to the Senate for its consideration. Prior to the 97th Congress, they were called *Senate Executive Documents*. These documents usually contain messages from the President and the Secretary of State. *Senate Executive Reports* contain the Senate Foreign Relations Committee's analysis of the treaty and its recommendation to the Senate as to approval. Both Treaty Documents and Senate Executive Reports are issued in numbered series which identify the Congress and sequence in which they were issued. Treaty Document No. 104–5, for example, is the fifth treaty transmitted in the 104th Congress. Treaties transmitted before the 97th Congress, of which a few are still pending, were

identified alphabetically; Executive H, 96–2 was the eighth treaty transmitted in the second session of the 96th Congress.

Legislative history research tools have been discussed more fully in Chapter 6, but several resources are particularly helpful in tracing the legislative history of treaties.

The *Congressional Index,* CCH's weekly looseleaf service, includes a table of treaties pending before the Senate. This is one of the most valuable status tables for determining actions taken on pending treaties. Treaty listings include references to Treaty Documents, Executive Reports, hearings, and ratifications. The treaties are listed chronologically by the session of transmittal and designated by Treaty Document number or Executive letter (for treaties before 1981). A country and subject index precedes the list of treaties. A sample page from the table is shown in Exhibit 83.

The *Legislative Calendar* of the Senate Foreign Relations Committee, the official status table of business before the committee, is perhaps the best list of pending treaties with actions taken thereon, but it is less widely available than the CCH service. Its information on hearings is particularly useful. The "Cumulative Record" final edition for each Congress includes a list of committee publications for both sessions.

Other standard legislative history tools are also useful in treaty research. The *CIS/Index* includes some coverage of treaties and provides access to documents and reports through several indexes, but it does not provide legislative history summaries as it does for statutes. The *CQ Weekly Report* contains occasional special re-

7054   Treaties—Nominations   23 6-9-95

December, 1979, establishes a mechanism to achieve international and domestic cooperation and coordination in facilitating the recognition of academic credentials, and improve the mobility of students, teachers and scholars.

96-2, Executive W (11/24/80)—Animals and wildlife—Canada—Migratory bird protection

The Protocol Amending the Convention of August 16, 1916 for the Protection of Migratory Birds in Canada and the U.S. modernizes the Convention's subsistence-taking and egg-collection provisions. The Protocol broadens subsistence-taking rights to "all indigenous inhabitants of the State of Alaska" in a racially nondiscriminatory way. Authorities in both countries determine what constitutes legitimate subsistence needs and establish hunting seasons.

97th CONGRESS—1st SESSION

97-15, Treaty Document No. (7/28/81)—Crime and criminal procedures—Extradition—Sweden

The Supplementary Convention on Extradition between Sweden and the U.S., signed at Washington, D.C. in May, 1981, expands the list of extraditable offenses to include tax evasion, obstruction of justice, offenses relating to the international transfer of funds, and conspiracy.

98th CONGRESS—1st SESSION

98-10, Treaty Document No. (10/4/83)—Foreign trade—Europe—Endangered species

The Amendment to the 1973 Convention on International Trade in Endangered Species of Wild Fauna and Flora (CITES), adopted in April, 1983, allows the European Community to become a party to the Convention as a community, thereby opening the Convention to regional economic integration organizations.

98-12, Treaty Document No. (11/17/83)—Income tax—Denmark

The Protocol to the Convention between the U.S. and Denmark for the Avoidance of Double Taxation and the Prevention of Fiscal Evasion with Respect to Taxes on Income was signed at Washington, D.C. in August, 1983.

The Protocol modernizes the original Convention (see Executive Q, 96-2) to conform with positions taken by the U.S. Senate on more recent income tax treaties, and changes to Danish tax laws since 1980.

Ordered reported: 5/8/84; 12/4/85

Reported: S. Ex. Rept. No. 98-23, 5/21/84; S. Ex. Rept. No. 99-5, 12/11/85

98th CONGRESS—2nd SESSION

98-14, Treaty Document No. (1/30/84)—Crime and criminal procedures—Consular rights—South Africa

The Consular Convention between the U.S. and South Africa was signed at Pretoria in October, 1982.

The Convention would provide certain consular rights when a national of either country is arrested and detained in the other country. These rights include free communication between a national and consul, notification of consular officers of the arrest and detention, and permission for visits by consuls to detained nationals.

96-2

Exhibit 83: A page of treaty summaries in the *Congressional Index*.

ports on major treaties, and includes chronologies, summaries of debates and messages, and general information about current treaties. The fortnightly and bound indexes to the *Congressional Record* list treaty actions and discussions appearing in the *Record,* under the heading "Treaties" and also occasionally under the name of a particular treaty or its subject matter. Although not very convenient for current use, the *Congressional Record* indexes are helpful for retrospective research into a particular treaty's legislative history.

The *CIS Index to US Senate Executive Documents and Reports* (1987) provides coverage up to the beginning of the general *CIS Index* in 1970. It lists the documents and reports chronologically from 1818 to 1969, with indexes by subject, treaty title, document number, and report number. This index is part of the CIS *Congressional Masterfile 1* on CD–ROM, and all the indexed documents are available as part of the CIS legislative history microfiche collection. The eight-volume *Reports of the Committee on Foreign Relations, 1789–1901,* S. Doc. No. 231, 56th Cong., 2d Sess. (1901), is a handy compilation of older executive reports.

§ 12–3. CASE LAW AND STATUTES

Many judicial decisions, particularly but not exclusively from the federal courts, reflect United States practice in international law. These cases can be found in the standard reporters described in Chapter 2, as well as in several specialized reporters.

American International Law Cases (1971–date), now in its third series, reprints American federal and state court decisions relating to international law. The cases are

arranged by subject, and looseleaf binders contain indexes and case tables.

The U.S. Court of International Trade was created in 1980 as a successor to the U.S. Customs Court, with a broader jurisdiction than its predecessor. Its decisions are reported officially in the *U.S. Court of International Trade Reports,* as well as in the *Federal Supplement.* Court of International Trade decisions are subject to review by the U.S. Court of Appeals for the Federal Circuit, which replaced the Court of Customs and Patent Appeals in 1982. The Federal Circuit's decisions in trade cases are published officially in *Cases Decided in United States Court of Appeals for the Federal Circuit* and commercially in the *Federal Reporter.*

Several federal administrative agencies issue decisions relating to international law, including the Federal Maritime Administration; Immigration and Naturalization Service; International Trade Commission; National Transportation Safety Board; and Treasury Department. Those decisions appear in the agencies' reports and in specialized databases of both WESTLAW and LEXIS. BNA's *International Trade Reporter* (1980–date) and Oceana's *United States International Trade Reports* (1981–date) include both judicial and administrative decisions on international trade.

International Legal Materials, the bimonthly compendium of documents, includes important federal and state decisions relating to international law. *International Law Reports,* a comprehensive reporter of the decisions of international tribunals and national courts, contains some American decisions.

§ 12–4. DIGESTS AND
RESTATEMENTS

The Department of State has published a number of encyclopedic digests of international law, offering authoritative statements of the United States international law practice as of the date of publication. Based on treaties, decisions, statutes and other documents reflecting the U.S. position on major issues of international law, these digests are essentially official restatements of American international law.

The most current of these digests (although long outdated) is M.M. Whiteman's *Digest of International Law* (15 vols., 1963–73), focusing largely on the period from the 1940s to the 1960s. Despite its confusing arrangement and lack of an overall table of contents, the contents are accessible through a general index and other finding aids.

The Whiteman *Digest* is supplemented by a Department of State series called *Digest of United States Practice in International Law*. Annual volumes were issued for 1973 through 1980, and two cumulative volumes covering 1981–88 have been published. More current materials are digested in "Contemporary Practice of the United States Relating to International Law," a feature in each quarterly issue of the *American Journal of International Law*.

The earlier digests of international law published by the Department of State, with slight variations in title, were by the following compilers: Francis Wharton (1886; 2d ed. 1887); John Bassett Moore (1906), covering the period 1776 to 1906 and effectively superseding Wharton; and G.H. Hackworth (1940–44), covering the period 1906 to 1939. Since the later digests do not reprint the

contents of the earlier ones, they retain their research value for the period covered.

The American Law Institute's *Restatement of the Foreign Relations Law of the United States (Third),* published in two volumes in 1987, is an unofficial but respected summary of American law and practice in international law and foreign relations. The *Restatement of Conflict of Laws (Second),* published in four volumes (1971–80), covers private international law from an American perspective. The format of these works is similar to that of the other Restatements described above in Chapter 9.

Appendices to the Restatements include abstracts of citing court decisions, and further references to cases and law review articles can be found through *Shepard's Restatement of the Law Citations* or online database searches.

§ 12–5. FOREIGN RELATIONS COLLECTIONS

International Legal Materials has already been mentioned as a source for current American documents related to international law. There are also several retrospective compilations relating to American foreign relations and international law. Many of the documents in these sets are also available in their primary form of publication, but are more conveniently accessible in these compiled editions.

Foreign Relations of the United States (1861–date) is a continuing series of official papers prepared by the Historical Office of the U.S. Department of State, providing a comprehensive record of material relating to treaties, their negotiation and adoption. Unfortunately, there is

a time lag of about twenty-five years between the original (often confidential) issuance of these documents and their publication in this series.

The Department of State also publishes documentary compilations on a more current basis. This series includes: *A Decade of American Foreign Policy: Basic Documents, 1941–1949* (1950); *American Foreign Policy: Basic Documents, 1950–1955* (2 vols., 1957) and *1968–1980* (3 vols., 1983); and annual volumes entitled *American Foreign Policy: Current Documents,* for the years 1956 to 1967 and 1981 to date. There is a two to five year time lag in the publication of these volumes.

The five-volume *United States Foreign Relations Law: Documents and Sources* (1980–84), compiled by Michael J. Glennon, Thomas M. Franck, and Robert C. Cassidy, Jr., is a convenient compilation of basic documents, arranged by subject.

§ 12–6. CONCLUSION

This brief survey of the literature of United States practice in international law highlights the extent and variety of available sources. With the increasingly global nature of business and legal relationships, and the frequent treatment of transnational legal issues by American courts, international law research is no longer an exotic specialty known only to a few practitioners.

CHAPTER 13

INTERNATIONAL LAW: GENERAL SOURCES

---

§ 13–1. INTRODUCTION

Having explored the sources of United States practice in international law, we turn now to the general materials in this field. Public international law regulates the relations between national states. Although its primary historical functions have been the preservation of peace and regulation of war, international law now governs an ever broader range of transnational activities. It regulates matters from copyright protection to the rights of

refugees, and agreements such as the North American Free Trade Agreement or the Maastricht Treaty have made international law an inherent aspect of commercial activity.

The classic statement of the sources of international law doctrine is found in Article 38 of the Statute of the International Court of Justice. The ICJ is to apply the following sources:

a. international conventions, whether general or particular, establishing rules expressly recognized by the contesting states;

b. international custom, as evidence of a general practice accepted as law;

c. the general principles of law recognized by civilized nations;

d. ... judicial decisions and the teachings of the most highly qualified publicists of the various nations, as subsidiary means for the determination of the rules of law.

The most important of these categories are the first two: international conventions or treaties, and the developing body of international custom. When a treaty is relevant to a problem involving its signatories, it is the primary legal authority. International custom consists of the actual conduct of nations, when that conduct is consistent with the rule of law. Custom is not found in a clearly delineated literature or collection of sources, but is established instead by evidence of the practices of a number of states. The materials described in Chapter 12 on United States practice are typical of the sources which can be researched for this purpose.

There is no general agreement as to what constitutes "general principles of law." The clause was probably included in Article 38 to discourage a tribunal from refusing to decide a case because there was no applicable law, but general principles are rarely invoked to support court decisions. Although such principles are not susceptible to research, lawyers and diplomats often argue that the positions they support are based on general principles. The most effective uses of this nebulous source are based on principles drawn from treaties, customary law, or notions of international equity.

The judicial decisions referred to in the Statute include decisions of both international tribunals and domestic courts. While the decisions of international tribunals are not considered binding precedents in subsequent disputes, they are evidence of international practice and can aid in treaty interpretation and in the definition of customary law. The "teaching of the most highly qualified publicists" refers to the writings of international legal scholars, but disagreement over which scholars are "the most highly qualified" has diminished the acceptance of particular sources for this purpose. Like judicial decisions, however, these sources are subsidiary to treaties and international custom.

Although not specified as a source in Article 38, the analysis of specific international incidents, including particularly the actions, reactions, and statements of states in these crisis situations, has become a new and more empirical area of investigation. This type of study is described in W. Michael Reisman & Andrew A. Willard, eds., *International Incidents: The Law That Counts in World Politics* (1988).

§ 13–2. PRELIMINARY RESEARCH AND BIBLIOGRAPHIES

A researcher facing a problem in international law can begin in any one of a variety of sources, depending on the nature of the problem. If the research deals with a particular topic which is covered by identifiable sources (such as an international organization's activities, a treaty, or the foreign relations of a particular country), one can proceed directly to the relevant documentation in that field.

For a general problem, without immediate references to specifically identifiable sources, one can begin with a reference work, a law review article, or a treatise for general information and for help in analyzing the issues involved. A general treatise, such as Michael Akehurst's *A Modern Introduction to International Law* (6th ed. 1987) or Ian Brownlie's *Principles of Public International Law* (4th ed. 1990), can provide an overview of an area of international law doctrine. Volume 1 (Peace) of the classic *Oppenheim's International Law* has been published in a 9th edition (1992), but volume 2 (Disputes, War and Neutrality) is still in a 7th edition (1952), and volume 3 (International Organizations) has yet to appear.

The *Encyclopedia of Public International Law*, edited by Rudolf Bernhardt and published under the auspices of the Max Planck Institute for Comparative Public Law and International Law, provides a comprehensive view of international law issues. Its articles are written by respected authorities, are short but informative, and provide brief bibliographies for further research. The set was originally published in 12 volumes between 1981 and 1990, with each volume devoted to one or more

specific subjects. It is in the process of being reissued in one alphabetical sequence, with some additional articles and addenda. Two volumes, A–D (1992) and E–I (1995), have been published.

Other encyclopedias that may provide helpful background or bibliographic references for further reading include Ervin Laszlo & Jong Youl Woo, eds., *World Encyclopedia of Peace* (4 vols., 1986); Edmund Jan Osmanczyk, *Encyclopedia of the United Nations and International Relations* (2d ed. 1990); and Edward Lawson, ed., *Encyclopedia of Human Rights* (1991).

A variety of important international law documents are reprinted in Ian Brownlie, ed., *Basic Documents in International Law* (4th ed. 1994); Chia–Jui Cheng, ed., *Basic Documents on International Trade Law* (2d ed. 1990); P.W. Birnie & A.E. Boyle, eds., *Basic Documents on International Law and the Environment* (1995); and CCH's *Basic Documents of International Economic Law* (1990), which is also available online in both WESTLAW and LEXIS.

A specialized dictionary, such as Clive Parry et al., *Parry and Grant Encyclopaedic Dictionary of International Law* (1986), or Robert L. Bledsoe & Boleslaw A. Boczek, *The International Law Dictionary* (1987), may be useful if problems of terminology arise.

Because the source materials involved in international law issues are published in diverse, elusive sources, bibliographies are often useful finding aids for materials in this field. Two current guides to research are Elizabeth Beyerly's *Public International Law: A Guide to Information Sources* (1991) and *Germain's Transnational Law Research* (1991–date), by Claire Germain.

Bibliographies useful for retrospective research include Simone–Marie Kleckner, *Public International Law and International Organization: International Law Bibliography* (rev. ed. 1988); Ingrid Delupis, *Bibliography of International Law* (1975); J.G. Merrills, *Current Bibliography of International Law* (1978); and Jacob Robinson, *International Law and Organization: General Sources of Information* (1967).

Public International Law: A Current Bibliography of Books and Articles (1975–date) is a comprehensive, semi-annual index of the literature in the field. The United Nations Library in Geneva publishes a *Monthly Bibliography* (1928–date, originally published by the League of Nations Library) of recent books, documents, and selected articles. Each issue of the *American Journal of International Law* contains an extensive section reviewing or noting new works in the field, and the *International Journal of Legal Information* regularly publishes bibliographies devoted to specific areas of foreign and international law.

§ 13–3. TREATIES

In addition to the United States treaty sources described in Chapter 12, there are three major treaty series of worldwide scope and a variety of publications by regional organizations and individual foreign countries. In addition, a number of guides and indexes are available for researching multinational treaties, whether or not the United States is a party.

a. Sources

The most comprehensive source for modern treaties is the *United Nations Treaty Series* (*UNTS*). Since 1946

this series has published all treaties registered with the United Nations by member nations (including the U.S.) and some filed by non-members. The treaties appear in their original languages, as well as in English and French translations. Initially, there were indexes published for every one hundred volumes of *UNTS*; more recent indexes cover fifty volumes apiece. The series consists of over twelve hundred volumes and is the most comprehensive treaty collection, but there is a time lag of almost ten years in its publication of treaties and about five more years in publication of indexes. Exhibit 84 shows the first page of a multilateral convention in *UNTS*.

A new publication edited by Igor Kavass, *United Nations Treaty Indexing Service*, provides more current access to *UNTS* than the official indexes. It consists of a paper *Current United Nations Treaty Index* covering recently published treaties, and an electronic *United Nations Master Treaty Index on CD–ROM*, which is in the process of providing complete retrospective coverage.

The *League of Nations Treaty Series* (*LNTS*)(205 vols., 1920–46), the predecessor to the *United Nations Treaty Series,* includes treaties ratified from the formation of the League to the creation of the United Nations. Its scope is similar to that of *UNTS*. The *LNTS* is accompanied by a series of nine index volumes.

A retrospective treaty collection, *Consolidated Treaty Series* (*CTS*)(243 vols., 1969–86), edited by Clive Parry, contains all treaties between nation states from 1648 to 1918. It is designed to provide a complete compilation of treaties up to the beginning of the *LNTS*. The treaties appear in the language of one of the signatories, usually

CONVENTION[1] ON THE REDUCTION OF STATELESSNESS

The Contracting States,

Acting in pursuance of resolution 896 (IX),[2] adopted by the General Assembly of the United Nations on 4 December 1954,

Considering it desirable to reduce statelessness by international agreement,

Have agreed as follows:

Article 1. 1. A Contracting State shall grant its nationality to a person born in its territory who would otherwise be stateless. Such nationality shall be granted:

(a) at birth, by operation of law, or

(b) upon an application being lodged with the appropriate authority, by or on behalf of the person concerned, in the manner prescribed by the national law. Subject to the provisions of paragraph 2 of this article, no such application may be rejected.

A Contracting State which provides for the grant of its nationality in accordance with sub-paragraph (b) of this paragraph may also provide for the grant of its nationality by operation of law at such age and subject to such conditions as may be prescribed by the national law.

2. A Contracting State may make the grant of its nationality in accordance with sub-paragraph (b) of paragraph 1 of this article subject to one or more of the following conditions:

(a) that the application is lodged during a period, fixed by the Contracting State, beginning not later than at the age of eighteen years and ending not earlier than

---

[1] Came into force on 13 December 1975 in respect of the following States, i.e., two years after the date of the deposit of the sixth instrument of ratification or accession with the Secretary-General of the United Nations, in accordance with article 18 (1):

State	Date of deposit of the instrument of ratification or accession (a)	
United Kingdom of Great Britain and Northern Ireland*	29 March	1966

With a declaration that:

(a) The Convention shall apply to the following non-metropolitan territories for the international relations of which the United Kingdom is responsible: Antigua, Bahamas, Barbados, Basutoland, Bechuanaland, Bermuda, British Guiana, British Honduras, British Solomon Islands Protectorate, Cayman Islands, Channel Islands, Dominica, Falkland Islands, Fiji, Gibraltar, Gilbert and Ellice Islands, Grenada, Hong Kong, Isle of Man, Mauritius, Montserrat, St. Helena, St. Kitts, St. Lucia, St. Vincent, Seychelles, Swaziland, Turks and Caicos Islands, Virgin Islands.

(b) The Convention shall not apply to Aden and the Protectorate of South Arabia; Brunei; Southern Rhodesia; and Tonga, whose consent to the application of the Convention has been withheld.)

Sweden	19 February	1969 a
Norway	11 August	1971 a
Austria*	22 September	1972 a
Ireland*	18 January	1973 a
Australia	13 December	1973 a

* See p. 248 of this volume for the text of the declarations made upon ratification or accession.

[2] United Nations, *Official Records of the General Assembly, Ninth Session, Supplement No. 21* (A/2890), p. 49.

Exhibit 84: The first page of a convention in the *United Nations Treaty Series*.

accompanied by an English or French translation. Although there is no subject index, the set includes a chronological list and an index to parties.

The most important regional compilations for American lawyers are those published by the Organization of American States and the Council of Europe. The *Organization of American States Treaty Series* (1957–date) and its predecessor, the *Pan American Union Treaty Series* (1934–56), contain multilateral treaties of Western Hemisphere countries, including the United States. The treaties appear in English and Spanish, with a few also in French or Portuguese. Treaties among European states are published individually in the *European Treaty Series* (1950–date) and cumulated in the bound volumes of *European Conventions and Agreements* (1971–date). New European agreements often appear in the annual *European Yearbook*.

National treaty series include *United Kingdom Treaty Series* (1892–date); *Canada Treaty Series/Recueil des Traités* (1928–date); and *Recueil des Traités et Accords de la France* (1958–date). Many foreign countries publish current treaties in their official gazettes.

A growing number of treaties and other documents are available through the Internet. One of the most extensive sources is the *Multilaterals Project* of the Fletcher School of Law & Diplomacy at Tufts University.

b. Indexes and Guides

In addition to the indexes accompanying *UNTS*, *LNTS,* and *CTS,* and the United States sources described in Chapter 12, there are several guides and indexes for finding treaties. Some of the most useful of these are limited to coverage of *multilateral* agreements.

Multilateral Treaties Deposited with the Secretary–General, published by the United Nations, is an annually revised listing of multilateral treaties arranged by subject. It provides citations, current information as to the status of each treaty, and the text of any reservations imposed by the individual signatories. The list is limited to treaties concluded under UN auspices or for which the Secretary–General acts as depository. Exhibit 85 shows the listing for the convention in Exhibit 84.

Statement of Treaties and International Agreements (United Nations) is a monthly supplement to *Multilateral Treaties Deposited with the Secretary–General.* It includes both bilateral and multilateral treaties. Most treaties are listed here long before they appear in *UNTS,* but there is still a delay of almost two years between filing and publication. Each issue of the *Statement* contains a cumulative index for the year by country and subject.

A popular source for current information on multilateral treaties is M.J. Bowman & D.J. Harris, *Multilateral Treaties: Index and Current Status* (1984, with annual supplements). This index provides information on almost a thousand agreements, including some predating or not deposited with the UN.

World Treaty Index, compiled by Peter H. Rohn (5 vols., 2d ed. 1983–84) is growing increasingly dated, but it provides comprehensive coverage of some 44,000 treaties, indexing *UNTS, LNTS,* and other sources for treaties from 1900 to 1980. It provides access by country, subject, date, and international organization.

V.4: Statelessness

4. CONVENTION ON THE REDUCTION OF STATELESSNESS

Concluded at New York on 30 August 1961

ENTRY INTO FORCE: 13 December 1975, in accordance with article 18.
REGISTRATION: 13 December 1975, No. 14458.
TEXT: United Nations, *Treaty Series*, vol. 989, p. 175.
STATUS: Signatories: 5. Parties: 17.

Note: The Convention was adopted and opened for signature by the United Nations Conference on the Elimination or Reduction of Future Statelessness, convened by the Secretary–General of the United Nations pursuant to General Assembly resolution 896 (IX)[1] of 4 December 1954. The Conference met at the European Office of the United Nations at Geneva from 24 March to 18 April 1959 and reconvened at the Headquarters of the United Nations at New York from 15 to 28 August 1961.

Participant	Signature	Ratification, accession (a), succession (d)	Participant	Signature	Ratification, accession (a), succession (d)
Armenia		18 May 1994 a	Israel	30 Aug 1961	
Australia		13 Dec 1973 a	Kiribati		29 Nov 1983 d
Austria		22 Sep 1972 a	Latvia		14 Apr 1992 a
Bolivia		6 Oct 1983 a	Libyan Arab		
Canada		17 Jul 1978 a	Jamahiriya		16 May 1989 a
Costa Rica		2 Nov 1977 a	Netherlands[6]	30 Aug 1961	13 May 1985
Denmark		11 Jul 1977 a	Niger		17 Jun 1985 a
Dominican Republic	5 Dec 1961		Norway		11 Aug 1971 a
France	31 May 1962		Sweden		19 Feb 1969 a
Germany[5]		31 Aug 1977 a	United Kingdom	30 Aug 1961	29 Mar 1966
Ireland		18 Jan 1973 a			

Declarations and Reservations
(Unless otherwise indicated, the declarations and reservations were made upon ratification, accession or succession.)

AUSTRIA

Declarations concerning article 8, paragraph 3 (a), (i) and (ii):
"Austria declares to retain the right to deprive a person of his nationality, if such person enters, on his own free will, the military service of a foreign State.

"Austria declares to retain the right to deprive a person of his nationality, if such person being in the service of a foreign State, conducts himself in a manner seriously prejudicial to the interests or to the prestige of the Republic of Austria."

FRANCE

At the time of signature of this Convention, the Government of the French Republic declares that it reserves the right to exercise the power available to it under article 8 (3) on the terms laid down in that paragraph, when it deposits the instrument of ratification of the Convention.

The Government of the French Republic also declares, in accordance with article 17 of the Convention, that it makes a reservation in respect of article 11, and that article 11 will not apply so far as the French Republic is concerned.

The Government of the French Republic further declares, with respect to article 14 of the Convention, that in accordance with article 17 it accepts the jurisdiction of the Court only in relation to States Parties to this Convention which shall also have accepted its jurisdiction subject to the same reservations; it also declares that article 14 will not apply when there exists between the French Republic and another party to this Convention an earlier treaty providing another method for the settlement of disputes between the two States.

GERMANY[2]

The Federal Republic of Germany will apply the said Convention:

(a) in respect of elimination of statelessness, to persons who are stateless under the terms of article 1, paragraph 1, of the Convention relating to the Status of Stateless Persons of 28 September 1954;

(b) in respect of prevention of statelessness and retention of nationality, to German nationals within the meaning of the Basic Law (Constitution) for the Federal Republic of Germany.

IRELAND

"In accordance with paragraph 3 of article 8 of the Convention Ireland retains the right to deprive a naturalised Irish citizen of his citizenship pursuant to section 19 (1) (b) of the Irish Nationality and Citizenship Act, 1956, on grounds specified in the aforesaid paragraph."

NIGER

With reservations in respect of articles 11, 14 and 15.

UNITED KINGDOM OF GREAT BRITAIN AND NORTHERN IRELAND

"[The Government of the United Kingdom declares that], in accordance with paragraph 3 (a) of Article 8 of the Convention, notwithstanding the provisions of paragraph 1 of Article 8, the United Kingdom retains the right to deprive a naturalised person of his nationality on the following grounds, being grounds existing in United Kingdom law at the present time: that, inconsistently with his duty of loyalty to Her Britannic Majesty, the person

"(i) has, in disregard of an express prohibition of Her Britannic Majesty, rendered or continued to render services to, or received or continued to receive emoluments from, another State, or

"(ii) has conducted himself in a manner seriously prejudicial to the vital interests of Her Britannic Majesty."

228

Exhibit 85: A page from *Multilateral Treaties Deposited with the Secretary-General*.

The status of Inter–American and European treaties can be determined from the periodically revised guides *Inter–American Treaties and Conventions: Signatures, Ratifications, and Deposits with Explanatory Notes*; and *Chart Showing Signatures and Ratifications of Council of Europe Conventions and Agreements*.

§ 13–4. INTERNATIONAL ORGANIZATIONS

Intergovernmental organizations play a vital role in the creation and enforcement of international law. They establish and promote multilateral conventions governing both political and commercial relations. Several international organizations have also established adjudicatory bodies by whose decisions nations agree to be bound. Even when not acting as lawmaking bodies, international organizations publish important research sources such as treaty collections and yearbooks.

The organic documents of several dozen international organizations are gathered in P.J.G. Kapteyn et al., eds., *International Organization and Integration: Annotated Basic Documents and Descriptive Directory of International Organizations and Arrangements* (5 vols., 2d ed. 1981–85); and in Amos J. Peaslee, *International Governmental Organizations: Constitutional Documents* (5 vols., 3d ed. 1974–79). Two useful bibliographic guides to the documentation of international organizations are Th.D. Dimitrov, ed., *World Bibliography of International Documentation* (2 vols., 1981); and Peter I. Hajnal, ed., *International Information* (1988).

The *Yearbook of International Organizations* (3 vols., biennial) contains descriptions and directory information for thousands of international groups and associations,

and includes indexes by name, country and subject. Information on major organizations is included as Part One of the *Europa World Year Book* (2 vols., annual), which also provides extensive background information and statistics on the nations of the world.

a. United Nations

The formation of the United Nations after World War II has greatly influenced the development of international law. The UN has given international activity an organizational forum and a center for the preparation and promotion of legislation and conventions. Its six principal organs are the General Assembly, Security Council, Economic and Social Council, Trusteeship Council, Secretariat, and International Court of Justice. The United Nations also coordinates the activities of specialized bodies such as the Food and Agriculture Organization, the World Health Organization, and UNESCO. The UN has produced a vast amount of documentation rich in sources for research on most international problems.

Basic information on UN activities can be found in *Everyone's United Nations* (10th ed. 1986), a handy but now somewhat dated deskbook for international law research. More current works providing coverage of the UN's structure and membership are *United Nations Handbook*, published annually by the New Zealand Ministry of External Relations and Trade, and *Who's Who in the United Nations and Related Agencies* (2d ed. 1992).

The *Yearbook of the United Nations* is one of the best starting points for historical research on the UN or its affiliated organizations. Although coverage is delayed several years, this publication summarizes major devel-

opments, reprints some of the more important documents, and provides short bibliographies after each entry. Each volume includes a thorough index. Other UN yearbooks include *Yearbook on Human Rights* (1946–date); *Yearbook of the International Law Commission* (1949–date); and *United Nations Juridical Yearbook* (1965–date).

Among the most important documents for UN research are the *General Assembly Official Records* (GAOR). The records of the meetings of the assembly and its committees are accompanied by *Annexes* containing the more important documents produced during the session, and by *Supplements* containing annual reports submitted to the General Assembly by the Secretary–General, the Security Council, the International Court of Justice, and various committees. The final supplement each year compiles all the resolutions passed by the General Assembly during the session.

United Nations Resolutions (1973–date) reprints resolutions of the General Assembly and the Security Council in separate series, with cumulative indexes in each volume. For subject access, *United Nations General Assembly Resolutions in Our Changing World* (1991), by Blaine Sloan, and *Resolutions and Statements of the United Nations Security Council (1946–1992): A Thematic Guide* (2d ed. 1993), edited by Karel C. Wellens, are helpful.

Despite the importance of United Nations publications, their indexing unfortunately has not always made access easy. The United Nations has successively used several different indexing systems. The current system, *UN-DOC,* in use since 1979, is far better than its predecessors, *United Nations Documents Index* (1950–73) and

UNDEX (1974–78). *UNDOC* is issued as a monthly index, with annual cumulations in both paper and microfiche. Each issue contains a checklist, "Documents and Publications," and indexes by subject, author, and title. More convenient access is provided by the electronic *Readex CD–ROM Index to United Nations Documents and Publications*, with cumulative coverage since 1976, searching by keyword, agency, or document number, and the full text of resolutions.

A wide variety of UN information is available over the Internet, including the texts of resolutions from the General Assembly, Economic and Social Council, and Security Council. Coverage of other documents is highly selective but can lead to information not easily available elsewhere.

Much of the work of the United Nations in particular subject fields is conducted by separate international organizations, affiliated to the UN by agreements under Article 57 of the Charter. Referred to by the Charter as "specialized agencies," these organizations submit their reports to the Economic and Social Council, which forwards them to the General Assembly. Several of these agencies have extensive law-related activities which produce documentation useful to the legal researcher. *UNDOC* does not index these materials, but some of the agencies have their own indexing systems, such as the ILO's *International Labour Documentation* and the *UNESCO List of Documents and Publications*.

b. World Trade Organization

The World Trade Organization, the successor to the General Agreement on Tariffs and Trade (GATT), was established in January 1995 as the principle internation-

al body administering trade agreements among member states. The WTO acts as a forum for trade negotiations, seeks to resolve trade disputes, and oversees national trade policies. It is governed by the Ministerial Conference which meets every two years, while most operations are handled by the General Council.

The basic documents which govern WTO operations are reprinted in *The Results of the Uruguay Round of Multilateral Trade Negotiations: The Legal Texts* (1994) and *The WTO Dispute Settlement Procedures: A Collection of the Legal Texts* (1995). *Guide to GATT Law and Practice 1947–1994* (1995) provides an article-by-article analysis of the history and application of GATT rules up to the establishment of the WTO. Joseph F. Dennin, ed., *Law and Practice of the World Trade Organization* (1995–date) is just beginning publication but may be a major collection of texts and commentary.

c. European Union and Other Regional Organizations

For American lawyers, the European Union is probably the most frequently encountered of the world's many regional organizations. The EU was established in 1993 by the Maastricht Treaty, as the more ambitious successor to the European Communities (European Atomic Energy Community, European Coal and Steel Community, and European Economic Community). As economic and social developments lead to increasing European unity, the EU can be seen more as a supranational government than as a regional organization.

The major institutions of the EU are the European Parliament, a large elected body exercising mostly advisory powers; the Council, the major decision-making

body consisting of one minister from each member country; the Commission, a permanent executive body responsible for implementing the organizing treaties and managing the Union; and the European Court of Justice (which will be discussed in § 13–5 with other regional courts).

The *Official Journal of the European Communities* consists of two series, *Legislation* (L) and *Information and Notices* (C), with European Parliament debates published as an annex. Indexes are issued monthly. The monthly *Bulletin of the European Union* reviews activities and reprints some important documents, and the annual *General Report on the Activities of the European Union* provides an excellent overview of developments. One of the most useful official publications is the semiannual *Directory of Community Legislation in Force.* Ian Thomson, *The Documentation of the European Communities: A Guide* (1989) provides information about the EU's many publications.

CCH's *Common Market Reporter* is one of the most useful starting points for American lawyers, because of its familiar looseleaf format, broad scope, and frequent supplementation. In addition to its primary emphasis on the European Union, it also provides limited coverage of other regional organizations and summarizes the domestic legislation of many European countries on a variety of subjects.

Hans Smit & Peter Herzog, *The Law of the European Community* (1976–date) is a multivolume, article-by-article commentary on the Treaty of Rome which established the Common Market in 1957. The analysis contains references to current court decisions and scholarly sources, and each section is preceded by a bibliography of

relevant secondary material. K.R. Simmonds et al., eds., *Encyclopedia of European Community Law* (1973–date) is in the process of being replaced by a new *Encyclopedia of European Union Law*, which should provide comprehensive coverage of EU issues upon completion in 1997.

The first volume of an *Oxford Encyclopedia of European Community Law*, covering institutional law, was published in 1990; subsequent volumes, if published, will cover substantive law and community policies. Useful one-volume works include P.J.G. Kapteyn & P. VerLoren van Themaat, *Introduction to the Law of the European Community* (1989); D. Lasok & K.P.E. Lasok, *Law and Institutions of the European Union* (6th ed. 1994); and P.S.R.F. Mathijsen, *A Guide to European Union Law* (6th ed. 1995). The monthly *European Current Law* (1992–date) provides information on legal developments in the EU and throughout Europe.

A wide variety of EU material is accessible online through both WESTLAW and LEXIS, including CELEX, the official legal database of the EU. Coverage includes treaties, secondary legislation, preparatory documents, parliamentary questions, and national provisions implementing EU directives. *OJ CD*, one of several CD–ROMs covering the European Union, includes legislation from the *Official Journal* as well as a variety of other EU documents.

Other important regional organizations include the Council of Europe, the major body of European political unity; and the Organization of American States, often considered the oldest regional organization. As noted in § 13–3, both of these organizations draft and promote multilateral treaties among their member states, and publish collections and indexes of these treaties. Both

organizations also work to protect human rights in their member countries, as will be discussed in the following section.

§ 13–5. ADJUDICATIONS AND ARBITRATIONS

Although most disputes between nations are resolved by direct negotiation between the parties, some are submitted to international tribunals, arbitral bodies, or temporary commissions convened for particular disputes. Adjudications by some international bodies are generally recognized as authoritative, even if they sometimes lack effective enforcement procedures. Courts established by regional organizations are developing a growing body of international human rights law. Decisions of domestic courts on matters of international law can also be important sources, particularly as evidence of international legal custom.

a. International Court of Justice

Of particular interest in legal research relating to international adjudication are the publications of the International Court of Justice (also known as the World Court), which succeeded the Permanent Court of International Justice of the League of Nations. The ICJ meets at the Hague to settle legal controversies between countries and to resolve a limited number of other cases involving serious questions of international law.

The World Court's decisions are published initially in individual advance sheets and later in the bound volumes of *Reports of Judgments, Advisory Opinions and Orders*. Because the Court's own publication system is rather slow, the best printed source for recent decisions is

International Legal Materials. Decisions are also available online in **WESTLAW**'s **INT–ICJ** database. Exhibit 86 shows the first page of a decision, as published officially by the Court.

The annual *Yearbook of the International Court of Justice* contains a summary of the Court's work since 1946 and is often the easiest introductory tool. The *Yearbook* also contains basic information about the Court and summarizes opinions issued during the year.

The most extensive commentary on the work of the court is Shabtai Rosenne, *The Law and Practice of the International Court* (2d ed. 1985). Rosenne is also the author of a shorter volume, *The World Court: What It Is and How It Works* (5th ed. 1995), and editor of a useful compilation of source material, *Documents on the International Court of Justice* (3d ed. 1991).

Court publications include *Pleadings, Oral Arguments and Documents,* containing the briefs and documents submitted by the parties; *Rules of the Court*; and an annual *Bibliography of the ICJ* listing books and articles written about the Court.

Similar publications were issued by the Permanent Court of International Justice, the ICJ's predecessor as World Court. An unofficial compilation of PCIJ decisions was published as *World Court Reports,* edited by Manley O. Hudson (4 vols., 1934–43).

International Law Reports (1956–date), now edited by E. Lauterpacht and C.J. Greenwood, and succeeding *Annual Digest and Reports of Public International Law Cases* (1932–55), includes all PCIJ and ICJ decisions.

90

INTERNATIONAL COURT OF JUSTICE

1995
30 June
General List
No. 84

YEAR 1995

30 June 1995

CASE CONCERNING EAST TIMOR

(PORTUGAL *v.* AUSTRALIA)

*Treaty of 1989 between Australia and Indonesia concerning the "Timor Gap".
Objection that there exists in reality no dispute between the Parties — Disagreement between the Parties on the law and on the facts — Existence of a legal dispute.*

Objection that the Application would require the Court to determine the rights and obligations of a third State in the absence of the consent of that State — Case concerning Monetary Gold Removed from Rome in 1943 *— Question whether the Respondent's objective conduct is separable from the conduct of a third State.*

Right of peoples to self-determination as right erga omnes *and essential principle of contemporary international law — Difference between* erga omnes *character of a norm and rule of consent to jurisdiction.*

Question whether resolutions of the General Assembly and of the Security Council constitute "givens" on the content of which the Court would not have to decide de novo.

For the two Parties, the Territory of East Timor remains a non-self-governing territory and its people has the right to self-determination.

Rights and obligations of a third State constituting the very subject-matter of the decision requested — The Court cannot exercise the jurisdiction conferred upon it by the declarations made by the Parties under Article 36, paragraph 2, of its Statute to adjudicate on the dispute referred to it by the Application.

JUDGMENT

Present: President BEDJAOUI; *Vice-President* SCHWEBEL; *Judges* ODA, Sir Robert JENNINGS, GUILLAUME, SHAHABUDDEEN, AGUILAR-MAWDSLEY, WEERAMANTRY, RANJEVA, HERCZEGH, SHI, FLEISCHHAUER, KOROMA, VERESHCHETIN; *Judges* ad hoc Sir Ninian STEPHEN, SKUBISZEWSKI; *Registrar* VALENCIA-OSPINA.

4

Exhibit 86: An International Court of Justice decision, from its *Reports of Judgments, Advisory Opinions and Orders.*

It also prints selected decisions of regional and national courts on international law issues.

b. Regional and National Courts

The decisions of the courts of regional organizations have assumed growing importance in international law, as the range of disputes over which they exercise jurisdiction grows. Among the most important of these regional courts are the European Court of Justice, the European Court of Human Rights, and the Inter–American Court of Human Rights.

The European Court of Justice, an organ of the European Union, publishes its decisions in several official languages, including English. A subordinate Court of First Instance was established in 1988 to handle certain classes of cases and reduce the Court of Justice's workload. The official *Reports of Cases Before the Court of Justice and the Court of First Instance* includes decisions from both courts. Several unofficial, commercial publishers also provide these decisions in English as part of larger services, including the CCH *Common Market Reporter,* described above, and *Common Market Law Reports* (1962–date). All decisions since 1954 are also available online from both WESTLAW and LEXIS. The Office for Official Publications of the EC publishes the *Digest of Case–Law Relating to the European Communities* (1981–date), a looseleaf guide for locating decisions of both EU and national courts.

The European Commission of Human Rights and the European Court of Human Rights were created under the European Convention of Human Rights of 1950, which established a system for the international protection of the rights of individuals. Through the Commis-

sion a citizen can seek redress against the acts of his or her own government; the Court decides cases referred to it from the Commission. The Commission's decisions are published in *Decisions and Reports* (1975–date). The Court publishes two series of documents: Series A, *Judgments and Decisions,* and Series B, *Pleadings, Oral Arguments and Documents.* Decisions of both the Commission and the Court are also reported commercially in *European Human Rights Reports* (1979–date), available online from LEXIS; and a variety of documents and decisions appear in the annual *Yearbook of the European Convention on Human Rights* (1958–date). A case-finding tool is the *Digest of Strasbourg Case–Law Relating to the European Convention on Human Rights* (6 vols., 1984–85, with looseleaf supplements).

The Inter–American Commission on Human Rights was created in 1959 and hears complaints of individuals and institutions alleging violations of human rights in the American countries. At least ten countries, not including the United States, have accepted its jurisdiction. The Commission, or a member state, can refer matters to the Inter–American Court of Human Rights, created in 1978. The Court's decisions are reported in two series of judgments and in its annual report. The *Inter–American Yearbook on Human Rights* (1985–date) covers the work of both the Commission and the Court and includes selected decisions and other documents. Thomas Buergenthal & Robert E. Norris, eds., *Human Rights: The Inter–American System* (5 vols., 1982–date) also contains a variety of basic documents and decisions.

Judicial decisions of national courts on matters of international law are valuable sources of information accessible through the reporters and case-finders for each

country. This jurisprudence is also summarized in national yearbooks, periodicals, and digests of international law, and is reprinted in a few international law case reporters (such as *British International Law Cases* and *Commonwealth International Law Cases*). The indispensable *International Law Reports* includes selected decisions of domestic courts as well as decisions of international tribunals.

c. Arbitrations

An increasing number of disputes, between nations and between commercial partners, are settled by arbitration. The Hague Peace Conferences of 1899 and 1907 regularized international arbitration and created the Permanent Court of Arbitration and the International Commission of Inquiry. Their decisions were published in the *Hague Court Reports,* edited by James B. Scott (2 vols., 1916–32). This set was continued by the United Nations series, *Reports of International Arbitral Awards* (1948–date), with retrospective coverage back to the end of Scott's reports. The awards now appear in English or French with bilingual headnotes. The set includes agreements reached by mediation or conciliation, as well as awards resulting from contested arbitrations, but is limited to disputes in which states are the parties.

Repertory of International Arbitral Jurisprudence (3 vols., 1989–91) collects arbitral decisions from 1794 to 1987 and arranges them by subject, and A.M. Stuyt, ed., *Survey of International Arbitrations, 1794–1989* (3d ed. 1990) provides an extensive digest of decisions.

Several sources cover international arbitrations between private parties, including *Yearbook: Commercial Arbitration* (1975–date) and Hans Smit & Vratislav Pe-

chota, *World Arbitration Reporter* (1986–date). Some coverage is provided in *International Legal Materials,* and selected decisions appear in the *American Review of International Arbitration* (1990–date).

Other major publications on commercial arbitration include Pieter Sanders, ed., *International Handbook on Commercial Arbitration* (1984–date) and Clive M. Schmitthoff, ed., *International Commercial Arbitration* (1979–date). Current awareness is provided by BNA's monthly *World Arbitration & Mediation Report* (1990–date).

§ 13–6. YEARBOOKS

International law yearbooks are of two kinds: annual reviews of a nation's practice in international law (often combined with a selection of articles on current topics), and annual statements of the activities of particular bodies, such as international organizations or learned associations.

The first type of yearbook is especially useful when the practice of a foreign government on some international law question must be found. Most include articles by international law scholars and reprint selected major documents. Countries with publications of this type include Australia, Canada, France, Germany, Japan, and the United Kingdom.

Yearbooks of the second type are the major tools for preliminary research in international organizations. They include several yearbooks mentioned earlier in this chapter: the numerous United Nations publications, the Council of Europe's *European Yearbook,* and the European and Inter–American human rights yearbooks.

In addition to documents published in national year-books, there are also documentary compilations from many countries similar to the U.S. foreign relations collections discussed in Chapter 12.   These include materials related to international law, foreign policy and diplomacy, and are published both in large retrospective collections primarily useful for historical research and in continuing series of contemporary documents.

§ 13–7.   CONCLUSION

In researching international law in this increasingly global age, it is important for American lawyers *not* to limit their research to U.S. sources.   Materials from international organizations and other countries can provide new perspectives and present solutions that may not be readily apparent from within the U.S. legal tradition. A facility with other languages assists greatly in broadening the scope of research, but as this chapter has shown there are a large number of English-language resources available for serious international law research.

CHAPTER 14

ENGLISH AND COMMONWEALTH LAW

---

§ 14–1. INTRODUCTION

The legal systems of most foreign countries can be described as either *common law* or *civil law*. Each system has its own history, its own fundamental principles and procedures, and its own forms of publication for legal sources. Under the common law, as explained in Chapter 1, legal doctrine is derived from specific cases decided by judges rather than from broad, abstractly articulated codifications. Judicial decisions are traditionally the most important and vital source of new legal rules in a common law system.

The common law system originated in England and spread to its colonies around the world. Most of these

315

nations, now known as the Commonwealth, continue to have legal systems modeled on the English common law. The resources discussed in this chapter, however, are limited to the law of England, Canada and Australia.

While related, the legal systems of these countries are quite distinct. England has no written constitution, and Parliament is the supreme lawmaking body. *English law* generally refers to the domestic law of England and Wales, part of the United Kingdom of Great Britain and Northern Ireland. The U.K. has been part of the European Community (now the European Union) since 1973 and is increasingly governed by EU treaties and legislation. The Canadian and Australian systems are more similar to the United States, with federal governments and written constitutions. The Australian Constitution has been in effect since 1901, while the Canadian Constitution Act 1982 dramatically changed Canadian law, adding an extensive new Charter of Rights and Freedoms.

Although the laws of England and its former colonies have developed separately in recent years, common law countries share a heritage which gives their decisions more persuasive value in each other's courts than that generally afforded the law of other countries. The similarity of publications and research procedures makes the legal doctrine more accessible to researchers in the United States and other common law countries.

§ 14–2. CASE LAW

Court reports are central to legal research in England and other common law countries, and research is simplified by the relatively small number of published deci-

sions. Fifty state jurisdictions and the federal system in this country have produced a quantity of cases that has long since eclipsed the number of reported English decisions dating back to the thirteenth century, necessitating the complex system of digests and citators that were the focus of Chapter 3. Case law research in other common law countries is similar to that in the United States, but is not burdened by so great a volume of decisions.

England has a relatively simple system of courts, with the House of Lords as the court of last resort. The Canadian and Australian court systems are more like that of the United States, although fundamental differences exist. In the U.S., for example, state supreme courts are the final arbiters on issues of state law, while any decision from a Canadian provincial court or an Australian state court is generally subject to review by the highest federal court in its country.

a. Publication of Cases

As in the United States, new decisions in most other common law countries are published first in weekly or monthly advance sheets and later in permanent bound volumes. Both advance sheets and volumes usually include case tables and indexes. Besides the official or authorized series of reports, there are often unofficial commercial reporters which provide quicker access to new cases and may contain more useful headnotes and digests.

As described above in Chapter 2 (at page 17), English law reporting has had a long and varied history. The recording of decisions began with the *Plea Rolls,* then developed into the *Year Books,* and next into the nominative reporters. Most nominative reports were cumu-

lated into the *English Reports: Full Reprint,* covering cases from 1220 to 1865 in 176 volumes. This invaluable set contains about 100,000 decisions originally published in some 275 series of nominative reporters. The volumes are arranged by court, star-paged to the original reporter, and accessible by a two-volume alphabetical table of cases. There is, however, no subject index. Another compilation of older cases, the *Revised Reports,* covers 1785 to 1866 in 149 volumes and includes some decisions not found in the *Full Reprint.*

For decisions since 1865, the standard source is the semi-official *Law Reports,* which now consists of four series: *Appeal Cases* (House of Lords and the Judicial Committee of the Privy Council); *Queen's Bench Division*; *Chancery Division*; and *Family Division.* Before appearing in these four separate series, new cases are published in *Weekly Law Reports* (1953 to date), which also includes some decisions unreported in the four *Law Reports* series.

All England Law Reports (1936–date) is a commercially published reporter which often issues new cases sooner than the *Weekly Law Reports* and contains some decisions which are not published elsewhere. As in the United States, there are also numerous specialized subject reporters published in England (as well as in Canada and Australia).

Canada and Australia both have authorized reports for their federal court of last resort (*Canada Supreme Court Reports,* and *Commonwealth Law Reports* for the High Court of Australia). Each nation also has a Federal Court with both trial and appellate jurisdiction, and an official series of reports for that court. In Canada, the commercially published *National Reporter* contains deci-

sions of the Supreme Court and the Federal Court of Appeal, and *Dominion Law Reports,* now in its fourth series, contains decisions from both federal and provincial courts. The High Court of Australia's decisions are also published in the *Australian Law Reports,* along with cases from lower federal courts and from state courts on federal issues; *Federal Law Reports* duplicates some of this coverage of lower court decisions. In addition, each country has reporters for the supreme courts of its provinces or states.

English cases since 1945, including those published in the *Law Reports, All England Law Reports,* and over two dozen specialized reporters, are available online from LEXIS, which also provides more selective coverage of cases from Canada and Australia. In the COMCAS (Commonwealth Cases) or INTLAW (International Law) libraries, these cases are in the ENGCAS, CANCAS and AUSCAS files respectively; there is also an ALL file with cases from all jurisdictions represented. WESTLAW provides access through a gateway to QL System's Quicklaw, Canada's major online legal database system.

b. Case Research Tools

Many of the same types of tools are available for case research in other common law countries as are found in the United States. Digests and encyclopedias are frequently used. *Shepard's Citations* has no real counterparts in other countries, but there are tools for finding later cases that have considered an earlier decision. In most common law countries, cases are usually referred to and researched by name rather than by citation.

Each country has a major national digest, somewhat similar to the West digest system: *The Digest: Annotat-*

ed British, Commonwealth and European Cases (3d ed. 1971–date); the *Canadian Abridgment* (2d ed. 1966–date); and the *Australian Digest* (3d ed. 1988–date). In each of these sets, case abstracts are arranged by subject into over one hundred topics. Each topic begins with an outline of its contents. All three sets include consolidated indexes and tables of cases. In *The Digest,* case summaries are followed by annotations of later cases in which the summarized case has been considered, making a *Digest* entry useful for both finding and updating cases. As its title suggests, it offers a wide range of decisions beyond those of English courts.

All three digests are updated regularly by bound or looseleaf supplements. The Canadian and Australian digests are further updated in the monthly issues of *Canadian Current Law Case Law Digests* and the *Australian Legal Monthly Digest.*

Another English service useful for both finding and updating cases is *Current Law.* Its *Monthly Digest* contains summaries of new court decisions arranged by subject and a Cumulative Table of Cases containing the names of both new decisions and earlier cases which have been judicially considered. The case summaries cumulate at the end of the year into the *Current Law Year Book,* and the case tables into the *Current Law Case Citator.* The *Case Citator* consists of two volumes covering 1947 to 1988 and an annual paperback supplement. It lists, by name, cases decided since 1947 and earlier cases which have been cited since that date. For those cases which have been judicially considered, the effect of each later case is indicated with notes such as "Overruled", "Applied", or "Considered."

Updating Canadian and Australian cases is possible through *Canadian Case Citations* and the *Australian Case Citator*. Like their English counterparts, tables in these works are arranged alphabetically by case name and are useful for finding citations as well as for determining later treatment of cited decisions. *Canadian Current Law* and *Australian Current Law* provide information on recent cases and other legal developments.

Indexes to particular sets of court reports are a genre of case research tool seldom found in the U.S. but common in other countries. The *Law Reports,* for example, are accompanied by a regularly updated *Consolidated Index* containing a subject index, a comprehensive table of cases reported, and citators for cases, statutes, and regulations. Similar indexes are available for many other English, Canadian and Australian reports. Among the report series accompanied by bound index volumes are *All England Law Reports,* Canada's *Dominion Law Reports,* and Australia's *Commonwealth Law Reports. Halsbury's Laws of England*, an encyclopedia described below at page 326, is also widely used as a case-finder.

§ 14–3. STATUTES

Statutes in other common law jurisdictions are published both in session laws and in compilations of statutes in force. The compilations, however, generally reprint acts alphabetically by name or chronologically, rather than by subject. There is no counterpart to the *United States Code,* in which each part of an act is systematically assigned to a title and given a section number as part of a general subject compilation of statutes. Instead, acts are permanently identified by their original name and date of enactment.

The current national session law publications are *Public General Acts* (for Britain), *Statutes of Canada,* and *Acts of the Parliament of the Commonwealth of Australia.* Each is published in annual volumes with subject indexes or tables of acts for each year. Statutes of the individual Canadian provinces and Australian states are published in similar annual volumes. Most jurisdictions publish new statutes in some more timely fashion; new Canadian federal statutes, for example, appear upon assent in Part III of the *Canada Gazette.*

The standard historical collection of English statutes is the *Statutes of the Realm,* covering 1235 to 1713 in nine volumes (1810–1822), with two volumes of indexes. Several other chronological collections were published during the 19th century under the title *Statutes at Large,* extending coverage to 1869.

Statutes in Force: Official Revised Edition (1972–date) is the current official compilation of statutes in the United Kingdom, consisting of a separate pamphlet for each act, in looseleaf volumes arranged by subject. Revised pamphlets are issued as necessary, and subject access is provided by an annual *Index to the Statutes.* An annual *Chronological Table of Statutes* lists all statutes enacted since 1235 and provides information on repeals, amendments and current status.

Britain also has a commercial, annotated compilation of statutes which is much more current and useful for most research. *Halsbury's Statutes of England and Wales* (4th ed. 1985–date) is an unofficial, well-indexed encyclopedic arrangement of acts in force, updated with annual bound supplements and two looseleaf volumes (*Current Statutes Service,* containing annotated versions of new statutes, and *Noter–Up Service,* providing refer-

ences to developments since the latest annual supplement). A consolidated *Table of Statutes and General Index* is published annually. *Halsbury's* is the most convenient subject compilation of English statutes and includes footnote annotations to judicial decisions.

English statutes in force are also available on LEXIS, in the STAT file of the ENGGEN or UK library. The online version is more current than any printed source, but it does not include the annotations found in *Halsbury's Statutes*.

Both Canada and Australia have bound compilations of statutes in force as of specific dates, although in both countries acts are simply arranged alphabetically by title. Neither country has an annotated, regularly updated publication similar to *Halsbury's Statutes*. The present compilation of Canadian federal statutes is the *Revised Statutes of Canada 1985,* proclaimed in force in 1988. A softcover index (2d ed. 1991) accompanies the set. The most recent bound compilation of Australian federal acts is *Acts of the Australian Parliament 1901–1973*; since 1979 reprinted acts have also been published in pamphlets filed in looseleaf binders. Subject access is available through the annual *Wicks Subject Index to Commonwealth Legislation.*

The AUSLAW file on LEXIS provides access to all Australian Commonwealth Acts since 1901, but Canadian statutes are only found through Canadian database systems such as QL Systems (available through a WEST-LAW gateway) and SOQUIJ (for Quebec law in French).

The major citator for British statutes is the *Current Law Legislation Citator,* published as part of the *Current Law* service. The *Citator* consists of a chronological list of statutes, with each statute followed by references to

later statutes and cases which affect it. Coverage includes any statutes amended, repealed, or considered in judicial decisions since 1947. Two volumes cover 1947 to 1988, with updating provided by annual supplements and monthly coverage in *Current Law Monthly Digest*.

A cumulative "Table of Public Statutes" in the *Canada Gazette* lists amendments and repeals since the latest *Revised Statutes of Canada*, and provides information on legislation enacted since the latest revision. Recent legislative activity by both federal and provincial governments is noted in *Canadian Current Law Legislation*, and references to citing cases can be found by using *Canadian Statute Citations*.

In Australia, *Commonwealth Statutes Annotations* and *Federal Statutes Annotations* both provide references to amendments and to cases citing federal statutes. Similar works are available for some Australian states, and information on federal and state legislative developments is available in such publications as the *Australian Legal Monthly Digest* and *Australian Current Law*.

While parliamentary debates and other legislative documents are also published in each of these countries, legislative history materials are generally considered less persuasive than in the United States for purposes of statutory interpretation. Courts are reluctant to look beyond the plain meaning of statutory language and less willing to acknowledge ambiguity.

§ 14–4. REGULATIONS

As in the United States, delegated legislation plays a vital role in the legal system of Commonwealth nations. Regulations, the most common form of delegated legisla-

tion, are known in Britain as *statutory instruments* and in Australia as *statutory rules*.

There has not been an official subject compilation of English statutory instruments since 1948, but annual *Statutory Instruments* volumes are published. The government also publishes two current finding tools: *Table of Government Orders* (a numerical list of orders and statutory instruments, indicating repeals and amendments) and *Index to Government Orders* (a subject index to orders and instruments currently in force).

The most useful source for research in English statutory instruments is the unofficial *Halsbury's Statutory Instruments* (4th ed. 1978–date). Similar in arrangement to *Halsbury's Statutes,* it contains the full text of many instruments and summarizes others. The set is updated by two looseleaf binders containing the texts of recent instruments, an annual supplement, and a monthly survey of new developments. An annual index provides subject access to the set.

The texts of all statutory instruments of general effect currently in force, including many not printed in *Halsbury's,* are available online from LEXIS. A combined file, STATIS, contains all current statutes *and* statutory instruments, except those that have only local effect.

Another source for information on British statutory instruments is *Current Law.* Its *Monthly Digests* and *Year Books* list new instruments and include them in their subject digests, and the *Current Law Legislation Citator* contains a "Table of Statutory Instruments Affected" noting amendments or revocations.

Access to Canadian and Australian regulations is similar to that for statutes, with infrequently revised compi-

lations and tables for finding more recent materials. The latest compilation of Canadian federal regulations is the *Consolidated Regulations of Canada 1978,* and new regulations are published biweekly in Part II of the *Canada Gazette.* Access is provided by the "Consolidated Index of Statutory Instruments" in the *Canada Gazette* or the commercially published *Canada Regulations Index.* Annual volumes of *Statutory Rules Made Under Acts of Parliament of the Commonwealth of Australia* contain the texts of Australian regulations, and the weekly *Commonwealth of Australia Gazette* contains notice of new regulations and amendments.

§ 14–5. SECONDARY SOURCES

The secondary literature of other common law countries parallels that of the United States, with a variety of treatises, practitioners' handbooks, looseleaf services, and other materials. This section examines only a few of the most basic resources.

a. Encyclopedias

Like *Am. Jur. 2d* and *C.J.S.,* legal encyclopedias in other nations contain concise statements of ruling law and extensive footnote references to primary sources. Foreign legal encyclopedias may be even more useful than those from one's own country, since they summarize unfamiliar legal doctrines and provide convenient references to materials that might otherwise be very difficult to find.

Halsbury's Laws of England (4th ed. 1973–date) is broader in scope than the American encyclopedias, since its coverage encompasses statutes and administrative sources as well as case law. Access to the set is provided

by a comprehensive index and by tables of cases and statutes cited. The encyclopedia is updated by cumulative annual supplements and a Current Service looseleaf volume, which includes a "Monthly Review" summarizing new developments.

While there is no general legal encyclopedia for all of Canada, two regional encyclopedias include coverage of Canadian federal law: the *Canadian Encyclopedic Digest (Ontario)* (3d ed. 1973–date), and the *Canadian Encyclopedic Digest (Western)* (3d ed. 1979–date). Two competing comprehensive Australian legal encyclopedias, *Halsbury's Laws of Australia* and *The Laws of Australia* (both 1992–date) are in the process of publication.

Martindale–Hubbell International Law Digest is hardly a substitute for an encyclopedic treatment and original sources, but it provides convenient, brief summaries of major legal principles for England, Canada, and Australia, as well as each Canadian province, Northern Ireland, Scotland, and several other common law countries.

b. Periodicals and Treatises

No other country has a profusion of legal periodicals to match that in the United States, but the forms of publication are similar. Each nation has a variety of academic law reviews and professional journals. The major American indexes (*Index to Legal Periodicals* and *Current Law Index/Legal Resource Index*) include coverage of most of the world's major English-language journals, but there are also indexes published in other countries that provide more thorough and specific coverage of legal issues in those countries.

The *Legal Journals Index* (1986–date) covers most law journals published in the United Kingdom (in 1993 its

publisher began a separate *European Legal Journals Index*, to cover those journals focusing on issues of European law), and *Current Law* includes references to relevant books and articles in its *Monthly Digests* and *Year Books*. The most comprehensive Canadian index is *Canadian Legal Literature*, covering both books and articles and published as part of the *Canadian Current Law* and *Canadian Abridgment* series. Another publication, the *Index to Canadian Legal Periodical Literature*, focuses solely on journal articles. References to recent Australian material appear in the *Australian Legal Monthly Digest* and *Australian Current Law*.

c. Dictionaries and Research Guides

Two resources that can help in researching another country's laws are legal dictionaries and guides to legal research. A dictionary ensures that words are understood in their proper context, and a foreign research guide contains more detailed and precise discussion than is possible in an American treatment.

The major English legal dictionary is *Jowitt's Dictionary of English Law* (2 vols., 2d ed. 1977, with 1985 supp.); two shorter but useful works are *A Dictionary of Law* (3d ed. 1994) and *Osborn's Concise Law Dictionary* (8th ed. 1993). *The Dictionary of Canadian Law* (2d ed. 1995) is the most substantial treatment of Canadian legal definitions, and Australian legal terms are defined in *Australian Legal Dictionary* (2d ed. 1985). David M. Walker's *Oxford Companion to Law* (1980) is a cross between a dictionary and an encyclopedia, providing concise explanations of basic concepts, documents, events, and institutions.

English legal research materials are discussed in R.G. Logan, ed., *Information Sources in Law* (1986), and Guy Holborn, *Butterworths Legal Research Guide* (1993). Similar treatment for Canada is offered by Margaret A. Banks, *Banks on Using a Law Library* (6th ed. 1994), and Douglass T. MacEllven, *Legal Research Handbook* (3d ed. 1993). The basic text for Australia is Enid Campbell et al., *Legal Research: Materials and Methods* (3d ed. 1988).

§ 14–6. CONCLUSION

While research in English, Canadian, or Australian law may be limited by the unavailability of some materials in most U.S. libraries, it need not be limited by differences in terminology or by a lack of understanding of basic tools. These common law jurisdictions have legal research materials that are quite similar to our own and are easily accessible to American legal researchers, either for comparative study or for analysis of legal problems arising in those nations.

Frequent or extended research in the law of another country calls for a more substantial introduction to its legal system than can be offered here. The legal research guides cited above provide introductory surveys and also refer to more substantial background sources.

CHAPTER 15

THE CIVIL LAW SYSTEM

---

§ 15–1. INTRODUCTION

Expanded foreign communication, travel, and trade have made the law of other countries increasingly significant to American social and economic life. The law of a foreign country may be relevant in American court proceedings involving international transactions, and American legal scholars and lawmakers use other legal systems as a basis for better understanding and improving our own system. Foreign law sources are also essential to the growing study of comparative law, by which the differences between the law of diverse countries and systems are analyzed.

Most countries outside the United States and the Commonwealth function under the civil law system. Although the term *civil law* is used in several contexts to

330

mean very different things, the *civil law system* refers to the legal tradition, arising out of Roman law and the European codes, which characterizes the countries of continental Western Europe, Latin America, and parts of Africa and Asia. There are several distinctive characteristics of the civil law system: the predominance of comprehensive and systematic codes governing large fields of law (civil, criminal, commercial, civil procedure, and criminal procedure); the strong influence of concepts, terms and principles from Roman law; little weight for judicial decisions as legal authority; and great influence of legal scholars who interpret, criticize and develop the law in their writings, particularly through commentaries on the codes.

The differences between the common law and civil law systems have become less marked in recent years, as each system adopts features of the other. Codes have been enacted in some American jurisdictions, for example, while judicial decisions are being given greater weight in some civil law countries.

There are also countries which do not fit clearly into either the civil law or common law systems, but are strongly influenced by customary law or traditional religious systems, particularly Hindu or Islamic law. The law of these countries (e.g. India, Israel, Pakistan and Saudi Arabia) may be a mixture of civil *or* common law and the religious legal system. Their publications tend to differ most markedly from those in this country and are the least familiar to American lawyers.

When starting research in the law of a country other than one's own, it is essential to have some sense of what publications are available and in what sources the research should be conducted. Bibliographic guides and

general introductions to law are available in English for many civil law countries. However, part of the difficulty of doing legal research in the civil law system stems from differences in language. Bilingual and multilingual legal dictionaries are available for many languages, but it is impossible to comprehend the law of a foreign country in an unfamiliar language with only the aid of a legal dictionary.

Translations and summaries of foreign law in English may be quite helpful, but research in translated texts of legal materials is no substitute for study of the original documents. Where a lack of knowledge of the original language precludes the use of primary sources, consultation with experts in the other legal system is necessary to adequately handle the interests of a client faced with a serious foreign law problem. English translations can, however, provide some familiarity with the basic concepts and issues.

Since research approaches in civil law vary from country to country and with the topic being researched, it is impossible to suggest one model procedure for all purposes. Obviously procedures will differ between research limited to English-language materials and research based on original sources. Because of the difficulty of covering the great variety of sources and procedures in foreign languages and the relative inaccessibility of such sources to most American lawyers, we will focus first on English translations and then briefly treat research in other languages.

§ 15–2. RESEARCH IN ENGLISH

Research in English-language materials on civil law begins with a general introduction to the law of the

country involved in the problem and, if available, an introduction to the specific subject in the law of that country. Such preliminary reading may be found in an encyclopedia, a treatise, or a periodical article. Footnote references in that source may provide leads for continuing the research. A bibliographic guide for the country or subject involved, usually covering both primary and secondary materials, can also be very useful. With some understanding of the basic concepts and terminology of the subject matter and a general sense of the publications available in English, one can then begin research in English translations and summaries.

a. Encyclopedias and Treatises

The most extensive survey in English of the law of various nations, including many in the civil law system, is the *International Encyclopedia of Comparative Law* (1971–date). This comprehensive work, still in progress, includes a series of "National Reports" on individual countries, with references to the main sources of law and topical bibliographies for each country. Most of the encyclopedia gives detailed information on specific legal topics, such as contracts and civil procedure. Even after twenty-five years, however, only the Torts volumes have been published in their final bound format.

More concise overviews of the civil law system can be found in general treatises such as René David & John E.C. Brierley, *Major Legal Systems in the World Today* (3d ed. 1985); John H. Merryman, *The Civil Law Tradition* (2d ed. 1985); and Alan Watson, *The Making of the Civil Law* (1981). Casebooks offering general introductions to foreign law include Merryman, Clark & Haley's *The Civil Law Tradition: Europe, Latin America, and*

East Asia (1994) and Schlesinger's *Comparative Law* (5th ed. 1988).

There are as well a number of guides in English to the legal systems of specific countries or regions. A sample of recently published titles includes Albert Hung–Yee Chen, *An Introduction to the Legal System of the People's Republic of China* (1992); J.M.J. Chorus et al., eds., *Introduction to Dutch Law for Foreign Lawyers* (1993); Christian Dadomo & Susan Farran, *The French Legal System* (1993); Nigel G. Foster, *German Law & Legal System* (1993); Francisco A. Avalos, *The Mexican Legal System* (1992); and F. Dessemontet & T. Ansay, eds., *Introduction to Swiss Law* (1995). Brief overviews of many national systems are included in Kenneth R. Redden, ed., *Modern Legal Systems Cyclopedia* (21 vols., 1984–date). Before looking for specific sources from a particular country, it may be worthwhile to see if a descriptive overview is available.

b. Bibliographic Guides

A wide variety of foreign law bibliographies are published, including some covering many subjects and many jurisdictions as well as specialized bibliographic surveys of particular countries, regions, or subjects.

The most useful and comprehensive multinational bibliography is Thomas H. Reynolds & Arturo A. Flores, *Foreign Law: Current Sources of Codes and Basic Legislation* (5 vols., 1989–date), covering almost every country in the world. It contains separate sections on individual countries, with descriptions of each legal system, notes on the major primary sources (including those available in English), and a detailed subject listing of codes and selected secondary sources.

The late Charles Szladits' *A Bibliography on Foreign and Comparative Law: Books and Articles in English* (1955–date), now edited by Vratislav Pechota, is an excellent multivolume bibliography, arranged by subject with geographical and author indexes. The bibliography is updated periodically by bound supplements, although there is a time lag of several years between coverage dates and publication.

Numerous research guides and bibliographies for specific regions, countries and subjects are available. A few examples of publications in English include: Paul Graulich et al., *Guide to Foreign Legal Materials: Belgium, Luxembourg, Netherlands* (1968); Charles Szladits & Claire M. Germain, *Guide to Foreign Legal Materials: French* (2d ed. 1985); Timothy Kearley & Wolfram Fischer, *Charles Szladits' Guide to Foreign Legal Materials: German* (2d ed. 1990); and Jacqueline D. Elliott, *Pacific Law Bibliography* (2d ed. 1990).

c. Translations and Summaries of Foreign Law

The growing literature on foreign law includes many translations of actual laws, as well as discussions of law on different subjects for various foreign countries. For the simplest information, English summaries of basic laws and procedures of over fifty countries appear annually in the *Martindale–Hubbell International Law Digest*.

Several commercially published collections issue foreign laws in translation, prominent among which are *American Series of Foreign Penal Codes,* compiled by the Comparative Criminal Law Project of the Wayne State University Law School; *Digest of Commercial Laws of the World* and *Digest of Intellectual Property Laws of the*

World, both edited by Lester Nelson; and *Investment Laws of the World,* prepared by the International Centre for Settlement of Investment Disputes. The International Bureau of Fiscal Documentation publishes several series covering taxation laws throughout the world, including *African Tax Systems, Guides to European Taxation, Taxation in Latin America, Taxes and Investment in Asia and the Pacific,* and *Taxes and Investment in the Middle East.*

Specialized international organizations publish regular collections of new legislation from countries throughout the world. These include the Food and Agriculture Organization (*Food and Agricultural Legislation,* semiannual); International Labour Office (*Labour Law Documents,* three times a year); and World Health Organization (*International Digest of Health Legislation,* quarterly).

The United States government publishes several useful guides to the legal and business environments in countries around the world. *Country Reports on Economic Policy and Trade Practices,* a biennial report from the Department of State to Congress, summarizes basic trade, investment, and employment laws. The Department of Commerce's International Trade Administration publishes *Overseas Business Reports,* an extensive series of brochures about marketing in specific countries. Much of this information is available electronically on the *National Trade Data Bank (NTDB),* a monthly government CD–ROM with a wide range of data from over a dozen federal agencies.

In addition, some of the major multinational accounting firms publish brief English-language guides to the

tax and commercial law of foreign countries. The most up-to-date and extensive sets are available from Ernst & Young and Price Waterhouse, both published under the title *Doing Business in [Name of Country]*.

The most current collection of foreign constitutions in English, translation is *Constitutions of the Countries of the World*, edited by Gisbert H. Flanz. For some foreign-language countries, the constitution in its original language is included as well. A supplementary series, *Constitutions of Dependencies and Special Sovereignties*, is also published.

Very few online databases offer access, in English, to foreign laws. Among the exceptions, available on both WESTLAW and LEXIS, are the CELEX database of European Union materials, and Chinalaw, containing laws and regulations of the People's Republic of China dating back to 1950. Both databases also have translations of legal texts from Central and Eastern European countries and Russia.

d. Periodical Indexes

Periodical literature in English on foreign law is covered in the basic legal periodical indexes discussed in Chapter 9, including the *Index to Legal Periodicals* and the *Legal Resource Index*. The *Index to Foreign Legal Periodicals* focuses on foreign and international legal issues in journals in both English and foreign languages. Szladits's *Bibliography on Foreign and Comparative Law* also indexes a wide range of periodical articles in English, although publication delays limit its usefulness for current research topics.

§ 15–3. RESEARCH IN ORIGINAL SOURCES

The most effective research in any legal system is likely to be in the language of the country whose law is being investigated. Before undertaking such research, background reading in the relevant sections of an encyclopedia, looseleaf service, or treatise may be helpful, both as an introduction to the subject and as a lead to further sources.

After the introductory study, the researcher must consult the relevant code (preferably in an edition with good commentary) or other statutes applicable to the problem being researched. One should then find administrative orders and judicial decisions implementing or interpreting the legislative norms. In the absence of citators, the current authority of decisions can be determined through digests or indexes to collections of decisions, if available, or from references in recent treatises and articles. The leading French legal periodicals, *Recueil Dalloz Sirey* and *La Semaine Juridique,* and the French looseleaf services of the *Juris–Classeurs* system are particularly useful in offering both legislative texts and judicial decisions, as well as scholarly articles.

This general procedure does not apply to every civil law country. In many countries, research will begin with the code itself, but almost never, as in the United States, with a review of judicial decisions.

a. Basic Legal Sources

Most countries in the civil law system have several separately published codes. These include the basic general codes (civil, criminal, commercial, civil procedure and criminal procedure) and minor codes which are often

simply statutory compilations on specific subjects (such as taxation, labor law, and family law). The codes are usually published in frequent unannotated editions, and also in larger editions with scholarly commentary, annotations and other aids. Despite the importance of the codes, there is no legal distinction between a code and other legislation, and code provisions can be amended or repealed by ordinary statutes.

In many countries, daily official gazettes contain the texts of new laws, decrees and administrative orders. These comprehensive gazettes are the official sources for new legislation, but in some countries cumulative indexes are issued infrequently. Research is often conducted, therefore, in periodicals with legislative sections or in looseleaf services with more effective indexes.

Since there are far fewer reported judicial decisions in civil law countries, there are, in most jurisdictions, fewer reporters of such decisions. Both official and commercial series do exist, however, for many countries. The commercial editions are often part of larger periodical or looseleaf services, which may also include statutes, decrees, regulations, and helpful commentary.

Legal databases are appearing with increasing frequency in civil law countries, but most are not yet available in the United States. An extensive library of French materials, however, is available through LEXIS, including laws and regulations (with the full text of the *Journal Officiel* beginning in 1955) as well as judicial opinions (for some courts, as far back as 1958). LEXIS also has more selective coverage of Italian and Mexican sources.

Just as it has in the United States, CD–ROM publication of legal material in other countries has increased dramatically. The annual *Directory of Law–Related CD–*

ROMs lists compilations and indexes available for over a dozen countries. Few of these, of course, will be available in many U.S. libraries.

b. Secondary Materials

Under the civil law system, scholarly commentaries and treatises by recognized experts have considerable weight as persuasive authority. They are discussed as "secondary materials" here in keeping with our own notion of authority, but in many instances they have greater weight than judicial decisions. The range of available texts, as in common law countries, is quite broad in both subject and quality. There are comprehensive scholarly treatises, highly specialized monographs on narrow topics, pragmatic manuals and guides for the practitioner, and simplified texts for students and popular use. For those with the necessary language skills, these works offer considerable help in legal research. Information about the literature available on specific topics can be found in legal bibliographies and guides published for particular countries; in Reynolds & Flores, *Foreign Law*; or in the selective bibliographies in the "National Reports" pamphlets of the *International Encyclopedia of Comparative Law*.

Foreign legal encyclopedias, particularly in France (*e.g.*, Dalloz *Nouveau Repertoire de droit*), are often of higher quality and reputation than those in this country. Their articles are frequently written by leading legal scholars.

Civil law countries have a multitude of legal periodicals covering general developments or specific topics, although many journals are hard to obtain in this country. Access to a large number of foreign-language legal peri-

odical articles is available through the *Index to Foreign Legal Periodicals,* which also covers *festschriften* and other collections of essays. There are periodical indexes published in some foreign countries which are limited to the literature of these countries.

Citation forms for foreign legal materials can be very confusing for American lawyers. Fortunately, *The Bluebook: A Uniform System of Citation* (15th ed. 1991) includes citation information for fifteen civil law countries and for basic Roman law sources. Its coverage is quite limited but still helpful.

§ 15–4. CONCLUSION

Lawyers who lack knowledge of languages other than English will be seriously handicapped in researching civil law problems. However, the increasing availability of secondary materials in English and translations of primary sources of foreign law now allow preliminary study of some legal problems for a number of countries. Such study may help the American lawyer to determine the general nature of a problem, and can facilitate communication with the foreign law specialist who may be called in to assist.

APPENDIX A

STATE RESEARCH GUIDES

Because of variations in legal materials from state to state, a general research guide like this *Nutshell* cannot provide the necessary detail for specific state sources. These guides are therefore suggested for further information on the materials of individual states.

There are also several articles in *Law Library Journal* and other law reviews discussing state practice materials and research methods, and a series of short but useful guides to state materials or government documents issued by the American Association of Law Libraries. These materials are generally listed here only if no other recent guide is available for that state.

Nancy Adams Deel & Barbara G. James, "An Annotated Bibliography of State Legal Research Guides," 14 Legal Reference Services Q., nos. 1/2, at 23 (1994) provides a more extensive, well-annotated list of state guides. Guides to legislative history research in specific states are listed and discussed in Jose R. Torres & Steve Windsor, "State Legislative Histories: A Select, Annotated Bibliography," 85 Law Libr. J. 545 (1993).

Alabama   Hazel L. Johnson & Timothy L. Coggins, *Guide to Alabama State Documents and Selected Law–Related Materials* (1993).
Lynne B. Kitchens & Timothy A. Lewis, "Alabama Practice Materials:

A Selected Annotated Bibliography," 82 Law Libr. J. 703 (1990).

Alaska   Aimee Ruzicka, *Alaska Legal and Law–Related Publications: A Guide for Law Librarians* (1984).

Arizona   Kathy Shimpock–Vieweg & Marianne Sidorski Alcorn, *Arizona Legal Research Guide* (1992).

Arkansas   Kathryn C. Fitzhugh, "Arkansas Practice Materials: A Selective Annotated Bibliography," 11 U. Ark. Little Rock L.J. 791 (1988); modified version printed in 81 Law Libr. J. 277 (1989).
Lynn Foster, *Arkansas Legal Bibliography: Documents and Selected Commercial Titles* (1988).

California   Daniel W. Martin, *Henke's California Law Guide* (3d ed. 1995).

Colorado   Gary Alexander et al., *Colorado Legal Resources: An Annotated Bibliography* (1987); also printed in 16 Colo. Law. 1795 (1987).

Connecticut   Shirley Bysiewicz, *Sources of Connecticut Law* (1987).
Lawrence G. Cheeseman & Arlene C. Bielefeld, *The Connecticut Legal Research Handbook* (1992).

District of Columbia   Leah F. Chanin, "Legal Research in the District of Columbia," in *Legal Research in the District of Columbia, Maryland and Virginia* (1995).

Florida   Niki L. Martin, *Florida Legal Research & Source Book* (1989).
Betsy L. Stupski, *Guide to Florida Legal Research* (4th ed. 1994).

Georgia   Leah F. Chanin & Suzanne L. Cassi-
                     dy, *Guide to Georgia Legal Research
                     and Legal History* (1990).
                     Nancy P. Johnson & Nancy Adams
                     Deel, "Researching Georgia Law," 9
                     Ga. St. U. L. Rev. 585 (1993).

Idaho   Patricia A. Cervenka et al., *Idaho
                     Law–Related State Documents: An
                     Annotated Bibliography* (1989).

Illinois   Frank G. Houdek & Jean McKnight,
                     "An Annotated Bibliography of Legal
                     Research Tools," 16 S. Ill. U. L.J. 767
                     (1992).
                     Laurel Wendt, *Illinois Legal Re-
                     search Manual* (1988).

Indiana   Linda K. Fariss & Keith A. Buckley,
                     *An Introduction to Indiana State
                     Publications for the Law Librarian*
                     (1982).

Iowa   Angela K. Secrest, *Iowa Legal Docu-
                     ments Bibliography* (1990).

Kansas   Fritz Snyder, *A Guide to Kansas Le-
                     gal Research* (1986).

Kentucky   Arturo L. Torres, "Kentucky Practice
                     Materials: A Selective, Annotated
                     Bibliography," 84 Law Libr. J. 509
                     (1992).

Louisiana   Win–Shin S. Chiang, *Louisiana Legal
                     Research* (2d ed. 1990).

Maine   William W. Wells, *Maine Legal Re-
                     search Guide* (1989).

Maryland   Pamela J. Gregory, "Legal Research
                     in Maryland," in *Legal Research in
                     the District of Columbia, Maryland
                     and Virginia* (1995).

Massachusetts   Margot Botsford & Ruth G. Matz,
                     eds., *Handbook of Legal Research in
                     Massachusetts* (2d ed. 1988).

Michigan	Richard L. Beer & Judith J. Field, *Michigan Legal Literature: An Annotated Guide* (2d ed. 1991). Nancy L. Bosh, *The Research Edge: Finding Law and Facts Fast* (1993).
Minnesota	Arlette M. Soderberg & Barbara L. Golden, *Minnesota Legal Research Guide* (1985).
Mississippi	Ben Cole, *Mississippi Legal Documents and Related Publications: A Selected Annotated Bibliography* (1987).
Missouri	Mary Ann Nelson, *Guide to Missouri State Documents and Selected Law–Related Materials* (1991).
Montana	Stephen R. Jordan, *A Guide to Montana Legal Research* (1993).
Nebraska	Ann C. Fletcher et al., *Michie's Research Guide to Nebraska Law* (1995).
Nevada	Katherine Henderson, *Nevada State Documents Bibliography, Part I: Legal Publications and Related Material* (1984).
New Jersey	Cameron Allen, *A Guide to New Jersey Legal Bibliography and Legal History* (1984). Paul Axel–Lute, *New Jersey Legal Research Handbook* (1985).
New Mexico	Patricia Wagner & Mary Woodward, *Guide to New Mexico State Publications* (2d ed. 1991). Mary A. Woodward, "New Mexico Practice Materials: A Selective Annotated Bibliography," 84 Law Libr. J. 93 (1992).
New York	Ellen M. Gibson, *New York Legal Research Guide* (1988).

North Carolina	Jean Sinclair McKnight, *North Carolina Legal Research Guide* (1994).
Ohio	James Leonard, "A Select, Annotated Bibliography of Ohio Practice Materials," 17 Ohio N.U. L. Rev. 265 (1990). Susan Schaefgen & Melanie K. Putnam, *Ohio Legal Research: Effective Approaches and Techniques* (1988).
Oklahoma	Christine A. Corcos, *Oklahoma Legal and Law–Related Documents and Publications: A Selected Bibliography* (1983).
Oregon	Lesley Ann Buhman et al., *Bibliography of Law Related Oregon Documents* (1984).
Pennsylvania	Joel Fishman, *Bibliography of Pennsylvania Law: Secondary Sources* (1992). Joel Fishman, *An Introduction to Pennsylvania State Publications for the Law Librarian* (1985).
Puerto Rico	Carlos I. Gorrín Peralta, *Fuentes y Proceso de Investigación Jurídica* (1991).
Rhode Island	Colleen McConaghy, *Selective Bibliography for the State of Rhode Island: State Documents and Law–Related Materials* (1993).
South Carolina	Paula Gail Benson & Deborah Ann Davis, *A Guide to South Carolina Legal Research and Citation* (1991).
South Dakota	Delores A. Jorgensen, *South Dakota Legal Research Guide* (1988).
Tennessee	Lewis L. Laska, *Tennessee Legal Research Handbook* (1977). D. Cheryn Picquet & Reba A. Best, *Law and Government Publications of*

the State of Tennessee: A Bibliographic Guide (1988).

Texas
Lydia M.V. Brandt, *Texas Legal Research: An Essential Lawyering Skill* (1995).

Karl T. Gruben & James E. Hambleton, eds., *A Reference Guide to Texas Law and Legal History: Sources and Documentation* (2d ed. 1987).

Vermont
Virginia Wise, *A Bibliographical Guide to the Vermont Legal System* (2d ed. 1991).

Virginia
John D. Eure & Robert D. Murphy, eds., *A Guide to Legal Research in Virginia* (2d ed. 1994).

Sarah K. Wiant, "Legal Research in Virginia," in *Legal Research in the District of Columbia, Maryland and Virginia* (1995).

Washington
Martin Cerjan et al., *Washington Legal Researcher's Deskbook 1994* (1994).

West Virginia
Sandra Stemple et al., *West Virginia Legal Bibliography* (1990).

Wisconsin
Richard A. Danner, *Legal Research in Wisconsin* (1980).

Wyoming
Nancy S. Greene, *Wyoming State Legal Documents: An Annotated Bibliography* (1985).

APPENDIX B

CONTENTS OF NATIONAL REPORTER SYSTEM

Coverage begins with decisions in the designated volumes of the following major state reports:

Atlantic Reporter (1886 to date): 53 Connecticut; 1 Connecticut Appellate; 18 Connecticut Supplement; 12 Delaware (7 Houston); 6 Delaware Chancery; 77 Maine; 63 Maryland; 1 Maryland Appellate; 63 New Hampshire; 47 New Jersey Law; 40 New Jersey Equity; 1 New Jersey; 1 New Jersey Superior; 108 Pennsylvania State; 102 Pennsylvania Superior; 1 Pennsylvania Commonwealth; 15 Rhode Island; 58 Vermont.

California Reporter (1960 to date): 53 California 2d; 176 California Appellate 2d.

New York Supplement (1888 to date): 1 New York (1 Comstock); 1 Appellate Division; 1 Miscellaneous.

North Eastern Reporter (1885 to date): 112 Illinois; 284 Illinois Appellate; 102 Indiana; 1 Indiana Appellate; 139 Massachusetts; 1 Massachusetts Appeals; 99 New York; 43 Ohio State; 20 Ohio Appellate; 1 Ohio Miscellaneous.

North Western Reporter (1879 to date): 1 Dakota; 51 Iowa; 41 Michigan; 1 Michigan Appeals; 26 Minnesota; 8 Nebraska; 1 Nebraska Appellate; 1 North Dakota; 1 South Dakota; 46 Wisconsin.

Pacific Reporter (1884 to date): 1 Arizona; 1 Arizona Appeals; 64 California; 1 California Appellate; 7 Colorado; 1 Colorado Appeals; 43 Hawaii; 1 Hawaii Appellate; 2 Idaho; 30 Kansas; 1 Kansas Appeals; 4 Montana; 17 Nevada; 3 New Mexico; 1 Oklahoma; 1 Oklahoma Criminal; 11 Oregon; 1 Oregon Appeals; 3 Utah; 1 Washington; 2 Washington Territory; 1 Washington Appellate; 3 Wyoming.

South Eastern Reporter (1887 to date): 77 Georgia; 1 Georgia Appeals; 96 North Carolina; 1 North Carolina Appeals; 25 South Carolina; 82 Virginia; 1 Virginia Appeals; 29 West Virginia.

South Western Reporter (1887 to date): 47 Arkansas; 1 Arkansas Appellate; 1 Indian Territory; 84 Kentucky; 89 Missouri; 93 Missouri Appeals; 85 Tennessee; 16 Tennessee Appeals; 1 Tennessee Criminal Appeals; 66 Texas; 21 Texas Appeals; 1 Texas Civil Appeals.

Southern Reporter (1887 to date): 80 Alabama; 1 Alabama Appellate; 22 Florida; 104 Louisiana; 39 Louisiana Annotated; 9 Louisiana Appeals; 64 Mississippi.

APPENDIX C

CURRENT STATUS OF MAJOR OFFICIAL STATE REPORTS

This listing does not include *unofficial* reporters unless they have received official recognition or are generally used in place of discontinued official reporters. See *The Bluebook: A Uniform System of Citation* (15th ed., pp. 169–218) for a fuller listing of state reports (with abbreviations), and Cohen, Berring & Olson, *How to Find the Law* (9th ed. 1989, Appendix B) for earlier reports.

Alabama	*Alabama Reports* (1840–1976) discontinued with volume 295; *Alabama Appellate Court Reports* (1910–76) discontinued with volume 57. Current official sources are West's *Alabama Reporter* and *Southern Reporter*.
Alaska	*Alaska Reports* (1869–1958) discontinued with volume 17. Current official sources are West's *Alaska Reporter* and *Pacific Reporter*.
American Samoa	*American Samoa Reports* (1900–date).
Arizona	*Arizona Reports* (1866–date) (includes Court of Appeals since 1976); *Arizona Appeals Reports* (1965–76) discontinued with volume 27.
Arkansas	*Arkansas Reports* (1837–date); *Arkansas Appellate Reports* (1979–

date), bound with *Arkansas Reports.*

California — *California Reports* (1850–date); *California Appellate Reports* (1906–date).

Colorado — *Colorado Reports* (1864–1980) discontinued with volume 200; *Colorado Court of Appeals Reports* (1891–1905, 1912–15, 1970–80) discontinued with volume 44. Current official sources are West's *Colorado Reporter* and *Pacific Reporter.*

Connecticut — *Connecticut Reports* (1817–date); *Connecticut Appellate Reports* (1983–date); *Connecticut Supplement* (1935–date); *Connecticut Circuit Court Reports* (1961–77) discontinued with volume 6.

Delaware — *Delaware Reports* (1832–1966) discontinued with volume 59. *Delaware Chancery Reports* (1814–1968) discontinued with volume 43. Current official sources are West's *Delaware Reporter* and *Atlantic Reporter.*

District of Columbia — Current official source is *Atlantic Reporter.*

Florida — *Florida Reports* (1846–1948) discontinued with volume 160. Current official sources are West's *Florida Cases* and *Southern Reporter.*

Georgia — *Georgia Reports* (1846–date); *Georgia Appeals Reports* (1907–date).

Hawaii — *Hawaii Reports* (1847–date); *Hawaii Appellate Reports* (1980–date).

Idaho — *Idaho Reports* (1866–date).

Illinois   *Illinois Reports* (1819–date); *Illinois Appellate Reports* (1877–date).

Indiana   *Indiana Reports* (1848–1981) discontinued with volume 275; *Indiana Court of Appeals Reports* (1890–1979) discontinued with volume 182. Current official sources are West's *Indiana Cases* and *North Eastern Reporter*.

Iowa   *Iowa Reports* (1855–1968) discontinued with volume 261. Current official source is *North Western Reporter*.

Kansas   *Kansas Reports* (1862–date); *Kansas Court of Appeals Reports* (1895–1901; 1977–date).

Kentucky   *Kentucky Reports* (1785–1951) discontinued with volume 314. Current official sources are West's *Kentucky Decisions* and *South Western Reporter*.

Louisiana   *Louisiana Reports* (1809–1972) discontinued with volume 263. Current sources (unofficial) are West's *Louisiana Cases* and *Southern Reporter*.

Maine   *Maine Reports* (1820–1965) discontinued with volume 161. Current official sources are West's *Maine Reporter* and *Atlantic Reporter*.

Maryland   *Maryland Reports* (1904–date); *Maryland Appellate Reports* (1962–date).

Massachusetts   *Massachusetts Reports* (1804–date); *Massachusetts Appeals Court Reports* (1972–date).

Michigan	*Michigan Reports* (1847–date); *Michigan Appeals Reports* (1965–date).
Minnesota	*Minnesota Reports* (1851–1977) discontinued with volume 312. Current official sources are West's *Minnesota Reporter* and *North Western Reporter*.
Mississippi	*Mississippi Reports* (1818–1966) discontinued with volume 254. Current official sources are West's *Mississippi Cases* and *Southern Reporter*.
Missouri	*Missouri Reports* (1821–1956) discontinued with volume 365; *Missouri Appeal Reports* (1876–1952) discontinued with volume 241. Current official sources are West's *Missouri Cases* and *South Western Reporter*.
Montana	*Montana Reports* (1869–date).
Navajo Nation	*Navajo Reporter* (1969–date).
Nebraska	*Nebraska Reports* (1860–date); *Nebraska Appellate Reports* (1992–date).
Nevada	*Nevada Reports* (1865–date).
New Hampshire	*New Hampshire Reports* (1816–date).
New Jersey	*New Jersey Reports* (1948–date), succeeding both *New Jersey Law Reports* (1790–1948, 137 volumes) and *New Jersey Equity Reports* (1830–1948, 142 volumes); *New Jersey Superior Court Reports* (1948–date).
New Mexico	*New Mexico Reports* (1852–date).

New York
New York Reports (1847–date); Appellate Division Reports (1896–date); Miscellaneous Reports (1892–date).

North Carolina
North Carolina Reports (1778–date); North Carolina Court of Appeals Reports (1968–date).

North Dakota
North Dakota Reports (1890–1953) discontinued with volume 79. Current official source is North Western Reporter.

Ohio
Ohio State Reports (1852–date) succeeding Ohio Reports (1821–52); Ohio Appellate Reports (1913–date); Ohio Miscellaneous Reports (1965–date).

Oklahoma
Oklahoma Reports (1890–1953) discontinued with volume 208; Oklahoma Criminal Reports (1908–53) discontinued with volume 97. Current official sources are West's Oklahoma Decisions and Pacific Reporter.

Oregon
Oregon Reports (1853–date); Oregon Reports, Court of Appeal (1969–date).

Pennsylvania
Pennsylvania State Reports (1845–date); Pennsylvania Superior Court Reports (1895–date); Pennsylvania Commonwealth Court Reports (1970–94) discontinued with volume 168; Pennsylvania District and County Reports (1921–date).

Puerto Rico
Puerto Rico Reports (1899–1972); Decisiones de Puerto Rico (1899–date).

Rhode Island
Rhode Island Reports (1828–1980) discontinued with volume 122.

Current official sources are West's *Rhode Island Reporter* and *Atlantic Reporter*.

South Carolina *South Carolina Reports* (1868–date).

South Dakota *South Dakota Reports* (1890–1976) discontinued with volume 90. Current official source is *North Western Reporter*.

Tennessee *Tennessee Reports* (1791–1971) discontinued with volume 225; *Tennessee Appeals Reports* (1925–71) discontinued with volume 63; *Tennessee Criminal Appeals Reports* (1967–71) discontinued with volume 4. Current official sources are West's *Tennessee Decisions* and *South Western Reporter*.

Texas *Texas Reports* (1846–1963) discontinued with volume 163; *Texas Criminal Reports* (1876–1963) discontinued with volume 172. Current sources (unofficial) are West's *Texas Cases* and *South Western Reporter*.

Utah *Utah Reports* (1855–1974) discontinued with volume 30, 2d series. Current official sources are West's *Utah Reporter* and *Pacific Reporter*.

Vermont *Vermont Reports* (1826–date).

Virgin Islands *Virgin Islands Reports* (1917–date).

Virginia *Virginia Reports* (1790–date); *Virginia Court of Appeals Reports* (1985–date).

Washington *Washington Reports* (1889–date); *Washington Appellate Reports* (1969–date).

West Virginia   *West Virginia Reports* (1874–date).

Wisconsin   *Wisconsin   Reports*   (1853–date);
West's *Wisconsin Reporter* (1941–
date) is co-official since 1975.

Wyoming   *Wyoming Reports* (1870–1959) discontinued with volume 80.   Cur-
rent official sources are West's *Wyoming Reporter* and *Pacific Reporter*.

APPENDIX D

TOPICAL LOOSELEAF AND CD–ROM SERVICES

This is a selective list of topical services useful in legal research. Print looseleaf services are shown in roman type and CD–ROM services in *italics*. This list should be used with caution since new services are issued frequently and others cease publication. The basic criteria for inclusion are frequent supplementation (at least monthly) and publication of primary documents (either abstracts or full texts). For fuller listings, see the annual publications *Legal Looseleafs in Print* and *Directory of Law–Related CD–ROMs*.

Abbreviation	Publisher
BNA	Bureau of National Affairs
Bender	Matthew Bender & Co.
CBC	Clark Boardman Callaghan
CCH	CCH Inc.
IHS	IHS Regulatory Products
LRP	LRP Publications
RIA	Research Institute of America
UPA	University Publications of America
WGL	Warren, Gorham & Lamont
WSB	Washington Service Bureau

Accounting

Accountancy Law Reports (CCH)

Cost Accounting Standards Guide (CCH)

SEC Compliance (WGL)

Advertising

Advertising Compliance Service (Greenwood Press)

Alcoholic Beverages

Liquor Control Law Reports (CCH)

Aviation

Aviation Law Reports (CCH)

Banking

Bank Compliance Guide (CCH)

The Banking Library (IHS)

BNA's Banking Report

Federal Banking Law Reports (CCH)

Federal Banking Law Service (A.S. Pratt & Sons)

Bankruptcy

Bankruptcy Law Reporter (BNA)

Bankruptcy Law Reports (CCH)

West's Bankruptcy Library

Carriers

Federal Carriers Reports (CCH)

Motor Carrier–Freight Forwarder Service (Hawkins Publishing Co.)

Rail Carrier Service (Hawkins Publishing Co.)

Commercial Law

Consumer Credit Guide (CCH)

RICO Business Disputes Guide (CCH)

Secured Transactions Guide (CCH)

UCCSEARCH: An Integrated Practice System (CBC)

Communications

Communications Regulation (Pike & Fischer)

Communications Regulation on CD–ROM (Pike & Fischer)

Media Law Reporter (BNA)

Computers

Guide to Computer Law (CCH)

Corporations

Business Strategies (CCH)

Capital Changes Reporter (CCH)

Corporate Practice Series (BNA)

Corporate Secretary's Guide (CCH)

Corporation (Aspen Law & Business)

Criminal Law

BNA Criminal Practice Manual

Criminal Law Reporter (BNA)

Disabilities

AIDS Law & Litigation Reporter (University Publishing Group)

BNA's Americans with Disabilities Act Manual

Disability Law on CD–ROM (LRP)

Individuals with Disabilities Education Law Reporter (LRP)

National Disability Law Reporter (LRP)

Elections

Federal Election Campaign Financing Guide (CCH)

Employment Practices

Employment and Training Reporter (MII Publications)

Employment Discrimination Coordinator (CBC)

Employment Practices Guide (CCH)

Employment Testing: Law and Policy (UPA)

Fair Employment Practices (BNA)

Federal Equal Opportunity Reporter (LRP)

Human Resources Fair Employment Practices (WGL)

Energy

Energy Management and Federal Energy Guidelines (CCH)

Natural Gas Policy Act Information Service (Thompson Publishing Co.)

Nuclear Regulation Reports (CCH)

Utilities Law Reports (CCH)

Environment

BNA's Environment Library on CD

Chemical Regulation Reporter (BNA)

Earth Law Environmental and Safety Library (IHS)

Environment Reporter (BNA)

Environmental Law Reporter (Environmental Law Institute)

The Environmental Law Reporter (CBC)

International Environment Reporter (BNA)

Right–to–Know Planning Guide (BNA)

Toxics Law Reporter (BNA)

Estate Planning and Taxation

Analysis of Federal Taxes: Estate and Gift (RIA)

Estate Planning & Taxation Coordinator (RIA)

Federal Estate and Gift Tax Reports (CCH)

Financial and Estate Planning (CCH)

Inheritance, Estate and Gift Tax Reports (CCH)

Successful Estate Planning Ideas & Methods (RIA)

United States Tax Reporter: Estate and Gift Taxes (RIA)

Excise Taxation

Analysis of Federal Taxes: Excise (RIA)

Federal Excise Tax Reports (CCH)

United States Tax Reporter: Excise Taxes (RIA)

Family Law

Family Law Reporter (BNA)

Family Law Tax Guide (CCH)

Federal Taxation (General and Income)

Analysis of Federal Taxes: Income (RIA)

CCH Access CD–ROM: CCH SmartTax

CCH Access CD–ROM: Federal Tax Guide

CCH Access CD–ROM: Standard Federal Tax Reports

CCH Federal Tax Service

Federal Tax Coordinator 2d (RIA)

Federal Tax Guide (CCH)

Kleinrock's Tax Library (Kleinrock Publishing)

RIA OnPoint System

RIA Tax Desk

Standard Federal Tax Reports (CCH)

Tax Action Coordinator (RIA)

Tax Advisors Planning Series (RIA)

Tax Analyst OneDisc (Tax Analysts)

Tax Ideas (WGL)

Tax Management (BNA)

Tax Management Tax Practice Series on CD (BNA)

Tax Management Portfolios Plus (BNA)

United States Tax Guide (RIA)

United States Tax Reporter (RIA)

United States Tax Reporter on CD–ROM (RIA)

West's Federal Taxation Library

Food and Drug

The Food and Drug Library (IHS)

Food Drug Cosmetic Law Reports (CCH)

Foundations and Charities

Charitable Giving and Solicitation (WGL)

Exempt Organizations Reports (CCH)

Tax Exempt Organizations (RIA)

Franchises

Business Franchise Guide (CCH)

Government Contracts

Government Contracts (Bender)

Government Contracts Reports (CCH)

West's Government Contracts Library

Government Information

Access Reports/Freedom of Information (Access Reports)

Ethics in Government Reporter (WSB)

Health Care

BioLaw (UPA)

BNA's Health Law Reporter

CCH Access CD–ROM: Medicare and Medicaid

CCH Pulse: The Resource Guide to Health Care Reform

The Medical Devices Library (IHS)

Medical Devices Reporter (CCH)

Medicare–Medicaid Guide (CCH)

The Medicare/Medicaid Library (IHS)

Housing and Real Estate

Fair Housing / Fair Lending (Aspen Law & Business)

Housing and Development Reporter (WGL)

Real Estate Coordinator (RIA)

Resort Development Law Reporter (Land Development Institute)

Immigration

Employers' Immigration Compliance Guide (Bender)

IRIS: Immigration Research Information Service (Federal Publications)

SearchMaster Immigration Law Library (Bender)

Insurance

INSource: The Red Books (NILS Publishing Co.)

Insurance Law Reports: Fire and Casualty (CCH)

Insurance Law Reports: Life, Health & Accident (CCH)

Intellectual Property

BNA's Patent, Trademark & Copyright Journal

Copyright Law Reports (CCH)

International Business and Taxation

Commercial Laws of the World (Foreign Tax Law Publishers)

Common Market Reports (CCH)

Doing Business in Europe (CCH)

Financing Foreign Operations (Economist Intelligence Unit)

Foreign Tax and Trade Briefs (Bender)

International Trade Reporter (BNA)

Investing, Licensing and Trading Conditions Abroad (Economist Intelligence Unit)

National Trade Data Bank (National Technical Information Service)

Tax Laws of the World (Foreign Tax Law Publishers)

U.S. Taxation of International Operations (WGL)

Labor Relations

BNA's Human Resources Library on CD–ROM

CCH Access CD–ROM: Human Resources Management

Collective Bargaining Negotiations and Contracts (BNA)

Employment Coordinator (CBC)

Employment PowerLink (CBC)

Federal Labor Relations Reporter (LRP)

Federal Merit Systems Reporter (LRP)

Government Employee Relations Report (BNA)

Guide to Employment Law and Regulation (CBC)

HR Series (CBC)

Human Resources Guide (WGL)

Human Resources Management (CCH)

Labor Law Reports (CCH)

Labor Relations Reporter (BNA)

Union Labor Report (BNA)

Lawyers and Legal Ethics

ABA/BNA Lawyer's Manual on Professional Conduct

National Reporter on Legal Ethics and Professional Responsibility (UPA)

Prepaid Legal Services Regulation Reporter (American Prepaid Legal Services Institute)

Legislation

CIS/Index (Congressional Index Service)

Congressional Index (CCH)

Maritime Law

Shipping Regulation (Pike & Fischer)

Native Americans

Indian Law Reporter (American Indian Lawyer Training Program)

Occupational Safety and Health

BNA's Safety Library on CD–ROM

Employment Safety and Health Guide (CCH)

Occupational Safety & Health Reporter (BNA)

Partnerships and S Corporations

Partnership & S Corporation Coordinator (RIA)

Partnership Tax Planning & Practice (CCH)

S Corporations (WGL)

S Corporations Guide (CCH)

Pensions and Compensation

BNA Pension & Benefits Reporter

BNA's Compensation & Benefits Library on CD–ROM

BNA's Payroll Library on CD–ROM

Compliance Guide for Plan Administrators (CCH)

Employee Benefits Compliance Coordinator (RIA)

Employee Benefits Management (CCH)

ERISA Update (WSB)

Executive Compensation (Aspen Law & Business)

Executive Compensation & Taxation Coordinator (RIA)

Federal Pay and Benefits Reporter (LRP)

Fringe Benefits Tax Guide (CCH)

Individual Retirement Plans Guide (CCH)

Payroll Administration Guide (BNA)

Payroll Guide (RIA)

Payroll Management Guide (CCH)

Pension and Profit Sharing (RIA)

Pension Coordinator (RIA)

Pension Plan Guide (CCH)

RIA Payroll Guide

RIA Pension & Benefits Expert

RIA's Guide to IRAs, SEPs, and KEOGHs

Products Liability and Consumer Safety

Consumer Product Safety Guide (CCH)

Product Safety & Liability Reporter (BNA)

Products Liability Reports (CCH)

Securities and Commodities

American Stock Exchange Guide (CCH)

Blue Sky Advantage for State Securities (CCH)

Blue Sky Law Reports (CCH)

CFTC Administrative Reporter (WSB)

CCH Access CD–ROM: Federal Securities Law Reporter

Chicago Board Options Exchange Guide (CCH)

Commodity Futures Law Reports (CCH)

Federal Securities Law Reports (CCH)

Mutual Funds Guide (CCH)

NASD Manual (CCH)

New York Stock Exchange Guide (CCH)

Securities Regulation & Law Report (BNA)

Securities Regulation Service (WGL)

The Securities Regulatory Library (IHS)

Securities Transfer Guide (CCH)

Tax Management Multistate Tax Portfolios Plus (BNA)

West's Federal Securities Library

State and Local Taxation

All–State Sales Tax Reports (CCH)

All States Tax Guide (RIA)

CCH Access CD–ROM: State Tax Reporters

Multistate Corporate Income Tax Guide (CCH)

State and Local Taxes (RIA) (for each state)

State Income Taxes (RIA)

State Tax Guide (CCH)

State Tax Reports (CCH) (for each state)

Supreme Court

United States Law Week (BNA)

United States Supreme Court Bulletin (CCH)

Taxation

See specific headings

Trade Regulation

Antitrust & Trade Regulation Report (BNA)

Trade Regulation Reports (CCH)

Unemployment Insurance / Social Security

Social Security Plus (CBC)

Unemployment Insurance Reports (CCH)

West's Social Security Library

Workers' Compensation

Benefits Review Board Black Lung Reporter (Bender)

Benefits Review Board Longshore Reporter (Bender)

Workers' Compensation Business Management Guide (CCH)

*

TITLE INDEX

References are to pages

Boldface references are to exhibits

*

SUBJECT INDEX

References are to pages

Boldface references are to exhibits

ABBREVIATIONS
Dictionaries, 9
In *Shepard's Citations,* 73–75, **74,** 151, **152**

ADMINISTRATIVE LAW
   Generally, 4, 192–93
Commonwealth countries, 324–26
Directories, 193–94, **195**
Federal agency decisions, 212–13, 285
Federal agency regulations
   Codification, 202–08, **203**
   Daily publication, 196–202, **198–200**
   Electronic sources, 201, 206–09
   Indexes, 201
   LSA pamphlets, 204, **205,** 206
   Research procedures, 208–11
   Shepardizing, 209, **210**
State agencies, 217–18

ADVANCE SESSION LAW SERVICES
See Session Laws

ADVANCE SHEETS, 21

ALMANACS, 257–60, **259**

AMERICAN DIGEST SYSTEM
See Digests

383

SUBJECT INDEX
Boldface references are to exhibits

†